DICTIONARY OF
AVIATION

DICTIONARY OF
AVIATION

An Illustrated History of the Airplane

Anthony Robinson

Foreword by
Air Vice-Marshal Donald Bennett

CRESCENT BOOKS NEW YORK

Acknowledgments

Illustrations were kindly supplied by the following sources:

API, Aeritalia, Aeroplane Supply Company Toronto, Air Portraits, Airsouth, J. Alexander, W. David Askham, Auckland Collection, Australian War Memorial, E. C. R. Baker, Adrian M. Balch Collection, BBC Hulton Picture Library, Beech Aircraft, Bell Aerospace, Bell Helicopters, Roger Bell, Bettman Archive, G. Bingham, Blitz Library, Boeing, Peter M. Bowers Collection, Chaz Boyer, Bristol Company, British Aircraft Corporation, British Airways, K. Brookes, A. J. Brown, Charles E. Brown, Bundesarchiv, COI, Camera Press, Department of National Defence Canada, Public Archives of Canada, Central Press, E. F. Cheesman, J. C. Cook, County Studio, Hugh Cowin, Crown Copyright, J. B. Cynk, Czechoslovak News Agency, Avions Marcel Dassault, Deutsches Museum München, Eshel Dramit Ltd, Carina Dvorak, ECPA, Fairchild, Fiat, Flight International, Flight Picture Library, Fokker-VFW International, Fox Photos, Roger Freeman, J. Fricker, Gamma, E. G. Gee, General Dynamics, Achile Ghizzardi, James Gilbert, James Goulding, Grumman Aerospace Corporation, Chris Harrison, Hawker Siddeley Aviation, Wallace Heaton, J. Heritage, Stuart Howe, M. Hooks, Robert Hunt Library, Hurlston Design, IGDA, Imperial War Museum, A. Imrie, P. A. Jackson, D. James, R. C. Jones, G. W. Kaelia, Keystone, Peter Kilduff Collection, D. J. Kingston, Klepacki, J. H. Lapsley, Legende Gaillard, Library of Congress, J. Lloyd, Lockheed, Lufthansa, MAP, Peter R. March, Glenn L. Martin Company, F. K. Mason, N. K. Matrenin, McDonnell Douglas, Ministry of Defence, Minnesota Historical Society, Philip Moyes, K. Munson, Musée de l'Air, Musée Royal de l'Armée, National Portrait Gallery, No 11 Group RAF Strike Command, Novosti, Heinz Nowarra, David Oliver, M. B. Passingham, L. Peacock, Stephen P. Peltz, Photri, Politik Deutschland/Berlin-Luftbrucke, K. Poolman, Popperfoto, Press Association, RNAS, E. Ritaranta, Bruce Robertson, Rolls-Royce, Royal Air Force Museum Hendon, Saab, Peter Sarson, Science Museum London, C. Seeley, F. Selinger, Hiroshi Seo, C. Shores, Shorts, Shuttleworth Collection, Sikorsky Aircraft, Georges Sirot Collection, Herman J. Sixma/IAAP, Smithsonian Institution, Robert Soubiron Collection, Southeastern Newspapers, Starliner Aviation Press, Stato Maggiore, E. Stewart, Sud Aviation, TASS, Z. Titz, Trans World Airlines, Michael Turner, US Air Force, US Army, US Navy, L. Valousek, Roger-Viollet, Vought Corporation, N. Wiltshire, Wojskowa Agencia Fotograficzna, Michael Young.

Half title page *Biplane glider built and flown by Otto Lilienthal in 1895 (Deutsches Museum, München).*

Frontispiece *Panavia Tornado IDS, or Interdictor Strike aircraft, built in the UK by British Aerospace (Richard Cooke).*

This 1984 edition published by Crescent Books, distributed by Crown Publishers, Inc.

ISBN 0-517-439379
Printed in Yugoslavia

h g f e d c b a

CONTENTS

2 AERIAL WARFARE

3 AEROPLANE MANUFACTURERS

FOREWORD

Daedalus and Icarus may have started it all, including a slight airworthiness problem, but we must not blame them for all the sluggishness of man's conquest of the air. The Chinese did some rather tricky gliding experiments about 4000 years ago and Jules Verne had one or two bright ideas, but it was only about 180 years ago that things really started to happen – and that was in England. Sir George Cayley designed and built gliders incorporating aerofoil wings, thus teaching the world the first real facts of flight.

Lighter-than-air machines, of which the French Montgolfier hot-air balloon won early fame, were developed with great success particularly for military observation purposes. In the 1890s the Royal Engineers were very active with both tied and free balloons and with gliders and man-lifting kites on Hartford Bridge flats (near Blackbushe Airport). All these things were, however, deficient in one respect: they lacked propulsion. A. V. Roe, Grahame-White, Sopwith and others succeeded in getting airborne with some very primitive power units, but Wilbur Wright was really the first to achieve sustained flight. Wilbur and Orville Wright set things moving; after that progress was meteoric. The First World War accelerated every aspect of aviation so that by the end of the war aircraft were making a genuine impact. Then civil aviation picked up the ball, and from 1919 to 1939 there were huge improvements in payloads, range, speeds and safety. The air routes of Imperial Airways, KLM, Air France and others soon served the whole world. Service aviation followed closely.

Those of us who have lived through the last seventy years of aviation history have been lucky – and privileged. We have seen enormous technical achievement – a real credit to mankind. We in Britain have also witnessed many political acts ranging from the good to the tragic. Nationally Great Britain, once the clear leader in most respects, has gone downhill. This has been caused, not by technical shortcomings, but by political defeatism. It is now the United States that leads the world in aircraft development, matched only by the Soviet Union in terms of quantity – if not quality – of aircraft produced. France, too, has developed many adventurous and effective aircraft designs, proving that it is not only the super-powers who are capable of producing successful aircraft.

The author of this Dictionary has taken on a tremendous task, covering three main areas of aviation – people, warfare and aircraft. The result of his labours gives us a reference book of great value worldwide. In view of the enormous field which he has covered it is surprising how little he has omitted. We must congratulate Tony Robinson on the extent of his coverage, and on the depth of research he has undertaken. We must hope, also, that when he up-dates the text for the second edition he will have masses of new and exciting material to add.

Air Vice-Marshal Donald Bennett

Left *Queen Elizabeth inspects the Path Finder force in February 1944. This unit was commanded by Air Vice-Marshal Donald Bennett.*

9

1

PILOTS AND PERSONALITIES

Above *The Eole's bulky steam engine was installed ahead of the pilot's seat and effectively blocked his forward view.*

Right *John Alcock (right) and his navigator Arthur Whitten Brown follow a ship's officer down the gangway of the Irish sea ferry on their return to England in July 1919.*

Below far right *Alcock (in suit) and Brown were fêted by the London crowds after their transatlantic flight.*

Below right *This plan view of Ader's Eole of 1890 shows the bat-like wing planform and its bamboo structure.*

Below *Clement Ader. His claims to be the first man to fly have long been a source of controversy.*

ADER

Clément Ader (1841–1925) was a French aviation pioneer who built the first man-carrying aeroplane to take off under its own power. By profession an electrical engineer, Ader completed this machine, which he named 'Eole', in 1890. It was a bat-like monoplane with a wingspan of 14m (45ft 11in), a length of 6·5m (21ft 4in) and a wing area of 28m² (300sq. ft). With an all-up weight of 296kg (652lb), the Eole was powered by a 20hp four-cylinder steam engine which drove a four-bladed tractor propeller.

Ader's pioneering flight was made in secret on 9 October 1890 from the grounds of Château Pereire at Armainvilliers. He claimed that it covered a distance of 50m (164ft) at a height of some 20cm (8in) above the ground. Clearly this was no more than a powered hop, but its significance was that for the first time a powered aeroplane had risen from level ground under its own power. As a flying machine the Eole had many disadvantages, quite apart from its inability to make a sustained flight. Most notable of these was its lack of control surfaces, which led Ader to comment on its instability. Furthermore, the bulky engine installation in front of the pilot's seat almost completely blocked off the pilot's view ahead.

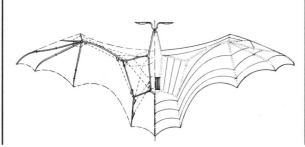

Ader attempted to interest the French army in a twin-engined aeroplane, the Avion III, which spanned 16m (52ft 6in) and had an all-up weight of 400kg (880lb). Unfortunately, it failed to leave the ground both times it was demonstrated (at Satory near Versailles) on 12 and 14 October 1897. In later life Ader was to claim that on the second occasion he completed a flight of over 275m (300yd). However, this assertion is discounted by most historians.

ALCOCK

Captain John Alcock (1892–1919) with his navigator Arthur Whitten Brown were the first men to fly across the Atlantic Ocean non-stop. The qualification is necessary because the first-ever Atlantic crossing by aeroplane was made by the US Navy's NC-4 flying boat in May 1919, with intermediate landings at the Azores and Lisbon. Alcock trained as an engineer and in 1912 he learned to fly, qualifying for the Royal Aero Club's pilot certificate on 26 November. On the outbreak of World War I he volunteered for service with the Royal Naval Air Service, being employed as a flying instructor until 1917. He was then posted to the Aegean where he served with distinction both as a single-seat scout pilot and as a long-range bomber pilot flying the Handley Page O/100. On 30 September 1917 he was brought down into the sea during a bombing raid with the HP O/100 and he remained a prisoner of the Turks until the end of the war.

In March 1919 Alcock was demobilized from the

RAF and he immediately approached the Vickers company to seek sponsorship for a transatlantic flight attempt. The immediate stimulus for this was a £10,000 prize offered by the press baron Lord Northcliffe for the first Atlantic crossing by air. Among the aeroplanes considered capable of attempting the Atlantic crossing in 1919 was the Vickers Vimy bomber. This twin-engined aircraft was designed for long-range bombing raids on Germany, but saw no operational service before the Armistice. Stripped of all military equipment and fitted with extra fuel tanks, the Vimy had

Alcock's Vimy ended the transatlantic flight ignominiously with its nose in an Irish peat bog. The Vimy is today preserved in the Science Museum, London.

a range of some 3860km (2400 miles). It was this aircraft that Alcock decided to fly across the Atlantic.

Accompanied by Brown and a team of engineers and mechanics from Vickers, Alcock sailed for Newfoundland in early May 1919, with the dismantled and crated Vimy following him by freighter. The west-to-east crossing was preferred because of the advantage given by the prevailing winds. The Vimy arrived in Newfoundland on 26 May, was assembled and test-flown on 9 June. Five days later the fuel-laden aircraft took off and headed for Ireland. For more than four hours the flight was through fog and cloud, so that navigation had to be entirely by dead reckoning. When Brown was finally able to take a sun shot, it was found that the Vimy was only a few kilometres off course. There followed ten hours of darkness and at daybreak the Vimy flew into storm clouds. Lashed by hail and tossed by violent air currents, the Vimy was forced down to a mere 30m (100ft) above the sea. As Alcock struggled to regain altitude, the Vimy flew into a snowstorm and began to ice up. Brown courageously clambered from his cockpit to clear the ice from the gauges and intakes of the wing-mounted engines. The Vimy finally broke through cloud at 3000m (11,000ft). Once clear of the clouds and within 160km (100 miles) of the Irish coast, Alcock dived down to 150m (500ft) to clear the ice from the engines and airframe.

Shortly after 8.15am the Vimy made its landfall, and, circling the Clifden radio masts, Alcock dropped down to land in what he took to be a convenient field. Unfortunately it was a peat bog and the Vimy ended its historic flight by nosing over into the spongy surface. The elapsed flight time was 16 hours 27 minutes.

Alcock and Brown returned to a hero's welcome in London and both received knighthoods. Tragically, Alcock died in an air crash in December 1919, when working as a test pilot for Vickers.

ARNOLD

General Henry H. 'Hap' Arnold (1886–1950) was Chief of Staff of the US Army Air Force from its formation in 1941 until 1946. He thus commanded the service throughout the crucial years of America's involvement in World War II and laid the foundations for the truly independent air service which came into being in 1947 after his retirement. Born at Gladwyne, Pennsylvania, on 25 June 1886, Arnold graduated from the US Military Academy at West Point in 1907 and was commissioned into the infantry. After service in the Philippines, he was assigned to the Signal Corps (then responsible for military aviation) and became one of the US Army's first qualified pilots after receiving instruction at the Wrights' school at Dayton, Ohio. Arnold did not see active service in Europe during World War I, but served in a number of senior

A formation of Boeing B-17 Flying Fortresses en route to bomb Germany in August 1944. Arnold was a firm believer in the employment of massed formations of strategic bombers in daylight raids, despite the opposition of his British allies to such tactics.

administrative posts in the United States, rising to the rank of full colonel by 1917 and becoming Assistant Director of the Office of Military Aeronautics.

By the end of World War I the US Army Air Service (formed in 1918 and to become the Army Air Corps in 1926) had gained a great deal of experience in air warfare in France. The early postwar years were a period of fierce controversy over the future of air power, with the flamboyant and outspoken Brigadier Billy Mitchell pressing the case for an independent air service with such vehemence that it led to his court-martial and disgrace in 1925. Arnold was a friend and admirer of Mitchell's, but although he shared the same aims his personality was less abrasive and his methods a good deal more cautious. Consequently the inter-war years saw his steady rise in rank and influence. In 1925 he became Chief of the Information Division in the Office of Chief of the Air Corps and in June 1929 he graduated from the Army's Command and General Staff School at Fort Leavenworth, Kansas. Arnold was appointed commander of the 1st Bombardment Wing at March Field, California, in November 1933 and the following year he led a flight of Martin B-10 bombers to Alaska and back in a test of air mobility.

In February 1935 Arnold was promoted to brigadier-general and became Assistant Chief of the Air Corps. On the death of his superior, Major-General Westover, Arnold became Chief of the Air Corps in 1938. Thereafter he became successively Army Deputy Chief of Staff for Air (October 1940), the Chief of the newly created Army Air Force (June 1941) and finally commanding general of the Army Air Force (March 1942). Whatever his title, from 1938 onwards Arnold was in a position to implement his beliefs in the effectiveness of air power. He masterminded the immense expansion of American warplane production and the parallel strengthening of the Army Air Corps. A staunch believer in the strategic bomber, he presided over the creation of the USAAF's Eighth Air Force, which began its air offensive against Germany in 1942. The American bombers operated in daylight against the advice of the more experienced RAF and the ever-increasing opposition of the Luftwaffe's defences. This policy was eventually to be vindicated by results and was to lead to an equally successful air offensive against Japan in 1944–5. As early as 1944 Arnold was planning for the postwar air force, but the strain of his immense responsibilities took its toll and he collapsed with a heart attack. Returning to work, he remained in office for the remainder of the war, but retired at his own request in 1945. He died on 15 January 1950.

BADER

Group Captain Sir Douglas Bader (1910–82) overcame the severe handicap of the loss of both of his legs in a flying accident to become one of the Royal Air Force's foremost fighter leaders in the early years of World War II. Bader was born in London on 21 February 1910 and was educated at St Edward's School, Oxford. He entered the RAF College Cranwell in 1928, gaining a prize cadetship. Two years later he was commissioned and joined No 23 Squadron at RAF Kenley, Surrey, flying Gloster Gamecock fighters. A keen sportsman, Bader represented the RAF in rugby and cricket and in 1931 he was a member of his squadron's aerobatic team for the RAF Air Pageant at Hendon. In that year No 23 Squadron began to convert to Bristol Bulldog fighters and it was while flying

low-level aerobatics with the new aircraft that Bader crashed and sustained his serious injuries.

After months in hospital Bader began to walk again with the help of artificial limbs, but his disability led to his discharge from the RAF on medical grounds. By the outbreak of World War II he had established himself in civilian life, working for the Shell Oil Company. However, he was determined to return to the RAF as a fighter pilot and by sheer force of character he persuaded the authorities to accept him for flying duties. In February 1940 Bader was posted to No 19 Squadron at Duxford (the RAF's first Spitfire squadron). Once the 30-year-old flying officer had proved his abilities, promotion was rapid. He first saw action over Dunkirk as a flight commander with No 222 Squadron (another Duxford-based Spitfire unit) and on the eve of the Battle of Britain he was

Top General 'Hap' Arnold commanded the US Army Air Force throughout World War II, but was forced to retire due to ill health in 1946.

Above Douglas Bader (fourth from right) with some of the pilots of No 242 Squadron in October 1940. At this time he often led the Duxford Wing in action.

promoted to squadron leader and assumed command of No 242 Squadron, a Hawker Hurricane unit largely manned by Canadian pilots.

Bader's first command was not an easy one, as No 242 Squadron had taken part in the disastrous Battle of France and morale was at a low ebb. However, the squadron soon regained its fighting spirit under Bader's forceful and inspiring leadership. As a part of RAF Fighter Command's No 12 Group, No 242 Squadron was not in the forefront of the Battle of Britain, which was largely fought by No 11 Group. However, No 12 Group did on occasions reinforce the hard-pressed squadrons in the south. In order to bring the greatest number of fighters into action against the Luftwaffe, Bader organized and led the three-squadron-strong Duxford Wing. This achieved some success and by the end of September Bader's personal victory tally stood at $12\frac{1}{2}$ (the fraction indicating a shared victory). Less happily, his successes led to an acrimonious controversy over Fighter Command's tactics. Yet what the proponents of wing tactics, Bader foremost among them, failed to realize was that the forward-based squadrons in No 11 Group did not have

sufficient early warning of enemy air raids to assemble a wing formation to meet them.

With the ending of daylight mass-bombing attacks by the Luftwaffe against Britain, Fighter Command prepared for offensive operations over enemy-occupied France. For such raids wing rather than squadron strength was considered necessary and Bader was appointed to lead the Tangmere Wing early in 1941. Flying Spitfires, the wing carried out fighter sweeps and bomber escort missions, often engaging enemy fighters in combat. In August 1941 Bader was forced to parachute into occupied France after his Spitfire had collided with a German Messerschmitt Bf 109. At this time his personal score stood at $22\frac{1}{2}$ victories, but it was as an inspiring fighter leader as much as a successful pilot that Bader excelled. After his capture, he made such a nuisance of himself, escaping and being recaptured on several occasions, that he was finally sent to Colditz Castle. There he was liberated by the Americans in 1945. He retired from the RAF in 1946 and returned to work for the Shell Company. Bader also devoted much time after World War II to giving practical help to the disabled.

BALL

Captain Albert Ball VC (1896–1917) was one of the first British fighter aces of World War I to achieve widespread popular acclaim. He was born in Nottingham on 14 August 1896 and was educated at Trent College. On the outbreak of war in August 1914 he volunteered for service with the Sherwood Foresters as a private soldier. In October 1914 he was commissioned and transferred to the North Midlands Cycle Corps, hoping to be sent with them to France. He was disappointed in this, however, and so began to take flying lessons at Hendon, gaining his Royal Aero Club

certificate in October 1915. Ball then transferred to the Royal Flying Corps, completed his flying training and was awarded his pilot's wings on 22 January 1916.

Ball's first operational unit was No 13 Squadron at Savay in France, which flew BE2c aeroplanes on reconnaissance and artillery observation duties. In May 1916 he transferred to No 11 Squadron, which flew both two-seat FE2b aircraft and single-seat Bristol Scouts and Nieuports. The individualistic and aggressive Ball much preferred flying the single-seaters and during the following two months he had many combats with enemy aircraft, his exploits being rewarded by the award of a Military Cross. In July he was posted to No 8 Squadron, a BE2c unit, for a rest, but Ball was irked by the lack of action and was soon back flying Nieuport 17 scouts with No 11 Squadron.

Towards the end of August 1916, Ball joined No 60 Squadron, again flying Nieuport scouts, and the following month he took command of the squadron's A Flight. He celebrated this promotion with a two-week spell of intensive air fighting during which he shot down eight enemy aircraft, plus one probable, and forced one machine to land. In September he was

Above A Hawker Hurricane of the RAF's Battle of Britain Memorial Flight is preserved in the markings of Bader's personal aircraft, which he flew when commanding No 242 Squadron in 1940.

Below Albert Ball combined an introspective and solitary nature with a reckless disregard for danger when in combat with the enemy.

awarded the Distinguished Service Order and bar, to which was added a second bar in November. In October 1916 Ball was posted back to England for a rest from combat flying. At that time he had shot down 12 German aeroplanes and one observation balloon, had sent one machine down out of control and had forced a further 19 to land. As a fighter pilot Ball was very much the lone wolf, flying by himself where and when he pleased. On the ground too he tended to prefer his own company. Yet the combat tactics of this withdrawn and self-sufficient young man were aggressive to the point of foolhardiness, as he would attack any enemy aircraft that he encountered and was undaunted by the odds against him.

On his return to England in October 1916 Ball found himself to be a national hero and his home town of Nottingham made him a Freeman of the City. Yet he longed to return to combat in France. In February 1917 he joined the newly formed No 56 Squadron at London Colney in Hertfordshire as commander of A

Right Francesco Baracca, Italy's leading fighter pilot of World War I, began his military career as a cavalryman. His certificate qualifying him to fly the Nieuport scout is illustrated.

Below The Nieuport 17 scout was Ball's favourite aeroplane and he continued to fly one even when serving with the SE5-equipped No 56 Squadron in 1917.

Bottom Baracca poses with one of his victims, an Austro-Hungarian Albatross DIII scout which he forced to land in June 1918.

He learned to fly in France, qualifying as a military pilot in July 1912, and by the time of Italy's entry into World War I in May 1915 he was an experienced military airman. His early wartime flights were in Nieuport two-seaters, but by the following spring he was flying single-seat fighters and he scored his first victory (over an Austro-Hungarian Aviatik two-seater) on 7 April 1916. Flying with the 70ª Squadriglia, he had destroyed five enemy aircraft by the end of the year. It was at this time that he adopted his famous prancing horse insignia, which is used as a unit emblem by the Italian air force to this day.

In May 1917, when his personal score stood at ten, Baracca was transferred from the 70ª Squadriglia to the newly formed 91ª Squadriglia which flew the Spad SVII. The following month he assumed command of this squadron and by the end of September he had shot

Flight, and accompanied the unit to France in April 1917, scoring the unit's first aerial victories later that month. No 56 Squadron was equipped with the new SE5 scout, which in its modified SE5a form was to become one of the classic fighter aeroplanes of World War I. Yet Ball disliked the SE5 and acquired a Nieuport scout which he flew whenever possible. His return to combat was at a time when the RFC was suffering heavy losses (indeed the month was to be recorded in history as Bloody April) and so the air fighting of the following weeks was to be the most intense of his career. It ended with his death in combat on 7 May 1917. At that time he was credited with the destruction of 23 German aircraft, a further two sent down out of control and 21 forced to land. Ball was awarded the Victoria Cross posthumously for his achievements.

BARACCA

Maggiore Francesco Baracca (1888–1918) was Italy's top-scoring fighter pilot in World War I. He was born on 9 May 1888 at Lugo di Romagna and in 1907 he entered the Military Academy at Modena, joining the 2nd Cavalry Regiment on completion of his training.

down 19 enemy aircraft. Towards the end of the year the air war over northern Italy intensified with the Austro-Hungarian victory at Caporetto in October. Baracca's unit re-equipped with the improved Spad SXIII at this time and the Italian airmen saw much hard fighting. At the end of the year his victory tally stood at 30 and he was awarded the Medaglia d'Oro al Valor Militare (Italy's highest award for valour). After a rest from combat, he returned to his squadron and on 15 June 1918 (the first day of the Battle of the Piave) he scored his 34th and final victory. Four days later, while leading a ground-attack mission, he was hit by an infantryman's bullet and died instantly.

BARKER

Wing Commander William George Barker RCAF (1894–1930) was one of the foremost fighter aces of World War I and one of the most highly decorated airmen of that conflict, his awards including the Victoria Cross, DSO and bar, MC and two bars, plus the French Légion d'Honneur and Croix de Guerre. Born in Manitoba, Canada, Barker enlisted in the Canadian Mounted Rifles on the outbreak of World War I and accompanied them to France. He then transferred to the Royal Flying Corps as an observer and was commissioned in April 1916. During his service as an observer with No 9 Squadron he shot down his first enemy aircraft on 29 July 1916. Early in 1917 he was selected for pilot training and after receiving his wings he returned to France to fly RE8 observation aircraft with No 15 Squadron.

Barker returned to England to become an instructor pilot, but instead he joined No 28 Squadron, a scout or fighter unit equipped with Sopwith Camels, in October 1917. He accompanied the squadron to France as a flight commander the same month. Barker was quick to demonstrate his skills as an air fighter, shooting down five enemy aircraft before his unit was trans-

Below Barker pictured after the award of the Victoria Cross, which he received for an epic single-handed combat against a formation of German Fokker DVII fighters.

Below Barker in front of his Sopwith Camel B6313 in which he gained all his victories over the Italian Front.

ferred to Italy in November 1917. This move was necessary to bolster the Italian defences following the disastrous defeat at Caporetto. Barker quickly resumed his run of successes, scoring his first victory over the new front on 29 November, and by the end of March 1918 he had accounted for ten aeroplanes and nine observation balloons.

In April 1918 Barker was given his first command, No 66 Squadron, which like his previous unit flew the Sopwith Camel on the Italian Front. Indeed Barker was able to take his personal Camel, serial number B6313, to his new unit. During his period in command of No 66 Squadron (from mid-April until mid-July) Barker was credited with shooting down 16 enemy aircraft. This period of intense air fighting coincided with the Austro-Hungarian offensive on the Piave in June and a grateful Italian government awarded Barker the Medaglia d'Argento al Valor Militare in recognition of his services. Barker then moved on to command No 139 Squadron, another Italian-based fighter squadron, which flew the two-seat Bristol F2B Fighter. Barker was reluctant to relinquish his single-seat Camel and this accompanied him to the Bristol Fighter squadron. Flying both types of aircraft, Barker gained a further six victories during this period. He also flew an Italian Caproni trimotor bomber over enemy territory to drop an Italian secret agent, a mission which earned him a second Medaglia d'Argento.

In September 1918 Barker returned to England as an instructor, but he longed to return to the active life of a front-line fighter pilot. Accordingly he persuaded the authorities to allow him to return to France for a short period, flying the new Sopwith Snipe on attachment to the Camel-equipped No 201 Squadron. On 27 October, the last day of his attachment, he found the action for which he craved. Flying alone he engaged and shot down an enemy two-seater, but was then surpised by a formation of Fokker D VII scouts. Enemy fire severely wounded him in the thigh, but he fought back despite passing out from the pain of his wound. Three enemy aircraft fell to his guns, but Barker was wounded again twice. He managed nevertheless to bring his badly damaged Snipe down in a crash-landing. Although for a time it was feared he would die from his injuries, he lived to receive the Victoria Cross which was awarded him for his last epic flight. After postwar service in the RCAF, Barker went into civil aviation and he was killed in a flying accident on 12 March 1930.

BARKHORN

Gerhard Barkhorn (born 1919) was the second-highest-scoring Luftwaffe air ace of World War II and with his compatriot Erich Hartmann the only fighter pilot to have shot down more than 300 enemy aircraft. Born at Königsberg in East Prussia on 20 March 1919, Barkhorn began his flying training with the Luftwaffe

in 1938. Two years later he fought in the Battle of Britain, serving with Jagdgeschwader 2 and JG 52, both equipped with the Messerschmitt Bf 109E fighter. However, he claimed no victories during this period and it was not until JG 52 moved east for the invasion of the Soviet Union in June 1941 that he began to score.

Barkhorn's first victory came on 2 July 1941 during his 120th combat sortie. Yet if he was slow to start scoring, thereafter his tally of enemy aircraft destroyed steadily increased. In August 1942, when he was awarded the Knight's Cross, his score stood at 59 victories and by the end of that year his victories had passed the 100 mark. In mid-1943 Barkhorn became *Kommandeur* of JG 52's II Gruppe and on 30 November that year his score reached 200. This run of successes was entirely against Soviet pilots, many of whom as Barkhorn himself has testified were poorly trained and inexperienced. It would be wrong, however, to suggest that all these victories were easy ones. Barkhorn fought against Soviet-operated Western fighters, including Spitfires, Hurricanes and Bell P-39 Airacobras, and he had considerable respect for the qualities of the Soviet Yakovlev Yak-9. During one combat mission in 1943, he fought a 40-minute duel with a Lavochkin LaGG-3 from one of the Soviet guards fighter regiments, at the end of which neither pilot had gained the advantage.

On 13 February 1944 Barkhorn shot down his 250th enemy aircraft, but his hitherto uninterrupted fighting career was shortly to meet with a serious setback. In May 1944, when his score stood at 273 victories, Barkhorn led a formation of Bf 109Gs which were providing fighter cover for the Ju 87 Stukas of the redoubtable Oberst Hans-Ulrich Rudel. It was Barkhorn's sixth mission of the day and no doubt his reactions were sluggish. A Soviet fighter dived through the German formation and sent Barkhorn's fighter crashing to earth. He survived, but spent the next four months in hospital recovering from his wounds. This period of inaction allowed the young Erich Hartmann to catch up with Barkhorn's score and to beat him to the honour of becoming the Luftwaffe's top-scoring fighter ace.

Barkhorn finally achieved his 300th victory on 5 January 1945, but he was to score only one more kill

Gerhard Barkhorn in the cockpit of his Messerschmitt Bf 109G fighter at the time of his 250th victory on the Eastern Front in February 1944.

Roland Beamont combined the careers of RAF fighter pilot and test pilot during World War II. After the war he became the English Electric Company's chief test pilot.

before he was transferred to command JG 6 in the west. Shortly thereafter he joined Jagdverband 44, an elite fighter unit commanded by former General of Fighters Adolf Galland, which flew the revolutionary new Messerschmitt Me 262 twin-jet fighter. Barkhorn flew only two missions on the Me 262, as on his second flight while attempting to intercept an American bomber formation he suffered engine failure. His crippled fighter was then engaged by one of the piston-engined P-51 Mustang fighter escorts and Barkhorn was forced to crash-land. His injuries effectively prevented him from participating in the closing air battles of World War II.

In the course of 1104 fighter missions, Barkhorn had scored 301 aerial victories, had been shot down nine times, baled out twice and wounded twice. However, 1945 did not see the end of Barkhorn's flying career, for in 1955 he joined the new West German Luftwaffe, in which he rose to the rank of *General*.

BEAMONT

Wing Commander Roland Prosper Beamont (born 1920) joined the Royal Air Force on a short-service commission in 1938 and completed his flying training in September 1939. With the outbreak of World War II he did not wait long for a posting to an operational unit and in November 1939 he joined No 87

Squadron, which flew Hawker Hurricanes from Lille/Seclin airfield in France as part of the Air Component of the British Expeditionary Force. This was the period of the 'phoney war' and the squadron saw little action until the German offensive against France and the Low Countries in May 1940. From 10 May until No 87 Squadron was evacuated to Britain ten days later, Beamont took part in numerous combats and claimed his first three victories. He then took part in the Battle of Britain and flew his single-seat Hurricane against Luftwaffe night raiders during the Blitz.

In June 1941 Beamont joined No 79 Squadron, also flying Hurricanes, as a flight commander and he remained with this unit until the end of the year. His next posting was to the Hawker aircraft factory at Langley as a production test pilot – the beginnings of a long and distinguished career in this field. Not only did he test-fly newly built Hurricanes, but he also took part in the testing of the new Hawker Typhoon fighter. At the end of this period of test flying he returned to operations and was posted to the first Typhoon units, assuming command of No 609 Squadron in October 1942. Under Beamont's leadership this squadron established the Typhoon as the RAF's outstanding ground-attack fighter of World War II. The aircraft had had numerous teething troubles and Beamont's experience as a test pilot with Hawker's helped to iron out many of its early problems.

In May 1943 Beamont returned to Hawker's as an experimental test pilot working on the new Tempest fighter. He then commanded the RAF's first Tempest Wing taking part in the battle against the V1s and then moving to France as part of the RAF's 2nd Tactical Air Force in support of the advancing Allied armies in October 1944. Beamont's wartime flying career came to an abrupt halt shortly afterwards, when he was shot down by ground-fire and made a prisoner of war.

After the end of World War II Beamont remained in the RAF only until the end of 1945. He then embarked on a career as a civilian test pilot, working briefly for the Gloster and de Havilland aircraft companies, before joining English Electric in 1947. In 1948 Beamont visited the United States, where he had the opportunity to test-fly some of the new American military jets. During a flight in the North American XP-86 Sabre prototype he made history by becoming the first Englishman to exceed the speed of sound in diving flight. Another milestone was reached in 1949 when Beamont made the first flight in the English Electric B3/45, prototype of the RAF's first jet bomber, the Canberra. Therefter, he was to test-fly the numerous variants of this aircraft produced for the RAF and for foreign customers. He also flew the aircraft on a demonstration tour of the United States, prior to the USAF ordering a licence-built version of the Canberra, the Martin B-57. In 1954 Beamont began test-flying the English Electric P1, an experimental prototype that was to evolve into the Lightning.

The last new aircraft to be flown by Beamont was the British Aircraft Corporation TSR-2 (English Electric had been absorbed by BAC in 1964), but this advanced tactical strike reconnaissance aircraft was cancelled in 1965. However, test-flying proceeded on new versions of the Canberra and Lightning and Beamont continued with this work until his retirement from professional flying in 1968.

Above left *Beamont at the controls of an English Electric Canberra B Mk 2, Britain's first jet bomber. In May 1949 he made the first flight in the Canberra prototype.*

Above *The Canberra design team pose in front of the first prototype with Beamont, who stands fourth from the right.*

Left *Beamont climbs from the cockpit of the experimental English Electric P1 in 1957. This aircraft was later developed as the Lightning fighter.*

BENNETT

Air Vice-Marshal Donald Bennett (born 1910) formed and led RAF Bomber Command's Path Finder Force in World War II. Born in Queensland, Australia, on 14 September 1910, Bennett joined the Royal Australian Air Force in 1930. However, due to the effect of stringent economies, there was no place for him in the RAAF and, after completing his initial flying training, he left for Britain on transfer to the RAF. Bennett's first posting to an operational unit took him to No 29 (Fighter) Squadron at North Weald in Essex, flying the Armstrong Whitworth Siskin. He then transferred to flying boats, serving with No 210 Squadron flying Supermarine Southamptons, whose CO was Squadron Leader A. T. Harris (later wartime C-in-C of Bomber Command).

Navigation was Bennett's speciality and he became a lecturer at the Navigation School at Calshot and later an instructor at the Flying Boat Training School. In 1934 he took part in the MacRobertson Air Race to Australia, acting as navigator of a Lockheed Vega, but his aircraft crashed at Aleppo in Syria and was put out of the race. In 1935 he left the RAF and the following year joined Imperial Airways, becoming captain of Short Calcutta, Kent and Empire flying boats on the Brindisi to Alexandria leg of the air route to India. One of Bennett's most interesting assignments with Imperial Airways was the testing of the Short-Mayo Composite. This consisted of a four-engined S20 seaplane mounted atop an S21 flying boat, which would carry the seaplane for part of its journey to increase its payload and range. Bennett piloted the S20 in route-proving flights across the Atlantic and from Britain to South Africa.

On the outbreak of war in September 1939, Bennett was despatched to Canada to organize the Atlantic Ferry Service, which flew American-built aeroplanes to Britain. He rejoined the RAF in mid-1941 and was given command of No 77 Squadron, which flew AW Whitleys in Bomber Command. His next command was No 10 Squadron, equipped with Handley Page Halifaxes, which he joined in April 1942. On the night of 28/29 April he led a raid against the battleship *Tirpitz* in Aasfiord, Norway. His aircraft was shot down by anti-aircraft fire, but he managed to evade capture and reach neutral Sweden, returning to Britain a month after being shot down.

By mid-1942 the C-in-C of Bomber Command, Bennett's former CO Air Chief-Marshal Sir Arthur Harris, was seriously worried about the standards of navigation and bomb-aiming accuracy within his command. In order to improve the situation, in July 1942 he formed a five-squadron-strong Path Finder Force under Bennett's command, which was to locate and mark targets for the main bomber force. The concept proved to be a success and with the introduction of new navigational aids such as the H2S ground-

Right *Air Vice-Marshal Donald Bennett formed and led RAF Bomber Command's Path Finder Force in World War II. He wears the Force's eagle badge beneath his medal ribbons.*

Below *One of Bennett's notable achievements in civil aviation was the testing of the S20 floatplane* Mercury, *the upper component of the Short-Mayo composite. In 1938 he flew* Mercury *from Britain to South Africa, establishing a long-distance seaplane record which still stands today.*

mapping radar and later the Oboe ground-directed bombing system, the accuracy of Bomber Command's attacks increased appreciably. This led to the expansion of the Path Finder Force and in January 1943 it became No 8 Group in Bomber Command. Bennett remained its Air Officer Commanding and was promoted to the rank of air vice-marshal. By the end of the war, the Path Finder Force had expanded to a strength of 20 squadrons, equipped with the highly effective four-engined Avro Lancaster and twin-engined DH Mosquito. The force had flown a total of more than 50,000 operational sorties and had marked over 3400 targets for the main force. Bennett retired from the RAF after the war and joined the board of British South American Airways. His active flying career was not at an end, however, and in 1948 he took part in the Berlin airlift.

BISHOP

Air Marshal William Avery 'Billy' Bishop (1894–1956) was the second-highest-scoring fighter pilot in the Royal Flying Corps in World War I. He was born in Ontario, Canada, on 8 February 1894, and at the age of 17 years he entered the Royal Military College. On the outbreak of World War I he joined a militia regiment and the following year he sailed to Britain with the 7th Canadian Mounted Rifles. In order to reach the fighting in France, he transferred to the RFC as an observer and he was posted to No 21 Squadron

Right The skilful and aggressive Canadian, William Avery Bishop, was the second-highest-scoring fighter pilot of the British air services in World War I.

Below Bishop stands beside his Nieuport 17 scout. It was while flying this aircraft that he made the single-handed attack on a German aerodrome which earned him the Victoria Cross.

at Netheravon. In January 1916 he accompanied the squadron to France, but six months later returned to Britain to train as a pilot.

After qualifying for his wings, Bishop served with a home defence unit until March 1917, when he was posted to France and joined No 60 Squadron, which flew Nieuport scouts. On 25 March he opened his score against the enemy by shooting down an Albatros scout, but a faulty engine forced him to crash-land in the forward British trenches. The following month was a period of intense aerial activity, which has gone down in history as 'Bloody April' because of the severe RFC losses. Bishop was in the thick of the battles, his score for the month being nine enemy aeroplanes shot down, plus two observation kite balloons destroyed in flames. His run of successes continued throughout May and by the end of that month he had scored 22 aerial victories. His work was rewarded by the award of the Military Cross and shortly afterwards by the Distinguished Service Order.

On 2 June 1917 Bishop carried out a daring single-handed attack on a German aerodrome, machine-gunning the hangars and shooting down three Albatros scouts which attempted to intervene. This exploit was brought to the notice of General Hugh Trenchard, commanding the RFC in France, and Bishop was awarded the Victoria Cross. He continued to engage enemy aircraft whenever the opportunity arose and by the end of July his score stood at 38 victories. By this time No 60 Squadron had replaced its Nieuport scouts with the Royal Aircraft Factory's superb SE5a. Flying the new aircraft, Bishop despatched nine more enemy aeroplanes in August, earning a bar to his DSO and a posting back to Britain for a well-deserved rest period. At this time he was the highest-scoring RFC pilot.

After leave in Canada, during which he wrote his classic account of air fighting, *Winged Warfare*, Bishop returned to Britain and was given command of the newly formed No 85 Squadron, which was working up on the SE5a scout at Hounslow. On 22 May 1918 Bishop led the squadron on a flight across the English Channel to its new base at Marquise in France. Five days later he celebrated the resumption of his fighting career with his 48th victory. Over the next three weeks he added 25 victories to his score-sheet, bringing his final total up to 72. His last combat flight on 19 June resulted in the destruction of four Pfalz DIII scouts and a German two-seater, and typified his aggressive fighting qualities. This last period of fighting brought him the award of the RAF's newly instituted Distinguished Flying Cross.

Bishop ended World War I as a lieutenant-colonel, commanding the Canadian Wing then forming in Britain. In 1919 he returned to Canada and partnered fellow ace Billy Barker many flying enterprises. During World War II he became a senior officer in the Royal Canadian Air Force and played a notable part in the administration of the British Commonwealth Air Training Plan. He died at Edmonton, Alberta, in September 1956.

back to base at Debden, Essex. Blakeslee's dissatisfaction with the Thunderbolt persisted, despite the fighter's popularity and excellent record with the rival 56th Fighter Group. In December he had the opportunity to lead the newly arrived 354th Fighter Group on operations and he was greatly impressed with the North American P-51 Mustang fighter which they flew. Consequently, he began to lobby for the 4th Fighter Group to be re-equipped with the new fighter and his influence was strengthened in January 1944, when he succeeded another Eagle Squadron veteran, Colonel Chesley Peterson, as CO of the 4th Fighter Group.

Blakeslee's wish was granted and in February 1944 the 4th Fighter Group converted to the P-51 Mustang. The transition was a smooth one and on 4 March Blakeslee led the new fighters over Berlin, the group

BLAKESLEE

Colonel Donald J. M. Blakeslee (born 1918) was one of the outstanding USAAF fighter leaders of World War II, who with some 500 combat missions to his credit was in action for longer than any other USAAF fighter pilot. After learning to fly at Willoughby Field, near his home town of Fairport Harbor, Ohio, Blakeslee joined the Royal Canadian Air Force. In May 1941 he was posted to Britain to join No 401 Squadron RCAF, flying Hawker Hurricanes from Digby in Lincolnshire. The squadron re-equipped with Spitfires and moved south to Biggin Hill in October and the following month Blakeslee destroyed his first enemy aircraft, a Messerschmitt Bf 109, over France. The following year he was posted to No 133 (Eagle) Squadron as a flight commander and during the fierce air fighting over Dieppe on 19 August 1942 he was credited with the destruction of a Focke Wulfe Fw 190 fighter and a further two damaged.

On 22 August 1942 the three American-manned RAF Eagle Squadrons were transferred to the control of the USAAF and combined to form the 4th Fighter Group, Blakeslee exchanging his RCAF flight lieutenant's uniform for that of a captain in the USAAF. Two months later Blakeslee assumed command of the group's 335th Fighter Squadron and was promoted to major in January 1943. Early in the new year the group gave up their beloved Spitfires and began to convert to the Republic P-47 Thunderbolt. Blakeslee himself scored the first victory with the massive new fighter on 15 April, catching up with an Fw 190 in a dive and sending it to the ground. Blakeslee afterwards commented acidly on the unpopular Thunderbolt: 'It ought to dive, it certainly won't climb.'

In May 1943 Blakeslee was promoted to lieutenant-colonel and became the 4th Fighter Group's operations officer, leading the unit on numerous escort missions. On 16 August his Thunderbolt was badly damaged by cannon-fire from Fw 190s during an escort mission to Paris, but he managed to nurse his damaged fighter

Top *Blakeslee pictured in the cockpit of his P-51D Mustang, after an escort mission over Berlin with the 4th Fighter Group.*

Above *Blakeslee's P-51D Mustang (nearest the camera) leads the 4th Fighter Group's 335th Fighter Squadron on a mission during the summer of 1944.*

destroying four enemy fighters for the loss of three Mustangs. Blakeslee himself did not score as the guns of his fighter jammed before he could fire a shot. Yet this mission was the start of a highly successful period for the 4th Fighter Group, which under Blakeslee's leadership claimed the destruction of 323 enemy aircraft between 5 March and 24 April for the loss of only 44 Mustangs. This effort earned the group a Distinguished Unit Citation and Blakeslee himself a Distinguished Service Cross.

On D-Day Blakeslee led the group's first fighter sweep over the Normandy beaches and later that month his fighters accompanied the Boeing B-17s on the first shuttle mission to Soviet territory and back.

For his leadership on these gruelling shuttle escort missions, which covered 9650km (6000 miles) and involved more than 29 hours' operational flying, Blakeslee received a bar to his DSC. In October 1944 he handed over command of the 4th Fighter Group to his successor and his combat career was at an end. His official score was 15½ victories, but the true figure is probably much higher, for Blakeslee was more concerned with leading his fighters in combat than with running up and confirming an impressive total of kills.

BLÉRIOT

Louis Blériot (1872–1936) was one of the foremost pioneers of early aviation, who is chiefly remembered for making the first crossing of the English Channel in an aeroplane. Born at Cambrai on 1 July 1872, Blériot trained as an engineer and then established a profitable business as a manufacturer of automobile headlamps, which gave him sufficient income to finance his experiments in aviation. His first flying machine, constructed in 1900, was an ornithopter (flapping wing) design, which not surprisingly did not leave the ground. Yet Blériot was undeterred and in 1903 he began work on a biplane, floatplane glider in association with another distinguished aviation pioneer, Gabriel Voisin. This aircraft crashed into the water on its first flight, nearly drowning Voisin. A second floatplane was built by Voisin for Blériot and this was a powered machine, but in spite of numerous power-plant modifications, it remained firmly waterborne.

Blériot next designed and built an unconventional canard (tail-first) monoplane, powered by a 24hp

Above *Louis Blériot was a successful manufacturer of automobile headlamps, who used the profits from his business to finance the building of his early aeroplanes.*

Right *Blériot pictured at the end of his cross-Channel flight in 1909 in a field near Dover Castle.*

Below *The Blériot Type XI monoplane is prepared for the Channel flight. This aeroplane was one of the most successful pre-World War I designs.*

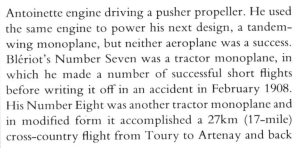

Antoinette engine driving a pusher propeller. He used the same engine to power his next design, a tandem-wing monoplane, but neither aeroplane was a success. Blériot's Number Seven was a tractor monoplane, in which he made a number of successful short flights before writing it off in an accident in February 1908. His Number Eight was another tractor monoplane and in modified form it accomplished a 27km (17-mile) cross-country flight from Toury to Artenay and back

– making two forced landings en route – on 31 October 1908. By the end of the year, Blériot had built three more aeroplanes: Number Nine was a monoplane, Number Ten a biplane, while Number Eleven – more usually designated Blériot XI – was the monoplane in which he achieved his cross-Channel success, and was arguably the most successful aeroplane of its day. The Blériot XI was a monoplane with a span of 7·8m (25ft 7in), length of 8m (26ft 3in) and weighing 300kg (660lb) loaded. Powered by a three-cylinder Anzani engine it reached a speed of 58km/h (36mph). The cost of the machine was £480 and many remained in service until the early years of World War I.

In 1909 Blériot determined to win the £1000 prize offered by the *Daily Mail* for the first Channel crossing by an aeroplane (a crossing had been made by balloon as early as 1785). His most serious rival, Hubert Latham, attempted the flight on 19 July and was forced down into the Channel 11km (7 miles) out. Blériot followed from Calais on 25 July and after a flight of 36 minutes he touched down near Dover Castle. His feat was acclaimed by enthusiastic crowds in both London and Paris and orders for the Blériot XI flooded in. However, his days as a pilot were all but over. In December 1909, while making a demonstration flight over Constantinople, his aeroplane stalled and crashed. Blériot was not seriously injured, but he resolved to give up flying and concentrate on the building of aeroplanes. His machines were built for private customers and newly emergent military air arms in France and abroad. During World War I Blériot became president of the Spad company, which built the successful Spad

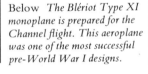

SVII and SXIII fighters. In 1934 the 25th anniversary of his Channel crossing was marked by making him a commander of the Légion d'Honneur.

BOELCKE

Hauptmann Oswald Boelcke (1891–1916) was one of the foremost German fighter aces of World War I and made an outstanding contribution to the development of fighter tactics. Born near Halle in Saxony on 19 May 1891, Boelcke joined the Prussian Cadet Corps in March 1911 and was commissioned the following year. He volunteered for the Air Service and completed his flying training just before the outbreak of war in August 1914. His first unit was Fliegerabteilung 13 in France and he and his brother Wilhelm, an observer with the unit, usually flew together. In April 1915 he transferred to Fliegerabteilung 62 and on 4 July he and his observer, Leutnant Wuehlisch, shot down a French Morane two-seater. That month Boelcke's unit received its first armed Fokker Eindecker single-seaters, which Boelcke and another squadron member, Leutnant Max Immelmann, then flew regularly. His second victory came on 19 August and then he was detached from his unit to Metz for bomber escort duties, scoring further successes. In January 1916 he brought down his eighth enemy aircraft, the same score as his comrade Immelmann, and both men were awarded the Pour le Mérite.

Above *Blériot's cross-Channel flight aroused tremendous popular enthusiasm, as this contemporary tapestry illustration indicates.*

Right *Oswald Boelcke was a pioneer tactician of air fighting, who formed and led one of the first German fighter squadrons in World War I.*

Boelcke's next posting was to Fliegerabteilung 203, another two-seater unit. By this time his views on fighter tactics were taking shape and he opposed the scattering of fighter aircraft in small groups among the reconnaissance units. His opinions were respected and in June 1916 he was ordered to form a specialized fighter flight, Kampfeinsitzer Sivry, for service on the Verdun sector. However, when Immelmann was killed in combat on 18 June, it was decided to give Boelcke a rest from combat flying. At that time he had scored 19 aerial victories and was the youngest *Hauptmann* in the German army.

After completing a tour of inspection of air units on the Eastern and Macedonian Fronts, Boelcke assisted in the formation of seven new specialized fighter squadrons, or *Jagdstaffel* – and was himself given command of Jasta 2. He took great care in selecting and training his fighter pilots, one of the recruits to Jasta 2 being Manfred von Richthofen. He also codified his ideas on fighter tactics into the 'Dicta Boelcke', which stressed the advantages of superior height and speed, surprise, and firing at close range. Boelcke's rules warned of the dangers of foolhardiness, but counselled that the best way of meeting a surprise attack was to turn into the enemy.

New fighter aircraft matched these refined tactics and Jasta 2 received Fokker D III and Albatros D I and D II scouts. Boelcke resumed scoring on 2 September,

Above *Boelcke's early successes were gained while flying the Fokker Eindecker, which first reached the front in 1915.*

Below right *Richard Bong became the highest scoring American fighter pilot of World War II while serving with the USAAF's Fifth Air Force in the Pacific.*

Below *Bong is interviewed by war correspondents after one of his successful combats in 1944. All of his victories were scored against the Japanese.*

shooting down a Royal Flying Corps de Havilland DH2 scout north of Thiepval. By the end of the month Jasta 2 had scored 21 victories, while Boelcke's personal tally stood at 29. Further successes followed and on 26 October Jasta 2's score-sheet recorded 51 victories, 21 of them Boelcke's, bringing his victories up to 40. Two days later Boelcke's luck ran out. While dogfighting with a formation of DH2s, Boelcke and his friend Erwin Boehme collided. Boelcke's Albatros span earthwards and he died of a fractured skull in the ensuing crash. His score of 40 enemy aircraft destroyed was at that time well ahead of that of any other German airman. Indeed it is a fitting tribute to Boelcke that Germany's leading ace at the end of the war was to be his protégé von Richthofen.

BONG

Major Richard I. Bong (1920–45) was the leading American air ace of World War II. Bong was born at Superior, Wisconsin, on 24 September 1920. After enrolling in the State Teachers' College, Bong decided to change his career and enlisted in the Army Air Corps as a flying cadet in May 1941. He completed his training and gained his wings in January 1942, but instead of the posting to combat theatre which he wanted, he was retained in the United States as a flying instructor. He chafed at the inaction and to relieve his frustration he decided to loop his aeroplane around the centre span of San Francisco's Golden Gate Bridge. This flagrant breach of flying discipline had the desired effect and he was posted to the Southwest Pacific Theatre.

In November 1942 Bong joined the 25th Fighter Group's 39th Fighter Squadron, which flew Lockheed P-38 Lightnings in New Guinea. On 27 December he claimed his first victories, shooting down an Aichi D3A Val dive-bomber and an escorting Mitsubishi A6M Zero. On 7 January he shot down two Nakajima Ki-43 Oscar fighters and the next day another, bringing his score to five. He then transferred to the 9th Fighter Squadron, 49th Fighter Group, which also flew the P-38 Lightning. Victories followed at regular intervals and at the end of his first year of combat, Bong's score stood at 21 enemy aircraft destroyed. He then returned to the United States on leave.

Early in 1944 Bong returned to combat. On 27 February he and fellow ace Lieutenant-Colonel Thomas Lynch strafed a Japanese staff transport aircraft just after it had landed, apparently killing a number of high-ranking Japanese officers. On 12 April he claimed two Ki-43 Oscars, bringing his score to 27 – one more than that of leading World War I American ace Eddie Rickenbacker. Congratulations were showered on Bong and his promotion to the rank of major was made effective from this date. At this time there was keen rivalry between the various up-and-coming aces in the Southwest Pacific Theatre, with such pilots as Neel Kearby, William Dunham, Thomas Lynch and Thomas McGuire all vying for top place. Lynch and Kearby were both killed in action at about this time, however, which led General Arnold to suggest that the top scorers be returned to the United States. As a compromise solution, Bong was only sent home on leave and spent three months touring training airfields to lecture to cadets.

In October 1944 Bong rejoined the 49th Fighter Group in the Philippines and reopened his scoring with two Japanese fighters brought down on 20 October. A month later Bong's score stood at 36, six ahead of McGuire, his closest rival. Now Bong began to fly missions with the 475th Fighter Group, to which McGuire belonged. While flying in the same formation as his rival, Bong scored his 40th victory on 17 December. This marked the end of his combat career, as he was immediately grounded and posted back to the United States. He had flown 146 combat missions, comprising 365 hours of flying. His decorations included the Distinguished Service Cross, two Silver Stars, seven Distinguished Flying Crosses and 15 Air Medals. To these was added the Medal of Honor in December 1944. Ironically Bong's return to the United States did not save his life, as he was killed while flying in August 1945.

BYRD

Rear-Admiral Richard Evelyn Byrd of the US Navy (1888–1957), the first man to fly over the North Pole, was a distinguished polar explorer who exploited the potential of the aeroplane in expeditions to both the Arctic and Antarctic regions. He was educated at Shenandoah Valley Military Academy, Virginia Military Institute and the University of Virginia before entering the US Naval Academy at Annapolis as a cadet. A keen athlete, Byrd sustained a serious foot injury which it appeared would force his retirement from the Navy. However, he successfully applied for transfer to the naval aviation branch and completed his flying training at Pensacola, Florida. In August 1918 Lieutenant Byrd was appointed to command the Naval Air Station at Halifax, Nova Scotia. He became an accomplished air navigator, developing a 'bubble' sextant for high-altitude use, a sun compass and a driftmeter. He was also involved in the organization of the US Navy transatlantic flying-boat flight in 1919.

In the years following World War I, Byrd worked with Rear-Admiral William Moffett to build up the US Navy's air arm. He was involved in the selection of sites for new air bases and it was at this time that he conceived the idea of a flight to the North Pole to gain public support for his service. He had to be content, however, with the less ambitious assignment of providing air support for Commander D. B. MacMillan's expedition to western Greenland in 1924. Yet Byrd was not to be deflected from his purpose and he applied for extended leave so that he could organize a private air expedition to the North Pole.

By 1926 a race to reach the Pole had developed between Byrd and the Norwegian explorer Roald Amundsen. Byrd had the backing of automobile magnate Henry Ford and had acquired a Fokker Trimotor (named *Josephine Ford* after his sponsor's daughter) and had enlisted the help of Floyd Bennett as his pilot. Amundsen was to fly in the Italian-built airship *Norge* and both flights were to start from King's Bay, Spitsbergen. In the event Byrd's Trimotor was the first to leave and achieved its objective in a 15½-hour flight, with Bennett at the controls, Byrd navigating and George Noville as flight engineer.

Above *Richard Byrd devoted his life to polar exploration by aircraft and he was the first man to fly over the North Pole in 1926.*

Below *Byrd and his rival Roald Amundsen inspect supplies at Spitsbergen in 1926, with the Fokker Trimotor* Josephine Ford *in the background.*

Bottom *The sturdy and reliable Fokker FVII trimotor transport aircraft were also used by Byrd on his Antarctic expedition of 1928.*

Other notable flights followed. In 1927 Byrd planned a non-stop New York to Paris flight in another Fokker Trimotor named *America*. Bennett was to have been his pilot, but he was badly injured in an air crash, so his place was taken by Bert Acosta. The *America* left New York on 29 June 1927, but was prevented by fog from landing at Paris and had to ditch off the French coast after a 42-hour flight.

Byrd now turned to Antarctic exploration and late in 1928 established a base camp on the continent, at Little America on the Bay of Whales. It was from here that he accomplished a flight over the South Pole on 29 November 1929, flying in a Ford Trimotor named *Floyd Bennett* in memory of his former pilot. On this occasion he was flown by Berndt Balchen. It was the start of a new series of Antarctic expeditions under his leadership. Promoted to the rank of rear-admiral in the US Navy, he carried out much scientific exploration and he named Marie Byrd Land in honour of his wife. The work was often arduous and in 1934 he spent the winter alone in a small hut at his advance base.

On the eve of World War II, Byrd was appointed commander of the US Antarctic Service, but the post was short-lived. After the war, in which he served as a staff officer, Byrd returned to the Antarctic, flying into Little America in January 1947 aboard an R4D transport aircraft launched from the carrier USS *Philippine Sea*. His last flight over the South Pole was in January 1956 and he died in Boston, Massachusetts, the following year. The United States named Byrd Station, Antarctica, in his honour.

CALDWELL

Group Captain Clive R. Caldwell DSO, DFC and bar, (born 1910) was not only the top-scoring Australian fighter pilot of World War II, but also an outstanding fighter leader, who played a prominent part in the air defence of Darwin in 1943. Born on 28 July 1910 and educated at Sydney Grammar School, he learned to fly with the Royal Aero Club of New South Wales in 1938. He joined the Royal Australian Air Force in September 1939, was awarded his pilot's wings in November 1940, and was commissioned as a pilot officer in January 1941.

Caldwell was posted to the Middle East, where he joined No 250 Squadron flying Curtiss Tomahawks from Aqir in Palestine. His first taste of action came with the Syrian Campaign, but it was not until his squadron moved to the Western Desert that he gained his first victories. On 26 June 1941 he opened his score by shooting down a German Messerschmitt Bf 109, while escorting Blenheim bombers. Further victories followed, but on 29 August the tables were turned and he was hit and wounded by fire from two Bf 109s during a combat over Tobruk. Revenge came on 5 December, when he shot down five Junkers Ju 87 Stuka dive-bombers during a single sortie.

Right *Group Captain Clive Caldwell pictured with his Spitfire, which records victories over German, Italian and Japanese aircraft.*

Below *The pilots of No 112 Squadron pose in front of a Kittyhawk painted with the unit's shark-mouth marking in 1942. Caldwell is third from the left in the front row.*

Caldwell constantly sought to improve his gunnery skills and this effort paid off, for by the end of 1941 he was a flight commander on No 250 Squadron with 18½ victories to his credit. In January 1942 he was promoted to the rank of squadron leader and given command of No 112 Squadron, which was converting from Tomahawks to the more powerful Kittyhawks. His first victory in air combat with his new squadron came on 21 February, when he shot down a Bf 109. More significantly, at this time Caldwell carried out tests to determine the Kittyhawk's suitability as a fighter-bomber and as a result one of this aircraft's most effective operational roles was introduced.

In May 1942 Caldwell relinquished command of No 112 Squadron and moved to England, where he flew on operations for a short while with the Spitfire-equipped Kenley Wing. Thereafter he travelled home to Australia by way of the United States, arriving in Brisbane in September 1942. After a short time instructing at an operational training unit, he became wing leader of the newly arrived No 1 Fighter Wing in January 1943. This unit comprised three Spitfire squadrons which had been despatched from Britain to assist in the air defence of Darwin. Their first success came on 6 February, when a Mitsubishi Ki-46 Dinah reconnaissance aircraft was shot down, and Caldwell's first victories against the Japanese were scored on 2 March. The wing's fortunes against the Japanese were mixed. On 2 May Caldwell led the interception of a

Japanese raid which resulted in the loss of 11 Spitfires for only six of the enemy. However, on 20 June the position was reversed and nine Japanese aircraft were destroyed against only two Spitfires. On 20 August Caldwell intercepted a Dinah reconnaissance aircraft which he shot down, his last victory of the war bringing his total score to 28½. Unusually these included victories over all three member nations of the Axis Pact: Germany, Italy and Japan.

In September 1943 Caldwell was posted to command No 2 Operational Training Unit at Mildura in Victoria. He returned to an operational unit in April 1944, and when promoted to group captain he formed No 80 Wing, equipped with Spitfire Mk VIII fighters. The wing moved forward to Morotai, beween New Guinea and Borneo, in October 1944, in anticipation of the invasion of the Philippines. However, the Americans refused Australian units a part of this operation, much to the disgust of Caldwell and his pilots, and so for him the war ended on a sour note. He retired from the RAAF in March 1946.

CAYLEY

Sir George Cayley, Bt (1773–1857) was one of the most remarkable early aviation pioneers, whose theoretical work and practical experiments laid the foundations of the science of aerodynamics. A Yorkshire baronet, Cayley began his aeronautical experiments in 1796 by building a flying model helicopter, based on earlier work by the Frenchmen Launoy and Bienvenu. He next turned to the design of a fixed-wing aeroplane and his sketches for this, engraved on a silver medal dated 1799, show a monoplane wing machine with a cruciform tail unit, powered by paddles. Although his means of propulsion were impractical, he had made the important step of separating lifting surfaces from the means of propulsion. This meant a move away from the flapping-wing ornithopter machine, based on a mistaken notion of bird flight, that was to lead many of the early aviation pioneers astray.

Although lighter-than-air flight had become a practical proposition with the Montgolfier brothers' balloon of 1783, Cayley was not to be seduced away from his work on heavier-than-air machines. During the decade 1799 to 1809, he carried out a series of important experiments, investigating the effects of different aerofoil sections and angles of incidence on lifting surfaces. He then produced a successful model glider, by attaching a kite-like wing to a pole and fitting it with a cruciform tail unit. This fruitful decade ended with Cayley's testing of a full-scale glider with a 28m² (300sq. ft) wing, which was tested without a pilot. He was certainly aware of the need for a suitable aeroplane power plant, but he had dismissed the steam engine as unsuitable due to its poor power/weight ratio and his experiments with a gunpowder motor proved to be entirely unsuccessful.

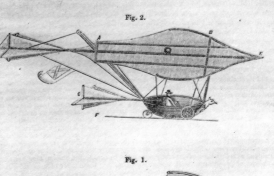

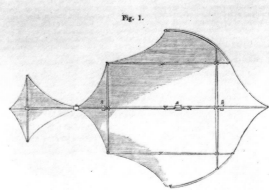

Above *Sir George Cayley. His theoretical work and practical experiments in the early nineteenth century laid the foundations of the science of aeronautics.*

Left *Cayley's design for a man-carrying glider, which was to be launched from a balloon, was illustrated on the cover of the* Mechanics Magazine.

The results of Cayley's experimental work were published in three parts in Nicholson's *Journal of Natural Philosophy, Chemistry and the Arts* in 1809–10 with the title 'On Aerial Navigation'. This classic treatise pointed out the basic aerodynamic forces acting on a fixed-wing aeroplane; it pointed out the effects of a wing's dihedral angle on lateral stability; it stated that a cambered aerofoil surface would provide greater lift than a flat one; it looked at the effects of movement of the centre of pressure on an aerofoil; and it described the basic principles of bird flight which had been consistently misunderstood up to this time. After the publication of this paper Cayley's interest in aviation languished and for 30 years he devoted his time to other interests.

In 1843, at the age of 70, Cayley resumed his work on aviation, stimulated by the publication of W. S. Henson's designs for an 'aerial steam carriage'. Cayley's 1843 design was for a 'convertiplane', which would take off using four helicopter rotors. Once airborne the rotors would close to form circular wings, and pusher airscrews would drive the machine forward. In 1849 there followed a triplane glider, which unlike the convertiplane was actually built and made a short towed flight carrying a ten-year-old boy. Four years later, Cayley built another glider in which his coachman – apparently much against his will – made a short gliding flight from one of the dales near Cayley's home at Brompton Hall in Yorkshire.

Perhaps the most fitting tribute to Cayley was made by Wilbur Wright, when he wrote in 1909: 'About 100 years ago an Englishman, Sir George Cayley, carried the science of flying to a point which it had never reached before and which it scarcely reached again during the last century.'

CHENNAULT

Lieutenant-General Clair Lee Chennault (1890–1958) formed and led the American Volunteer Group in China against the Japanese invader and rose to command the USAAF's 14th Air Force in World War II. After training as a teacher, Chennault enlisted in the US Army in 1917 and was later commissioned into the infantry. He then transferred to the Army Air Service and qualified as a pursuit (fighter) pilot in 1919. Two years later he was posted to the 1st Pursuit Group at Ellington Field, Texas, where he served alongside veterans of World War I and gained a valuable insight into fighter tactics.

At a time when most airmen were staunch advocates of the bomber, Chennault began to champion the cause of pursuit aviation, which properly handled, he argued, could defeat any bomber offensive. His views did not endear him to senior officers in the Army Air Corps, but Chennault was a natural rebel and persisted in publicizing his ideas on the role of the fighter. In 1933 he graduated from the Air Corps Tactical School at Maxwell Field, Alabama, and returned there as an instructor in pursuit aviation. At this time he formed a famous aerobatic team 'Three Men on the Flying Trapeze', whose Boeing P-12 fighters toured much of the United States. More importantly he published his ideas in a book entitled *The Role of Pursuit Aviation*. Yet his days in the Air Corps were numbered and in 1937 his critics in the service forced his retirement on

Chennault talks to Mustang maintenance men of the fourteenth Air Force during a tour of inspection.

Lieutenant-General Clair Chennault formed the American Volunteer Group for service in China and later commanded the USAAF's Fourteenth Air Force in that theatre.

the grounds of ill-health. The 46-year-old major, in common with many other pilots of his generation, had become deaf due to the effects of engine noise in an open cockpit.

Chennault's career as an airman was far from finished and immediately after his retirement he set out for China at the invitation of Chiang Kai-shek. On arrival he was appointed as Chiang's air adviser, with the rank of colonel, and set about creating an air-defence system to repel Japanese air raids. He found the task dauntingly difficult, as the Chinese pilots were inexpert fliers and the foreign volunteers little better. However, the situation improved in January 1941, when the US government offered China 100 Curtiss P-40 fighters and gave Chennault permission to recruit volunteer pilots for them from the US flying services. This was the origin of the American Volunteer Group (AVG) – or more popularly the Flying Tigers – which was to provide China with its first effective defensive fighter force.

Chennault, by then a brigadier-general in the Chinese air force, deployed two squadrons of the AVG at Kunming to protect the vital Burma Road supply route and the third he despatched to Burma to bolster the RAF's slender defences. The Flying Tigers fought well against the invading Japanese and by the time that Rangoon fell in March 1942 had claimed about 150 enemy aircraft destroyed. On 4 July 1942 Chennault and his AVG rejoined the US armed forces, the AVG becoming the USAAF's 23rd Fighter Group and Chennault's command the China Air Task Force. By this date the Flying Tigers' claims stood at 272 aerial victories, plus 225 enemy aircraft destroyed on the ground. In March 1943 Chennault's command became the 14th Air Force and he was raised to the rank of major-general. By the end of the year the 14th Air Force controlled 188 fighters, 51 heavy bombers, 23 medium bombers and various transport and reconnaissance aircraft. By the end of the war, Chennault's fighter squadrons had claimed the destruction of over 2300 Japanese aircraft. He returned to the United States in August 1945, but shortly afterwards went back to China to organize the China Air Transport airline. Chennault died in July 1958.

CHESHIRE

Group Captain Leonard Cheshire VC (born 1917) was one of the RAF's leading bomber pilots of World War II. Born in Chester on 7 September 1917, he completed his education at Merton College, Oxford, and became a member of the University Air Squadron. He was commissioned as an RAF reserve officer in 1937 and on the outbreak of war in September 1939 was mobilized to complete his flying training. He qualified for his pilot's wings in December 1939 and in June 1940 was posted to No 102 Squadron, which flew Armstrong Whitworth Whitley bombers from Driffield in Yorkshire. On the night of 12/13 November 1940, during a raid on Cologne, his aircraft was badly damaged by the premature ignition of a flare. Cheshire nevertheless succeeded in bringing the Whitley back to base and this accomplishment was recognized by the award of the Distinguished Service Order.

Cheshire completed his first tour of operations in January 1941 and, on volunteering for a second tour, was posted to No 35 Squadron at Linton-on-Ouse, Yorkshire, which flew the RAF's new Handley-Page Halifax four-engined bomber. By the end of 1941 Cheshire had been promoted to the rank of squadron leader and had added a bar to his DSO and received the Distinguished Flying Cross for his work on bomber operations. From January to August 1942 he served as an instructor at No 1652 Heavy Conversion Unit at Marston Moor, Yorkshire.

Right A sequence of photographs showing the marking of the Gnôme-Rhône factory at Limoges by Cheshire's Lancaster on the night of 8/9 February 1944.

Left Group Captain Leonard Cheshire was awarded the Victoria Cross in 1944 after taking part in more than 100 bombing missions in World War II.

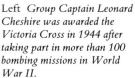

At the start of his third operational tour Cheshire was appointed to the command of No 76 Squadron, which flew Halifaxes from Linton-on-Ouse. He has written about his time on this squadron in his book *Bomber Pilot*. There followed promotion to group captain – at the age of 25 – and command of RAF Marston Moor, an appointment usually reserved for officers of far greater seniority. However, in September 1943 Cheshire willingly reverted to the rank of wing commander in order to take command of No 617 Squad-

ron – the legendary Dam Busters. This unit remained to some degree an elite squadron, with crews of above-average experience and ability, and consequently was called upon to carry out some very demanding missions. On the night of 8/9 February 1944, No 617

Squadron carried out a precision night attack on the Gnôme-Rhône factory at Limoges, with Cheshire marking the target from a height of only 60m (200ft). He repeated this success over Munich on the night of 24/25 April, while flying a twin-engined de Havilland Mosquito.

During the build-up to D-Day the squadron continued to attack precision targets and on the eve of the invasion they created a 'phantom' invasion fleet of their own off the Pas de Calais, dropping Window (metallized foil strips) in such a way as to create a radar echo similar to that of a group of ships. Three days after the landings, Cheshire marked the entrance to the Saumur railway tunnel, an incredibly difficult target which was nonetheless successfully blocked by bombing, thus delaying German reinforcements en route to Normandy. Thereafter the Dam Busters' special skills were put to good use in attacking V-weapons sites, Cheshire often using a single-seat Mustang fighter as a marker aircraft. On 6 July he flew his 100th operation and was then taken off combat flying. The award of the Victoria Cross followed in September. On 9 August 1945 Cheshire witnessed the detonation of the atom bomb on Nagasaki, flying as an observer aboard a Boeing B-29 Superfortress. He left the RAF in 1946 and has since devoted his life to charitable causes.

CLOSTERMANN

Pierre Clostermann (born 1921) was one of the Free French pilots who joined the RAF after the fall of France in June 1940 and by the end of the war, with 33 victories to his credit, he was one of the most successful and highly decorated French fighter pilots. In June 1940 Clostermann made his way to Britain from Brazzaville in the French Congo, where his father was serving. He learned to fly at Cranwell and then trained on Spitfires at No 61 Operational Training Unit. His first posting to an operational unit came in January 1943, when he joined the Free French No 341 (Alsace) Squadron.

Led by Commandant René Mouchotte, the squadron's Spitfires took part in fighter sweeps over occupied France as part of the Biggin Hill Wing. Clostermann flew on these missions as wingman to a more experienced pilot and so it was not until 27 July that he had the opportunity to open his score. On this day, the Biggin Hill Wing was escorting USAAF Marauders to Triqueville and on leaving the target they were bounced by a formation of Focke Wulf Fw 190 fighters. A confused dogfight developed during which Clostermann was able to shoot down two of the enemy fighters. On 27 August he flew as wingman to Mouchotte on an escort mission to St Omer. Enemy fighters split up the Spitfire formation and, although Clostermann succeeded in bringing down an Fw 190, his leader failed to return from the mission.

In October 1943 Clostermann was posted to No 602 Squadron at Detling in Kent, which was then engaged in Spitfire fighter-bomber attacks on V1 launching sites in the Pas de Calais region. In the new year the squadron moved north to the Orkneys to deal with high-flying reconnaissance aircraft over Scapa Flow. In the early summer the squadron returned south to participate in the Normandy invasion and from mid-June began to operate from a beach-head landing-strip – Clostermann being the first member of his squadron to land on French soil. At this time combats with enemy aircraft were infrequent and much of the action was against enemy ground forces. However, on 2 July, No 602 Squadron became engaged with a formation of 40 German fighters near Caen. Clostermann shot down two of them and shortly afterwards was awarded the Distinguished Flying Cross.

Posted back to Britain for a rest from operations, Clostermann then attended a course at the Advanced Gunnery School at Catfoss and in March 1945 returned

Below right *Pierre Clostermann (left) pictured with fellow pilot Ken Charney, when serving with No 602 Squadron equipped with Spitfire Mk IXs.*

Below *The Tempest pilots of No 3 Squadron pose for the cameraman at Volkel in Holland in 1945. Clostermann stands second from the left.*

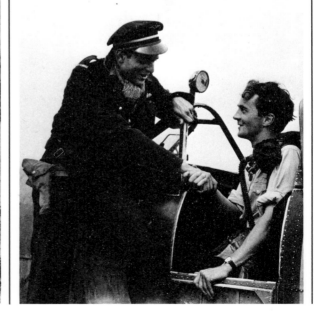

to the Continent. His new unit was No 274 Squadron, which flew the new Hawker Tempest fighter from Volkel in Holland. The last weeks of the war in Europe were to be a period of intense air combat for Clostermann. He reopened his scoring on 5 March, when he shot down one of a formation of four Messerschmitt Bf 109s. After transferring to No 56 Squadron, also flying Tempests, he continued to add to his score. On 5 April the squadron engaged 16 German fighters over Dummer Lake, Clostermann sharing in the destruction of two of them. He was then posted to No 3 Squadron as a flight commander, taking part in numerous attacks on air and ground targets right up until the end of the war. His total claims included 33 aerial victories, plus 24 aircraft destroyed on the ground. He left the RAF in August 1945 and settled in France, where he wrote *The Big Show*, a vivid account of his time with the RAF. He returned to military flying during the Algerian War, when he was recalled as a reservist to the Armée de l'Air.

air route to India. He set out on 20 November in a DH50 biplane, accompanied by engineer Arthur Elliott. They went as far as Rangoon in Burma and on his return Cobham had covered 27,360km (17,000 miles) in 220 flying hours over a period of four months. The authorities were favourably impressed by Cobham's reports and the following year he was asked to survey an air route to South Africa for Imperial Airways. Again flying a DH50, Cobham completed the 13,060km (8115-mile) flight to Cape Town – only the second time that this had been accomplished. On his return flight, despite being delayed by torrential rains, he arrived in Britain two days before the *Union Castle* liner which had left Cape Town at the same time.

Cobham's DH50 was converted to a floatplane in 1926 for a flight to Australia. However, when flying over Iraq, the aircraft was hit by a bullet fired by an Arab tribesman, injuring Cobham's engineer Elliott and severing a fuel line. Cobham made a hasty landing at Basra, but Elliott died of his injuries that night.

Below *Cobham's DH50J floatplane alights on the River Thames in October 1926, on his return from Australia. This flight earned him a knighthood.*

COBHAM

Sir Alan Cobham (1894–1973) did more perhaps than any other pioneer to foster air-mindedness among the British public between the wars. After serving in the Royal Field Artillery for three years of World War I, Cobham transferred to the Royal Flying Corps as a pilot. In 1919 he purchased a war-surplus Avro 504K trainer and formed Berkshire Aviation Tours to provide joyrides for members of the public. Poor weather during the summer of 1920 forced the firm to close and Cobham moved on to fly for de Havilland Hire Service. There followed a variety of flying jobs, including air mail flights to Spain, aerial tours of North Africa and ferrying the ultra-light de Havilland DH53 Humming Bird to Brussels for an exhibition.

In 1924 Cobham was chosen by the Director of Civil Aviation, Sir William Sefton Branker, to survey an

Left *Sir Alan Cobham, pictured on his return from India in 1925, took a leading part in developing civil air routes in the years between the two World Wars.*

Right *Former Wild West showman Samuel Cody pioneered heavier-than-air flying in Britain and he won the 1912 Military Aeroplane Trials.*

Cobham intended to abandon the flight, but was persuaded to continue, accompanied by an RAF NCO. He reached Australia in August and, on his return to Britain, landed the DH50 on the Thames beside the Houses of Parliament to a hero's welcome from the London crowds. He received a knighthood for his services to civil aviation.

In 1927–8 Cobham completed a 59,550km (37,000-mile) circumnavigation of Africa in a Singapore flying boat, the first time that this had been done. He was back in Africa in 1931, flying a Short Valetta seaplane on a survey of the Belgian Congo. Then for the following five years he devoted his energies to his 'National Aviation Day' touring airshows, which covered most of the United Kingdom, giving over 12,000 air displays and carrying more than one million

CODY

Samuel Franklin Cody (1861–1913), one of the most flamboyant of the early aviation pioneers, played an important part in the establishment of military aviation in Britain. A Texan of Irish-American stock, Cody first came to Britain as a Wild West showman – in the style of his famous compatriot and namesake 'Buffalo Bill' Cody. It was while there in 1899 that he became interested in the current craze for kite flying, which had been started by the Australian aviation pioneer Lawrence Hargrave. Cody scaled up the Hargrave box kite to the point where a string of them could lift a man aloft, and he interested the War Office in this invention, which could be used in winds too high to allow observation balloons to be flown.

Cody then progressed to the construction of man-carrying gliders, with wings constructed on the Hargrave box-kite principle, and the first of these took to the air in 1905. Like all Cody's flying machines, it was a massive aircraft for its day, spanning 15·5m (51ft). The glider was flown by various army officers at Aldershot before it crashed, severely injuring the inventor's son. Cody then became involved in the construction of the army's Dirigible No 1 – otherwise known as *Nulli Secundus* – which first flew with him aboard on 10 September 1907. By this time he was a familiar figure at the Army Balloon School at Farnborough, Hants, astride his white horse with his long beard and flowing shoulder-length hair.

Yet Cody's showmanship concealed a genuine enthusiasm for aviation. His work on *Nulli Secundus* had given him an insight into the workings of the petrol engine and he determined to apply this to the construction of a powered aeroplane. His machine, the Army Aeroplane No 1, was built at Farnborough in 1908. It is uncertain whether this or A. V. Roe's aeroplane was the first to fly in Britain, but what is certain is that the early flights of Cody's aeroplane were bedevilled by a series of crashes. He persevered and on 14 May 1909 succeeded in remaining airborne over a distance of 1·6km (1 mile). In 1910 Cody became a

Above *Cobham's DH50J is moored on the River Thames near the Houses of Parliament in October 1926 after its flight from Australia.*

passengers on joyrides. During the same period Cobham began to experiment with ways of increasing an aeroplane's range by in-flight refuelling. In 1934, accompanied by Squadron Leader William Helmore, he attempted to fly an Airspeed Courier non-stop from Portsmouth to Karachi, refuelling four times en route. The flight only reached Malta before the Courier was forced to land, but the concept had proved to be workable and Cobham formed Flight Refuelling Ltd to develop his ideas. It was not until the 1950s, however, that aerial refuelling became widely used by military operators and Cobham's company reaped the benefits of its pioneering work.

In January 1917 Collishaw was posted to No 3 (Naval) Squadron, a Sopwith Pup-equipped scout unit which was operating on the Western Front in support of the Royal Flying Corps. On 15 February he gained his first victory and later that month his squadron moved airfields from Vert Galand to Bertangles, near Amiens. On 24 March Collishaw's Pup was badly damaged in combat and his goggles smashed. Although he managed to return to his airfield, his face was badly frostbitten and he had to return to Britain to recover.

When Collishaw returned to France on 26 April he was posted to No 10 (Naval) Squadron, flying Sopwith Triplanes at Furnes in Belgium. Taking over command of the squadron's B Flight, Collishaw celebrated his promotion by destroying an enemy scout

naturalized British subject and at that time he was the most experienced aeroplane pilot in the country.

In 1911 the *Daily Mail* offered a £10,000 prize for the winner of the Circuit of Britain Race over a 1600km (1000-mile) course. Cody produced a new biplane to compete for the prize and it was the only British-built aeroplane to complete the course – but it finished three days behind the winner. Yet the ebullient Cody was not discouraged and he went on to win two Michelin Trophies and to establish a new British endurance record of 5 hours 15 minutes in the air.

Cody constructed a new monoplane powered by a 120hp Austro-Daimler engine to compete in the Military Aeroplane Trials at Larkhill on Salisbury Plain in July 1912. When this crashed, he transferred its engine into his Circuit of Britain biplane and entered this in the Trials. To the amazement of all, it was declared the winner (the excellent government-built BE2 was ineligible for the competition). Cody received £5000 in prize money and turned his attention to designing a floatplane to compete in a round-Britain race for seaplanes. It was while testing this machine (fitted with a land undercarriage) at Laffen's Plain, Farnborough, on 7 August 1913, that Cody crashed to his death.

Above Cody tests the controls of his 1910 biplane, in which he established a British endurance record by remaining airborne for four hours 47 minutes.

Right Raymond Collishaw chats to one of his Camel pilots in July 1918, when he commanded No 203 Squadron of the newly formed Royal Air Force.

on 28 April. The following month the squadron moved to the Ypres sector and during a period of intense air fighting from May until July Collishaw's flight claimed the destruction of 67 enemy aircraft. Collishaw's personal score was 32 victories, and his 'Black Flight', composed entirely of Canadian pilots, was one of the most successful units of its size in France.

At the end of July 1917 Collishaw was given three months' home leave in Canada. On returning to France he joined the RNAS Seaplane Defence Squadron at St Pol, which flew Sopwith Camels. In December he was appointed to command the squadron, but in January he returned to No 3 (Naval) Squadron as commanding officer. For his first four months in command (at the end of which the unit was retitled No 203 Squadron RAF), Collishaw saw no action, as at this time the CO was not expected to fly in combat. However, in June Collishaw began to lead his squadron in the air and resumed scoring on 11 June. Thereafter, until relieved of his command in October, he flew three or four combat patrols each week, bringing his score to 60 victories, which made him the third-highest-scoring ace of the British services.

COLLISHAW

Air Vice-Marshal Raymond Collishaw (1893–1976) was the third-ranking air ace of the British flying services in World War I and went on to attain high command in the RAF during World War II. Born on 22 November 1893 on Vancouver Island in Canada, Collishaw joined the Canadian fisheries protection service on leaving school. With the outbreak of World War I he volunteered for service as a pilot with the Royal Naval Air Service. After completing his training in 1916 he joined No 3 Wing RNAS, which was equipped with Sopwith 1½-Strutters and Short Bombers, at Manston in Kent. In September the wing flew across the Channel to Luxeuil-les-Bains and began bombing raids into Germany.

Left *Collishaw was a highly successful fighter pilot in World War I, and when Italy entered World War II in June 1940 he commanded the RAF in Egypt.*

After the Armistice, Collishaw remained in the RAF, commanding No 47 Squadron which flew against the Bolsheviks in south Russia during 1919–20. He then commanded No 30 Squadron in Iraq and No 41 Squadron in Britain. After attending Staff College, Collishaw was promoted to group captain in 1935. He commanded the RAF in Egypt when Italy entered World War II and used his meagre forces to good effect against a much more numerous enemy. In mid-1943 he retired with the rank of air vice-marshal.

COPPENS

Willy Coppens (born 1892) was the leading Belgian air ace of World War I. Born at Watermael near Brussels on 6 July 1892, he was serving with the 3rd Battalion of the 2nd Grenadier Regiment on the outbreak war. In September 1915 his request to transfer to the Aviation Militaire was granted and he learned to fly in Britain at the Ruffy-Baumann School at Hendon. Returning to Belgium in December 1915, he completed his training on Maurice Farman biplanes at Etampes and was posted to the 6ᵉ Escadrille as a reconnaissance pilot. This was not to Coppens's liking, as he wanted to fly fighter aircraft. The life of a reconnaissance pilot was not entirely dull, however. While flying a Sopwith 1½-Strutter, Coppens was attacked by four German fighters over Houthulst Forest and returned to base in an aircraft riddled with 32 bullet holes.

In July 1917 Coppens was posted to 1ᵉ Escadrille at Les Moeres, which flew Nieuport 17 fighters. Among this unit's pilots were the aces Jan Olieslagers, André de Meulemeester and the unit's commander Fernand Jacquet. At first, success in aerial combat eluded Coppens, even when he changed his Nieuport for the newer Hanriot HD1. On 18 March 1918 he attacked a German observation balloon, but its crew winched it down before it was damaged. A second attempt on a balloon on 11 April was no more successful.

Coppens finally scored his first victory on 25 April, when a patrol of Belgian fighters attacked a formation of 20 German aircraft. Yet Coppens was still intent on shooting down observation balloons and he devised special tactics to deal with them. As supplies of incendiary ammunition were very limited, he would only carry four on each mission, but would press his attack to within 50m (160ft) of the target to be sure of hitting it. This technique had the desired effect, except that when he first tried it Coppens nearly rammed his intended victim. He soon established his reputation as a 'balloon buster' and whenever he heard of a new German balloon he would go after it and shoot it down. On one sortie in September 1918, he destroyed a balloon with a single incendiary round and was able to bring a second down in flames with his remaining ammunition.

Coppens's remarkable career as a balloon buster came to an end on 14 October 1918. Diving onto a balloon over Praet Bosh, he was hit in the leg by anti-aircraft fire. Despite the severe pain, he continued his attack. His aircraft then went into a spin, but Coppens managed to recover and to regain the Belgian lines. Once over friendly territory his aircraft crashed and the wounded pilot was rushed to hospital, where doctors had to amputate his leg.

Coppens's final score was 37 aerial victories, 28 of which were observation balloons. He was the highest-scoring Belgian ace by a considerable margin, his

Below *Willy Coppens (right) is pictured with fellow Belgian aces André de Meulemeester (second from right) and Fernand Jacquet (third from right).*

Above *The leading Belgian air ace of World War I, Coppens specialized in the destruction of enemy observation balloons.*

Below right *John Cunningham, pictured climbing into the DH Vampire jet fighter, became the the de Havilland company's chief test pilot after wartime service with the RAF.*

Below *Cunningham (left) examines the official badge of No 85 Squadron. He commanded this unit, flying Mosquito night fighters, from early 1943 until February 1944.*

nearest rival being his former squadron colleague de Meulemeester with 11 victories. After the war Coppens remained in the Belgian air force.

CUNNINGHAM

Group Captain John Cunningham (born 1917) was one of the RAF's most successful night-fighter pilots of World War II and in the postwar years he became the de Havilland company's chief test pilot. Born at Addington in Surrey on 17 July 1917, Cunningham joined de Havilland as a technical apprentice in 1935 and while studying at the company's Technical School at Hatfield, he learned to fly with No 604 (Middlesex) Squadron of the Royal Auxiliary Air Force.

On the outbreak of World War II, Cunningham's squadron was equipped with Bristol Blenheims, which flew air cover over coastal convoys. This monotonous duty continued until June 1940, when the squadron began to train for night fighting. In September No 604 Squadron received the first Bristol Beaufighters and on 20 November Cunningham scored his first victory at night. Promoted to flight lieutenant and by then a flight commander, Cunningham scored his second victory, a Heinkel He 111 of the pathfinder unit KGr 100, on 23 December. Following his third victory on 2 January 1941, Cunningham was awarded the Distinguished Flying Cross.

Early in 1941 Cunningham teamed up with Sergeant C. F. Rawnsley, who was to become his regular radar operator for the rest of the war. April proved to be a successful month for Cunningham, bringing him the award of the Distinguished Service Order and raising his score to ten victories (nine of them by night). The high point of the month was on the 15th, when he destroyed three enemy aircraft in a single night. In June Cunningham was promoted to wing commander and assumed command of No 604 Squadron. Shortly afterwards the squadron moved from Middle Wallop in Hampshire to Coltishall in Norfolk, where it was better placed to intercept German raiders heading for the industrial Midlands. In August Cunningham and Rawnsley had a narrow escape when return fire from a German bomber knocked out one of their Beaufighter's engines. However, Cunningham maintained control and bought the damaged fighter back to base.

At the end of the summer No 604 Squadron returned to Middle Wallop. Cunningham was by this time the most experienced and skilled British night-fighter pilot and, in addition to his squadron duties, he played an important part in the development of new

techniques and equipment for night fighting. His old firm, de Havilland, was working on the Mosquito night fighter, while the Telecommunications Research Establishment at Malvern was developing new radars and the Fighter Interception Unit at Ford evaluated tactics. In July 1942 Cunningham relinquished command of No 604 Squadron for a rest period of non-operational duties.

Cunningham began his second operational tour as CO of No 85 Squadron flying Mosquitoes in February 1943. During his year with the squadron he enjoyed considerable further success, notably against Focke Wulf Fw 190 night-fighter-bombers. His personal score then stood at 20 victories. He saw no further combat and after the war rejoined de Havilland, becoming chief test pilot and flying such famous aircraft as the Comet, Sea Vixen and Trident.

DEERE

Air Commodore Alan Deere (born 1918) was one of the most successful New Zealand fighter pilots in the RAF during World War II. After working on a sheep farm and in a solicitor's office in New Zealand, he came to Britain in 1937 to join the RAF as a pilot. After completing his flying training, he was posted to No 74 Squadron flying Gloster Gauntlets and then was posted to No 54 Squadron. On the outbreak of war this unit was flying Spitfires, but it was not until May 1940 that it went into action. Deere's first victories came on 23 May, when he and another pilot escorting a Miles Master training aircraft were intercepted by Messerschmitt Bf 109s. In the ensuing dogfight Deere shot down two enemy fighters.

Deere next saw action over Dunkirk, covering the evacuation of the British expeditionary force, and on 28 May his aircraft was hit by return fire from a Dornier Do 17 bomber and forced down. Fortunately he landed in British-held territory and was able to

Above *Alan Deere (right), serving as wing leader with the Biggin Hill Wing, confers with Squadron Leader J. Charles (centre), CO of No 611 Squadron, and the Station Commander Group Captain 'Sailor' Malan.*

Right *King George VI decorates Deere with the Distinguished Flying Cross at RAF Hornchurch in 1940. Air Chief-Marshal Sir Hugh Dowding, C-in-C Fighter Command, looks on.*

Left *A tough and pugnacious New Zealander, Deere fought with RAF Fighter Command over Dunkirk and during the Battle of Britain, becoming a wing leader in 1943.*

return to his unit aboard one of the evacuation ships. No 54 Squadron then withdrew to Catterick for a rest period, before returning south to Hornchurch in mid-June. As the Battle of Britain opened, Deere became a flight commander. He was forced to crash-land again on 9 July, after colliding with a Bf 109 during a dogfight over the Channel. This was one of a series of mishaps that led Deere to entitle his RAF memoirs *Nine Lives*.

By early August No 54 Squadron was operating from Manston, one of Fighter Command's forward bases in the Battle of Britain. Deere's personal score then stood at 11 victories and he had been decorated with the DFC and bar. Back at Hornchurch on 31 August, Deere had perhaps his narrowest escape of the war. He was taking off at the head of a section of three Spitfires when enemy bombs burst beneath them just after lift-off. All three Spitfires were destroyed, but their pilots escaped with minor injuries. The squadron was then pulled out of action. However, Deere was involved in a mid-air collision during a training flight shortly afterwards, and injured his back after baling out.

After serving as a fighter controller during a short rest period, Deere was posted to No 602 Squadron as a flight commander in May 1941. Shortly afterwards the squadron moved to Kenley in Surrey and began cross-Channel fighter sweeps. On 1 August Deere was promoted to command the squadron and celebrated this event with his first victory for over a year. His second tour of operations was completed at the end of the year and he departed on a liaison mission with the United States. Returning in February 1942, he assumed command of No 403 Squadron, but on 2 June this unit suffered heavy losses at the hands of Focke Wulf Fw 190s and was withdrawn from the fighting. Deere was then posted to a staff appointment at No 13 Group Headquarters. In February 1943 he was briefly attached to the Biggin Hill Wing to gain combat experience with the new Spitfire Mk IX. Shortly thereafter he was back at Biggin Hill as wing leader. By the summer his score had risen to 22 enemy aircraft destroyed, but illness then forced him to relinquish this command. After serving at the Central Gunnery School, he finished the war as a staff officer in the 2nd Tactical Air Force. He remained in the RAF after World War II, rising to the rank of air commodore.

DOOLITTLE

Lieutenant-General James H. Doolittle (born 1896) combined the careers of record-breaking and racing pilot and military airman between the wars, rising to a position of high command in the USAAF in World War II. He is probably best remembered for the audacious raid he led against Tokyo in 1942. Born at Alameda, California, on 14 December 1896, Doolittle joined the US Army Air Service in 1917 and learned

Above *A B-25 Mitchell of Doolittle's Tokyo raiding force lifts off from the carrier USS Hornet at the start of its mission.*

Right *In April 1942 James Doolittle led the USAAF's first bombing raid on the Japanese homeland. He then held a series of senior commands before his retirement in 1946.*

Below *Doolittle (fifth from left) and his crew pictured after successfully abandoning their bomber over China at the end of the Tokyo mission.*

to fly on Curtiss Jennies. He saw no action in World War I, but in September 1922 he made a notable coast-to-coast flight across the United States in a de Havilland DH4 biplane, taking 21 hours 19 minutes to cover 3480km (2163 miles). This was the first occasion on which the country had been crossed in under 24 hours.

In 1925 Doolittle took part in the Schneider Trophy seaplane contest, piloting a Curtiss R3C-2 floatplane. Not only did he beat his British and Italian rivals to gain the Trophy for the United States in that year, but he also established a world air speed record for seaplanes. The following year he toured South America to demonstrate the Curtiss-Wright P-1 Hawk biplane fighter. In 1928–9 he worked as a test pilot to develop blind flying instruments, making the first flight 'under the hood' on 24 September 1929. In 1930 he resigned his commission in the US Army Air Corps and went to work for the Shell Oil Company. His air-racing activities continued and in 1931 he won both the Bendix and Thompson races.

In mid-1940 with Europe at war Doolittle was recalled to military service and with the rank of major he supervised the conversion of automobile production plants to aeroplane assembly. Yet more exciting and congenial work was in prospect. In January 1942 he was given the task of organizing a raid on the Japanese capital Tokyo. No American air bases were within range of this target so Doolittle's force of 16 twin-engined North American B-25 Mitchell bombers had to operate from the flight deck of the carrier USS *Hornet*. Aircraft of the Mitchell's size and weight had never previously operated from a carrier deck, but after practising take-offs from a dummy deck marked on the runway of Eglin Field, Florida, Doolittle was confident that it could be done.

His force of 16 Mitchells embarked aboard the *Hornet*, which sailed from San Francisco on 12 April. Six days later the carrier was within 1000km (620 miles) of the Japanese home islands and at 0800 hours Doolittle lifted his Mitchell from the *Hornet*'s deck. The following bombers formed up into five three-aircraft flights, three of them bound for Tokyo, one for Yokohama and one for Osaka. All but one of the Mitchells, which had to jettison its load when engaged by enemy fighters, delivered their bombs on target and the bombers then set course for Chuchow airfield in China. This landing ground was at extreme range for the Mitchells, however, and had no navigation aids to guide the bombers in. Consequently, they had to force-land wherever they could. Doolittle's crew and those of five other bombers made it to friendly territory and were returned to the United States. The raid gave a tremendous boost to morale and Doolittle received the Medal of Honor and was promoted to brigadier-general. He went on to command the Twelfth, Fifteenth and Eighth Air Forces of the USAAF, becoming the youngest lieutenant-general in the US Army. In 1946 he retired from active duty to resume his business career.

DOWDING

Air Chief-Marshal Lord Dowding (1882–1970) was the architect of RAF Fighter Command's victory in the Battle of Britain, Germany's first major defeat of World War II. Born on 24 April 1882, Hugh Dowding entered the Royal Military Academy at Woolwich in 1899 and a year later was commissioned into the Royal Garrison Artillery. In 1913 while attending the Staff College at Camberley, Surrey, he learned to fly and in October 1914 he went to France with No 6 Squadron RFC. He remained in France until 1917, serving on the staff and with squadrons in the field. By the following year he had reached the rank of brigadier-general and he was granted a permanent commission as a group captain in the postwar RAF.

In the inter-war years he served in Iraq and Palestine as well as in various appointments in the United Kingdom. In 1929 he commanded the Fighting Area of Air Defence of Great Britain (forerunner of Fighter Command) and then went to the Air Ministry, joining the Air Council as Air Member for Supply and Research. His work here led to the development of the eight-gun monoplane Spitfire and Hurricane fighters. In 1936 Dowding became the first C-in-C of RAF Fighter Command and prepared the air defences of the United Kingdom for the coming war with Germany. The quality of his work stood the test of combat during the summer of 1940, when RAF Fighter Command decisively defeated the Luftwaffe in the Battle of Britain, albeit by the narrowest of margins. This outstanding victory was shabbily rewarded when Dowding was relieved of his command in November 1940 and offered no comparable senior position. Uncomplainingly, he retired from the RAF in the following year.

Above *Dowding talks to former Battle of Britain pilots on the fifth anniversary of the Battle. He stands fourth from the left, with Douglas Bader to his left.*

Left *Air Chief-Marshal Sir Hugh Dowding was the first air officer commanding RAF Fighter Command and he led this force to victory in the Battle of Britain.*

DUKE

Squadron Leader Neville Duke (born 1922) was the top-scoring Allied fighter pilot in the Mediterranean and Middle East in World War II and as a test pilot after the war he established a new world air speed record flying the Hawker Hunter fighter. He was born at Tonbridge, Kent, on 11 January 1922 and in 1940 he volunteered for pilot training with the RAF. He gained his pilot's wings in February 1941 and in April was posted to No 92 Squadron, then the top-scoring unit in Fighter Command, which flew Spitfire Mk VBs from Biggin Hill in Kent. Duke took part in numerous fighter sweeps over France and on 25 June 1941 he scored his first victory, shooting down a Messerschmitt Bf 109 over Dunkirk.

In October 1941, with two victories to his credit, Duke was posted to Egypt, where he joined No 112

Below *Neville Duke pictured in the cockpit of a Hunter fighter when he was chief test pilot for the Hawker Aircraft Company in the 1950s.*

Bottom *In 1929 Ira Eaker (second from right) was one of the crew of the Fokker C-2A which set a world endurance record. Carl Spaatz stands on his left.*

Squadron at Sidi Henesh. Flying Curtiss Tomahawks, Duke reopened his scoring on 23 November, when he downed a Bf 109 from the Luftwaffe's elite Jagdgeschwader 27. This success was not typical of RAF fortunes at this period and before the end of the year Duke had been shot down himself on two occasions, but without suffering serious injury. In January 1942 the squadron re-equipped with Curtiss Kittyhawks and on 14 February accounted for 16 enemy aircraft for no loss to themselves, Duke's share being an Italian Macchi MC200.

From March to November 1942 Duke served as an instructor in the Canal Zone and then returned to operations with No 92 Squadron flying Spitfire Mk VCs from Gambut. In January 1943, with 11 victories to his credit, he was promoted to flight lieutenant and became a flight commander on his squadron. In March he added seven victories to his score and was awarded the Distinguished Service Order. In April he was taken off operations again and posted to No 73 Operational Training Unit at Abu Sueir as chief flying instructor with the rank of squadron leader.

In February 1944 Duke was appointed CO of No 145 Squadron, flying Spitfire Mk VIIIs at Caserta in Italy. His successes against enemy aircraft continued, earning him a second bar to his DFC. On 7 June his Spitfire was damaged by ground-fire during a strafing attack and he was forced to bale out over Lake Bracciano. He was picked up by two Italian boys in a boat and, evading capture, he regained the Allied lines. By this time enemy aircraft were seldom encountered, and the squadron began dive-bombing sorties, each Spitfire carrying a 226kg (500lb) bomb. On 3 September he handed over command of his squadron and his combat career was at an end. He had flown a total of 496 operational sorties and was credited with 28 confirmed kills, plus six probables and ten enemy aircraft damaged.

On his return to Britain Duke was posted to the Hawker Aircraft Company at Langley as a production test pilot, flying the Tempest Mk II and Mk V. After completing the Empire Test Pilots' School course, he joined the RAF High Speed Flight, which gained the world air speed record in 1946. Two years later he joined Hawkers as a test pilot and as chief test pilot from 1951 to 1956 he tested the RAF's new Hunter fighter. On 7 September 1953, piloting the Hunter Mk 3, Duke gained the world air speed record.

EAKER

Lieutenant General Ira C. Eaker (born 1896) was one of the champions of air power in the United States during the inter-war years and rose to high command during World War II. Eaker was born on 13 April 1896 at Llano, Texas, and was commissioned in the infantry before transferring to the Army Air Service in

November 1917. He saw no active service in World War I, but his postwar assignments included service in the Philippines (1919–22) and command of the 5th Aero Squadron at Mitchell Field, New York. In Janaury 1929 he commanded the Fokker C-2A *Question Mark*, which made a record endurance flight of 150 hours with the help of in-flight refuelling. In 1936 he made the first 'blind' transcontinental flight across the United States, using the instruments developed by Elmer Sperry. After commanding the Boeing P-26-equipped 17th Pursuit Group in the early 1930s, Eaker went to Washington as a staff officer. By 1940 he was executive officer to General 'Hap' Arnold, Chief of the Air Corps, with whom he collaborated in writing the book *Winged Warfare*.

In the autumn of 1941 Eaker came to Britain in order to observe the air war in Europe at first hand. Then after the United States entered the war against Germany he returned to Britain as commander of the US Eighth Air Force's Bomber Command. Despite the scepticism of his RAF counterparts, he pressed ahead with plans for massed daylight bomber raids over Germany. On 17 August 1942, Boeing B-17s of the Eighth Air Force made their first bombing raid over enemy-occupied France and Eaker himself was aboard one of the bombers for the mission.

In December 1942 Eaker became commanding general of the Eighth Air Force, a position that he was to hold for the most crucial year of the American daylight bombing offensive against Germany. In January 1943 Eaker flew to Casablanca, where Churchill and Roosevelt were conferring, and his arguments convinced the war leaders that the USAAF should be allowed to persevere with its daylight bombing campaign. This decision was confirmed in a policy directive, which called upon the RAF and USAAF to coordinate strategic air attacks on Germany by night and day. The RAF's experience of daylight bombing raids had been disastrous and they had been forced to switch their attacks to the hours of darkness. Senior

General Ira Eaker assumed command of the USAAF Eighth Air Force's bomber units early in 1942 and he accompanied the B-17 crews on the first mission over enemy territory.

RAF commanders urged the Americans to follow suit. When the Eighth Air Force began deep penetration raids into Germany it seemed that the RAF had been right. Losses were prohibitively high, 60 US bombers failing to return out of a force of 291 B-17s which attacked Schweinfurt on 14 October. But Eaker was not deflected from his belief in daylight bombing tactics and persevered with his plans to develop a long-range fighter escort force for the bombers, as well as radar bombing aids and pathfinder techniques to improve the accuracy of the Eighth Air Force's bombing.

Eaker did not remain with the Eighth Air Force to see the results of this work in 1944, as in January that year he was transferred to the Mediterranean theatre as commander of the Mediterranean Allied Air Forces. He remained there until the end of the war, building up the Fifteenth Air Force for strategic raids on southern Germany and providing air cover for the invasion of the south of France in August 1944. Nor did he lose his taste for experiencing combat at first hand, for in June 1944 he flew on the 15th AF's first shuttle mission to the Soviet Union. After the war he became deputy commanding general of the USAAF, holding this post until his retirement in 1947.

EARHART

Amelia Earhart (1898–1937) was one of the best-known women record-breaking pilots of the inter-war years and the mystery surrounding her disappearance in 1937 has still to be solved. Born on 24 July 1898, she served as a military nurse in Canada during World War I. In 1928 she became the first woman to fly the Atlantic as a passenger aboard a Fokker FVII/3m float-plane. The hollowness of this achievement spurred her to attempt the crossing piloting the aircraft herself. By early 1932, with a thousand hours of flying in her log-book, she was ready for the flight. On 20 May that year she took off from Harbour Grace, Newfoundland, at the controls of a Lockheed Vega monoplane, and headed out into the Atlantic. Battling through rain and fog, she reached the Irish coast and after a flight

Amelia Earhart is greeted in London by the United States ambassador Andrew Mellon, after completing the first solo Atlantic flight by a woman in May 1932.

lasting 15 hours 8 minutes landed in a meadow on the outskirts of Londonderry. She was the first woman to fly solo across the Atlantic and her achievement was recognized by the United States government awarding her the Distinguished Flying Cross.

The next record that Amelia Earhart attempted was the coast-to-coast crossing of the United States. This she accomplished on 25 August 1932 in a flight of 19 hours 5 minutes from Los Angeles to New York, the first time that a woman had made the flight non-stop. The following year she covered the same route and was able to take nearly two hours off her previous flight time. In January 1935 she became the first person to fly from Hawaii to California – a distance of some 3860km (2400 miles) over open ocean. That same year she made the first solo flights from Los Angeles to Mexico City and from Mexico City to Newark, New Jersey. Her flights led to the International League of Aviators awarding her the prestigious Harmon Trophy in 1936.

The next flight on which Amelia Earhart had set her sights was to be the most gruelling she had ever contested – a 43,500km (27,000-mile) flight around the world. For this she purchased a twin-engined Lockheed 10E monoplane, which was fitted with additional fuel tanks to give it a 7250km (4500-mile) range. On 17 March 1937 she took off from Oakland, California,

bound for Hawaii, with a three-man crew aboard the Lockheed 10E. Three days later, as she was taking off from Wheeler Field, Hawaii, the starboard undercarriage leg collapsed and the aircraft was seriously damaged, needing extensive repairs.

Ten weeks later, Amelia Earhart was ready to start her flight around the world for the second time. Carrying only one other person, her navigator Fred Noonan, she took off from Miami, Florida, on 1 June and set course for Puerto Rico. From the Caribbean, she flew south in stages to Brazil and then crossed the Atlantic to Dakar. Her route then took her across Africa to Khartoum and eastwards to Karachi, Calcutta, Bangkok, Singapore and Australia. On arriving at Lae, New Guinea, she had covered 35,500km (22,000 miles) in 30 days. The next leg of the flight to Howland Island, a distance of over 4000km (2500 miles), would be a taxing feat of navigation. Yet in spite of problems with the aircraft's navigation equipment, Amelia was determined to continue. The aircraft took off from Lae on 2 July 1937 and disappeared without trace. A full-scale search was organized, but despite rumours that Amelia Earhart and Noonan had become prisoners of the Japanese, their fate remains one of the mysteries of the air.

EDWARDS

Air Commodore Hugh Idwal Edwards VC (1914–82) was one of the RAF's outstanding low-level bomber pilots in World War II. Born in Fremantle, Western Australia, on 1 August 1914, he enlisted as a private soldier in the Australian Army in 1934. The following year he transferred to the Royal Australian Air Force and qualified for his pilot's wings in June 1936. Later that year he transferred to the RAF and on arriving in Britain was posted to No 15 Squadron at Abingdon, which flew Hawker Hind biplanes. In 1937 he was posted to No 90 Squadron, which began to re-equip with the new Bristol Blenheim monoplane. It was while flying this aeroplane that he crashed and suffered a serious leg injury.

Left *Amelia Earhart pictured in Britain in 1928, after she became the first woman to cross the Atlantic by air, as a passenger aboard a Fokker Trimotor floatplane.*

Below *Wing Commander Hugh Edwards commanded No 105 Squadron, flying the DH Mosquito bomber on daylight raids over Europe in 1942–3.*

It was not until April 1940 that Edwards was again fit for flying duties. In February 1941 he joined No 139 Squadron flying Blenheim Mk IV bombers and in May became CO of the similarly equipped No 105 Squadron. On 15 June he led his squadron in a daring attack on enemy shipping for which he received the Distinguished Flying Cross. On 4 July he led a force of 15 Blenheims drawn from his own and No 107 Squadron against an industrial complex at Bremen. Flying at low level to confuse the defenders, the Blenheims ran the gauntlet of an intense barrage of flak to reach the target. Despite his aircraft being repeatedly hit and his gunner wounded, Edwards circled the target to assess the effect of the attack. His gallantry and determination on this occasion were recognized by the award of the Victoria Cross.

At the end of July 1941 Edwards led No 105 Squadron to Malta, where they flew anti-shipping strikes over the central Mediterranean. Back in Britain in October, Edwards left the squadron to carry out a tour of the United States. He then served as an instructor, before returning to No 105 Squadron in August 1942. The unit was now flying the de Havilland Mosquito, undoubtedly the finest low-level bomber of the war, and Edwards led many daylight raids into occupied Europe and Germany. On 29 August his bomber was intercepted by a group of Focke Wulf Fw 190s, which succeeded in knocking out one of his engines. Despite this handicap the Mosquito showed the pursuers a clean pair of heels and Edwards nursed the damaged bomber into a wheels-up landing at Lympne. On 6 December he took part in a large-scale daylight attack on the Philips factory at Eindhoven in Holland, which involved not only Mosquitoes but also Boston, Mitchell, Ventura and Blenheim bombers.

On 5 January 1943 Edwards was awarded the Distinguished Service Order. A month later he was pro-

Above Edwards talks to Australian Prime Minister John Curtin during the latter's visit to RAF Station, Binbrook, which Edwards commanded in 1944.

Right Lieutenant-Commander Eugene Esmonde was awarded the Victoria Cross for leading the Fleet Air Arm's attack on the German battlecruisers Scharnhorst *and* Gneisenau *in the English Channel on 12 February 1942.*

moted to group captain and took command of the Bomber Command station at Binbrook, Lincolnshire. Although he was not obliged to fly on operations, he nonetheless flew more than a dozen night-bombing missions with the Lancasters of No 460 Squadron, a Royal Australian Air Force unit stationed at Binbrook. At the end of 1944 he was posted to the Far East, becoming Group Captain, Bombing Operations at Air Headquarters, Southeast Asia, based at Kandy in Ceylon. He remained in the RAF after the war, rising to the rank of air commodore, and he retired in 1963.

ESMONDE

Lieutenant-Commander Eugene Esmonde (1909–42) was the Fleet Air Arm officer who led the attack by Fairey Swordfish torpedo bombers on the German battlecruisers *Scharnhorst* and *Gneisenau* during their Channel Dash in February 1942. For this action he was posthumously awarded the Victoria Cross. Esmonde was born on 1 March 1909 and he joined the RAF in 1928 on a five-year engagement, serving with a fighter squadron and with the Fleet Air Arm. He then became a pilot with Imperial Airways, but in 1939 he rejoined the Fleet Air Arm (which in 1937 had been transferred from the RAF to the Royal Navy) and was given the rank of lieutenant-commander.

On the outbreak of World War II Esmonde commanded the Swordfish-equipped No 825 Squadron and with this unit he took part in the hunt for the German battleship *Bismarck* in May 1941, leading a torpedo attack against the warship which won him the Distinguished Service Order. In the following November his squadron was aboard HMS *Ark Royal* when she was torpedoed and sunk by a German U-boat. There followed the heroic attack against the *Scharnhorst* and

Gneisenau on 12 February 1942, made in the face of intense opposition from flak and fighters. The six Swordfish of No 825 Squadron, flying from a shore base at RAF Manston in Kent, were shot from the sky. Esmonde and 12 of his comrades lost their lives and only five of the Swordfish crew members survived.

FONCK

René Fonck (1894–1953) was not only the top-scoring Allied pilot of World War I, but was second only to von Richthofen among the fighter pilots of all the combatant nations. Born in Saulcy-sur-Meurthe, France, Fonck was posted to an aviation training school at Dijon after his mobilization in August 1914. Within a month he was transferred to an engineer unit and for five months was engaged in building trenches before he was allowed to resume his pilot training. After qualifying as a pilot Fonck was posted to a reconnaissance unit, Escadrille C47, flying twin-engined Caudron G4 biplanes over the Vosges sector.

In July and August 1915 Fonck's unit was heavily engaged in low-level reconnaissance work, moving north to the Champagne sector in this period. On 22 August Fonck was commended for his reconnaissance work in an official citation. Meanwhile the pace of operational flying continued. On 25 September Fonck's Caudron was forced down by a broken fuel line, but he managed to regain French territory before crash-landing. In November Escadrille C47 shifted its operations to the Oise sector and it was here that Fonck gained his first aerial victory, albeit unconfirmed. This was a Fokker monoplane which fell to his guns on 1 March 1916. In July 1916 Escadrille C47 became a fighter unit, the change in role being effected simply by fitting the Caudron G4s with a fixed, forward-

Right René Fonck carries the standard of the Aviation Militaire during the 1919 Bastille Day parade in Paris.

firing machine gun. On 6 August Fonck forced a German two-seater to land behind Allied lines for his first officially confirmed victory. In March 1917 Fonck scored another success and this led to his transfer to *Les Cigognes* – Groupe de Chasse No 12 – on 15 April 1917.

On joining France's elite fighter unit, Fonck was allocated to Escadrille SPA 103 flying the Spad SVII. From then on Fonck steadily began to score victories over his opponents and by the middle of January 1918 he had destroyed 21 enemy aircraft. A superb shot and a methodical and self-assured man, he seldom took unnecessary risks. Nonetheless, he could on occasions outshine even such brilliant and headstrong contemporaries as Nungesser and Guynemer. One such demonstration came on 9 May 1918, when Fonck took off on his first sortie of the day at 1600 hours, after waiting for mist to clear. He engaged a formation of three two-seaters, all of which he shot down. After refuelling and rearming, he took off again at 1730 hours and encountered and shot down another two-seater. He then came across a formation of 11 enemy scouts, which he engaged, shooting down both the formation leader and the rearmost machine to bring his score for the day up to six. This performance was certainly no matter of luck for on 26 September he again brought down six opponents.

At the beginning of August Fonck's total score stood at 57 victories, making him the highest-scoring French ace, as Guynemer had 54 victories at the time of his death. Fonck's last victory of the war came on 1 November 1918, when he brought down a German two-seater which was dropping propaganda leaflets. His official total stood at 75, but Fonck maintained that the true figure was some 120. After the war he became a stunt flier and attempted some record flights. He later rejoined the Armée de l'Air and in 1937 became Inspecteur de l'Aviation de Chasse, retiring in 1939.

Below René Fonck, pictured in front of his Spad SVII scout, was the leading Allied air ace of World War I with 75 victories to his credit.

GABRESKI

Colonel Francis Gabreski (born 1919) was the third-ranking American fighter ace and his victories include both German aircraft in World War II and Communist Chinese MiG-15s over Korea. Born of Polish immigrant parents at Oil City, Pennsylvania, Gabreski intended to become a doctor. However, in June 1940 he abandoned his studies and enlisted in the Army Air Corps as an aviation cadet. On completing his flying training, he was posted to the 45th Pursuit Squadron, which flew Curtiss P-40s from Wheeler Field, Hawaii. He was one of the fighter pilots who managed to get airborne to meet the Japanese attack on Pearl Harbor on 8 December 1941, but he gained no victories on this day.

Gabreski returned to the continental United States in October 1942 and joined the 56th Fighter Group, the first unit to equip with the Republic P-47 Thunderbolt. He was appointed a flight leader with the group's 61st Fighter Squadron and, when the Thunderbolts arrived in Britain, was detached to gain operational experience with the RAF's No 315 (Polish) Squadron at Northolt. His Polish background made him immediately acceptable on the squadron and he gained much valuable experience in the course of 13 operational missions, flying the Spitfire Mk V. The 56th Fighter Group began operations in April 1943 and in June Gabreski was promoted to major and assumed command of the 61st Fighter Squadron.

During the summer of 1943 the Thunderbolts penetrated ever deeper into enemy air space, escorting the USAAF's four-engined heavy bombers. Gabreski's first victory came on 24 August, when he shot down a Focke Wulf Fw 190, and he repeated the success in September. By the end of the year his score stood at eight victories.

Above Francis Gabreski briefs the pilots of the 61st Fighter Squadron prior to an escort mission over enemy-occupied Europe.

Right Gabreski in the cockpit of his Republic P-47 Thunderbolt during his service with the 56th Fighter Group. He gained 28 victories in World War II.

1944 was a year of intense air fighting for the aircraft of the Eighth Air Force, and the 56th Fighter Group was to see more than its share of the action, ending the war as the second-top-scoring fighter unit in the command. Gabreski was the group's deputy executive and operations officer in the early months of 1944, gaining a further ten combat victories during the period. In April he resumed command of the 61st Fighter Squadron with the rank of lieutenant-colonel. On 22 May he claimed the destruction of three Fw 190s and during June he shot down another five German fighters. His last victory of World War II, all of them gained while flying the Republic P-47 Thunderbolt, was a Messerschmitt Bf 109 downed on 5 July. He was then top-scoring Eighth Air Force pilot on combat duty. He had destroyed 28 enemy aircraft in the air, the majority of them single-engined fighters, and in addition had knocked out one German aircraft on the ground. It was while attempting to increase his ground-strafing score on 20 July 1944 that Gabreski's World War II combat career came to an abrupt end. While attacking Bassinheim airfield near Coblenz, he struck the ground with his propeller and was forced to crash-land. For the remainder of the war he was a POW in Stalag Luft 1.

On his return to the United States, Gabreski became a test pilot at Wright-Patterson Air Force Base, Ohio. Then after a brief spell out of uniform, he was posted back to a fighter unit. In 1950 the Korean War broke out and Gabreski was posted to the combat theatre, initially as deputy commander of the 4th Fighter Wing and later in command of the 51st Fighter Wing. These

units flew F-86 Sabre jet fighters against the Communist MiG-15s. Gabreski scored $6\frac{1}{2}$ victories over the enemy jets, bringing his total score to $34\frac{1}{2}$.

GALLAND

General Adolf Galland (born 1912) was one of the Luftwaffe's leading fighter tacticians of World War II, rising to the position of General of Fighters and gaining a personal score of 104 victories. He was born on 19 March 1912 at Westerholt and began his flying training as a glider pilot. In 1932 he was accepted for pilot training by the German airline Lufthansa and after the Nazis came to power in 1933 he received clandestine training as a fighter pilot in Italy. In 1935 when the existence of the Luftwaffe was openly acknowledged, Galland joined II Gruppe, Jagdgeschwader 132 flying Heinkel He 51 biplane fighters from Juterborg-Damm. Galland's first taste of combat came in May 1937, when he was sent to Spain to join the Condor Legion fighting alongside the Nationalist Air Force. He commanded 3 Staffel, Jagdgruppe 88, an He 51 *Staffel* largely employed on ground-attack duties, and so he

scored no victories in air combat during his period in Spain. Recalled to Germany in August 1938, he remained with ground-attack units, flying Henschel Hs 123s biplanes with II Gruppe, Lehrgeschwader 2 during the Polish Campaign in September 1939.

Early in 1940 Galland's repeated requests to be transferred to a fighter unit were granted and he was appointed adjutant to JG 27, which flew the Messerschmitt Bf 109E. During the assault in the west in May 1940 he was in action against the Belgian and

Left *Adolf Galland rose to fame as a fighter leader during the Battle of Britain in the summer of 1940, serving with the Luftwaffe's Jagdgeschwader 26.*

Below *Galland climbs out of the cockpit of his Messerschmitt Bf 109E at the end of a mission. His personal emblem is painted beneath the fighter cockpit canopy.*

French air forces and by early June he had scored 12 victories. On the eve of the Battle of Britain Galland was appointed to command III Gruppe, JG 26, based at Caffiers on the Channel coast. During the course of the battle, he was outspoken in his criticism of the misguided German tactics which tied the Bf 109s to the bomber formation that they were escorting, rather than giving them a free hand to hunt out and engage the RAF fighters whenever they might be met. Yet in spite of the Luftwaffe's defeat, the Battle of Britain was a personal success for Galland. His victory score had risen to 40, he had been given command of JG 26 and was only the second German pilot to have been awarded the Oakleaves to the Knight's Cross. During the early months of 1941, the Luftwaffe fighter units were on the defensive in France, operating against RAF fighter sweeps and small-scale bomber raids. However, action was brisk enough to allow Galland to raise his victory score to 70 by June 1941.

In November 1941 Werner Moelders, the Luftwaffe's General of Fighters, was killed in an air crash and Galland was appointed to succeed him. He was promoted to the rank of *Generalmajor* and was the youngest general in the German armed forces. Over the next three years Galland battled for the expansion of the German fighter force in the face of high-level apathy and even opposition. He had his moments of triumph, notably when he organized the fighter cover for the battlecruisers *Scharnhorst* and *Gneisenau* during their Channel Dash in February 1942. However, the growing weight of American air attacks on the German homeland in 1943–4 placed an increasingly insupportable strain on Germany's comparatively slender fighter resources. Indeed the situation was so serious that the Allied Normandy invasion in June 1944 was virtually unopposed by German fighters. Another cause of serious disagreement not only with Goering and the Luftwaffe high command, but with Hitler himself, was the tactical employment of the Messerschmitt Me 262 jet fighter, which was being misused as a fighter-bomber rather than in its intended air-defence role. At the end of 1944 Galland relinquished his post of General of Fighters and spent the last months of the war flying the Me 262 as commander of the elite Jagdverband 44.

GARROS

Roland Garros (1882–1918) was a pioneer racing and record-breaking pilot in France, who became one of the first successful fighter pilots of World War I. Garros's flying career began in 1910, when he learned to fly at the Blériot School at Buc. The following year he took part in the 1400km (874-mile) Paris-to-Madrid air race, which started from Issy-les-Moulineaux on 21 May. The contest was bedevilled by crashes and forced landings – one competitor crashing into the assembled dignitaries on take-off, killing the Minister for War and injuring the Prime Minister. Garros was rather more successful, reaching the vicinity of San Sebastián before he was forced down and crash-landed. Undeterred, he returned to Paris to prepare for the forthcoming Paris–Rome–Turin race. This started badly for him, when his Blériot crashed in the Rhône delta, but he secured a replacement and set off in pursuit of the leader Jean Conneau (who raced under the pseudonym Lieutenant Beaumont). The second machine carried him as far as Pisa, where it too crashed. Another replacement allowed him to reach Rome a day behind Conneau, where the two agreed to abandon the last stage of the race and to split the prize money.

In 1911 Garros set a world altitude record of 3910m (12,828ft) flying a Blériot XI and two years later he raised it to an altitude of 5610m (18,405ft). On 23 September 1913 he made the first successful flight across the Mediterranean, covering the 730km (453 miles) from Saint-Raphael to Bizerte, Tunisia, in 7 hours 53 minutes. By that time he was working for the Morane-Saulnier company and like his compatriot Adolphe Pegoud was an exponent of the newly discovered skills of aerobatic flying. He reached second place in the first aerobatic contest held in Juvisy in June 1913 and also pioneered precision aerobatic flying with the Ballet Aérien.

On the outbreak of war in August 1914 Garros joined France's Aviation Militaire. He soon became dissatisfied with the armament of the early military machines and urged his friend and former employer Raymond Saulnier to devise an interruptor mechanism which would allow a machine gun to fire forward through the arc of a revolving propeller without the bullets damaging the propeller blades. Saulnier had already looked at such a device, as had several other inventors, but concluded that the erratic firing rates of the early machine guns made it worthless. As a rudimentary alternative, Garros's Morane-Saulnier Type L was fitted with steel wedges to deflect any bullets hitting the propeller. With this aircraft Garros

scored his first kill on 1 April 1915 and within a fortnight he had added four more victories to his scoresheet to become the first air ace in history. His triumph was to be short-lived, however, for on 19 April, while attacking a German infantry column, he was brought down by ground-fire and he and his aircraft were captured. This incident stimulated the young Dutch aircraft designer Anthony Fokker to develop a true interruptor gear for his new Fokker Eindecker design. Thus was born the 'Fokker Scourge' which dominated the skies over the Western Front in 1915–16. Garros himself finally escaped from German captivity and returned to France. Rejoining the Aviation Militaire, he was killed in action on 5 October 1918.

Above left Roland Garros *was the first air ace in the history of air combat, shooting down five German aeroplanes in April 1915.*

Above Garros, *pictured at the controls of a Santos-Dumont Demoiselle, was a notable racing pilot in France before World War I.*

GIBSON

Wing Commander Guy Penrose Gibson (1918–44) led the famous Bomber Command raid on the German dams in May 1943 for which he was awarded the Victoria Cross. Born in Simla, India, on 12 August 1918, Gibson joined the RAF on a short-service commission in 1936 and on completing his pilot's training was posted to No 83 Squadron at Scampton, Lincolnshire. In September 1938 the squadron converted from Hawker Hind biplanes to the Handley Page Hampden twin-engined monoplane bomber. Gibson's first war mission was flown on 3 September 1939, the day war broke out, and was an unsuccessful armed reconnaissance in search of German warships. There followed a lull in operations until the spring of 1940. Thereafter Gibson was in action until late September, winning the Distinguished Flying Cross. He then spent a short period as an instructor before being posted to No 29 Squadron at Digby, Lincolnshire, a night-fighter unit operating Bristol Beaufighters.

On 12 March 1941 Gibson scored his first night victory, intercepting a German bomber near Skegness. Two nights later he scored again and then the squadron moved south to West Malling in Kent. Gibson's night-fighter tour came to an end in December 1941 after 99 operational sorties, during which he had claimed three enemy bombers destroyed, plus one probable and three damaged. Gibson was then promoted to squadron leader and was awarded a bar to his DFC.

After another spell as an instructor, Gibson returned to night-bomber operations in April 1942 as CO of No 106 Squadron at Coningsby, Lincolnshire. The squadron flew the unsatisfactory Avro Manchester, but these were soon replaced by the superlative four-engined Lancaster. For nearly a year, until mid-March 1943, Gibson led No 106 Squadron on night raids over Germany and Italy. He was promoted to the rank of wing commander on taking over the squadron and in

Below Wing Commander Guy Gibson (in hatch) and his crew prepare to board the Lancaster which they flew on the famous Dams raid in May 1943.

Bottom Gibson (right) was awarded the Victoria Cross for leading the Dams raid.

November 1942 he was awarded the Distinguished Service Order.

After relinquishing command of No 106 Squadron, Gibson was asked if he was prepared to volunteer for one more special operation. He agreed, but only later was told that his objective was to be the dams which provided hydro-electric power for most of the industrial Ruhr. As he set about forming a new unit (No 617 Squadron) for the operation he learned that he had been awarded a bar to his DSO. After a period of intensive training with the Barnes Wallis 'bouncing bomb', the squadron was ready for action. On the evening of 16 May 1943 Gibson led the first of three formations of specially modified Lancasters off the runway at Scampton in Lincolnshire and set course for the Möhne dam. After dropping his own bomb, Gibson circled the target area to direct the other bombers. Both the Möhne and Eder dams were breached, but eight of the 19 Lancasters despatched on the raid failed to return. A total of 34 awards for gallantry were shared among the surviving crews, with Gibson himself receiving the Victoria Cross.

In August 1943 Gibson gave up his command of No 617 Squadron and accompanied the Prime Minister, Winston Churchill, to the Quebec Conference. He then went on to visit the United States, returning to a staff job in the Air Ministry in December. During the next eight months, during which he occasionally flew on operations without official sanction, Gibson pleaded for a return to a front-line squadron. On 19 September 1944 he was allowed to fly on a raid to München-Gladbach as Master Bomber. He successfully completed his direction of the raid, but on the return flight his Mosquito was shot down and Gibson was killed.

GOERING

The titular head of the wartime Luftwaffe, Reichsmarschall Hermann Goering (1893–1946) began his career as an airman during World War I. Born on 12 January 1893, Goering was commissioned into the infantry in 1912 and in 1915 he transferred to the Air Service as an observer. In 1916 he learned to fly, joined a fighter unit and by June 1918 he had shot down 21 enemy aircraft and was awarded the Pour le Mérite. He then took command of the elite Jagdgeschwader 1 'Flying Circus' after the death of von Richthofen and had added one more victory to his score by the time of the Armistice. Refusing to surrender to the Allies, Goering disbanded his unit and ordered the aircraft to be set on fire in defiance of the terms of the Armistice.

In 1919–22 he worked as a civil pilot in Sweden, but then returned to Germany and joined the Nazi party. When Hitler came to power in 1933 Goering was appointed Aviation Minister and presided over the clandestine rebuilding of a German air force under the cover of civilian aviation. When the Luftwaffe was

Left Hermann Goering was created Reichsmarschall in 1940, the only German officer to hold this rank. His leadership of the Luftwaffe in World War II was almost totally ineffective.

Below Georges Guynemer (second from right) is photographed in front of his Morane-Saulnier parasol on the day of his first aerial victory, 19 July 1915.

officially reborn in March 1935 Goering became its commander with the rank of *General*. A vain and indolent man, Goering delegated the operational and administrative tasks to subordinates. He was in no sense an operational commander and his occasional attempts to direct air operations were often disastrous, one example being the débâcle of the Stalingrad airlift. He was captured by the US Army in 1945 and committed suicide the following year.

GUYNEMER

Georges Guynemer (1894–1917) was the most famous French fighter pilot of World War I and at the time of his death was the Aviation Militaire's top-ranking ace. He was born in Paris on 24 December 1894 and despite his ill-health was accepted by the Aviation Militaire for training as an air mechanic in 1914. The following year he qualified as a pilot and was posted to Escadrille MS3, which flew Morane-Saulnier scouts from Vauciennes. On 19 July he gained his first victory and was awarded the Médaille Militaire for his aggression and determination as a fighter pilot. He still had much to learn about the tactics of air fighting, however, and in September he was himself shot down. Fortunately he managed to crash-land in no-man's land and to reach the French lines unscathed.

By March 1916 Guynemer had gained eight victories, but on the 15th of that month he was wounded in air combat. In July 1916 he began flying the Nieuport 11 biplane scout. Towards the end of the year he began a run of success in air combat, gaining 30 victories by the end of January 1917. The following month he was promoted to *capitaine* and on 16 March destroyed three opponents in one day. On 5 June his score rose to 45 enemy aircraft destroyed and he was awarded the rank of Chevalier de la Légion d'Honneur for this achievement.

An unlikely hero, this frail and consumptive youth, aged only 23 at the time of his death, was driven by a relentless desire to excel as a fighter pilot. Seemingly heedless of danger, he had been wounded twice in combat, but the strain of continuous action was begin-

ning to tell. Guynemer was given the opportunity to retire from combat after his 45th victory, but he determined to continue. By then flying the Spad SVII fighter, his personal aircraft being named *Vieux Charles*, Guynemer raised his score to 48 by early July and on 20 August he accounted for victim number 53. At this time he was given the opportunity of testing a cannon-armed Spad, but he discovered that the vibration set up when the weapon was fired made accurate aiming impossible and so he reverted to a conventional machine-gun-armed aircraft. In August he was again given the opportunity to rest from combat. The French high command feared that the loss of such a celebrated airman would have a disastrous effect on public morale. Although he was now physically and emotionally exhausted he again refused.

On 6 September Guynemer scored his 54th victory. Five days later he set out on morning patrol accompanied by Lieutenant Bozon-Verduraz. The two aircraft entered cloud and on emerging Guynemer's companion was alone. Guynemer's body was never found and, although the Germans belatedly claimed to have shot him down, it is just as likely that he became disorientated in cloud and crashed to his death.

Below Guynemer stands beside his Spad SVII fighter Vieux Charles in 1917, when he was serving with Escadrille SPA3.

HARRIS

Marshal of the RAF Sir Arthur Harris (1892–1984) directed the RAF's night-bomber offensive against Germany during the crucial years 1942–5. Born on 13 April 1892 in Britain, Harris was taken to Rhodesia as a child and in 1914 enlisted in the Rhodesia Regiment for service in East Africa. He transferred to the Royal Flying Corps the following year and ended the war in command of No 45 Squadron flying Sopwith Camels. Granted a permanent commission in the peacetime RAF, he served in India and Iraq, as well as in various staff and flying appointments in Britain.

On the outbreak of World War II Harris was given command of No 5 Group in Bomber Command, with the rank of air vice-marshal. He then served as deputy chief of the air staff and led an RAF delegation to the United States. In February 1942 he became C-in-C of Bomber Command, directing the night-bomber offensive against Germany with a ruthlessness and determination which earned him the nickname of the Butcher (usually shortened to Butch) from his bomber crews. A firm believer in the controversial policy of area bombing, he mounted the Thousand-Bomber Raids of 1942, and the following year launched major offensives against the Ruhr, Hamburg and Berlin. Although he never succeeded in his aim of knocking Germany out of the war by bombing, the RAF's night offensive against Germany made a decisive contribution to the eventual Allied victory. Harris retired from the RAF in 1945.

HARTMANN

Erich Hartmann (born 1922) was the Luftwaffe's top-scoring fighter pilot of World War II and his combat record of 352 enemy aircraft destroyed has never been exceeded. He was born at Weissach in Württemberg on 19 April 1922 and on leaving school joined the Luft-

waffe to train as a pilot. His first posting to an operational unit came in October 1942, when he joined Jagdgeschwader 52's 9 Staffel, which flew the Messerschmitt Bf 109F (shortly to be replaced by the BF 109G) over the southern sector of the Russian Front. His initiation into combat flying was a gentle one, for there was little air activity in JG 52's area of operations in the winter of 1942–3. In five months Hartmann completed a hundred combat missions and accounted for the destruction of seven Soviet aircraft.

In 1943 Hartmann gained invaluable experience flying as the wingman of his *Geschwader Kommodore*, Hermann Graf. Graf was himself an impressively high scorer on the Eastern Front, finishing the war with a total of 212 victories. His combat technique was to close in to short ranges so that difficult deflection shooting was avoided and his fire had maximum effect. It was a doctrine that Hartmann was to follow with singular success. During the bloody and decisive Battle

Erich Hartmann was the Luftwaffe's top-scoring fighter pilot in World War II and his total of 352 air victories has never been exceeded by any other pilot.

to score until the very end of the war. It is an illustration of the shrinking perimeters of Nazi Germany that a number of Hartmann's final victories were over USAAF aircraft. Well over two-thirds of his final total of 352 enemy aircraft destroyed were fighters. Hartmann spent ten years after the war in Soviet prison camps and on his repatriation to West Germany joined the re-formed Luftwaffe, retiring with the rank of *Oberst* in 1973.

HAWKER

Major Lanoe Hawker VC (1890–1916) was one of the Royal Flying Corps' most successful fighter pilots in the early years of World War I. The son of a naval officer, he was born in 1890 and commissioned into the Royal Engineers in 1911. Hawker learned to fly in 1913 and the following year he transferred to the RFC. In October 1914 he accompanied No 6 Squadron to France, taking part in early reconnaissance and bombing operations. One of his notable exploits was the bombing of the German Zeppelin shed at Gontrude on 18 April 1915. Shortly afterwards he was awarded the Distinguished Service Order and assumed command of No 6 Squadron's A Flight on promotion to captain.

In June 1915 Hawker modified a single-seat Bristol

of Kursk, which opened on 5 July 1943, Hartmann began his fighting career in earnest and within a period of some two months he had increased his score to 61 enemy aircraft destroyed. On 20 August Hartmann's Bf 109G was damaged in combat and he was forced down in Soviet territory, but he managed to escape from his captors and regain the German lines.

On 29 October Hartmann was awarded the Knight's Cross for his exploits and at this time his score stood at 148 victories. This was by no means an exceptional score for Luftwaffe pilots operating on the Russian Front, where targets were more plentiful and kills were easier than in the western combat theatres. Conditions were to become tougher in 1944, with the withdrawal of Luftwaffe fighter units to Germany to defend the Reich against American daylight bombing raids. Hartmann's JG 52 remained on the Eastern Front, but had to assume responsibility for an ever-increasing area of operations. On 2 March Hartmann's score reached 200 (a distinction shared by only 14 other Luftwaffe pilots) and he was awarded the Oakleaves clasp to his Knight's Cross. July and August 1944 was a time of intense aerial activity and Hartmann shot down eight enemy aircraft on 23 August and 11 the following day. On 25 August when his score stood at 301 he was awarded the Diamonds clasp to the Knight's Cross.

In October 1944 Hartmann was promoted to *Hauptmann* and took command of JG 52's 4 Staffel. In February 1945 he became *Kommodore* of JG 52 and continued

Above Hartmann pictured in the cockpit of his Messerschmitt Bf 109G fighter, which carries his personal insignia. The majority of his victories were over Soviet aircraft on the Eastern Front.

Right Major Lanoe Hawker was the Royal Flying Corps' pioneer tactician in the new science of air fighting during 1915–16.

Scout biplane with a machine-gun mounting that enabled a Lewis gun to fire forward but outside the arc of the propeller. With this aircraft he quickly scored two victories over German two-seaters, before wrecking the Scout in a landing accident. With a similarly modified replacement aircraft he continued this run of success, which was rewarded by the award of a Victoria Cross in August 1915.

In September 1915 Hawker returned to England to assume command of the newly formed No 24 Squadron at Hounslow. This unit, equipped with the de Havilland DH2, was the first RFC squadron to be completely equipped with single-seat fighters (then known as scouts). In February 1916 the squadron flew to France and, although Hawker as the CO was not expected to fly in combat, he frequently did so. On 23 November 1916 Hawker and two of his pilots were engaged by Albatros scouts of Jasta 2 near Bapaume. Hawker was attacked by an Albatros flown by the rising German ace Manfred von Richthofen. After a combat lasting over half an hour, the German gained the advantage and Hawker was shot down and killed.

HINKLER

Herbert 'Bert' Hinkler (1892–1933) was the first man to fly solo from Britain to Australia. He was born at Bundaberg in Australia on 8 December 1892 and his first interest in aviation was in gliding. He then sailed to Britain, where he joined the Sopwith Aircraft Company as a mechanic. On the outbreak of World War I Hinkler joined the Royal Naval Air Service and in 1916 he became a gunner flying in Sopwith 1½-Strutters of No 3 Wing RNAS on bombing raids into Germany. He was awarded the Distinguished Flying Medal for this work. In the final year of the war he qualified as a pilot and joined No 28 Squadron of the newly formed RAF, flying Sopwith Camel scouts in Italy.

After leaving the RAF in 1919, Hinkler attempted to fly back to Australia in an Avro Baby biplane. He departed from Croydon in May 1920, but on reaching Italy the authorities refused him permission to continue the flight and he was forced to turn back. He was then employed by Avro as a test pilot.

Hinkler did not give up his ambition to fly to Australia and in February 1928 he set out from Croydon in his Avro Avian biplane. His flight took him to Rome, Malta, Benghazi, Palestine, Jask, Karachi, Calcutta, Rangoon, Penang, Singapore, Bima and finally to Darwin in Northern Australia. He had covered the 17,700km(11,000-mile) route in 134 flying hours, taking in all 16 days. It was a remarkable achievement not least because his planning had been put smoothly into effect without fuss or untoward incident. His flight brought him many rewards, including £10,000 in prize money, the Air Force Cross and an honorary commission as squadron leader in the Royal Australian Air Force.

Hinkler left the Avro company and attempted to design his own aircraft, but this venture was not a success. He then tried to establish an air-freight company in Canada, flying a de Havilland Puss Moth, but this enterprise also failed. In 1931 he returned to long-distance flying, making a non-stop flight from New York to Jamaica, a distance of some 2575km (1600 miles), in 18 hours. He then continued to Natal in

'Bert' Hinkler received a hero's welcome at Hanworth Aerodrome, Middlesex, after his first solo crossing of the South Atlantic in 1931.

Brazil, from where he began a flight across the South Atlantic, which ended at Bathurst in Gambia, West Africa. This was the first time that the flight had been accomplished solo. On his return to Britain, after completing a flight totalling more than 16,000km (10,000 miles), Hinkler was again honoured for his achievement, receiving the Britannia Trophy, the Seagrave Trophy and Royal Aero Club's Gold Medal.

In 1932 a new Britain-to-Australia solo record was set up by C. W. A. Scott and Hinkler determined to challenge it. On 7 January 1933 he set out in a Puss Moth on the first stage of his flight. The weather was unfavourable from the start and he had to battle with strong headwinds in crossing the Channel. He succeeded in crossing the Alps and then headed south. Flying through flurries of snow, he approached the Apennines, but got no further. The following spring a group of charcoal burners found the wreckage of Hinkler's plane with his body nearby. He was buried in Florence with full military honours.

IMMELMANN

Oberleutnant Max Immelmann (1890–1916) was one of the most successful of the early German fighter pilots in World War I. He was born at Dresden in Saxony on 21 September 1890 and at the age of 15 became an army cadet. He interrupted his army career to study engineering and became interested in aviation. On the outbreak of war in August 1914 he was recalled to army service and in November that year he transferred to the Fliegertruppe. After receiving pilot training at Adlershof, he was assigned to Fliegerabteilung 10 in April 1915. This was an artillery-spotting unit based at Vrizy in France. Immelmann soon transferred to Fliegerabteilung 62, which was then forming at Doberitz under the command of Hauptmann Hermann Kastner.

In May 1915 Immelmann accompanied his new unit to Arras in France, where he flew LVG BI biplanes on reconnaissance patrols. However, more exciting

Right Oberleutnant Max Immelmann, one of Germany's first air aces of World War I, is best remembered for the manoeuvre bearing his name, the Immelmann turn.

Below Immelmann poses with the wreckage of his seventh victim, a Morane-Saulnier Parasol of No 3 Squadron RFC, which he shot down on 15 December 1915.

work was in prospect. A fellow squadron member was Oswald Boelcke, who had experimented with armed two-seaters and then went on to fly the unit's first Fokker Eindecker monoplane fighter. Immelmann was quick to emulate him and on 1 August 1915 piloted the Fokker and succeeded in bringing down a BE2c flown by Lieutenant W. Reid of No 2 Squadron RFC. A second victory followed on 26 August and by the end of the year Immelmann had run up a score of seven enemy aircraft destroyed.

The early German fighter aircraft operated alone and on patrol would climb to their operational ceiling, about 3000m (10,000ft), to give them the advantage of height and speed at the outset of a combat. Immelmann's particular contribution to early air-fighting tactics was the turn that bears his name. Although it is not certain that he was the first pilot to use this manoeuvre, he certainly developed it for combat use. The Immelmann turn was in fact a slow roll off the top of a half-completed loop. This meant that a pilot could reverse his direction of flight while gaining altitude. In its practical application, it allowed a fighter pilot to dive down onto his victim, pull away and, by executing an Immelmann turn, be in a position to dive again from the opposite direction, if his first attack had not succeeded.

Decorations were showered on Immelmann in reward for his early successes, including the Knight's Cross of the Order of Albert from his native Saxony and Prussia's highest award for military valour, the

Pour le Mérite. This acclaim spurred him to greater efforts during the early months of 1916, and by the end of April he had gained another seven victories, to bring his score to 14. The Fokker Eindeckers, although manoeuvrable and fast machines in comparison with contemporary biplane two-seaters, were not without their faults. This Immelmann was to discover on 31 May 1916, when after his interruptor gear failed and he shot off his own propeller, the Fokker suffered structural failure and almost broke up in the air. Immelmann gained his 16th victory on the afternoon of 16 June, in combat with the FE2bs of No 25 Squadron RFC. That evening he again engaged No 25 Squadron, shooting down one of their machines for his 17th victory. However, in the process he came under fire from Corporal J. Waller, the gunner in the FE2b flown by Lieutenant G. R. McCubbin. Immelmann's Fokker plunged earthward and broke up before impact with the ground. His death shocked and sobered the German nation and even resulted in a tribute from his opponents in the RFC.

JOHNSON, AMY

Amy Johnson (1903–41) was one of the most accomplished women aviators of the inter-war years. Born at Hull in Yorkshire on 1 July 1903, she learned to fly in 1929. On 5 May the following year she set out on a solo flight to Australia in her de Havilland Gypsy Moth named *Jason*. It was a daunting prospect for any pilot with less than a hundred hours' solo flying experience. Yet within six days she had reached India, and battling through monsoon rains she arrived at Singapore on 19 May. Five days later she reached Darwin, the first woman to make the solo flight from Britain to Australia.

More record flights followed. In 1931 she flew from Britain to Tokyo, Japan, by way of Moscow, in a record nine days. In 1932 she married fellow record-

breaking pilot James Mollison and in November that year beat her husband's record in a flight from Lympne in Kent to Cape Town, South Africa, in a DH Puss Moth.

The two combined forces in 1933 to fly a DH Dragon in an attempt at the world distance record, but the enterprise ended in a crash at Bridgeport, Connecticut. In 1934 they took part in the MacRobertson Trophy race to Australia, flying a DH 88 Comet, but were forced to drop out at Baghdad in Iraq. Amy's marriage to Mollison did not survive these vicissitudes and after another flight to the Cape in 1936 she disappeared from the public eye. In 1940 she joined the Air Transport Auxiliary and was lost on a ferry flight in January 1941 when the Airspeed Oxford she was flying ran into dense fog. She was forced to abandon the aircraft off Herne Bay in Kent, but was drowned after parachuting into the sea.

Top Amy Johnson's Gipsy Moth lifts off from the airfield at Croydon at the start of her solo flight to Australia in May 1930.

Above Amy Johnson's DH Gipsy Moth Jason, *in which she flew to Australia in 1930, is preserved in the Science Museum, London.*

Left Amy Johnson made her first solo record-breaking flight, from England to Australia in 1930, when she was a relatively inexperienced pilot with only 80 hours' solo flying in her logbook.

Top *'Johnny' Johnson pictured with his labrador Sally in front of his Spitfire Mk IX on an advanced landing ground in France shortly after the Normandy Invasion in June 1944.*

Above *In March 1943 Johnson became leader of the Kenley Wing, which comprised three Spitfire Mk IX Squadrons of the Royal Canadian Air Force.*

JOHNSON, JAMES

Air Vice-Marshal James 'Johnny' Johnson (born 1915) was one of the RAF's most outstanding fighter leaders in World War II. He was born at Loughborough, Leicestershire, and joined the RAF Volunteer Reserve before the outbreak of World War II. After completing his flying training in the summer of 1940 he was posted to No 19 Squadron flying Spitfires at Duxford, Cambridgeshire. However, the unit was too heavily engaged in the Battle of Britain to absorb new and inexperienced pilots and so Johnson moved on to No 616 Squadron. This squadron also flew Spitfires, but was based at Kirton-in-Lindsey, Lincolnshire, well away from the main battle. At this time, trouble from an old collarbone injury forced Johnson to go to hospital to have the bone reset. He returned to No 616 Squadron in December and shortly afterwards took part in an inconclusive combat with a Dornier Do 17.

In February 1941 No 616 Squadron moved south, joining the Tangmere Wing led by Wing Commander Douglas Bader. The wing leader was quick to spot Johnson's potential as a fighter pilot and he often flew in Bader's section, sometimes as his wingman, on sweeps over enemy-occupied France. This gave him an excellent opportunity to learn fighter tactics, but as the wingman's job was to cover his leader, he had few chances of attacking enemy fighters. Nonetheless, Johnson began scoring, and in September 1941, when he had accounted for six enemy fighters and completed more than 50 operations over enemy territory, he was awarded the Distinguished Flying Cross. By this time Johnson was a flight commander with No 616 Squadron and he remained with the unit until July 1942.

Johnson's next posting was as CO of No 610 Squadron, flying Spitfire Mk VBs from West Malling in Kent. He led the unit during the great air battles over Dieppe on 19 August, when his personal score was one Focke Wulf Fw 190 destroyed and a Messerschmitt Bf 109F shared with two other pilots. In March 1943 Johnson was promoted to wing commander and became leader of the Canadian Wing at Kenley. The wing was engaged in offensive fighter sweeps, often escorting USAAF bombers over occupied Europe, and so there were many opportunities for air combat. Furthermore, the Canadians were flying the Spitfire Mk IX, the first mark of Spitfire that was a match for the Luftwaffe's Fw 190 fighter. Johnson made the most of his opportunities and the Canadian Wing under his leadership was the top-scoring wing in Fighter Command. At the same time his personal score mounted up, reaching 25 by the time he left the wing in September 1943. However, as Johnson himself has pointed out in his memoirs *Wing Leader*, one of the classic accounts of air fighting in World War II, his job was to ensure that his pilots operated effectively against the enemy and personal scores were a secondary consideration.

After a rest from operations in a staff job, Johnson returned to operations as leader of another Canadian unit, No 144 Wing in 2nd Tactical Air Force. Its job was to provide air cover for the Normandy invasion and thereafter support the advancing Allied armies. During this period Johnson increased his score to 38 victories, all of them against single-engined fighter aircraft. This was officially the highest score of an RAF pilot, although postwar research has suggested that the South African pilot Squadron Leader M. St J. Pattle exceeded this. Johnson remained in the RAF after the war, rising to the rank of air vice-marshal and commanding Air Forces Middle East before his retirement from the service in 1965.

KINGSFORD-SMITH

Sir Charles Kingsford-Smith (1897–1935) was the first man to cross the Pacific Ocean by air. He was born at Brisbane in Queensland, Australia, on 9 February 1897. He served in the Royal Flying Corps during World War I and was awarded the Military Cross. In 1921 he returned to Australia and went to work for West Australian Airways as a pilot. In 1927

accompanied by C. T. P. Ulm he flew around the Australian continent in a Bristol Tourer, taking 11 days to complete the flight.

Kingsford-Smith then determined to attempt a trans-Pacific flight and in July 1927 he left for the United States to obtain financial backing. He bought a Fokker F-VII trimotor monoplane from Polar explorer Sir Hubert Wilkins and named it *Southern Cross*. On 31 May 1928, accompanied by Ulm, Harry Lyon as navigator and James Warner as radio operator, he took off from Oakland, California, on the first leg of his 11,750km (7300-mile) flight. As most of the flight was over open ocean, the navigation problems were considerable. Although also troubled by cloud and turbulence, the *Southern Cross* successfully landed at Wheeler Field, Hawaii, after more than 27 hours in the air. For the next stage of the flight, Kingsford-Smith had to take the *Southern Cross* to a runway on the beach at Kauai Island, as the fuel-laden Fokker F-VII had an insufficient take-off run at Wheeler Field. On 3 June the next stage of the flight to Fiji began.

In spite of bad weather and trouble with both radio and engines, this was accomplished after a gruelling flight lasting 34 hours 28 minutes. The remaining 2800km (1750-mile) leg of the journey to Australia was flown through particularly bad storms and turbulence, but the *Southern Cross* finally touched down at Eagle's Farm, Brisbane. It had flown a total of more than 83 hours during the crossing.

Kingsford-Smith intended to continue his flight to Britain but before doing so he made the first non-stop flight across Australia and then flew across the Tasman Sea to New Zealand. He then flew the *Southern Cross* to Britain, taking 13 days for the journey. After Fokker had overhauled the *Southern Cross*, it left for Newfoundland in June 1930. From there Kingsford-Smith flew it to California, completing the first round-the-world flight by way of Australia. In October 1930 Kingsford-Smith established a new solo record for the Britain–Australia flight flying an Avro Avian, and three years later set another record with a Percival Gull.

In 1934 Kingsford-Smith, by this time knighted for his achievements, teamed up with P. G. Taylor (himself later to receive a knighthood) to take part in the MacRobertson Trophy race flying a Lockheed Altair. Before setting out from Australia they established a number of Australian inter-city records with the Altair. Then in October they left Brisbane on the first Pacific crossing from Australia to the United States. Delayed by bad weather, they finally arrived in California on 3 November. This was the first trans-Pacific flight by a single-engined aeroplane, but they were too late to compete in the MacRobertson race. In May 1935 Kingsford-Smith piloted the *Southern Cross* on its last major flight, to New Zealand. That November he set out in an Altair from Britain en route to Australia, but he and the aircraft disappeared over the Bay of Bengal.

Right *This Lavochkin La-7 fighter was flown by Ivan Kozhedub in the final air battles of World War II and carries his combat score marked in red stars.*

Right *Soviet ace Ivan Kozhedub shot down more German aircraft than any other Allied fighter during World War II.*

KOZHEDUB

The top-scoring fighter pilot of the Allied nations in World War II was the Soviet airman Colonel–General Ivan Kozhedub (born 1919). He joined the Soviet air force in 1940 and, because of his natural aptitude as a pilot, he was retained as a flying instructor during 1941–3. He thus escaped the carnage inflicted on the Soviet air force by the victorious Luftwaffe fighter pilots in the early months of the war on the Eastern Front. Second-line training duties were not, however, to Kozhedub's taste and he frequently requested transfer to an active-service fighter regiment.

Kozhedub's wish for a combat assignment was eventually granted and in March 1943 he attended a brief operational course on the Lavochkin LaGG-3 fighter. He was then posted to a fighter regiment serving with the 16th Air Army in the Kharkov sector of the Central Front. After the German defeat at Stalingrad, the situation had begun to improve for the Soviet forces and in the summer of 1943 Kozhedub took part in the great tank battle at Kursk, which proved to be one of the turning points of the war. On 5 July, the first day of the battle, Kozhedub's formation of Lavochkin La-5 fighters was engaged by a superior force of Focke Wulf Fw 190s and the Soviet pilot narrowly escaped with his life. The tables were turned the next day when Kozhedub shot down a Junkers Ju 87D for his first victory. Over the following weeks he continued to score and by the end of the month was credited with eight victories, including two Messerschmitt Bf 109s.

In September 1943 Kozhedub was promoted to captain and took command of a fighter squadron. He took part in the battle to recapture Kiev, which was reoccupied on 6 November. This was a hard-fought battle for Kozhedub, and he scored 11 victories within a period of ten days. He was then flying the La-5FN and his squadron's tasks included ground-attack sorties and escort for Ilyushin Il-2 Shturmovik attack aircraft. Early in the following year he was transferred to an elite guards fighter regiment and was made 'Hero of the Soviet Union'. His area of operations was the central and southern sectors of the war zone. Promotion to the rank of lieutenant-colonel followed and in May he was presented with a personal La-5FN which was donated by public subscription. Over the next three months Kozhedub gained 20 victories while flying this aircraft.

In July 1944 Kozhedub began to fly the improved Lavochkin La-7. His score then stood at 47 victories, but with the return of many Luftwaffe fighters to Germany for the defence of the Reich against USAAF bombers, combats were less frequent. Nonetheless by the end of 1944 his score had increased to 57. By this time he was a full colonel and deputy commander of his fighter regiment. On 12 February 1945 he shot down two Fw 190s, bringing his score to 59, the same as that of the hitherto top-scoring Soviet ace Colonel Aleksandr Pokryshkin. Later that month Kozhedub surprised a Messerschmitt Me 262 and shot it down before the speedy jet could make its escape. His final victories came on 19 April, when he shot down two Fw 190s. He had gained a total of 62 victories during 520 combat missions. He remained in the Soviet air force after the war, rising to high rank.

LACEY

Flight Lieutenant J. H. 'Ginger' Lacey (born 1917) was one of the top-scoring RAF pilots in the Battle of Britain. A pre-war member of the RAF Volunteer Reserve and an instructor with the Yorkshire Aeroplane Club, Sergeant Lacey was posted to No 501 Squadron flying Hawker Hurricanes from Filton near Bristol in September 1939. In May 1940 the squadron moved to France and was soon in action against the Luftwaffe. Lacey gained his first victories on 13 May. However, with the German advance into France the squadron was forced to evacuate on 18 June, by which time Lacey had gained five victories.

No 501 Squadron was heavily engaged during the Battle of Britain, with the Hurricanes making as many as six scrambles a day. Lacey's first victory of the battle came on 20 July and by the time the air fighting had died down in October, his score stood at 23. He was awarded the Distinguished Flying Medal and early the following year was commissioned. In the course of that year his squadron converted to Spitfires and Lacey became a flight commander. From August 1941 to March 1942 he served as an instructor, then he resumed operations with No 602 Squadron flying Spitfire Mk Vs. In March 1943 he was posted to India, where he ended the war as CO of No 17 Squadron flying Spitfire Mk VIIIs. His final score was 28 enemy aircraft destroyed.

LANGLEY

Samuel Pierpont Langley (1834–1906) was a distinguished American scientist, who made important theoretical and practical contributions to the invention of the aeroplane. His interest in aviation began in the 1890s, when he designed and built a series of powered model aeroplanes that gave him a means of testing his aerodynamic theories. By 1896 he had built two models, Aerodromes 5 and 6, which were capable of sustained flights for distances of more than 1200m (1300yd) under the power of small steam engines. These were the first mechanically propelled, heavier-than-air machines capable of sustained flight.

In 1898 Langley received US government support to build and test a man-carrying aeroplane. This was a tandem-wing monoplane with a 15m (48ft) span,

Below left *'Ginger' Lacey first saw action during the Battle of France in 1940 and ended the war commanding a Spitfire squadron in Burma.*

Below *Professor Samuel Langley (right) poses with the Aerodrome's pilot Charles Manley aboard the houseboat from which the aircraft was unsuccessfully launched.*

powered by a 55hp petrol engine developed by Charles Manley, who was to be the machine's pilot. On 7 October the machine was catapulted from the roof of a houseboat on the Potomac River, but it fouled its landing gear and fell into the river. Another attempt on 8 December was no more successful. Langley then abandoned his experiment.

Le MAY

General Curtis E. Le May (born 1906) was an outstanding American bomber commander of World War II, who played a major part in shaping Strategic Air Command in the postwar years. Born on 15 November 1906 at Columbus, Ohio, Le May joined the Army Air Corps in 1928. His early service was largely on fighter aircraft, but in 1937 he transferred to bombers. He took part in the early Boeing YB-17 Flying Fortress long-range proving flights to South America.

Promoted to captain in January 1940, he formed a squadron within the 34th Bombardment Group and then organized a ferry route for B-24s to Africa. On the outbreak of war he organized and trained a number of new bombardment groups, one of which, the 305th BG, he accompanied to Britain. Beginning combat in November 1942, Le May quickly made his mark, introducing successful new formation flying and bombing tactics. In July 1943 he was promoted to brigadier-general and given command of the Eighth Air Force's 4th Bomber Wing. He returned to the United States in June 1944 and then took command of the 20th Air

Left *Curtis Le May (centre) discusses the tactics of B-29 Superfortress raids on Japan with his officers in 1945, when he was in command of the 20th Air Force.*

Below *A characteristic portrait of Le May at the control of a Boeing KC-135 tanker aircraft, during his period as the USAF's Chief of Staff in the early 1960s.*

Force Bomber Command in India, operating B-29s from forward bases in China against the Japanese homeland. He moved to the 21st Air Force in January 1945 and the following August became the commanding general, directing the B-29s' strategic offensive against the Japanese homeland. Important postwar commands with the USAF included C-in-C of Strategic Air Command from 1948 to 1957 and Air Force Chief of Staff from 1961 until his retirement in 1965.

LILIENTHAL

Otto Lilienthal (1848–96) was one of the most influential aviation pioneers of the 19th century. He was the first man to build and fly a successful glider and this work paved the way for heavier-than-air flight in powered aeroplanes. Lilienthal was born at Anklam in Prussia in 1848 and from the age of 14 he experimented with flying machines, basing his work on the study of bird flight. His early attempts to build a successful ornithopter (a flapping-wing machine) convinced him that such a craft was impracticable and thereafter he devoted his energies to gliding flight.

In 1889 Lilienthal published the results of his theoretical studies in *Der Vogelflug als Grundlage der Fliegkunst* (Bird Flight as the Basis of Aviation), a book that was greatly to influence later pioneers. He began to build gliders in the same year, although it was not until 1891 and his third attempt that he produced one that flew. This aircraft was a bat-like monoplane with a fixed tailplane and fin, constructed of peeled willow wands covered with waxed cotton cloth. It was flown as a hang glider, with Lilienthal suspended by the shoulders from the wing and using movements of his body to control the glider by shifting its centre of gravity. In order to assist his early test flights with this glider, Lilienthal built a 15m (50ft) high artificial hill at Berlin-Lichterfelde.

Right Otto Lilienthal's gliding experiments in the late nineteenth century marked an important milestone in the history of manned flights.

Right In 1895 Lilienthal built and flew three biplane gliders, which he claimed were more successful than his earlier monoplane machines.

Below The inspiration that Lilienthal drew from his studies of bird flight can be appreciated from the design of his monoplane gliders.

Over the following five years Lilienthal modified and refined his glider designs, using wing-warping for control, increasing lift by means of a biplane wing and even building an unsuccessful powered machine fitted with a 2hp carbonic acid motor. But in 1896 Lilienthal crashed while testing a new control harness and died from his injuries. At that time he had made over 2000 successful flights, proving beyond doubt that heavier-than-air flight was a practical proposition.

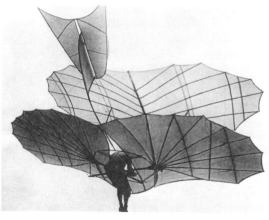

LINDBERGH

Charles Lindbergh (1902–74) was the first man to fly solo across the North Atlantic, making the flight from New York to Paris non-stop in May 1927. Lindbergh was born at Detroit, Michigan, of Swedish parentage on 4 February 1902. He learned to fly as a member of the US Army Air Corps Reserve in 1923 and then worked as an air mail pilot, gaining valuable experience in long-range navigation, often by night. With 2000 hours' flying experience in his logbook, he determined to attempt the North Atlantic crossing alone.

After obtaining the backing of a syndicate of St Louis businessmen, Lindbergh bought the Ryan NYP monoplane which he named *Spirit of St Louis* in their honour. This was a development of the Ryan M-1, fitted with increased fuel tankage and blind-flying instruments especially for the New York–Paris flight – hence the NYP designation. After taking delivery of the NYP at Ryan's San Diego factory, Lindbergh flew it non-stop to St Louis in a 14-hour 30-minute flight. He then took it to Roosevelt Field, New York, in preparation for the Atlantic flight. After a sleepless night, Lindbergh took off on the morning of 20 May, barely clearing a row of telegraph poles on the airfield's perimeter in his heavily laden machine. He was then faced with a 5800km (3600-mile) crossing, having never previously made a long flight over water. His aircraft performed well, however, and his navigation was very accurate. Icing proved to be a problem at one stage of the flight, but his greatest battle was with his tiredness on the 33-hour 30-minute flight. Lindbergh has vividly recorded his struggle to keep awake in his beautifully written book *The Spirit of St Louis*. He finally arrived safely at Le Bourget airport, to be mobbed by thousands of welcoming Frenchmen. Not only was this the first solo Atlantic flight, but it was also a new world distance record.

Lindbergh's achievements made him a celebrity overnight and gave the cause of aviation a much-

Above *Charles Lindbergh brings the* Spirit of St Louis *into the crowd-packed Croydon airport in May 1927, following his historic New York-to-Paris flight.*

Left *Lindbergh's solo flight over the Atlantic in 1927 captured the imagination of the American public to a greater degree than any other aviation exploit.*

Below *Lindbergh's Ryan NYP monoplane* Spirit of St Louis *is preserved in the Smithsonian Institution's National Air and Space Museum in Washington DC.*

needed boost. From Paris, Lindbergh flew the *Spirit of St Louis* to London and then he travelled back to the United States aboard the cruiser USS *Memphis*. He was promoted to the rank of colonel in the Air Corps Reserve and awarded the Distinguished Flying Cross. The Ryan NYP was also shipped back to the United States and Lindbergh flew the aircraft on a tour of Latin America, where he met Anne Morrow, the daughter of the US Ambassador in Mexico, who was to become his wife. The *Spirit of St Louis* was preserved and it is now on display at the Smithsonian Institution's National Air and Space Museum in Washington DC.

Lindbergh joined the airline Transcontinental Air Transport (TAT) as chairman of its technical committee, TAT later becoming the famous TWA. He also worked for Pan American Airways, for whom he made two impressive route-proving flights, accompanied by his wife. The first in 1931 was across the North Pacific, flying a Lockheed Sirius floatplane. His route took him from New York to Canada, Alaska, the USSR, Japan and China. Two years later he surveyed the North Atlantic, covering Scandinavia, Iceland, Greenland, the United Kingdom and the USSR. Tragedy then struck the Lindberghs, when their young son was kidnapped and brutally murdered. During World War II Lindbergh served briefly in the Southwest Pacific Theatre, advising fighter pilots on fuel economy and himself flying a number of combat missions.

LITVAK

Junior Lieutenant Lydia Litvak (1921–43) was the most successful woman fighter pilot of the Soviet Union during World War II. The Soviet air force is unique in having assigned women pilots to front-line combat duties, an expedient forced on it by acute shortages of trained pilots during the German offensive of 1941. Lydia Litvak, known as Lilya, was born in Moscow in 1921. She learned to fly at the Kherson flying school when aged 16. Between 1937 and 1941 she was a flying instructor with Osoaviakhim, an organization to promote popular interest in aviation which provided

Lydia Litvak (top, on the left, and above) was the most successful of the Soviet Union's women fighter pilots in World War II. No other nation permitted women to fly in combat.

facilities for sports flying and pre-military flying training for young Russians.

In October 1941 Lydia Litvak joined the Soviet air force and the following year she was assigned to the 73rd Guards Fighter Regiment, which was equipped with Yakovlev Yak-1 fighters. In this regiment she served alongside male fighter pilots, although an all-woman fighter unit, the 586th Fighter Regiment, was formed in 1942. She was quick to show her aptitude for air fighting, scoring two victories against Luftwaffe fighters on her first offensive patrol. Over the following year she flew 130 combat sorties and engaged in over 60 air battles, taking part in the defence of Stalingrad and Rostov. Her score stood at 12 victories by 1 August 1943, when she failed to return from an engagement with Junkers Ju 88 bombers and their fighter escort.

LUKE

Lieutenant Frank Luke Jr (1897–1918) was the US Army Air Service's second-ranking ace, gaining all his 18 victories during a meteoric two-month combat career. Born in Phoenix, Arizona, of German parentage, Luke enlisted in the US Army in September 1917 and trained as a pilot at Austin, Texas, and San Diego, California. He was commissioned as a second lieutenant in January 1918 and posted to France. On arrival he attended a training course at Issoudun and then served for a time as a ferry pilot, before being assigned to the 27th Aero Squadron, flying Spad SXIIIs.

A loner and something of a maverick, Luke did not take kindly to military discipline. Yet his combat flying was beyond reproach. On 4 August 1918 he claimed his first victory and during the St Mihiel offensive, which opened on 12 September, he began to attack enemy observation balloons. These targets were to become his speciality. His greatest day was on 18 September, when he accounted for three balloons

Left Soviet air force men and women pilots photographed with a Bell P-39 Airacobra supplied by the United States under Lend-Lease.

and two enemy aeroplanes, making him the top Army Air Service ace at that time. He returned with his aircraft riddled with enemy bullets. By 27 September his cavalier attitude to authority had reached such a pitch that his superiors considered court-martialling him. However, after shooting down another three balloons, he was brought down in enemy territory after a dogfight and died in a gun battle with his would-be captors. His score stood at 14 balloons and four aeroplanes destroyed and he was awarded a posthumous Medal of Honor.

McCAMPBELL

Captain David McCampbell (born 1910) was the leading US Navy air ace of World War II with 34 victories to his credit. A graduate of the US Naval Academy at Annapolis in 1933, McCampbell trained as a naval pilot at Pensacola, Florida, in 1937–8 and was then posted to fighter squadron VF-4 aboard the carrier USS *Ranger*. In 1940 he was assigned to the USS *Wasp* as Landing Signal Officer and was promoted to lieutenant-commander in October 1942. McCampbell then assumed command of VF-15, equipped with the Grumman F6F Hellcat fighter.

As commander of Air Group 15 aboard USS *Essex* McCampbell was in action from May until November 1944, taking part in the 'Great Marianas Turkey Shoot' (the Battle of the Philippine Sea), the Battle of Leyte Gulf and the subsequent invasion of the Philippines. His most succesful combat was on 24 October, when he engaged some 40 Zeroes and shot down no fewer than nine of them. His wingman on this occasion claimed a further six Japanese fighters. By the time that

Above Lieutenant Frank Luke Jr poses with his Spad SXIII fighter, which he flew with the US Army Air Service's 27th Aero Squadron in 1918.

Above right Commander David McCampbell photographed in the cockpit of his Grumman F6F-5 Hellcat. He was the US Navy's top-scoring pilot of World War II with 34 victories.

the *Essex*'s combat cruise had ended, McCampbell's personal score stood at 34 aerial victories, plus another 20 Japanese aircraft destroyed during ground strafing. His combat service was not confined to air fighting, however. On 25 October 1944 he coordinated an air strike by three carrier groups against Japanese shipping, which sank a carrier, a light cruiser and two destroyers. For this action he was awarded the Navy Cross and in January 1945 President Roosevelt awarded him the Medal of Honor.

McCONNELL

Captain Joseph McConnell (1922–54) was the USAF's leading ace in the Korea War. A veteran of World War II in which he had served as a navigator on Consolidated B-24 Liberators, McConnell then trained as a pilot, finishing his training on Lockheed F-80 Shooting Star jet fighters in February 1948. In 1951 he volunteered for combat duty in Korea, but did not receive this assignment until the autumn of 1952, when he joined the 51st Fighter Interceptor Wing, which flew North American F-86 Sabres. On 14 January 1953 he shot down his first MiG-15 and in just over a month he destroyed another four, becoming the 27th jet ace of the conflict.

On 12 April 1953, with his score standing at eight, McConnell's Sabre was badly damaged by anti-aircraft fire. He managed to nurse the crippled fighter to the coast, where he baled out into the icy waters of the Yellow Sea. Fortunately for him the rescue services had been alerted and he was winched aboard a Sikorsky H-19 helicopter of the 3rd Air Rescue Group within minutes. McConnell was now out for revenge and

before the end of the month two more MiG-15s had fallen to his guns. The following month saw numerous combats with the MiG-15s, USAF pilots scoring 56 kills between 8 and 31 May. McConnell's share comprised single victories on 13, 15 and 16 May, followed by a highly successful day on 18 May when he brought down three MiG-15s in two sorties. His combat tour then came to an end and he returned to the United States. The following year, while serving as a test pilot at Edwards Air Force Base, California, he crashed to his death while piloting the F-86H Sabre.

McCUDDEN

Major James McCudden VC (1895–1918) rose from the ranks of the Royal Flying Corps to become a squadron commander and fourth-ranking British air ace. He was born on 28 March 1895, the son of a soldier in the Royal Engineers. He joined the same corps as a boy soldier in 1910, but transferred to the RFC as an air mechanic in 1913. He accompanied No 3 Squadron to France in August 1914 and by April the following year had been promoted to sergeant. He then began flying with No 3 Squadron as an observer, receiving the French Croix de Guerre for his work.

At the end of January 1916, following in the steps of an elder brother, McCudden was accepted for pilot training. He gained his wings on 30 May 1916 and returned to France in July, joining No 20 Squadron which flew FE2b two-seaters. In August he transferred to No 29 Squadron, a scout squadron equipped with de Havilland DH2s, and on 6 September he gained his first victory. He was awarded the Military Medal in October and in the new year received his commission

Left *Captain Joseph McConnell was the top-scoring ace of the Korean War, scoring 16 victories when flying F-86 Sabres with the USAF's 51st Fighter Interceptor Wing.*

Right *James McCudden pictured shortly after his transfer from the Royal Engineers to the Royal Flying Corps in 1913.*

Right *McCudden rose from the rank of air mechanic in the Royal Flying Corps to command a squadron in the newly formed Royal Air Force in 1918.*

as a second lieutenant. By mid-February his score stood at five enemy aircraft destroyed and he was awarded the Military Cross, returning to Britain later that month as an instructor.

McCudden returned to France in August 1917 and became B Flight commander on No 56 Squadron, a highly successful unit equipped with the SE5a scout. He quickly regained his old form, adding four victories to his score before the month was out. At this time the squadron experienced a period of technical problems with its guns and ammunition, resulting in the guns jamming during combat. McCudden, with his technical background, determined to eradicate the problems, stripping down the guns and synchronizing gear to ensure that they were in perfect mechanical working order. This was typical of his approach – he often subjected the engine and airframe of his fighter to the same minute technical examination.

On the evening of 23 September there occurred one of the great air combats of the war, when McCudden's flight engaged the Fokker Dr I triplane flown by German ace Werner Voss. For ten minutes the German ace fought five of the RFC's most experienced pilots

before he finally fell to the guns of Lieutenant A. Rhys Davids. By the end of the month McCudden's score stood at 15 victories and in October he was awarded a bar to his Military Cross. A German LVG CV brought down in November provided McCudden with the non-standard spinner which he fitted over the propellor hub of his SE5a. December was a successful month in which he scored 14 victories and received the Distinguished Service Order, to which he added a bar in January 1918. His 50th victory came on 16 February and by the time he left No 56 Squadron on 5 March his score stood at 57. On 29 March he was awarded the Victoria Cross. Like so many outstanding air aces, his death was due not to enemy action but to a commonplace accident. On 9 July while flying to take up his appointment as CO of No 60 Squadron, McCudden's SE5a crashed and he died from his injuries.

McGUIRE

Major Thomas McGuire (1921–45) was one of the leading USAAF aces in the Pacific theatre in World War II. Graduating as a pilot in February 1942, he was assigned to the Southwest Pacific in early 1943, initially joining the 49th Fighter Group and then transferring to the 475th Fighter Group flying Lockheed P-38 Lightnings. During his first successful combat on 18 August, he destroyed one Kawasaki Ki-61 Tony and two Nakajima Ki-43 Oscar fighters. On 21 August he added two more Oscars to his score, becoming an ace in two combats. For the remainder of 1943 the air fighting over New Guinea was heavy and McGuire's score had reached 16 by the end of that time. A lull then followed in the early months of 1944.

McGuire resumed scoring in May 1944, bringing his tally to 21 by the end of July. He was then out of action with an attack of dengue fever for two months

and did not add to his score until 14 October, when he downed three Japanese fighters during a bomber escort mission over Borneo. Further opportunities for combat came with the invasion of the Philippines at the end of October, and McGuire claimed four kills in November, including two of the new Mitsubishi J2M Jack fighters. The following month he raised his total score to 38 and was then grounded for a short period. Resuming combat on 7 January 1945, his formation was attacked by a lone Mitsubishi A6M Zero and while manoeuvring against it, McGuire's P-38 spun into the ground.

MALAN

Group Captain Adolph 'Sailor' Malan (1910–64) was the RAF's top-scoring fighter pilot during the early years of World War II. He was born at Wellington, South Africa, and served in the Merchant Navy before joining the RAF in 1935. The following year he was commissioned and posted to No 74 Squadron, which flew Gloster Gauntlet fighters from Hornchurch in

Below 'Sailor' Malan was one of the RAF's most successful fighter pilots during the early years of World War II and he ended the war with 32 victories, all scored in 1940 and 1941.

Bottom Major Tommy McGuire became the second-highest-scoring American pilot of World War II, flying P-38 Lightnings with the 475th Fighter Group in the Southwest Pacific.

Essex. By the outbreak of war in September 1939 Malan was a flight commander with the squadron, which was then flying Supermarine Spitfires. Malan first saw action when he covered the evacuation of the British Expeditionary Force from Dunkirk, claiming his first victory on 21 May. After a week's intense fighting over Dunkirk the squadron was withdrawn to Leconfield in Yorkshire for a brief rest period.

In early June No 74 Squadron returned to Hornchurch and Malan became the squadron's commanding officer on 8 August. He was awarded the Distinguished Flying Cross for his actions over Dunkirk and later in June he received a bar to this decoration for shooting down two enemy bombers at night. This was the first occasion during World War II on which an RAF single seater fighter pilot had scored at night. In July No 74 Squadron became engaged in the opening skirmishes of the Battle of Britain, which

generally took place over coastal convoys. The following month Malan's squadron was intercepting raids over Britain and on 11 August he shot down two Messerschmitt Bf 109s and two days later accounted for a Dornier Do 17.

After this period of heavy fighting, No 74 Squadron was withdrawn to No 12 Group to rest and to train new pilots. Malan had by this time made his mark as a fighter tactician and his *Ten Rules of Air Fighting* was widely circulated within Fighter Command. As a squadron commander he was a stern disciplinarian, in contrast to the free-and-easy attitude of most of his contemporaries. In October Malan led the squadron south to Biggin Hill and they went into action against high-flying German fighters and fighter-bombers. By the end of the year Malan's personal score stood at 18 victories and he was awarded the Distinguished Service Order.

Early in 1941 Malan became one of the first wing leaders in Fighter Command, when he was appointed to lead the Biggin Hill squadrons. The RAF had then gone over to the offensive, flying numerous fighter sweeps and bomber escort missions over France. Combat with enemy Messerschmitt Bf 109 fighters was frequent and in June 1941 alone Malan accounted for nine of them. At the end of the summer he was taken off operations and awarded a bar to his DSO. Malan was at this time the RAF's highest-scoring fighter pilot with 32 victories officially confirmed. In October he was sent on a tour of the United States, where he had the opportunity of flying the Lockheed P-38 Lightning and Bell P-39 Airacobra. On returning to Britain, he went to the Central Gunnery School at Sutton Bridge, Lincolnshire, as an instructor. In October 1942 he was promoted to group captain and the following January became station commander at RAF Biggin Hill. He then commanded a fighter wing of the 2nd Tactical Air Force and in July 1944 took command of the Central Gunnery School at Catfoss, where many leading aces attended courses. Malan then took the RAF Staff College course, but not wishing to serve as a regular officer in the peacetime RAF, he retired after the war and returned to his native South Africa.

MANNOCK

Major Edward 'Mick' Mannock VC (1887–1918) was the leading British air ace of World War I. He was born in Ireland on 24 May 1887 and left school at the age of 13 to contribute to the family's income. Mannock was working in Turkey as a telephone engineer in November 1914 when that country entered World War I, and was interned under appalling conditions. Broken in health, he was repatriated to Britain in April 1915. He then enlisted in the Royal Army Medical Corps and the following year, after being commissioned into the Royal Engineers, applied for pilot training in the Royal Flying Corps. He was accepted, despite the handicap which he concealed of being partially blind in one eye. On completion of his training he was posted to France and joined No 40 Squadron in April 1917.

Although Mannock was involved in numerous combats during his first month with No 40 Squadron,

Below Malan's combat report for 19 June 1940, when he destroyed two enemy bombers at night while flying a Spitfire day fighter – a hitherto unprecedented feat.

Below right Major Edward 'Mick' Mannock, despite the handicap of being blind in one eye, became the top-scoring fighter pilot of the British air services in World War I.

it was not until 7 May that he scored his first success, sending a German observation ballon down in flames. Further successes followed in June and July and Mannock was awarded the Military Cross. He was then promoted to captain and became a flight commander on No 40 Squadron. Unlike his great hero Albert Ball, Mannock believed in teamwork in air fighting and undoubtedly the changing conditions of air warfare favoured formation rather than individual tactics. Mannock was also particularly concerned that inexperienced pilots should be initiated into the grim business of air fighting as gently as possible, and he took special pains to train newcomers. His personal run of success continued and between the end of July and leaving the squadron in early January 1918 he added more than 20 victories to his score-sheet.

In February 1918 Mannock was posted to No 74 Squadron, a new unit working up on SE5a scouts at London Colney, Hertfordshire. Mannock assumed command of the squadron's A Flight and in March flew with them to France. The squadron's first kill fell to Mannock's guns on 12 April and May was the most successful month in his fighting career with 24 victories added to his score. He opened June with a triple victory over a formation of German Pfalz scouts and by the time he left No 74 Squadron on 18 June he was recognized as one of the RAF's most accomplished fighter pilots.

After a short leave, Mannock was posted to command No 85 Squadron in succession to Billy Bishop. Four days after assuming command, Mannock led the squadron's SE5a's into combat against a formation of Fokker D VIIs, bringing down one of the enemy fighters himself and causing two others to collide and crash. Further victories followed and on 26 July, flying with a newcomer to the squadron, Lieutenant D. C. Inglis, he shot down a DFW two-seater for his 73rd. Mannock was flying low over enemy trenches just after the attack, through a barrage of small-arms fire,

Mannock (left) poses with fellow pilots of No 74 Squadron in France. He was commander of the Squadron's 'A' Flight in the spring of 1918.

Hans-Joachim Marseille poses with his Messerschmitt Bf 109F fighter, with which he scored the majority of his 158 combat victories before his death in September 1942.

and his companion saw his leader's SE5a start to burn and then crash in flames. Inglis himself only just managed to regain the Allied lines in an aircraft riddled with bullet holes. Nearly a year after his death, Mannock was awarded a posthumous Victoria Cross.

MARSEILLE

Hauptmann Hans-Joachim Marseille (1919–42) was the Luftwaffe's top-scoring fighter pilot against the Western Allies in World War II. At the age of 18 he enlisted in the Luftwaffe and after completing his flying training was posted to the Channel Front during the Battle of Britain. By the end of 1940 he had gained his first seven victories, but had also been forced to bale out of his own aircraft six times. Intolerant of military discipline and inclined to be scruffy and slapdash, Marseille was not very well thought of by his superiors. In January 1941 he was posted to I Gruppe, Jagdgeschwader 27 and in April this unit moved to North Africa to provide air support for Rommel's Afrika Korps.

It was in North Africa that Marseille was to make his reputation as a fighter pilot and he opened his score in the new theatre on 23 April 1941, shooting down an RAF Hurricane. Later that day the RAF evened the score and Marseille was forced to crash-land his badly damaged Messerschmitt Bf 109E. On 24 September he had a particularly successful combat, shooting down four RAF fighters. That autumn I/JG 27 replaced their Bf 109Es with the more powerful Bf 109F. Back in combat in December, Marseille gained 11 victories to bring his score to 36. On 8 February he again scored four victories in a day, becoming the top-scoring Luftwaffe pilot in North Africa. That month he was awarded the Knight's Cross.

After a period of leave in Germany Marseille returned to North Africa in April and resumed his brilliant air fighting career. In June 1942 alone he scored 33 victories and, on his score reaching 100 enemy aircraft destroyed, he was sent to Berlin to receive the Oakleaves clasp to the Knight's Cross from the Fuehrer's own hand. The secrets of his success were superb markmanship – he needed an average of only 15 rounds of ammunition per kill – coupled with great skill as an aerobatic pilot, above-average eyesight, an aggressive nature and the courage to pit these skills against his opponents.

On 1 September 1942 Marseille claimed an incredible 17 victories in one day and at least 12 of these victories can be corroborated from RAF records. This success brought him the award of the Diamonds clasp to the Knight's Cross. In mid-September his score reached 150 victories and he was promoted to *Hauptmann* and became commander of JG 27's 3 Staffel. Ironically, his death on 30 September was caused by a flying accident that could have befallen any pilot. The engine of Marseille's Bf 109 caught fire in flight and when baling out he struck the fighter's tailplane and was knocked unconscious, so he was unable to open his parachute. His final score was 158 kills and at the time of his death he was not yet 23 years old.

MITCHELL

Major-General William 'Billy' Mitchell (1879–1936) was a lifelong and outspoken champion of the cause of air power. Mitchell was commissioned into the US Army in 1899, and served in the Signal Corps. In 1916 he learned to fly at his own expense and was then assigned to the Signal Corps' Aviation Section. In 1917 he went to Europe to observe and report on military

Above left *Marseille was the Luftwaffe's most successful fighter pilot in the North African theatre during World War II.*

Above (both pictures) *The former German battleship Ostfriesland served as a target for Mitchell's bombers in a controversial demonstration of the impact of air power on naval warfare in 1921.*

Below *Major-General Billy Mitchell was an outspoken champion of the cause of air power in the United States during the 1920s.*

aviation developments. With the entry of the United States into World War I, he was appointed Aviation Officer to the American Expeditionary Force. He assumed command of the first US air units to reach the front and himself flew on operational missions. In 1918 he was awarded the Distinguished Service Cross and by the end of the war was commanding the air units of the US First Army.

On his return to the United States, Mitchell was appointed Director of Military Aeronautics, but his forthright opinions on the potential of air power were an embarrassment to the military establishment in Washington. In 1921–3 he conducted a series of much-publicized trials which showed that bombers could sink battleships, although his targets were unmanned and undefended ships at anchor. In 1925 Mitchell was posted to a backwater in Texas, but he would not be

silenced. He accused the military establishment of criminal negligence. His court-martial was inevitable. In 1926 he was found guilty of insubordination and resigned his commission. It was only in 1947, 11 years after his death, that Mitchell was rehabilitated and given the rank of major-general.

Right Oberst Werner Moelders was responsible for the highly effective combat tactics employed by the Luftwaffe during the early years of World War II.

MOELDERS

Oberst Werner Moelders (1913–41) was one of the early Luftwaffe aces in World War II and he did much to formulate German fighter tactics in that conflict. He was born at Gelsenkirchen on 18 March 1913 and joined the Luftwaffe in 1934. On completing his pilot training, he was commissioned as a *Leutnant* and posted to a fighter unit. In the summer of 1938 he was sent to Spain, taking command of the Condor Legion's 3 Staffel, Jagdgruppe 88 which flew the Messerschmitt Bf 109C fighter. Moelders proved to be a brilliant fighter pilot in action, gaining a personal score of 14 victories to make him the leading German ace of the Spanish Civil War. More important was his contribution to fighter tactics. Instead of the traditional three-

aircraft 'vic' formation, he instituted the two-aircraft element of leader and wingman, which operated in a loose, mutually supporting formation of four known as the *Schwarm* by the Luftwaffe.

In September 1939 Moelders was serving as *Staffel-kapitän* of 3 Staffel, Jagdgeschwader 53 on the Western Front. He then took command of III Gruppe, JG 53, and during the period of the 'phoney war' in 1939–40 he gained nine further victories. When the German assault in the west opened in May 1940, Moelders was in the thick of the fighting, gaining a further 16 victories over the next three weeks. In late May he was awarded the Knight's Cross, the first German fighter pilot to be so decorated. On 5 June he engaged a formation of French Dewoitine D520 fighters and his Messerschmitt Bf 109E was set on fire, forcing Moelders to bale out. He remained a prisoner of war until released after the armistice with France on 25 June.

Moelders was promoted to *Major* in July and

Above A jubilant Moelders climbs from his Messerschmitt Bf 109E fighter after a successful combat mission over England in October 1940, during the final phase of the Battle of Britain.

became *Kommodore* of JG 51, setting up his head-quarters at Wissant on the Channel coast. On 28 July he was slightly wounded in combat with the Spitfires of No 74 Squadron, but he continued to fly in combat, raising his score in World War II to 40 victories on 21 September 1940. He was awarded the Oakleaves clasp to the Knight's Cross in that month, only the second German serviceman to receive it. By the end of the Battle of Britain in October 1940, he had destroyed 50 enemy aircraft.

The following spring JG 51 moved east in preparation for the assault on the Soviet Union. The obsolescent aircraft of the Soviet air force proved to be easy victims and JG 51 soon became the first Luftwaffe fighter unit to destroy 1000 enemy aircraft. Moelders's personal score rose equally rapidly, passing the 100 mark within three weeks of the opening of the assault in the east. He was awarded the Diamonds clasp to the Knight's Cross and was then ordered back to Germany to take up the post of Inspector General of Fighters. This gave him the opportunity to tour front-line fighter units and to fly on operations with them. Consequently he was able to add a further 14 victories to his score-sheet.

In November 1941 the famous World War I ace Ernst Udet committed suicide, and Moelders, then inspecting fighter units on the Eastern Front, was summoned to the funeral in Berlin. The Heinkel He 111 in which he was flying suffered engine failure and came down in bad weather. Moelders died in the crash.

MOLLISON

James Mollison (1905–59) was one of the best-known record-breaking pilots of the 1930s. After learning to fly with the Royal Air Force he worked as an airline pilot with Australian National Airways. He then deter-

squadron and his first action took place on 3 August 1936. His first victory came on 12 August, when his Nieuport Delage NiD 52 fighter shot down a Republican Vickers Vildebeest. Later that month he was allocated one of the Heinkel He 51 fighters despatched by Germany to the Nationalists. However, he soon exchanged this for an Italian Fiat CR32 biplane, the type that he was to fly for the remainder of the war. He gained his fifth vitory on 11 September, his first with the Fiat CR32, and on 13 November brought down a Soviet Polikarpov I-15 during a great air battle over Madrid.

At the end of 1936 Morato took command of an independent fighter flight known as the *Patrulla Azul* (Blue Patrol). On 18 February Morato's three Fiat CR32s were engaged by 36 Republican I-15s and Morato managed to shoot down one and damage another before Italian fighters came to his rescue. In April 1937 he was promoted to major and his command expanded into a two-squadron *grupo*. He con-

mined to fly a light plane from Australia to England and, after an abortive first attempt, he made the flight in July–August 1931, piloting a de Havilland Gipsy Moth. He had covered 17,700km (11,000 miles) in just under nine days, winning £7000 in prize money. His next record attempt from Britain to Cape Town, South Africa, ended in Egypt, where a fault in the fuel system forced him to crash-land his DH Moth.

Mollison made another attempt to reach Cape Town in March 1932, flying a DH Puss Moth. His route this time lay across the Sahara Desert and then down the coast of West Africa. He reached Cape Town 4 days, 17 hours and 50 minutes after leaving Britain. There followed his marriage to Amy Johnson, and then in August he made the first east-to-west crossing of the Atlantic in a light aircraft. In February 1933 he crossed the South Atlantic from Thies, near Dakar, to Natal in Brazil in his Puss Moth. He thus became the first man to fly both the North and South Atlantic from east to west (against the prevailing winds). There followed a series of flights made with his wife, culminating in their unsuccessful entry in the MacRobertson Trophy race in 1934. In 1936 Mollison made a solo crossing of the North Atlantic, establishing a new speed record, and he flew this route many more times as a ferry pilot in World War II.

Above Record-breaking pilot James Mollison leaves the cockpit of his Bellanca Flash, in which he established a new transatlantic speed record in October 1936.

Right The leading Spanish Nationalist fighter ace of the Spanish Civil War was Joaquín García Morato, with 40 victories to his credit.

tinued to score victories and by January 1939 his score had reached 40. Shortly after the end of hostilities, on 4 April 1939, Morato was killed in a flying accident.

MORATO

Joaquín García Morato y Castaño (1904-39) was the leading Nationalist fighter pilot of the Spanish Civil War. He was commissioned into the infantry at the age of 19 and then transferred to the air service, learning to fly on Avro 504 biplanes. He first saw action flying de Havilland DH9A reconnaissance bombers against insurgents in Spanish Morocco. On the outbreak of the Civil War he joined a Nationalist fighter

NUNGESSER

Charles Nungesser (1892–1927) overcame serious wounds and injuries to become France's third-ranking air ace in World War I. He learned to fly in Argentina before the war and, after service in a hussar regiment which earned him the Médaille Militaire, he transferred to flying duties in January 1915. In April he joined Escadrille VB 106 at Saint Pol, near Dunkirk, and after the unit moved to Nancy in May he gained his first victory flying the cumbersome Voisin bomber, a feat which earned him the Croix de Guerre. Nungesser

Left *Charles Nungesser and his navigator Coli set out on the transatlantic flight attempt during which they disappeared without trace in May 1927.*

During the heavy air fighting over Verdun, Nungesser suffered further wounds and injuries, breaking his jaw again and dislocating a knee. Nonetheless, he continued to fight and raised his score to ten victories. By September he had destroyed 17 enemy aircraft, a total only exceeded by Guynemer. His wounds forced him to go into hospital in late December, at which time he had 21 victories to his credit and had received the British Military Cross for going to the assistance of Royal Flying Corps aircraft under attack from German fighters. Returning to combat in the spring of 1917 he raised his score to 30 victories by mid-August, but his injuries troubled him to such a degree that he could hardly walk. His condition was not helped when he had a car accident, sending him to hospital yet again. This unbelievably determined pilot returned to combat in 1918, gaining his 45th and final victory on 15 August. After the war he started an unsuccessful flying school and then took up barnstorming in the United States. In 1927, while attempting a transatlantic flight, his aircraft disappeared without trace.

was then transferred to a fighter squadron, Escadrille N65, which flew Nieuport Bébé scouts. Nungesser's personal aircraft was decorated with a macabre insignia, consisting of a black heart on which were painted a white coffin and skull and crossbones, flanked by two candles. On 29 November he gained his first victory while flying Nieuports.

In January 1916 Nungesser suffered the first of a series of injuries that were to bedevil his flying career. He crashed while on a test flight, fracturing both legs and dislocating his jaw. Two months later he was out of hospital on crutches and was flying again. He rejoined N65 at the end of March and the following month resumed his scoring, sending down an observation balloon on 2 April. He was commissioned later that month and on 25 April engaged a formation of two-seaters escorted by three fighters. One of the two-seaters fell to his guns, but he only escaped from the escort with a badly damaged aircraft.

OLDS

Brigadier-General Robin Olds (born 1922) had a remarkable career as a fighter pilot in the American air services, becoming top-scoring ace of his fighter group in World War II and then towards the end of his service life fighting MiG-21s over North Vietnam. He was born in Honolulu, Hawaii, on 14 July 1922, the son of a US Army Air Service pilot. He entered the US Military Academy at West Point in 1940 and then trained as a pilot. In May 1944 he came to Britain, flying Lockheed P-38 Lightnings with the USAAF's 479th Fighter Group. Olds's early combat missions included flying patrols over the Normandy beachheads in June 1944, where the distinctive, twin-

Below left *Nungesser stands beside his Nieuport scout, with its macabre personal insignia. Although wounded and injured in crashes many times, Nungesser persevered to become France's third-ranking ace in World War I.*

Below right *Colonel Robin Olds pictured in 1966, when he became the commander of the 8th Tactical Fighter Wing – the Wolfpack – at Ubon air base in Thailand.*

rose to the rank of colonel and took command of the 81st Tactical Fighter Wing, based in Britain at Bentwaters in Suffolk.

In 1966 he was assigned to Southeast Asia, taking command of the 8th Tactical Fighter Wing at Ubon air base in Thailand on 30 September. At the age of 44, Olds found himself again in combat, flying McDonnell Douglas F-4C Phantoms against the North Vietnamese fighter force. On 2 January 1967 Olds mounted Operation Bolo, in which his F-4s simulated a bomb-laden air strike force to lure the North Vietnamese into combat. The plan worked and the 8th TFW claimed the destruction of seven MiG-21s for no loss to themselves. Olds himself scored one of these kills. On 4 May, while escorting a strike force of Republic F-105s, Olds's wingman spotted two MiG-21s closing on the formation and his leader fired an AIM-9 Sidewinder missile at one of the MiGs, which went down out of control. On another escort mission on 20 May a dozen MiG-17s engaged eight F-4s led by Olds, who accounted for two of the four enemy aircraft destroyed in that fight. In all during Olds's period of command the 8th TFW destroyed 24 MiGs. His next assignment was as Commander of Cadets at the USAF Academy, Colorado Springs, after which he retired from the service.

PARK

Air Chief-Marshal Sir Keith Park (1892–1975) was one of the RAF's outstanding tactical commanders of World War II, leading No 11 Group, Fighter Command throughout the Battle of Britain. Born in New Zealand on 15 June 1892, he enlisted in the New Zealand Field Artillery in August 1914 and served in Gallipoli and on the Western Front before volunteering for the Royal Flying Corps. After pilot training he was

boomed P-38 could not be mistaken for a German aircraft by over-enthusiastic Allied AA gunners. Olds began to build up his score of German aircraft destroyed and in September the 479th Fighter Group exchanged its P-38s for North American P-51 Mustangs. At the end of the year Olds returned to the United States on leave, but in January 1945 rejoined the group and took command of its 434th Fighter Squadron. The unit was based at Wattisham in Suffolk and operated on long-range bomber escort missions. By the end of hostilities, Olds had taken part in 107 combat missions and destroyed 13 enemy aircraft in the air, plus a further 11½ during strafing attacks against enemy airfields.

Olds remained in the postwar USAF, and was a founder-member of the first jet aerobatic team, flying Lockheed P-80 Shooting Stars. In 1948 he returned to Britain to serve with the RAF on an exchange posting, commanding No 1 Squadron, which flew Gloster Meteor jet fighters from Tangmere in Sussex. After service in the United States, Germany and Libya, he

Above *Colonel Robin Olds (right) prepares to add four MiG kills to the 8th Tactical Fighter Wing's scoreboard after a successful combat over North Vietnam on 20 May 1967.*

Right *Park seated in the cockpit of his North American Harvard. During the Battle of Britain he toured the units of No 11 Group flying his personal Hawker Hurricane fighter.*

71

posted to No 48 Squadron, flying Bristol F2B Fighters in early 1917. By the end of the year he had shot down 15 enemy aircraft and had himself been shot down twice. Early in 1918 he was appointed to command No 48 Squadron, finishing the war with 20 victories.

Park was granted a permanent commission in the RAF after the war and served in Egypt and Iraq in the 1920s. He then commanded Nos 25 and 111 Squadrons, before going to Buenos Aires as air attaché. In 1938 he became Dowding's Senior Air Staff Officer at Headquarters Fighter Command and in early 1940 was appointed to command No 11 Group. He directed the air fighting over Dunkirk and then played a decisive part in the Battle of Britain, as his group bore the brunt of the fighting. His tactical skills were ill-rewarded, for in October 1940 (at the same time as Dowding was superseded) he was posted to a back-water in Training Command.

In July 1942 Park was appointed to command Malta's air defences and his brilliant handling of his squadrons was rewarded by a knighthood. In January 1944 he became Air Officer Commanding Middle East Command and in February 1945 moved on to command the air units of South East Asia Command. In the Far East Park directed the air operations which contributed to the reoccupation of Burma. In 1946 he retired from the RAF and returned to New Zealand.

PATTLE

The little-known South African fighter pilot Squadron Leader M.T. St J. 'Pat' Pattle (1914–41) was probably the leading RAF ace of World War II, with an estimated 50 victories to his credit. He was born at Butterworth, South Africa, on 23 July 1914, and in 1936 came to Britain to join the RAF. After completing his flying training, he was posted to No 80 Squadron flying Gloster Gladiators and accompanied the squadron to Egypt in the spring of 1938. When Italy entered the war, Pattle was a flight commander. He first saw action on 4 August, shooting down an Italian Fiat CR32 and a Breda Ba 65, but was then forced to bale out of his damaged Gladiator. He landed behind Italian lines, but evaded capture and made his way back to the British side. On 8 August he was again in action and shot down two Fiat CR42 fighters.

In November 1940 No 80 Squadron was sent to Greece to help repel the Italian invaders. Pattle was in action on 19 November, claiming two Fiat CR42s destroyed. Further victories followed in December, but then severe winter weather greatly hampered further operations. Air action increased again in February and by the middle of the month Pattle's personal score stood at 15 victories. No 80 Squadron then began to receive Hawker Hurricane fighters and Pattle scored his first kill flying a Hurricane on 20 February. An intense air battle developed over the front line on 28 February when 19 RAF fighters intercepted many Italian formations, destroying 26 enemy aircraft for the loss of one Gladiator. Pattle's share in this bag was two Fiat BR20 bombers shot down. In early March, with 23 kills to his credit, he was awarded a bar to his Distinguished Flying Cross and promoted to squadron leader.

Pattle then assumed command of No 33 Squadron, a Hurricane unit newly arrived in Greece. His first mission with the squadron was a bomber escort operation over Albania on 23 March during which Pattle destroyed one Fiat G50 in the air and a further three during a strafing attack on their airfield. On 6 April Germany entered the war in the Balkans and thereafter

Squadron Leader 'Pat' Pattle (fifth from right) photographed with the Hurricane pilots of No 33 Squadron, the unit that he commanded in Greece in 1941. The little-known Pattle may have been the RAF's top-scoring pilot of World War II.

the air war became a great deal more intense. On 6 April Pattle's Hurricanes engaged Luftwaffe Messerschmitt Bf 109s for the first time and were fortunate to shoot down five of them. Pattle was continually in action over the following two weeks, at the end of which the RAF fighters were forced to withdraw from the forward airfields to the Athens area. On 20 April on his third sortie of the day he engaged a formation of German bombers over Eleusis Bay and brought two of them down before his Hurricane came under attack from a Messerschmitt Bf 110 and Pattle was shot down into the sea. As the records for this period were lost during the RAF's evacuation from Greece, official confirmation of Pattle's final score is impossible, but it is believed to stand at some 50 enemy aircraft destroyed.

PICKARD

Group Captain P.C. Pickard (1915–44) was one of the most remarkable pilots of RAF Bomber Command in World War II. He was born on 16 May 1915 and was commissioned in the RAF in 1937. His first posting to a front-line squadron took him to No 214 Squadron at Feltwell, Norfolk, flying Handley-Page Harrows. He spent the early months of World War II in a training unit, but then was posted to No 99 Squadron, which flew Vickers Wellington bombers. In July 1940 he was awarded the Distinguished Flying Cross and transferred to No 311 Squadron, a newly formed Czech bomber unit, to assist in its operational training. The squadron was soon declared operational and Pickard remained with the unit, flying night bomber missions, until March 1941. He was then awarded the Distinguished Service Order and the Czech Military Cross. It was at this time that he became well known to the public as captain of Wellington 'F-for-Freddie' in the documentary film 'Target for Tonight', which followed the fortunes of a night bomber on a typical mission.

Pickard was then promoted to squadron leader and was posted to No 9 Squadron at Scampton, Lincolnshire, where he met navigator Flight Sergeant Bill

Broadley, who was to fly with Pickard for much of the remainder of his career. Later in 1941 Pickard was appointed to command No 51 Squadron, whose Armstrong Whitworth Whitleys carried the parachutists who executed the Bruneval raid in February 1942. This daring coup secured the secrets of the German Würzburg radar for RAF technical intelligence. For his part in the raid Pickard was awarded a bar to his DSO.

In November 1942 Pickard took command of No 161 (Special Duties) Squadron at Tempsford, Bedfordshire. The squadron's task was to deliver agents into enemy-occupied Europe and to supply resistance forces with arms and other supplies. Among the aircraft that No 161 Squadron flew on these hazardous tasks were Westland Lysanders and Lockheed Hudsons, which often landed in enemy territory to drop off and collect agents and resistance leaders, and HP Halifaxes for the supply-dropping tasks. For his work with this unit Pickard was awarded a second bar to his DSO.

On leaving No 161 Squadron Pickard was promoted to group captain and took command of RAF

Below *Group Captain Percy Pickard's remarkable wartime flying career included a period in command of No 161 Squadron, which delivered agents into enemy-occupied Europe.*

station Sculthorpe, Lincolnshire. In October he moved on to command No 140 Wing in the 2nd Tactical Air Force. This wing was made up of three Mosquito FB Mk VI squadrons, which specialized in low-level daylight attacks on pinpoint targets. On 3 October 1943 Pickard led the wing against just such a target, a power station at Pontchâteau in France. In 1944 the wing was called upon to carry out the famous raid on Amiens Gaol, which was successfully accomplished on 18 February. However, on leaving the target area, Pickard's Mosquito was shot down by enemy fighters and he and his navigator, Flight Lieutenant Bill Broadley, were killed.

POST

Wiley Post (1901–35) was an outstanding American long-distance flier of the inter-war years. His first contact with flying came in 1919, when he joined a barnstorming outfit as a parachutist. He soon went back to working in the oilfields, where by ill-fortune he was blinded in one eye by a steel splinter. The compensation he received for this accident allowed him to buy his own aeroplane – a Canadian-built Curtiss Jenny – and learn to fly. Over the next few years he earned a precarious living as a barnstorming pilot, but then in 1930 he was appointed as personal pilot to the oil magnate F. C. Hall. Hall's aircraft was a Lockheed Vega monoplane which was named *Winnie Mae* in honour of his daughter. The Vega was entered in the 1930 National Air Races and Post flew it to victory in the Nonstop Derby over a course stretching from Los Angeles to Chicago.

Left *Wiley Post (left) and his navigator Harold Gatty pictured at the end of their gruelling around-the-world, record-breaking flight on 1 July 1931.*

Post next set his sights on the round-the-world record, intending to beat the airship *Graf Zeppelin*'s time of 21 days by a flight lasting less than ten days. He teamed up with Australian navigator Harold Gatty and the pair set off from Roosevelt Field, New York, on 23 June 1931. The first refuelling stop was at Harbour Grace, Newfoundland, and then Post intended to fly direct to Berlin. However, bad weather forced a change of plan and Post landed in Britain at RAF Sealand in Cheshire. Berlin was finally reached 23 hours 30 minutes after leaving New York. The following day Post and Gatty set course for Moscow and then headed across the Soviet Union for the Pacific coast of Siberia. At one landing place the Vega became bogged down in mud and had to be towed free by a tractor. On 30 June they finally reached Solomon

Below *Post's record-breaking Lockheed Vega* Winnie Mae *is today preserved in the Smithsonian Institution's National Air and Space Museum in Washington DC.*

Beach, Alaska, and after replacing a damaged propellor they set course for New York. The Vega arrived at Roosevelt Field at 2047 hours on 1 July, having taken 8 days, 15 hours and 51 minutes to cover 25,000km (15,500 miles).

Two years later Post determined to break his own record, this time flying solo, but with the help of an autopilot. He took off in *Winnie Mae* from Floyd Bennett Field, New York, on 15 July 1933. Despite problems with bad weather and a faulty gyroscope, Post landed back at Floyd Bennett Field on 22 July, having knocked nearly a day off his previous record. Post's second round-the-world flight had lasted 7 days, 18 hours and 36 minutes.

Post next turned his attention to high-altitude flight, developing a special electrically heated pressure suit for himself and a supercharger for the *Winnie Mae*'s Pratt & Whitney Wasp engine. Thus equipped he attained altitudes up to 16,750m (55,000ft). In 1935 the *Winnie Mae* was retired and replaced by a Lockheed Orion floatplane. Accompanied by humorist Will Rogers, Post set out to survey a new air route over Siberia. At Point Barrow, Alaska, the Orion crashed on take-off and Post and Rogers were killed.

REITSCH

Hanna Reitsch (1912–79) was a highly skilled woman test pilot, who participated in the development flying of German combat aircraft in World War II. She was born in Hirschberg, Silesia, on 29 March 1912, and first learned to fly on gliders at Grunau. She then progressed to powered flying, but continued to pilot gliders. In

German airwoman Hanna Reitsch first established her reputation as a glider pilot, but went on to test-fly a wide range of powered aeroplanes.

1933 she went to South America with an expedition that was to use gliders to study thermal currents in the region. On her return she joined the Institute for Glider Research at Darmstadt, test-flying new glider designs and carrying out research into the problems of long-distance and high-altitude gliding flight. Her test-flying work earned her the honorary title of *Flugkapitän*.

In September 1937 Hanna Reitsch began work as a test pilot at the Luftwaffe's test centre at Rechlin. One of the first machines that she tested was the Focke-Achgelis FA 61 twin-rotor helicopter. With this machine she established a new distance record for helicopters in a flight from Bremen to Berlin in October 1937. Then following February she flew the machine inside the Deutschlandhalle in Berlin. She also test-flew

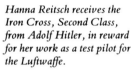

Hanna Reitsch receives the Iron Cross, Second Class, from Adolf Hitler, in reward for her work as a test pilot for the Luftwaffe.

the DFS 230 troop-carrying glider, which was produced in quantity for the Luftwaffe. Other flying included work on cable-cutter devices, which was extremely hazardous as it involved flying bombers into balloon cables with only an untried cable-cutter for protection. Her courage was recognized by the award of the Iron Cross, which she received from Hitler in March 1941.

In the summer of 1942 Hanna Reitsch joined the Messerschmitt Me 163 test programme, flying unpowered glider versions of this rocket-powered interceptor. On one test flight the jettisonable undercarriage failed to release and she had to land on this rather than the usual under-fuselage skid. The undercarriage was not stressed for landing loads and as a result of the subsequent heavy landing she spent the next five months in hospital. When she had recovered from her injuries, she returned to her test-flying work on the Me 163. An even more dangerous aeroplane that she flew was the Fieseler Fi 103R, a piloted version of the V1 flying bomb. It was intended that the pilot would fly this aircraft to the target and put it in a dive towards it, baling out at the last minute. It was never used in combat, however. In the final days of World War II, Hanna Reitsch flew Luftwaffe General von Greim into Berlin, avoiding the Soviet air defences, and was thus one of the last people to see Hitler alive. After the war she was imprisoned by the Allies, but continued flying after her release. In 1970 she established a new German gliding record.

RICHTHOFEN

Manfred von Richthofen (1892–1918), the legendary 'Red Baron', was the top-scoring German fighter pilot of World War I. He was born at Breslau on 2 May 1892, a member of the minor nobility, and was commissioned into a cavalry regiment in 1912. When the fighting of World I bogged down into trench warfare, in which the cavalry could play little part, von Richthofen transferred to the Air Service as an observer. In the summer of 1915 he served with Fliegerabteilung 69 on the Eastern Front and then transferred to the west, flying in bombers with the Brieftauben Abteilung Ostende (Ostend Carrier Pigeon Unit, a cover name to conceal the squadron's true role). In October 1915 von Richthofen began his pilot training and was then posted to Kampfstaffel 2 on the Western Front.

On 26 April 1916 von Richthofen claimed his first aerial victory, a Nieuport scout which he brought down over Verdun, although it was not officially confirmed. His unit then moved east, but von Richthofen soon transferred to Oswald Boelcke's newly formed fighter squadron Jasta 2. On 17 September he scored his first officially confirmed victory, a Royal Flying Corps FE2b, and by the end of the year his score stood at 15 enemy aircraft destroyed. His hardest fight of this period was on 23 November 1916, when he shot down the British ace Major Lanoe Hawker. In January 1916 von Richthofen received the Pour le Mérite, Prussia's highest award for gallantry.

Early in 1917 von Richthofen formed and led his own fighter squadron, Jasta 11. Equipped with Albatros scouts which were technically far superior to most Allied aircraft of the period, his pilots inflicted high casualties on their opponents during 'Bloody April' 1917. By this time von Richthofen's score was 52 victories. While on leave he learned that his brother Lothar, a pilot with Jasta 11, had been wounded and this made the air war a matter of personal vengeance for him. A cold and calculating man, von Richthofen scored many of his victories against vulnerable two-seaters. A superb marksman, he was like many of the great aces keen on hunting and shooting for sport. He

Manfred von Richthofen, popularly known as the 'Red Baron' because his personal aircraft were painted red, was Germany's leading fighter pilot of World War I.

Richthofen decorated a room with trophies from his victims' aircraft. The serial number 5964 comes from the DH2 flown by Major Lanoe Hawker.

often took a ghoulish delight in the fate of his victims and collected trophies from their crashed aircraft whenever he could.

In June 1917 von Richthofen took command of Jagdgeschwader I, a fighter unit made up of four *Jastas* and dubbed by the RFC the 'Flying Circus'. Most of von Richthofen's victories were scored while flying the Albatros scout, but in this latter part of his fighting career he flew the Fokker Dr I Triplane, scoring some 20 kills with it. In July 1917 von Richthofen had been wounded in the head during an air combat and afterwards he suffered from frequent headaches. Yet he continued to run up an impressive series of victories and with 80 confirmed kills he was the highest-scoring pilot of any nation in Word War I. On 21 April 1918 he was involved in a dogfight with Sopwith Camels of No 209 Squadron RFC and was shot down and killed with a single bullet through the heart. Whether the fatal shot was fired by Captain Roy Brown's Camel or by ground gunners has long been a matter of controversy.

RICKENBACKER

Captain Eddie Rickenbacker (1890–1973) was the leading ace of the US Army Air Service in World War I. Born at Columbus, Ohio, on 8 October 1890, his early interest was in automobiles and he became an expert mechanic and driver. At the age of 26 he became one of the United States' leading motor racing drivers and established a new land speed record in 1916. The following year, when the United States entered World War I, he enlisted in the army and became driver to General John Pershing. But Rickenbacker wanted to transfer to the Air Service to fly fighters and, despite his age (the average age for fighter pilots in World War I was around 20) and his lack of formal education, he was accepted.

Rickenbacker learned to fly at the 3rd Aviation Instruction Centre at Issoudun in France and in January 1918 he was appointed as engineering officer at Issoudun. In March he was posted to the 1st Pursuit Group, joining the 94th Aero Squadron whose 'Hat in the Ring' insignia he was to make famous. Lafayette Escadrille ace Raoul Lufbery led the squadron's Nieuport 28s on their first war patrol on 19 March. Richenbacker scored his first victory, an Albatros DVa, on 29 April. Another Lafayette Escadrille veteran, James Norman Hall, was shot down, wounded and taken prisoner on 7 May and during this fight Rickenbacker scored his second victory, although it was not officially confirmed at the time. On 22 May he scored his fourth victory, but was beaten to the honour of becoming the first American-trained fighter ace by Lieutenant Douglas Campbell.

Rickenbacker was kept out of the air war from June until August 1918 by a serious ear infection. He made up for this period of inaction in September, shooting

down four Fokker D VII fighters, a Halberstadt two-seater and an observation balloon. By this time the squadron was flying the Spad SXIII fighter. On 25 September he became CO of the 94th Aero Squadron. An especially noteworthy combat took place on 25 September, when Rickenbacker took on a formation of five Fokker D VIIs and two Halberstadt two-seaters, accounting for one of each of them. This air fight was mentioned in the citation of Rickenbacker's Medal of Honor, which he belatedly received in 1930.

During October Rickenbacker claimed 14 more victories and by the time of the Armistice his score stood at 22 enemy aircraft destroyed plus four observation balloons. After the war he ran the Rickenbacker Motor Company, which failed in 1927, and more successfully Eastern Airlines. During World War II he served in the USAAF. While inspecting air bases in the Pacific

Below Captain Edward Rickenbacker, a noted American motor-racing driver before World War I, became the US Army Aviation Service's top-scoring fighter pilot.

Bottom Rickenbacker poses with his Spad SXIII fighter, which carries the 94th Aero Squadron's Famous 'hat-in-the-ring' insignia.

Theatre the Boeing B-17 in which he was flying crashed and he spent 22 days in a liferaft before being rescued. After a long and eventful life he died peacefully at the age of 83.

RUDEL

Hans-Ulrich Rudel (1916–82) was the Luftwaffe's most outstanding dive-bomber and ground-attack pilot of World War II. Born at Konradswaldau, Silesia, on 2 July 1916, he enlisted in the Luftwaffe in 1936. His first posting was to the dive-bomber unit I Gruppe, Stukageschwader 168, and he then served with a reconnaissance unit, winning the Iron Cross for his work in the Polish Campaign of September 1939. In 1940 he returned to dive-bombers, but saw no action that year.

Rudel was posted to I Gruppe, StG 2 flying the Junkers Ju 87B in Greece in April 1941 and he was to remain with that *Geschwader* for the rest of his wartime career. With the start of the war against the Soviet Union, Rudel was soon in action, flying four missions on the first day of the campaign. In July he was appointed technical officer to III/StG 2. In a notable raid on the Soviet Fleet at Kronstadt on 23 September, Rudel dive-bombed and sank the battleship *Marat*. By the end of 1941, he had flown 400 missions and in January 1942 he was awarded the Knight's Cross and rested from operations.

Rudel returned to StG 2 in August 1942, when the unit was operating the Ju 87D over the southern sector of the Eastern Front. He was appointed *Staffelkapitän* and took part in numerous operational sorties, so that by February 1943 he had over 1000 missions to his credit. He was promoted to *Hauptmann* and began to fly anti-tank sorties with the 37mm-cannon-armed Ju 87G. He quickly ran up an impressive score of knocked-out tanks, his tally passing the 100 mark in October. During 1943 he added the Oakleaves and Swords clasps to his Knight's Cross. Promotion to *Major* followed in March 1944 and he took command of III Gruppe, Schlachtgeschwader 2 (as StG 2 had been redesignated).

The Luftwaffe's ground-attack units were heavily engaged on the Eastern Front during 1944 as the German armies retreated. On 20 March Rudel landed his Ju 87 behind enemy lines to pick up the crew of a shot-down aircraft. However, waterlogged ground prevented his taking off again. Wounded in the shoulder by pursuing Soviet troops, he made his escape and regained German lines by swimming the icy waters of the Dniester. Ignoring his wound, he continued to fly on operations and the award of the Diamonds clasp to the Knight's Cross followed. Rudel was shot down and wounded again in August and the following month took command of SG 2. At the end of the year his outstanding combat record was recognized by the award of the Golden Oakleaves clasp to the Knight's Cross, the only time this decoration has ever been bestowed. In February 1945 Rudel received another wound and his right foot was later amputated. Even this did not ground him and he fought on to the end of the war. He had flown over 2500 operational sorties and had destroyed over 500 enemy tanks, a record unsurpassed by any other airman.

SAMSON

Air Commodore Charles Rumney Samson (1883–1931) was one of the foremost pioneers of naval aviation. He joined the Royal Navy at the age of 15 as a cadet and in 1911 he was one of four naval officers

Below Oberst Hans-Ulrich Rudel was the Luftwaffe's most outstanding ground-attack pilot of World War II, winning the unique Golden Oakleaves clasp to the Knight's Cross.

Bottom Rudel prepares to lead a sortie of bomb-laden Junkers Ju 87D Stuka dive-bombers on the Eastern Front. By early 1943 he had taken part in a thousand such missions.

selected for pilot training. He then established a naval airfield at Eastchurch, where future pilots were trained and experiments carried out in naval air operations. In 1912 he flew a Short biplane off the deck of HMS *Africa* and later that year flew from HMS *Hibernia* while she was under way. The following year he carried out night-flying and armament trials and, when King George V reviewed the Fleet at Spithead in July 1914, Samson led a flypast of naval aircraft.

In August 1914 Samson's Eastchurch Squadron was despatched to France, where it carried out reconnaissance sorties. Yet the swashbuckling Samson was not content with this passive role and formed an armoured car squadron to harrass the flank of the advancing German armies. His aircraft also carried out bombing attacks. The German advance on the Channel coast eventually forced the squadron back to Dunkirk and it was withdrawn to Britain in early 1915. The squadron then moved to the Dardanelles and was based

at Imbros, carrying out reconnaissance and bombing missions against the Turkish forces. The unit was expanded to become No 3 Wing RNAS, but with Allied evacuation from the Dardanelles it returned to Britain in December 1915.

Samson's next command in May 1916 was the seaplane-carrier *Ben-my-Chree*, which operated from Port Said in Egypt against Turkish forces until January 1917, when it was sunk by a shore battery. Returning to Britain that spring, Samson then served as a staff officer in the Air Department at the Admiralty. In November 1917 he took command of the flying-boat base at Great Yarmouth, moving to Felixstowe in April (when the Royal Naval Air Service merged with the Royal Flying Corps to form the Royal Air Force) to command a group of east coast air stations. In May 1918 Samson achieved another experimental 'first', flying a Sopwith Camel from a lighter towed behind a warship. This procedure was successfully used by

Right *A raid by seaplanes from the carrier HMS* Ben-my-Chree, *which Samson commanded, was carried out on the Turkish-held Chilkaldir Bridge on 27 August 1916.*

Right *Wing Commander Charles Samson stands in front of a Nieuport two-seater, which he flew when he commanded No 3 Wing RNAS in the Dardanelles theatre in 1915.*

Lieutenant S. D. Culley to intercept a German airship on 11 August 1918.

After World War I Samson elected to remain in the RAF, rather than return to the navy, although characteristically (and against normal regulations) he retained his beard in the new service. During the 1920s he led a number of route-proving flights, including a 17,700km (11,000-mile) round trip from Heliopolis, Egypt, to Cape Town, South Africa, and back with four Fairey IIIFs in 1927. He retired from the RAF with the rank of air commodore in 1929.

SANTOS-DUMONT

Alberto Santos-Dumont (1873–1932), the Brazilian-born aviation pioneer, made the first successful aeroplane flight in Europe in 1906. Santos-Dumont had come to live in Paris at the age of 19 and in 1897 he took up the then-popular sport of ballooning. A wealthy man of leisure, he then turned his attention to airships, making his first ascent over the French capital in 1898 in an airship built to his own requirements. In the summer of 1901 he twice attempted to win the prize offered by Henri Deutsche de la Meurthe for the first airship flight from St Cloud to the Eiffel Tower and back within 30 minutes. Both flights ended in forced landings, but on 19 October he finally succeeded. Santos-Dumont owned 14 airships at various times, his favourite being the No 9, which he regularly used for journeys around Paris and its suburbs.

In 1904 during a visit to the United States Santos-Dumont learned of the Wright Brothers' work and this aroused his interest in the powered aeroplane. The first such machine that he built, the 14 bis (so designated because it was first tested beneath his airship No 14), was a 10m (33ft) span biplane. It was built as

Far left *The swashbuckling Samson pictured on his charger at Tenedos during the Dardanelles campaign, when he commanded No 3 Wing RNAS.*

Left *The dapper little Brazilian Alberto Santos-Dumont pictured at the controls of one of his airships, in which he used to travel around the Paris suburbs.*

Left *Santos-Dumont's aeroplane the 14 bis made the first flight of more than 100 metres' distance in Europe, at Bagatelle outside Paris on 23 October 1906.*

a canard (with the tailplane mounted ahead of the wings) and was powered by a 24hp Antoinette engine. It proved to be underpowered with this engine and Santos-Dumont substituted a 50hp Antoinette. In this form it took to the air on 23 October 1906 and covered a distance of some 60m (200ft), winning the Archdeacon prize for the first European flight of more than 25m (80ft). On 12 November, after the 14 bis had been further modified by the fitting of ailerons, Santos-Dumont covered a distance of over 210m (700ft). These were the first true aeroplane flights in Europe.

In 1908 Santos-Dumont produced another aeroplane design, his No 19 Demoiselle. This was a small, lightweight machine powered by a 20hp engine, and few could have left the ground in it but the diminutive Santos-Dumont, who weighed only 50kg (108lb). Nonetheless the Demoiselle was put into series production by the Clement-Bayard company. It was the more successful of his aeroplanes, despite being tricky to fly. In 1910 Santos-Dumont's failing health forced him to give up flying, but he had the consolation that his pioneering work had helped to usher in the European aviation age.

SCHNAUFER

Major Heinz-Wolfgang Schnaufer (1922–50) was the Luftwaffe's leading night-fighter ace of World War II. He was born on 16 February 1922 and joined the Luftwaffe in 1940. After learning to fly, he trained as a night-fighter pilot and was posted to II Gruppe, Nachtjagdgeschwader 1 in April 1942. The *Gruppe* operated the Messerschmitt Bf 110 twin-engined fighter from St Trond airfield in Belgium against the RAF's night bombers. On 2 June 1942 Schnaufer gained his first night victory and during the next year of operational flying he raised his total score to 21. In August 1943 Schnaufer was appointed *Staffelkapitän* of 12 Staffel, NJG 1.

The rudder of Schnaufer's Messerschmitt Bf 110G night fighter, preserved in the Imperial War Museum, London, attests to this pilot's remarkable skill in attacking RAF night bombers.

By the summer of 1943 the German night fighters' task became more difficult, as RAF Bomber Command made use of electronic countermeasures, escorting night fighters and sophisticated tactics to penetrate the Reich's night air defences. A determined pilot, however, could still operate successfully, as Schnaufer demonstrated on the night of 16 December 1943. He took off in very bad weather to intercept a raid bound for Berlin and managed to shoot down four enemy bombers before safely regaining his base. At the end of the year, with 42 victories to his credit, he was awarded the Knight's Cross.

The new year began with Schnaufer's promotion to *Hauptmann* and he took command of IV Gruppe, NJG 1. On the night of 25 May he was especially successful, bringing down five RAF bombers, and for this feat he received the Oakleaves clasp to his Knight's Cross. At the end of July he was awarded the Swords

Major Heinz-Wolfgang Schnaufer (fourth from right), the Luftwaffe's leading night-fighter ace of World War II, parades for Reichsmarschall Hermann Goering.

to the Knight's Cross, at which time his score stood at 89 night victories. Schnaufer became *Kommodore* of NJG 4 in November and by the end of the year his score had risen to 106, making him the top-scoring night-fighter pilot. Another notable success came on 21 February, when he shot down seven Lancasters within a 20-minute period during a raid on Duisburg. He survived the war with a score of 121 night victories, but was killed in a motor accident in 1950. The rudder of his Bf 110, marked with his 121 victories, is today preserved in the Imperial War Museum, London.

SMITH

Sir Ross Smith (1892–1922) piloted the first aircraft to fly from Britain to Australia. In August 1914 he enlisted in the Australian Army and served at Gallipoli, until he contracted enteric fever and was evacuated to Britain. In 1916 he returned to the Middle East and transferred to the Australian Flying Corps, joining No 1 Squadron AFC as an observer. The following year he trained as a pilot and rejoined No 1 Squadron AFC, flying Bristol F2B Fighters. He then flew the first Handley Page O/400 twin-engined bomber to arrive in the Middle East.

At the end of the war, Smith piloted an HP O/400 carrying Brigadier-General A. E. Borton and Major-General W. Salmond from Egypt to India. This was the first time that the route had been flown. Smith set off on 29 November 1918 and, with intermediate stops at Damascus, Baghdad, Bushire, Bandar Abbas and Chabbar, arrived at Karachi on 10 December. The HP O/400 then flew on to Calcutta, but was later wrecked during a storm.

In 1919 Ross Smith decided to try to win the £10,000 prize that the Australian government had offered for the first flight from Britain to Australia.

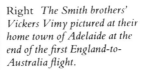

Right The Smith brothers' Vickers Vimy pictured at their home town of Adelaide at the end of the first England-to-Australia flight.

Left Ross Smith, accompanied by his brother Keith and two mechanics, made the first flight from England to Australia in 1919.

It was stipulated that the winners must be Australian and that the flight should take no more than 30 consecutive days. Vickers made a Vimy bomber available and Smith chose his brother Keith as navigator and Sergeants Bennett and Shiers as mechanics. They left from Hounslow, Middlesex, on 12 November and the Vimy battled through clouds and snow to Lyons. On the next stage, the aircraft became bogged down at Pisa and bad weather dogged the flight as far south as Crete. However, on 18 November they arrived at Cairo with the first 4000km (2500 miles) of the flight behind them. The next stage was to Karachi and then on to Bangkok, which was reached on 1 December. Flying on to Singora the Vimy met what Ross Smith described as the worst flying conditions he had ever encountered. At Singora the airstrip was waterlogged and the landing had to be made downwind, but the Vimy got down with only its tailskid broken.

The flight then continued to Singapore, the Dutch East Indies and on to Darwin, which was reached on 10 December. It had taken nearly 28 days and so qualified for the government prize. From Darwin the Vimy flew on to Adelaide, the Smiths' home city, which they reached on 23 March 1920. Both brothers received knighthoods and their mechanics the Air Force Medal. In 1922 Sir Ross Smith planned a flight around the world, but while testing a Vickers Viking IV amphibian at Brooklands in Surrey he crashed to his death.

SMITH-BARRY

Wing Commander Robert Smith-Barry (1886–1949) was the man who devised the first proper system of flying instruction in the British armed forces. He learned to fly in 1911 and the following year he was

commissioned in the Royal Flying Corps, attending the first course of the Central Flying School. On the outbreak of World War I he accompanied No 5 Squadron to France, flying reconnaissance missions during the retreat of the British Expeditionary Force from Mons. On 18 August 1914 he was badly injured when his BE8 crashed, breaking both his legs and smashing a kneecap. He began flying again in 1915 and in May 1916 returned to France as a flight commander with No 60 Squadron. In July the squadron's CO was killed in action and Smith-Barry was appointed to succeed him, remaining in command until December 1916.

On his return to Britain, Smith-Barry voiced his criticisms of the generally poor standard of pilot training and was given the opportunity of improving the situation as commander of No 1 Reserve Squadron at

Above The Avro 504K was one of the training aircraft used by Smith-Barry's School of Special Flying at Gosport in 1917.

Left Robert Smith-Barry devised the first truly effective system of flying training in the world for RFC pilots during World War I.

Gosport, Hampshire. There he instituted systematic training in all aspects of flying and in May 1917 produced his *Notes on Teaching Flying* for instructors. The Gosport System proved to be highly effective and formed the basis of RAF flying training for nearly 30 years. Smith-Barry was promoted to lieutenant-colonel and took command of the newly formed School of Special Flying at Gosport. In 1918 he became a brigadier-general in command of a training group, but he rebelled against the administrative work, was demoted to lieutenant-colonel and returned to Gosport. He retired from the RAF in 1918, but in World War II, after a period as a ferry pilot, he rejoined the RAF, serving as a station commander and ground instructor.

SPAATZ

General Carl 'Tooey' Spaatz (1891–1974) was the first commander of the USAAF's Eighth Air Force in World War II and the newly formed US Air Force's first Chief of Staff in 1947. He was born in Boyertown, Pennsylvania, on 28 June 1891 and entered the Military Academy at West Point as a cadet in 1910. He served as an infantryman until 1915, when he began flying training. In 1916 he joined the 1st Aero Squadron and flew reconnaissance missions over the Mexican border during the expedition against 'Pancho' Villa. Spaatz was promoted to captain in May 1917 and sent to France to command the American training base at Issoudun. The following year he saw combat with the 2nd Pursuit Group and was credited with the destruction of three enemy aircraft.

In 1920 Spaatz was promoted to major and appointed to command Kelly Field, Texas. The following year he moved on to command the 1st Pursuit Group

Left *Carl Spaatz ended World War II as commander of the American strategic air forces in the Pacific theatre and in 1947 became the newly independent US Air Force's first Chief of Staff.*

and then attended the Tactical School at Maxwell Field, Alabama. After a staff appointment in Washington, he commanded the Fokker C-2A *Question Mark* on its endurance flight in January 1929. There followed command of the 7th Bombardment Group and 1st Wing in California before another period of staff work in Washington.

Spaatz became a colonel in 1939 and the following year went to Britain to observe developments in the air war. He returned there in July 1942 as commander of the Eighth Air Force. He then moved on to North Africa as commander of Allied tactical and strategic air forces. At the time of the Normandy invasion he commanded all the USAAF's strategic bomber forces in the European theatre of operations and he ended the war in a similar command in the Pacific. In February 1946 he became commanding general of the USAAF. He then planned and executed the formation of the USAF, an air force truly independent of the army, before his retirement in 1948.

STEINHOFF

General Johannes Steinhoff (born 1913) was one of the Luftwaffe's most skilled fighter leaders in World War II and, despite the handicap of severe burns, he rose to high rank in the postwar West German air force. Born on 15 September 1913, he joined the Luftwaffe before World War II, serving during the Polish Campaign as a fighter pilot with Jagdgeschwader 26. In February 1940 he joined JG 52, becoming commander of the unit's 4 Staffel. The *Staffel* was heavily engaged during the Battle of Britain, flying the Messerschmitt Bf 109E, and by the end of the battle Steinhoff's personal score was six enemy aircraft destroyed.

JG 52 was transferred to the east in the spring of 1941 in preparation for the coming war with the Soviet Union. During the first month of the campaign Steinhoff destroyed 28 enemy aircraft and was awarded the Knight's Cross. He had proved to be an able fighter leader and in February 1942 he took command of JG 52's II Gruppe, with the rank of *Hauptmann*. The opportunities to make kills on the Eastern Front were exceptionally good, especially when JG 52 began flying the Messerschmitt Bf 109F. By the end of August 1942 Steinhoff's score had reached 100 and he received the Oakleaves clasp to the Knight's Cross. In February 1943 his score reached the 150 mark.

Steinhoff left II/JG 52 in March 1943 and departed for Tunisia to take command of the hard-pressed JG 77 whose last *Kommodore*, Joachim Müncheberg, had been killed in combat. In contrast to the air fighting on the Eastern Front, in the Mediterranean the Luftwaffe was on the defensive and JG 77 was forced to pull back first to Sicily and then to the Italian mainland. As the USAAF's stategic bombers came into action in the Mediterranean, JG 77 was deployed to cover the vital Romanian oil refineries towards the end of 1943.

In April 1944 Steinhoff returned to Germany to convert from the Messerschmitt Bf 109, various versions of which he had flown since the beginning of the war, to the radical new Me 262 twin-jet fighter. He took command of JG 7, the first *Jagdgeschwader* to fly the new fighter, going into action against US heavy bombers over the German homeland. In February 1945, following the 'Revolt of the Aces' against Goering's mismanagement of the air war, Steinhoff was ordered to hand over command of JG 7, and he then joined Galland's Jagdverband 44. This was an élite unit manned by some of the Luftwaffe's most experienced fighter pilots. On 18 March his Me 262 crashed on take-off and Steinhoff suffered appalling burns before he was rescued from the wreck of his fighter. He had flown more than 900 missions in World War II and was credited with

Below Johannes Steinhoff was one of the most experienced German fighter pilots of World War II and reached high rank in the postwar West German Luftwaffe.

176 enemy aircraft destroyed. After the war he overcame the physical and psychological handicaps of his injuries, joined the new Luftwaffe in the 1950s and in 1971 became the service's inspector-general.

he succeeded Sir David Henderson as commander of the RFC in France, a position that he held until the end of 1917. A tireless administrator, he was less successful as a tactical commander. His inflexible insistence on offensive action by the RFC squadrons irrespective of their strength or the quality of their aircraft led to heavy casualties. In 1918 he became the RAF's first Chief of the Air Staff, but soon disagreed with his Air Minister Lord Rothermere and resigned. He then commanded the Independent Force RAF, which was formed to carry out strategic bombing of the German homeland.

In 1919 Trenchard again became Chief of the Air Staff and held the post until his retirement in 1929. During these years he did his most valuable work, preserving his service from the short-sighted attempts of the army and navy to have it disbanded, and laying the foundations of a peacetime air force which could be quickly expanded in time of crisis. His influence in matters of strategy within the air force was again harmful, however, as he formulated a doctrine of air warfare which emphasized the role of the bomber to an unwarranted degree.

TRENCHARD

Marshal of the Royal Air Force Lord Trenchard (1873–1956) exerted immense influence on the RAF during the first decade of its existence, earning the reverential title, Father of the RAF, and the less dignified nickname of 'Boom'. Hugh Montague Trenchard was born on 3 February 1873 and was commissioned into the Royal Scots Fusiliers in 1893. In 1912 he learned to fly at his own expense at the Sopwith School, Brooklands, and transferred to the Royal Flying Corps. He was appointed adjutant of the Central Flying School, Upavon, and on the outbreak of war found himself left behind at Farnborough, Hampshire, to organize reinforcements for the RFC in the field. Although a trained pilot, he never became a skilled airman, his forte being administration and command.

Trenchard moved to France in November 1914 to take command of No 1 Wing and then in August 1915

TUCK

Wing Commander Robert Stanford Tuck (born 1916) was one of the RAF's most successful fighter pilots in the early years of World War II. He was born at Catford, London, on 1 July 1916 and in 1935 joined the RAF on a short-service commission. After completing his flying training, he was posted to No 65 Squadron, flying Gloster Gauntlets from Hornchurch in Essex. The following year the squadron converted to the Gloster Gladiator and it was when flying one of these in 1938 that Tuck suffered a mid-air collison and was lucky to escape with a severe cut to the face.

Shortly after the outbreak of World War II Tuck was posted to No 92 Squadron, flying Supermarine Spitfires. The squadron was heavily engaged over the Dunkirk beaches in May/June 1940, Tuck scoring his **first** victories and temporarily taking over the squadron when the CO, Squadron Leader Roger Bushell,

down a Messerschmitt Bf 109. On 11 November, when Tuck was away on leave, the squadron intercepted an Italian raid off the Suffolk coast and brought down eight enemy aircraft. This action fully restored the squadron's fighting spirit and Tuck's success as a squadron commander was recognized by the award of the Distinguished Service Order. His personal score was also growing and by the end of the year he had 20 victories to his credit.

On 21 June 1941 Tuck fought a single-handed battle with a formation of Messerschmitt Bf 109s, shooting down two before he was forced down into the Channel. He was soon rescued and returned to his unit. The following month he became leader of the Duxford Wing and, after a liaison visit to the United States, leader of the Biggin Hill Wing. Action during fighter sweeps over France brought his score up to 29 victories, but then on 28 June 1942 he was shot down by ground-fire and made prisoner of war. In 1945 he managed to escape and succeeded in linking up with the advancing Soviet armies.

Above Squadron Leader Robert Stanford Tuck pictured in the cockpit of his Hawker Hurricane Mk 1, when he was commanding officer of No 257 (Burma) Squadron.

Below Tuck (left) and fellow prisoner-of-war Squadron Leader Roger Bushell were imprisoned in Stalag Luft III at Sagan, from which Bushell masterminded 'The Great Escape' in 1944.

was shot down and taken prisoner. After a brief rest from operations, the squadron was back in action flying from Northolt in June and Tuck raised his score to seven victories, receiving the Distinguished Flying Cross. There followed a lull during the early weeks of the Battle of Britain, when the squadron operated from Pembrey in Wales on the very edge of the fighting. Nonetheless, Tuck saw some action against German bombers, raising his score to 13 and receiving a bar to his DFC.

In early September Tuck was promoted to squadron leader and took command of No 257 Squadron which flew Hawker Hurricanes from Debden in Essex. The loss of experienced pilots on the squadron had somewhat lowered morale, but Tuck soon rectified the situation. The squadron was in action on 15 September 1940 (one of the decisive days of the battle and now celebrated as Battle of Britain Day) and Tuck brought

UDET

Generaloberst Ernst Udet (1896–1941) was the highest-scoring German fighter pilot to survive World War I, but his service as a senior commander in the Luftwaffe during World War II was rather less distinguished. Born on 26 April 1896 at Frankfurt am Main, Udet was a founder-member of the Aero Club of Munich in 1909. On the outbreak of World War I he volunteered for army service as a despatch rider and then applied for transfer to the Air Service. When he was turned down, he then learned to fly at his own expense and was finally accepted as a military pilot. His first posting, in July 1915, was to Fliegerabteilung (A) 206, flying Aviatik two-seaters. Although the unit's main task was observation for the artillery, Udet took part in a number of bombing missions and his eagerness for action resulted in his transfer to one of the early fighter units.

Udet was attached to the Kampfeinsitzer-Kommando-Habsheim, flying the Fokker E I monoplane. His first encounter with the enemy, on 12 March 1916, resulted in his fighter being peppered by fire from his intended victim, a French Caudron. However, on 18 March he was more successful, bringing down a Farman and being awarded the Iron Cross 1st Class. In 1916 Udet's unit became Jagdstaffel 15 and by December he had scored two more victories, bringing down a Breguet and a Caudron, and was commissioned as a *Leutnant* in the New Year.

In 1917 Jasta 15 suffered many losses and although Udet claimed eight victories only three of them were officially confirmed. The disgruntled fighter pilot then obtained a transfer to Jasta 37 in Flanders and flying against the British units on this sector of the front Udet raised his score to 15 by the end of the year. In March

1918 he joined von Richthofen's Jagdgeschwader I, becoming *Staffelführer* of Jasta 4. He was awarded the Pour le Mérite in April and in June scored 12 victories. On 29 June he had a narrow escape when his Fokker D VII was shot down by a French Breguet, Udet parachuting to safety. He fought on through the fierce air battles of the summer and ended the war as an *Oberleutnant* with 62 victories to his credit.

After the war Udet stayed in aviation, flying for the airline Rumpler-Luftverkehr and giving air displays. He ran his own aircraft manufacturing company for a while, but then returned to stunt flying, taking part in several flying films. After the Nazis came to power the reluctant Udet was persuaded to join the newly formed Luftwaffe, becoming inspector of fighters and dive-bombers and then head of the technical office. A convivial man with a deep-rooted love of flying, Udet was completely unsuited to a high administrative position. Nevertheless, in February 1939 he became Director-General of Luftwaffe Equipment. He found it increasingly difficult to cope with the problems of an expanding aircraft industry and in a fit of depression in November 1941 he took his own life.

VOSS

The German World War I ace Leutnant Werner Voss (1897–1917) destroyed 48 enemy aircraft during less than a year of air fighting and at one time it seemed that he would rival the performance of Manfred von Richthofen. Born of Jewish parentage at Krefeld on 13 April 1897, he enlisted in a hussar regiment on the outbreak of war in 1914 and transferred to the Air Service in 1915. His first operational service was with

Above Ernst Udet stands in front of his Fokker D VII fighter in 1918, when he commanded the elite Jagdgeschwader I. He was the highest-scoring German ace to survive World War I.

Above right In 1936 Udet joined the Luftwaffe as inspector of fighters and dive-bombers, but he detested administrative work as this cartoon he drew in 1937 bears witness.

Below Leutnant Werner Voss prepares for a mission in his personal Albatros DIII, when he commanded Jasta 5 in the spring of 1917.

Kampfstaffel 20, flying bombing missions over Verdun. On 25 November 1916 he joined Jasta 2, flying the Albatros DII, and two days later scored his first two victories. There followed a lull in the air fighting, but in February 1917 Voss resumed scoring, bringing down eight enemy aircraft that month. Although on the ground Voss was meticulous in checking the condition of his aeroplane and its machine guns, in the air he was reckless. His flying displayed an *élan* that befitted an ex-cavalry man, but which contrasted sharply with von Richthofen's calculating tactics.

During March Voss brought his score up to 22 victories, making him the top pilot in Jasta Boelcke (as Jasta 2 had been redesignated in honour of the pioneer air fighter). Voss was on leave for most of 'Bloody April' 1917, following his receipt of the Pour le Mérite on 8 April. He was then posted as acting *Staffelführer* to Jasta 5, moving on to Jastas 29 and 14, before settling

Above *Leutnant Werner Voss (right) is framed by the wings of his Fokker Dr I Triplane as he talks with staff officers of the Imperial Army Air Service.*

in command of Jasta 10, which was part of von Richthofen's 'Flying Circus', Jagdgeschwader I. In August 1917 Voss began flying the new Fokker Dr I Triplane, an aircraft which delighted him with its superb manoeuvrability in contrast to the rather heavy Albatros scouts. During the first three weeks of September he steadily added to his score, gaining his 48th kill on the morning of 23 September. That afternoon he was engaged by the SE5a scouts of the elite No 56 Squadron Royal Flying Corps and was shot down and killed after an epic dogfight with some of the leading British aces of the day.

WARNEFORD

Flight Sub-Lieutenant R. A. J. Warneford (1891–1915) was the first Allied airman to bring down a Zeppelin in combat during World War I, earning a Victoria Cross for the exploit. Warneford was born in India on 15 October 1891 and enlisted in the army in January 1915. The following month he transferred to the Royal Naval Air Service as a probationary pilot. He gained his Royal Aero Club Certificate at Hendon and then completed his flying training at the Central Flying School, Upavon, Wiltshire.

On 7 May 1915 Warneford flew an Avro 504 from Eastchurch to St Pol airfield near Dunkirk to join No 1 Squadron RNAS. One month later, on 7 June, Warneford's squadron commander was alerted that three Zeppelins were returning to their bases from a night attack on Britain. Warneford, operating on detachment from Furnes airfield in Belgium, was ordered into the air in his Morane Type L parasol-wing monoplane just after midnight.

Warneford spotted airship LZ37 just to the north of Ostend and gave chase. As he closed on the Zeppelin its gunners opened fire on his Morane, but their aim was poor. Warneford then manoeuvred his aircraft into position above the LZ37 and released his 9kg (20lb) Hales bombs, the only armament he carried. The airship exploded into flames and crashed onto a convent in the Mont St Amand district of Ghent, all but one of its crew of ten being killed. Shortly afterwards Warneford had to make a forced landing behind enemy lines to repair a severed fuel line. He succeeded in taking off again before he was detected and returned safely to Furnes.

Warneford was widely acclaimed as a hero and on 11 June he was awarded the Victoria Cross. Six days later the Henri Farman F27 that he was piloting crashed and Warneford died of his injuries.

Right *Flight Sub-Lieutenant Rex Warneford was awarded the Victoria Cross for his successful engagement with Zeppelin LZ37 in June 1915.*

Left *Air Commodore Sir Frank Whittle portrayed with a diagram of the turbojet engine which he invented. He first developed his theories when he was a cadet at the RAF College, Cranwell.*

Below *Whittle's W1 turbojet first took to the air on 15 May 1941, installed in the Gloster E28/39. The aircraft is today preserved in the Science Museum, London.*

Bottom *The historic first flight of the Wright Flyer – the first successful powered aeroplane – took place at Kitty Hawk, North Carolina, on 17 December 1903 with Orville at the controls.*

attended a flying instructor's course at the Central Flying School before being posted to No 2 Flying Training School, Digby, Lincolnshire, as an instructor. He then became a test pilot at the Marine Aircraft Experimental Establishment at Felixstowe, Suffolk, and in 1932 took an engineering course at RAF Henlow, Bedfordshire, before taking a degree in Mechanical Science at Cambridge University.

While at Cambridge, Whittle obtained financial backing from a company, Power Jets Ltd, to develop his ideas. In 1937 a jet engine was successfully run on the test bench and the Air Ministry seconded Whittle to the Special Duties List to continue his work. The Gloster Aircraft Co. was contracted to build the first jet-propelled aircraft and this (the E28/39) first flew on 15 May 1941. It was followed by a twin-jet fighter for operational service, the Gloster Meteor, which first flew in March 1943. Whittle continued his work on jet engines, but resigned from the RAF with the rank of air commodore in 1948.

WRIGHT BROTHERS

Wilbur Wright (1867–1912) and his brother Orville (1871–1948) made the first successful flights in a powered heavier-than-air machine and are generally acknowledged as the inventors of the aeroplane. In December 1892 the two brothers opened a bicycle shop in Dayton, Ohio, and the money they earned from this business financed their experiments in aviation. After trials with control surfaces attached to a kite, the brothers built a full-sized glider. This they test-flew at Kill Devil Hill, Kitty Hawk, North Carolina, the scene of all their early flights during the period 1901–3. By 1902 they had produced a glider that was controllable in all three axes of flight.

WHITTLE

Air Commodore Sir Frank Whittle (born 1907) designed and built the first successful British jet engine. He was born in Coventry on 1 June 1907 and enlisted in the RAF as a boy apprentice in 1923. He was then selected for officer training, becoming a cadet at the RAF College, Cranwell, in 1926. It was during his final term at the college that he developed his ideas on jet propulsion, arguing that such a power plant would enable an aircraft to fly much faster than the conventional piston engine and propeller. Whittle's thesis on jet propulsion was published in the *RAF Journal* in 1928, but no official interest in his ideas resulted.

On passing out from Cranwell, Pilot Officer Whittle was posted to No 111 Squadron flying Armstrong Whitworth Siskins. He was a superb pilot and in 1929

YEAGER

Brigadier-General Charles 'Chuck' Yeager USAF (born 1923) was the first man to fly faster than the speed of sound in level flight. Yeager enlisted in the USAAF as a mechanic at the age of 18 and then trained as a pilot, qualifying in March 1943. He was assigned to the 357th Fighter Group training in the United States on Bell P-39 Airacobras. In November 1943 the group became part of the Eighth Air Force in Britain and re-equipped with the North American P-51 Mustang. Yeager's early operations were eventful for on his seventh mission he destroyed a Messerschmitt Bf 109 for his first victory. He was himself shot down over France two days later, but evaded capture and returned to his unit by way of neutral Spain and Gibraltar. On 12 November while flying an escort mission to Bremen Yeager destroyed no fewer than five aircraft and the following month he added a Me 262 jet fighter and four Focke Wulf Fw 190s to his score. When he completed his combat tour, after 64 missions, in February 1945, he was credited with 13½ victories.

On returning to the United States Yeager became a test pilot at Wright Field, Ohio, working on the Lockheed P-80 and Republic P-84 development programmes and evaluating captured Axis fighters. He was then assigned to the Bell XS-1 test programme at Muroc, California (later Edwards Air Force Base). Flying this rocket-powered experimental aircraft, he reached a speed of Mach 1·05 on 14 October 1947, the first supersonic flight. In 1954 he gave up test-flying to command a USAF fighter squadron in Germany. In 1966 he took command of the 405th Fighter Wing

The Wrights then built a powered machine, using an engine and propellers of their own design. On 17 December 1903 Orville made a flight of 36m (120ft) in this machine and later that day both brothers bettered that distance. They determined to keep their work secret to avoid their ideas being pirated and so the first practical aeroplane flight in history did not attract the publicity it deserved. In 1904 they built an improved Flyer (name they gave to all their powered machines) and offered it to the governments of the United States, Britain and France, but without success.

It was not until 1908 that the Wrights achieved the acclaim that their obsessive secrecy had hitherto denied them. A contract was agreed with the US War Department to provide an aircraft at a cost of $25,000. Unfortunately, while Orville was demonstrating this machine at Fort Meyer, it crashed, severely injuring him and killing his passenger Lieutenant Thomas Selfridge. Wilbur was in France, where his demonstrations at Le Mans and Pau met with wide acclaim.

Awards were showered on the brothers, including gold medals from both the Royal Aero Club and Royal Aeronautical Society in Britain and a similar award from the President of the United States. In November 1909 the Wright Company was formed in the United States, and licences were granted to manufacture Wright machines in Britain and Germany. In May 1912, however, Wilbur Wright died of typhoid fever. It was he who had provided the inventive genius to complement his brother's mechanical and piloting skills, so it was then left to others to further the development of powered flight.

Top The early Wright Flyers took off from a length of trackway, with a weight and pulley system providing the aircraft's initial momentum. This apparatus can be seen in the illustration of a Wright Flyer A at Ft Myer, Virginia, in 1909.

Above Wilbur Wright (in cap) pictured at the controls of the Wright Flyer A, with King Alfonso XIII of Spain, during his triumphal tour of Europe in 1909.

Right Charles 'Chuck' Yeager (left), the first man to fly faster than the speed of sound in level flight, pictured with British test pilot Peter Twiss.

in Southeast Asia and completed 127 combat missions on the North American F-100 Super Sabre. He retired as a brigadier-general in 1975, having flown over 10,000 hours in 155 different types of aircraft during his flying career.

ZEMKE

Colonel Hubert 'Hub' Zemke (born 1914) commanded the 56th Fighter Group, one of the top-scoring fighter units of the USAAF's Eighth Air Force in World War II. A pre-war US Army Air Corps pilot, Zemke was sent to Britain in 1941 to study fighter equipment and tactics in the European war. He then moved on to the Soviet Union to supervise the reassembly of US-supplied Curtiss P-40 fighters and also to study the air war on the Eastern Front. Then he moved to the Middle East and North Africa with a similar brief, returning to the United States in the spring of 1942 with an unrivalled knowledge of modern fighter tactics.

Above The rocket-powered Bell XS-1 research aircraft in which Yeager made his historic flight over the Muroc dry lake in California in October 1947.

Below left Hubert Zemke commanded the USAAF's first operational P-47 Thunderbolt unit, the 56th Fighter Group – nicknamed the Wolfpack – which went into action in the spring of 1943.

Right Zemke congratulates two of his group's most successful pilots, Robert Johnson (left) and Walker Mahurin (right) after the USAAF's daylight raid on Berlin on 6 March 1944.

Below Zemke (left) confers with three of the 56th Fighter Group's leading pilots: Frederick Christensen (second from left), Francis Gabreski (third from left) and David Schilling.

At the beginning of 1943 Zemke returned to Britain as commander of the 56th Fighter Group, flying the massive Republic P-47 Thunderbolt. The group became operational that April and Zemke opened his score with two Focke Wulf Fw 190s shot down on 13 June. At first the P-47 was not successful in combat, being slow to accelerate and having a poor rate of climb. However, Zemke set out to devise tactics which compensated for these shortcomings and capitalized on the fighter's good altitude performance, fast diving speed and tremendous firepower. On 2 October 1943 he gained his fifth victory, becoming his group's second ace. At the end of the month he returned to the United States, with seven enemy aircraft to his credit.

Zemke returned to the 56th FG in January 1944 and resumed scoring the following month. In March he was awarded the Distinguished Service Cross for his leadership of the 56th FG, his personal score then standing at ten. Transferring to the 479th FG, flying Lockheed P-38 Lightnings and then North American P-51 Mustangs, Zemke brought his score to 19½ victories. On 30 October 1944 Zemke was forced to bale out over Germany, when his P-51 began to break up in a violent storm. He remained a POW until the end of the war.

AERIAL WARFARE

ADVANCED AIR STRIKING FORCE 1939–40

In September 1939 RAF Bomber Command despatched the squadrons of its No 1 Group to bases in France, where the formation was redesignated the Advanced Air Striking Force (AASF). The move was a very necessary one, as the ten squadrons of the AASF flew the Fairey Battle light bomber which had insufficient range to reach enemy targets when operating from UK bases. Underpowered and with inadequate

Above *RAF ground crew begin to clear the snow and ice from a Fairey Battle light bomber of the Advanced Air Striking Force during the bitter winter of 1939–40.*

Left *The Fairey Battles of No 88 Squadron flying in 'vic' formation. The Battle's poor performance and inadequate defensive armament resulted in many being shot down.*

defensive armament, the Battles were unable to cope with the Luftwaffe's flak and fighter defences. Two squadrons of Hawker Hurricane fighters, Nos 1 and 73 Squadrons, were therefore attached to the AASF to provide fighter escort.

The early sorties of unescorted Battles over enemy territory had led to heavy losses and the bombers were confined to night-time missions, for which they were ill-designed. When the 'phoney war' ended with Germany's assault in the west in May 1940, the AASF had some 100 Battles on strength operating with eight squadrons (two squadrons having been withdrawn to convert to Bristol Blenheims). The Battles were thrown into the attack on 10 May in a vain attempt to stem the German advance through Luxembourg. They suffered heavy losses, mostly from the highly effective German flak. For example, on 11 May seven Battles of a formation of eight drawn from Nos 88 and 218 Squadrons failed to return from a mission over Luxembourg.

On 12 May the AASF was given the task of destroying two vital bridges over the Albert canal, which had been captured intact by the Germans. Six Battle crews from No 12 Squadron volunteered for the attack and a fighter escort was provided by eight Hurricanes of No 1 Squadron. One of the Battles was forced to abort the mission and the remaining five were all accounted for by flak and fighter defences over the target. The escorting Hurricanes were outnumbered by Messerschmitt Bf 109s and could do little to help the bombers. The Battle flown by Flying Officer Donald Garland managed to release its bombs on one of the target bridges, before crashing in flames. Garland and his navigator Sergeant Thomas Gray were posthumously awarded the Victoria Cross for this action.

By the afternoon of 13 May the AASF's bomber strength had been reduced to 62 serviceable Battles and this force was committed to an attack on pontoon bridges in the Sedan region. The enemy shot down 35 of the bombers. These severe losses and the need to withdraw to new airfields to avoid being overrun by the German advance reduced the AASF to making isolated night attacks over the following three weeks.

On 13 June with the Germans advancing on Paris,

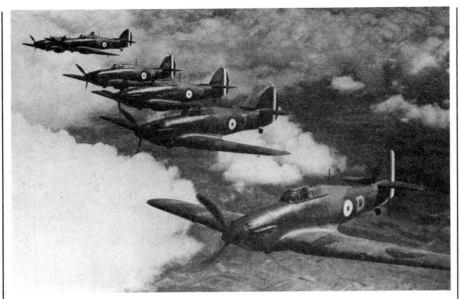

Fortresses fitted with the APS-20A radar) served until 1951, giving the early warning of air attack on naval forces that had been lacking off Okinawa and the Japanese home islands.

The US Navy continued to take the lead in developing and deploying AEW aircraft, with conversions of the Grumman TBF Avenger and Douglas AD Skyraider which unlike the PB-1Ws could operate from aircraft carriers. These aircraft used the APS-120 radar, which was also fitted to the Fleet Air Arm's Fairey Gannet AEW Mk 3 aircraft and remained in service until the early 1980s with the RAF's Avro Shackleton AEW Mk 2s. In the late 1950s the APS-120 was overtaken by the improved APS-82 radar with increased range and a greater degree of target discrimination. This was fitted in a saucer-shaped aerial carried atop the Grumman E-1 Tracer carrier-borne AEW aircraft. Land-based AEW systems were also deployed by the US Navy, which produced the Warning Star variant of the Lockheed Super Constellation civil airliner, as well as non-rigid airships (blimps) fitted with an AEW radar in the nose. Naval airships continued in use until 1961.

A further improvement in carrier-based AEW capability came in 1964 with the US Navy's introduction of the Grumman E-2A Hawkeye and its APS-96 search radar. The Hawkeye was itself further developed and the current E-2C version with its APS-125 radar system is a highly effective AEW aircraft. During the Southeast Asia conflict the US Navy used Hawkeyes to direct air strikes over North Vietnam, warning the strike forces of enemy fighter activity and monitoring the progress of each mission. During the air battles between Syria and Israel in 1982 over the Beqa' Valley,

the remnants of the AASF carried out attacks on enemy forces crossing the Seine and Marne rivers. It was to be the Battles' swansong, for two days later the AASF bomber units were ordered to withdraw to Britain. In operations between 10 May and the date of withdrawal 115 Battles had been lost. The two Hurricane squadrons of the AASF had seen equally hard action, but their limited strength had not enabled them to give the Battles proper protection. No 73 Squadron was the last unit of the AASF to leave France, flying to Britain on 18 June. The RAF's losses had been heavy during the Battle of France, but RAF Fighter Command remained a force to be reckoned with.

Above A formation of Hawker Hurricane Mk I fighters of No 73 Squadron, one of two fighter units assigned to the Advanced Air Striking Force in September 1939.

Below The US Navy's Grumman E-2C Hawkeye is a carrier-based AEW aircraft.

Bottom The Shackleton AEW Mk 2 entered service with No 8 Squadron RAF in 1971 and is due to be replaced by the Nimrod AEW Mk 3 in 1984.

AIRBORNE EARLY WARNING

The limitations of ground-based radar in detecting low-flying aircraft had been recognized as early as 1939, but it was not until 1947 that the first airborne early warning (AEW) or radar picket aircraft entered operational service. Significantly, the user was the US Navy, which had experienced great problems in intercepting incoming kamikaze suicide missions in the closing months of the Pacific War. Its PB-1W radar pickets (converted USAAF Boeing B-17 Flying

Israeli E-2Cs directed her fighters to such good effect that none was lost while inflicting heavy losses on the Syrians.

The US Air Force made use of EC-121 AEW aircraft in Southeast Asia and has since developed the Boeing E-3A Sentry AWACS (airborne early warning and control system). Mounting an APY-1 radar with a range of well over 320km (200 miles), the Sentry can carry an airborne commander and his battle staff to direct tactical air operations in areas such as the Middle East, where ground control facilities are few. Alternatively it can be used to supplement the coverage of ground radars in the air defence role, and it is for this purpose that the NATO AWACS force is primarily intended.

Surveillance missions over the sea are an important aspect of the AEW mission and the RAF's recent BAe Nimrod AEW Mk 3 is particularly capable in this respect. Developed from the Nimrod MR Mk 1 maritime patrol aircraft, the Nimrod AEW Mk 3 will plug a significant gap in the air defences of the United Kingdom by providing comprehensive radar warning of the approach of low-level raiders. The Soviet Union's early warning Tupolev Tu-126 Moss aircraft, which first appeared at the beginning of the 1970s, is expected to be replaced by an AEW version of the Ilyushin Il-76 in the mid-1980s.

Above A Bristol F2B fighter of the RAF flying over north-west India in the 1920s.

Below The Boeing E-3A Sentry is the most advanced AEW aircraft in service anywhere in the world.

AIR CONTROL

Air control was the name given to the use of military aircraft to subdue rebellious tribesmen in colonial territories during the inter-war years. It was first proposed by the RAF's Chief of the Air Staff, Sir Hugh Trenchard, at the Cairo Conference in 1920 as an alternative to maintaining costly army garrisons in the newly mandated territories of Iraq, Palestine and Transjordan. Raiding and inter-tribal feuds were a way of life for many of the nomadic peoples of the Middle East, as they were for the tribesmen of India's Northwest Frontier. The traditional means for a colonial power to restore the peace was to send a military expedition against the disaffected tribe, at high cost in money and sometimes also in lives. Aircraft could react to trouble more quickly than an army column and could apply punitive measures at far less cost.

The methods of air control applied by the RAF in the Middle East, notably in Iraq, did not simply involve an indiscriminate bombing of tribal villages in reprisal for outrages. Normally, the rebels would be invited by political officers to submit to the government's judgment. If they refused, leaflets were dropped warning them to evacuate the villages, which were then bombed. The consequent disruption to everyday life was usually sufficient to bring the tribesmen to terms. A more serious threat to peace than the endemic minor tribal wars arose in Iraq in 1923, when a Turkish-inspired Kurdish revolt broke out in northeast Iraq. However, the RAF garrison was equal to the challenge, flying in troop reinforcements to the region, which with the support of air attack managed to quell the revolt.

Air control as successfully applied in Iraq, the Aden Protectorate, Palestine and Transjordan meant the reduction, but not the complete elimination, of ground forces. The garrison in Iraq in the mid-1920s (by far the largest) consisted of eight RAF squadrons,

supported by RAF armoured car squadrons and locally enlisted Iraqi levies. Overall command of the forces was exercised by Air Marshal Sir John Salmond, the Air Officer Commanding Iraq. It is probable that similar methods of air policing could have proved effective on the Northwest Frontier of India, where there were comparable peacekeeping problems. This region, however, was the jealously protected preserve of the British and Indian armies, which continued to employ the traditional methods of punitive expeditions against the unruly Pathan tribesmen. Nevertheless, RAF squadrons were used in a supporting role.

Other colonial powers, notably France and Italy, made considerable use of aircraft in controlling their overseas territories, but they were employed generally in an army support role rather than for true air control operations. The military problems of France in Morocco and Italy in Libya were more akin to those of an army of occupation. In Syria, however, the Armée de l'Air did play an important part in suppressing a rising of the Jebel Druse tribesmen in 1925–6.

Apart from its financial advantages, air control provided a *raison d'être* for the RAF at a time when the

Above The Westland Wapitis of No 55 Squadron RAF were stationed in Iraq for air control duties from 1930 until 1937, replacing DH9A bombers in this role.

Below Hawker Hardy army-cooperation aircraft of No 30 Squadron RAF guarded by a member of the Iraq Levies at Mosul, Iraq, in 1935.

concept of an independent air service was under attack. However, with the development of more sophisticated techniques of guerrilla warfare and latterly of effective man-portable surface-to-air missiles, air forces have been forced to evolve the more complex tactics of counter-insurgency.

AIR DEFENCE

The effective defence of friendly air space from incursions by enemy aircraft requires that five basic conditions be fulfilled. The first element in the air defence mission is early warning of attack, which enables the defence forces to be alerted. The enemy then has to be positively identified and precisely located. Finally he has to be intercepted and destroyed, or neutralized by some other method. All air defence systems from World War I until the present day have sought to fulfil these basic mission requirements.

During World War I it became necessary to build up an air defence system to guard those points of Britain that could be attacked by airships or bomber aircraft operating from the Continent. It was found that early warning of airship raids in 1915–16 was often provided by the interception of enemy radio transmissions. However, identification and location of the raiders was a largely hit-or-miss affair. Interceptor aircraft were assigned regular patrol lines, which it was hoped would bring them into contact with the airships. On occasions it did so. For example, on 7 June 1915 Flight Sub-Lieutenant Rex Warneford successfully intercepted Zeppelin LZ 37 over Belgium and brought it down in flames. The weapons used by the early interceptors included bombs, explosive darts and incendiary machine-gun ammunition. Ground-based defences included anti-aircraft guns, searchlights and even the rifles of mobile cyclist battalions. Bringing these weapons to bear was no easy task, for if an airship

wished to avoid trouble, it could jettison ballast and rise far more quickly than the best rate-of-climb of contemporary interceptor aircraft. Nevertheless, with the addition of a chain of forward observers in coastal stations, linked by telephone to a central headquarters to report visual sightings of intruders, this system inflicted heavy loses on the German airships, and had mastered this threat by the autumn of 1916.

In the summer of 1917 the British air defences were faced with a new problem, when high-flying and fast formations of Gotha twin-engined bombers began to raid London. The system evolved to meet this menace, although it was not properly tested in action in its fully developed form, was in many ways the prototype of that of 1940. An expanded network of observer posts enabled the raiders to be plotted overland, although in practice this system did not always work efficiently. New high-performance defending aircraft, such as the Sopwith Camel and Bristol F2B Fighter, could meet

Below *The air defence of Great Britain depended on biplane fighters, such as these Bristol Bulldogs of No 17 Squadron, during the inter-war years.*

effectiveness. The need for an efficient means of early warning was recognized and an attempt was made to use sound location for this means. A 60m (200ft) long 'sound mirror' was built on Romney Marshes but proved to have a range of only some 25km (16 miles) and was clearly inadequate. A more effective improvement in the air defence forces was the introduction of a radio link between interceptor aircraft and ground controllers. This allowed a fighter, once airborne, to be directed onto the enemy, whereas under the earlier system the pilot received no information on the position of the enemy after take-off.

When the British air defences were expanded to meet the threat from Nazi Germany in the late 1930s, the early warning problem was solved by Sir Robert Watson-Watt's invention of radar. During the Battle of Britain the radar chain provided invaluable advanced warning of German raids. At this time radar coverage of incoming planes ended at the coast and

the attacking bombers with the advantage of speed and manoeuvrability. Anti-aircraft artillery zones were created and separated from the fighter patrol lines.

The World War I air defence system coped reasonably well with the small-scale day raids and with the night attacks that followed. However, there remained a number of basic weaknesses in the air defences which were tackled in the 1920s with varying degrees of

Below *A Hurricane Mk I of No 1 Squadron in October 1940. The Hawker Hurricane was the mainstay of Britain's fighter defences in the Battle of Britain.*

the movements of raiders beyond that point had to be reported by the Observer Corps. Identification of hostile aircraft was at this stage by visual recognition, although a device known as IFF (identification friend or foe) provided radar controllers with a coded response from friendly aircraft to aid long-range recognition. Nonetheless, the positive identification of hostile aircraft was (and remains today) a problem for controllers and aircrew alike. In 1939 there was fought an inglorious battle, known to history as the Battle of Barking Creek, between RAF Hurricanes on one side and RAF Spitfires on the other – dramatically illustrating the genuine difficulties of differentiating friend from foe in the air.

RAF Fighter Command in the Battle of Britain represented a fully developed air defence system, although by no means a fool-proof one, when it came to dealing with daylight raiders. It provided the RAF's tactical commanders with sufficient information to deploy their hard-pressed and outnumbered squadrons to the best effect, with little energy or effort wasted. Yet above all it stood the acid test of combat and inflicted the first major defeat on Germany of World War II. However, when the Luftwaffe turned to night bombing attacks, a new system had to be evolved to counter the new tactics. Night defences were slow to

Left *The crew of a Gloster Javelin F(AW) Mk 5 prepare for a night sortie in the late 1950s. By that time the specialized night fighter had given way to the dual-role, all-weather fighter.*

Far right *A Westland Whirlwind HAR Mk 10 turboshaft-powered rescue helicopter winches a survivor aboard. The earlier piston-engined Whirlwind HAR Mk 2 first entered RAF service in 1955.*

evolve, but with the deployment of GCI (ground control of interception) radars with full overland coverage and short-range radar in the night fighters themselves, an effective defence took shape.

It was not until the latter half of World War II that Germany was faced with the urgent need to develop strong air defences to counter American daylight raids and RAF Bomber Command's night offensives. So long as Germany occupied much of western Europe, ample early warning and a defence in depth was relatively easy to achieve. Yet a major weakness was the lack of resources – and especially of fighter aircraft – allocated to the defences. Unescorted USAAF bombers, relying on close formation to allow mutual fire-support from their heavy defensive armament, were badly mauled by the Luftwaffe until long-range escort fighters were developed. Then in 1944–5 far-ranging North American P-51 Mustangs not only provided a close escort for the American bomber formations, but also sought out the Luftwaffe's fighters before they had a chance to intercept, even attacking them on their own airfields before they were able to take off. Despite such brilliant technical innovations by Germany as the jet-powered Messerschmitt Me 262 (often misused as a fighter-bomber) and the rocket-powered Me 163, the USAAF gained control of the air over the Reich during the hours of daylight. An equally hard-fought battle took place at night. The Luftwaffe's night force reached its peak effectiveness in early 1944, inflicting Bomber Command's heaviest losses of the war on the Nuremberg raiders on the night of 30 March 1944. The RAF countered with night-fighter escorts and electronic jamming of the Luftwaffe's radars and radio links, such protection being provided by Bomber Command's No 100 Group. Towards the end of the war, German air defence operations were greatly hampered by a shortage of fuel which grounded many aircraft.

Present-day air defence networks make extensive use of computer processing for rapid assessment of hostile threats. Radar coverage is extensive; for example NATO's NADGE network stretches from Norway to Turkey. Additional radar coverage is obtained from AEW aircraft and the entire system is linked together to form an integrated command and control network. Missile-armed interceptors can react rapidly to any threat and belts of surface-to-air missile defences have largely replaced heavy anti-aircraft artillery. Yet the basic principles of air defence have not changed since World War I.

Above *A Lightning F Mk 2A of No 19 Squadron pictured in the 1970s. The BAC Lightning is a fast-climbing interceptor ideally suited to the defence of high-value targets such as airfields.*

AIR/SEA RESCUE

Rescuing the crews of military aircraft forced down into the sea was undertaken during World War I on an *ad hoc* basis by marine craft, floatplanes and flying boats as an additional role to their primary duties. The

Above right *A Westland Lysander air/sea rescue aircraft of No 277 Squadron RAF carrying a dinghy pack attached beneath the stub wings on its undercarriage leg.*

Right *A Vickers Warwick of No 282 Squadron RAF carried an airborne lifeboat. It was photographed at the time of the Normandy Invasion in June 1944.*

same arrangements continued in the RAF between the wars, the service maintaining its own force of marine craft primarily to act as tenders for flying boats and floatplanes. With the increased need for air/sea rescue (ASR) services following the outbreak of World War II, 12 Westland Lysander aircraft, able to drop survival packs to aircrew in the sea, and more than a score of high-speed launches were earmarked for this duty. In February 1941 the RAF's Air/Sea Rescue Service was formed under the operational control of Coastal Command.

The Luftwaffe was generally better equipped than the RAF for ASR early in the war. Its dinghies and life jackets were better designed and aircrew were issued with a packet of fluorescent dye to mark their position in the sea for rescuers. In 1940 the English Channel was covered by Heinkel He 59 floatplanes equipped for ASR, and rescue floats, which provided good shelter, food and water, were positioned in mid-Channel. As the Luftwaffe's area of operations grew, so its rescue service, or *Seenotdienst* expanded. By the beginning of 1943 its coverage extended around the

coasts of all German-occupied Europe, covering the Black Sea, Mediterranean, Arctic Ocean, North Sea and English Channel. A *Seenotstaffel* operated such aircraft as the Dornier Do 18 and Do 24 flying boat, in cooperation with the surface vessels of a *Seenotflotille*.

The RAF's Air/Sea Rescue Service reached its peak strength in 1944, with 169 aircraft in service. A wide variety of aircraft were used for ASR, including Super-

Right The USAF's Aerospace Rescue and Recovery Service operated Sikorsky HH-3E helicopters – nicknamed Jolly Green Giants – during the Vietnam War.

marine Walrus amphibians, Lysanders, Boulton Paul Defiants and Spitfires. Whereas the Walruses could alight on the sea to pick up survivors, the other aircraft could only drop rescue packs and summon the help of ASR launches or other vessels. However, Lockheed Hudson and Vickers Warwick aircraft were specially modified to carry an airborne lifeboat, which could be parachuted to airmen in the sea. Other rescue aids included the Thornaby Bag and Bircham Barrel, buoyant containers filled with survival gear which could be dropped by virtually any aircraft. The Lindholme equipment was even more efficient, comprising a dinghy pack with attached buoyant supply containers. It remains in use to this day. During World War II the RAF Air/Sea Rescue Service saved 13,626

lives and the service continued to maintain specialized ASR squadrons in peacetime. In 1953 the first helicopter-equipped ASR squadron was formed and nowadays two RAF helicopter squadrons carry out search and rescue duties.

The United States Air Force pioneered the use of the helicopter for rescue missions during the Korean War, and in the Vietnam War the USAF Aerospace Rescue and Recovery Service saved 3883 lives. Many of these rescues were achieved under enemy fire deep inside North Vietnam and the Sikorsky HH-53 Super Jolly Green Giant rescue helicopter was armed with three rapid-fire machine guns to suppress ground-fire.

US Navy helicopters operating off ships of the Sixth Fleet in the Gulf of Tonkin also carried out many notable rescues. The primary responsibility for rescue operations off the United States' seaboard rests with the Coast Guard, which maintains rescue flights equipped with Sikorsky HH-3F Pelican and HH-52 Seaguard helicopters, supported by Lockheed HC-130 Hercules and various other fixed-wing aircraft.

AIR SUPERIORITY

Air superiority differs from air defence in that its aim is the positive one of gaining control of an area of airspace, rather than the defence of an area which is already controlled. The air superiority fighter seeks to dominate the skies over a particular area, be it a battlefield, an invasion beachhead or perhaps a portion of the front which has been selected for a breakthrough by ground forces. The aim will be to clear the skies of enemy aircraft, so that they cannot intervene in land operations nor hamper air operations by friendly forces. Although the air superiority mission is usually flown in support of land operations, this is not necessarily so, and in World War II fighter aircraft of the USAAF established air superiority over the German homeland to allow their strategic bomber forces to operate at will. However, what all such missions have in common is the contest between opposing fighter forces to dominate the skies.

British fighter operations over the Western Front during World War I offer a classic illustration of the process of seeking to gain command of the air over a battlefield and its rear supply areas. Major-General Sir Hugh Trenchard, the commander of the Royal Flying Corps in France during 1915–17, firmly adhered to an offensive doctrine. He aimed to cover the enemy lines with offensive fighter patrols from dawn until dusk, yet the technical and numerical superiority which such a policy realistically required was often lacking. For instance 'Bloody April' of 1917 saw unnecessarily high losses (1270 British aeroplanes destroyed between March and May 1917) as a result of Trenchard's offensive policy. Yet when air superiority could be gained, the advantages were impressive. This was shown in Palestine, where the RAF had gained air mastery by September 1918 through a combination of superior equipment and aggressive tactics. It used this command of the air to carry out extensive reconnaissance and bombing raids on the Turkish forces and, as the Turks were denied information from air reconnaissance, effective deception tactics could be

The Sopwith Camels of No 4 Squadron, Australian Flying Corps, engage the fighters of von Richthofen's 'circus' in March 1918, in a mêlée typical of the fighting over the Western Front at this time.

used by Allenby in the campaign which culminated in the capture of Jerusalem.

In Germany the lesson that a successful army must enjoy some measure of air superiority was well learned. The early successes of blitzkrieg tactics were the outcome of German mastery of the air, as much as the innovative use of armoured formations on land. In the Polish Campaign in September 1939 and the assault in the west in May 1940 the Luftwaffe's first objective was the elimination of the enemy's air arm. Once this was achieved, there followed the exploitation of the valuable intelligence gained from air reconnaissance and the merciless air attacks on ground forces which were an integral feature of blitzkrieg. The Luftwaffe's swiftly gained air mastery was not simply the result of the Germans possessing superior fighter aircraft and using them with greater tactical skill than their opponents, although these factors were of course important. Germany's enemies lost command of the air by default, as they had not realized the crucial importance of air superiority and were seriously deficient in both equipment and tactics. It is not by chance that Germany's first defeat came in the Battle of Britain, as only then was the Luftwaffe opposed by a well-equipped fighter force, backed by a superb system of command and control.

In the spring of 1941 the bulk of the Luftwaffe's fighter force moved eastwards. In the Balkans and during the initial assault on the Soviet Union it again succeeded in eliminating the enemy air forces. The Soviet fighter regiments were equipped with obsolescent aircraft – notably the Polikarpov I-16, which ironically had been one of the most advanced fighters of its day

when it first entered service in 1934. The Soviet air force was also at a disadvantage because its fighters had been misdeployed by being concentrated on forward airfields where they were easy targets for the marauding Luftwaffe.

Not until 1944 did the Soviet air force begin to wrest air superiority from the Luftwaffe. By this time the former was equipped with such workmanlike fighter aircraft as the Lavochkin La-5, Yakovlev Yak-9 and Yak-3. However, it was not by superiority of equipment that the Soviet air force overcame its redoubtable opponent, but rather through sheer weight of numbers, amounting to a superiority of about five-to-one. The Luftwaffe's first priority by this time was defence

Top This Luftwaffe Messerschmitt was shot down by RAF Spitfires on 5 September 1940 during the Battle of Britain. Its pilot was the German ace Franz von Werra of JG 3.

Above A P-51B Mustang of the 354th Fighter Group. The USAAF's North American P-51 Mustang fighter defeated the Luftwaffe in the fight for air superiority over Germany in 1944.

relatively ill-equipped North Korean air force. However, due to politically imposed restrictions on air action, which were to become a recurring feature of limited wars in the post-World War II era, the Communists were able to build up a fighter force of MiG-15 jets in Manchuria, where the airfields were safe from attack. Hence the fight for air superiority over North Korea was restricted to air-to-air combat, with the Communists having the advantage of choosing the time and the place of the encounter. This advantage and the Mig-15s' superior altitude performance over the USAF's North American F-86 Sabres were not fully exploited and the Communist jets seldom seriously hampered American air operations. This illustrates the importance of a further factor in a fight for air superiority, namely pilot morale and training. In contrast to the skilled and aggressive Sabre pilots, many of their opponents were inexperienced and prone to panic in combat. There were several instances of MiG pilots ejecting with little or no cause.

In the battle for air superiority over North Vietnam between 1965 and 1972, American pilots had to deal not only with enemy interceptor aircraft, but also with a formidable array of surface-to-air missiles (SAMs) and anti-aircraft guns defending key targets. Although defending North Vietnamese fighters enjoyed some successes, the attacking force was generally well protected by combat air patrols of McDonnell Douglas F-4 Phantoms. The SAMs were either neutralized by electronic countermeasures or directly attacked by defence suppression aircraft (codenamed Wild Weasels). The air superiority mission remains an important commitment for the air forces of both NATO and the Warsaw Pact countries.

AMERICAN VOLUNTEER GROUP 1941–42

The American Volunteer Group (AVG) – more popularly known as the Flying Tigers – was formed in 1941 by Clair Chennault to assist the Chinese Nationalist forces in their fight against the Japanese invaders. It was equipped with 100 Curtiss Tomahawk Mk IIB fighters which had originally been built for the RAF and it was manned by volunteers recruited in the main from the US armed forces. The Tomahawk fighters (usually referred to by the AVG as P-40s) were shipped to Rangoon in Burma during July 1941 and were then assembled at the nearby airfield of Mingaladon. By the end of August, 22 P-40s were available and intensive training in fighter tactics began at Kyedaw airstrip in Burma.

By the time of the Japanese attack on Pearl Harbor the AVG had been organized into three pursuit

of the homeland; the Eastern Front was starved of modern fighter aircraft and had insufficient fighter forces to re-establish air superiority.

The primary reason for the Luftwaffe's hard-pressed state in 1944 was the massive strategic air offensive mounted by the USAAF. This was not only an attack on vital industrial targets, but also a bid to wrest command of the air over Germany from the Luftwaffe. The USAAF's North American P-51 Mustang long-range escort fighters were capable of sorties lasting seven hours, bringing targets in Poland within range of their bases in Britain. Not only did the American fighters provide escort for the bombers, but they also sought out the Luftwaffe's fighters when parked on their airfields, after take-off when they were assembling for an attack on the box formations of bombers and – when they were most vulnerable – approaching their bases to land, short of fuel and ammunition after engaging the bombers.

At the outset of the Korean War in 1950 the USAF swiftly established superiority over the small and

A North Vietnamese MiG-17 fighter under attack from a USAF fighter. The US Air Force and Navy McDonnell Douglas F-4 Phantoms established a degree of air superiority over the North Vietnamese during the Southeast Asia conflict (1965–72).

squadrons, each with a strength of 18 fighters. On 10 December the group flew its first war mission, a reconnaissance of Bangkok in Japanese-occupied Thailand. Two days later the AVG's 3rd Squadron joined No 67 Squadron RAF at Mingaladon to provide an air defence force for Burma. The 1st and 2nd Squadrons then flew to Kunming in China, and on 20 December they intercepted a force of Japanese bombers, forcing them to jettison their bombs. Three days later the 3rd Squadron was in action in defence of Rangoon, scoring six kills for the loss of three P-40s and two pilots. On Christmas Day after an intense air battle the 3rd Squadron claimed 28 victories, but a Japanese attack on Mingaladon on 28 December so battered the unit that they had to be relieved by the AVG's 2nd Squadron. At the end of January, the 1st Squadron took over the air defence of Rangoon, but despite many successful air combats the deteriorating situation on the ground forced the AVG to withdraw northwards. The ten-week air defence of Rangoon had resulted in nearly

Above Curtiss P-40 fighters painted with the American Volunteer Group's famous shark-mouth marking are lined up on a waterlogged airstrip.

Right General Clair Chennault, who formed the AVG as part of the Chinese air force in 1941, pins the Service Medal onto the chest of 23rd Fighter Group ace, Lt-Col Bruce Holloway.

Below A Chinese soldier stands guard over a shark-mouth P-40 of the 23rd Flight Group, the USAAF unit which inherited the traditions of the Flying Tigers.

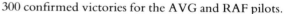

300 confirmed victories for the AVG and RAF pilots.

The AVG continued to fight alongside the RAF during the retreat through Burma, even going briefly onto the offensive with a successful attack on a Japanese fighter airfield in northern Thailand on 24 March 1942. However, the loss of Burma was by then a foregone conclusion and in May the AVG turned to the defence of the heavily bombed Chinese cities. The 1st Squadron was based at Kweilin, the 2nd Squadron covered Hengyang, with a detachment at Chungking, and the 3rd Squadron defended the main AVG base at Kunming. On 13 June the 1st Squadron had a particularly successful combat, claiming 11 Japanese aircraft destroyed for the loss of two P-40s.

On 4 July 1942 the AVG became the USAAF's 23rd Fighter Group, as part of the China Air Task Force which Chennault commanded. Few of the AVG's volunteer pilots remained with the new unit, however, largely because of insensitive treatment of them by the USAAF authorities. During some 30 weeks of air combat the AVG had accounted for 297 Japanese aircraft officially confirmed as destroyed, for the loss of 13 pilots killed in action, nine in training accidents and three made prisoners-of-war. The top-scoring AVG ace was Robert H. Neale, commander of the 1st Squadron, with 15½ victories to his credit.

AMIENS RAID 1944

One of the most daring and brilliantly executed of the low-level pinpoint bombing raids for which the RAF de Havilland Mosquito became famous was the attack on Amiens Prison. The object was to breach the prison walls so that the 700 Resistance fighters imprisoned there would be given a chance to escape. This called for absolute precision in the bombing and the crews of No 140 Wing RAF were carefully briefed for the attack.

After several postponements due to bad weather, three formations of Mosquito FB Mk VIs drawn from Nos 21, 464 and 487 Squadrons took off from Huns-

Top A DH Mosquito FB Mk VI releases its bombs over Amiens gaol during the raid on 18 February 1944.

Above The breach in the outer wall of Amiens gaol can be clearly seen in this photograph taken immediately after the raid. More than 250 Resistance fighters escaped in the confusion following the bombing.

don in Hertfordshire on 18 February 1944. They were led by Group Captain P. C. Pickard DSO, DFC, DFM, and escorted by the Hawker Typhoons of No 198 Squadron. En route to the target the weather was poor, with intermittent snow squalls, but it cleared as the French coast was approached. Flying at low level to avoid radar detection, the Mosquitoes headed for Amiens, where they picked up the long, straight Amiens–Albert road that was to lead them to the prison. Attacking in 'vic' formations of three, the bombers ran in at very low level and aimed their two 226kg (500lb) bombs at the base of the prison wall. They were flying so low that they had to pull up to clear the 18m (60ft) high wall. Succeeding formations attacked the German guards' quarters. Pickard, circling the target in his Mosquito, saw that the walls were holed and that prisoners were escaping, so he called off the last formation's attack.

As the Mosquitoes withdrew, Focke Wulf Fw 190 fighters appeared on the scene. They succeeded in shooting down Pickard's aircraft and he and his navigator, Flight Lieutenant Bill Broadley, were killed. A second Mosquito was shot down by flak, while three seriously damaged bombers struggled back to England. More than 250 prisoners escaped from the prison and some 50 Germans were killed by the bombing.

ANTI-SUBMARINE WARFARE

The aircraft is today one of the submarine's most effective enemies, taking its place beside the surface escort vessel and hunter-killer submarine in the anti-submarine warefare (ASW) armoury. The beginnings of the aircraft's battle against the submarine in World War I were hardly auspicious, although some air actions were successful. For example in 1916 two Austro-Hungarian Lohner flying boats surprised the French submarine *Foucault* travelling at periscope depth in the Adriatic, blew her to the surface with their bombs and forced her captain to scuttle her by further attacks. Such achievements were, however, the exception rather than the rule.

The Royal Naval Air Service made particularly strenuous efforts to develop effective anti-submarine aircraft and tactics. Flying boats such as the Curtiss H-12 and Felixstowe F-2A operated over the North Sea on 'Spider Web' patrols (named after the shape of the search pattern), intended to intercept U-boats in transit from their bases to the English Channel. Other ASW aircraft included non-rigid airships or blimps, more than a hundred of which were in service by the end of 1917. They were particularly useful as convoy escorts, as they had better endurance than aeroplanes. (Surprisingly, the US Navy continued to operate

attacks was the Leigh Light, a powerful searchlight which could illuminate the target submarine during the aircraft's run-in to attack. However, these aids were of little use until the RAF's anti-submarine weapons could be improved. Depth bombs used early in the war proved to be more of a menace to the aircraft dropping them than to the target. Modified naval depth charges were a partial solution, but did not became truly effective until they were fused to explode at far shallower depths than was at first thought necessary.

A number of efficient maritime patrol aircraft were in service with RAF Coastal Command early in the war, including the Lockheed Hudson land plane and the Consolidated Catalina and Short Sunderland flying boats. However, there was a pressing need for very long range patrol aircraft, which was only met when Consolidated Liberators reached Coastal Command from mid-1942. Operating from Iceland, they had sufficient range to close the mid-Atlantic gap in air patrol coverage. A further solution to this problem was the escort carrier, able to operate a small number of ASW Fairey Swordfish or Grumman Avenger aircraft, but these were not generally available until late in 1943.

As the war progressed a number of important technical developments contributed to the aircraft's war against the submarine. American scientists developed a device known as MAD (magnetic anomaly detector), which would detect the presence of a submerged submarine at close range by the slight variation in the earth's magnetic field caused by its metal hull. This was useful in accurately delivering a depth-charge attack. MAD-equipped Consolidated PBY flying boats of the US Navy Squadron VP-63 were especially successful over the Straits of Gibraltar in 1944. Another important American invention was the sonobuoy – a small floating sonar, which could pick up the sound of a U-boat's propeller and transmit the bearing to its parent aircraft. When dropped in patterns, data from sonobuoys could be used to give the precise position of a submarine through cross-bearings. The development of offensive ASW weapons for aircraft was not neglected and the Americans developed an acoustic-homing torpedo, which guided itself onto a submerged U-boat.

By May 1943 the Allied ASW forces had mastered the U-boats in the Atlantic and the war ended before the German submarines could regain the initiative. A total of 892 German, Italian and Japanese submarines were sunk by the Allies in World War II. Of these, surface ships accounted for $394\frac{1}{2}$, other submarines sank 64 and aircraft sank $433\frac{1}{2}$. The majority of the sinkings by aircraft were achieved by land-based patrol bombers, which accounted for $303\frac{1}{2}$. Submarines lost to other causes included 66 destroyed in port during raids by bomber aircraft and 64 sunk at sea by naval aircraft operating from carriers.

By the end of World War II the aircraft had reached full maturity as an ASW weapon. However, in 1954 the task of all anti-submarine forces became considerably more difficult with the appearance of the nuclear-

blimps throughout World War II on ASW duties.) Another expedient was 'Scarecrow' patrols flown by unarmed trainer aircraft such as the de Havilland DH6, which could be effective in frightening off a U-boat. DH Tiger Moths performed the same role early in World War II. Aircraft were therefore primarily of value as a deterrent to submarine attack in World War I.

By the outbreak of World War II the value of the aircraft as an anti-submarine weapon had been largely forgotten. At first it was believed in naval circles that ASDIC provided a complete defence against submarines, but since Admiral Doenitz's U-boats generally attacked while running on the surface at night, this fallacy was soon exposed. Radar-equipped aircraft would clearly be of value in countering the U-boat's new tactics and by the end of 1940 an ASV (air-to-surface vessel) radar set was in service. A further aid to night

Above The Blackburn Kangaroo anti-submarine patrol aircraft served with No 246 Squadron RAF in 1918. Note the depth-charge armament beneath the wing centre section.

Below A Short Sunderland of No 10 Squadron RAF over the Eddystone Lighthouse in 1940. The Short Sunderland flying boat was one of RAF Coastal Command's most effective patrol aircraft at the start of World War II.

powered submarine. This new foe was capable of remaining submerged throughout its patrol, unlike the diesel-electric powered boats of World War II which had periodically to surface (or at any rate raise a schnorkel tube) to recharge their batteries. Yet the ASW task has not become impossible and many improvements in detection devices and weaponry have been developed in the post-World War II period. Sonobuoys and the acoustic processing equipment carried aboard aircraft have been greatly improved in range and accuracy. ASW helicopters have come into service equipped with dunking sonar, MAD gear and acoustic-homing torpedoes, thus greatly increasing the reach of ASW surface vessels. Not all modern submarines are nuclear-powered and so equipment has been produced (known as Autolycus in the RAF, or Sniffer in the US Navy) which can detect the diesel fumes of a schnorkelling submarine. It may even be possible to locate a submerged submarine using an infra-red detector mounted on a satellite.

The development of ASW aircraft has kept pace with the improvements in detection equipment. The US Navy maintains a front-line strength of 24 patrol squadrons equipped with the Lockheed P-3 Orion aircraft. A conversion of the four-turboprop-powered Electra civil airliner, the Orion can remain on patrol for more than 17 hours and is equipped with a wide range of ASW detection equipment and up to 6800kg (15,000lb) of offensive weapons. The RAF operates four squadrons of jet-powered BAe Nimrods, with an endurance of 12 hours which can be extended by in-flight refuelling. Faced with a Soviet submarine fleet of some 300 vessels, these ASW aircraft have a more important role in maritime strategy than ever before.

ARMY AVIATION

There are many ways in which aircraft can intervene in the land battle. They can provide valuable intelligence through reconnaissance and observation; they can keep the skies above the battlefield clear of enemy forces; they can mount interdiction missions to cut off the enemy from reinforcement and resupply; they can swiftly fly-in urgently needed supplies and reinforcements; and they can directly attack enemy forces in the field.

Army aviation in fact is more than a century older than heavier-than-air flight, for the French Revolutionary armies used observation balloons in battle as early as 1794. Yet it was in World War I that aircraft became firmly established as essential adjuncts to mili-

offensive. Once an attack went 'over the top' communications between forward troops and the rear headquarters were often severed. Therefore contact patrol aircraft were used to locate friendly troops and swiftly pass the positions back to headquarters. The culmination of the airmen's efforts to cooperate with ground forces came with the development of tactics and aeroplanes to join in the ground battle. Specialized ground-attack aircraft, such as the British Sopwith Salamander and German Junkers JI, were produced in the final year of the war.

The opening campaigns of World War II showed that the Germans had achieved an impressive degree of cooperation between air and land forces. Ground attacks, spearheaded by tanks and motorized infantry, were supported by a balanced force of fighter, bomber and reconnaissance aircraft. The first task of the bombers, assisted by escorting fighters, was to knock

tary operations. Reconnaissance was an important role as early as 1914, when aircraft of the Royal Flying Corps provided the intelligence that led to the halting of the German army's advance in the Battle of the Marne. When the war of movement gave way to trench fighting, aerial photography allowed accurate maps of the enemy's defences to be swiftly produced. During the Battle of the Somme (July to November 1916) no less than 19,000 aerial photographs were taken of enemy positions and the fast-developing art of photographic interpretation allowed much valuable intelligence to be gleaned from this source.

The great concentrations of artillery on the Western Front also benefited from air support, as artillery observation aircraft could direct fire onto targets out of sight of ground observers. The Germans were quick to realize the specialized nature of this work and 14 *Artillerie Flieger Abteilungen* were formed in the latter half of 1915 exclusively for this task. By August 1916 over half the German observation units were for artillery observation. Another problem of trench warfare which the aircraft helped to solve was that of finding out how far friendly troops had advanced during an

Left The DFS 230 was the standard German troop-carrying glider in the early years of World War II. It could lift nine infantrymen, plus its pilot.

opponents. A key weapon in the Soviet air armoury was the Ilyushin Il-2 Shturmovik ground-attack aircraft, armed with a heavy-calibre cannon, bombs and rockets.

Since World War II many armies have formed their own air arms, largely equipped with helicopters, which are distinct from the air forces. An important innovation of the late 1960s was the armed attack helicopter, which is capable of knocking out enemy tanks. Specialized close-support aircraft currently in service include the RAF's V/STOL (vertical/short take-off and landing) BAe Harrier and the USAF's Republic A-10A Thunderbolt II tank-buster, armed with a massive rapid-fire 30mm cannon.

out the enemy air force and thereafter attack troop concentrations and strongpoints on the ground. A potent new weapon in the Luftwaffe's armoury was the Junkers Ju 87 Stuka dive-bomber, which was used as flying artillery against targets on the battlefield and in rear areas. Strategic and tactical reconnaissance aircraft provided intelligence to ground commanders at all levels and airborne troops were available to seize especially important objectives.

The Western Allies were slow to follow Germany's lead in organizing their army-support air forces into commands made up of a mixture of fighter, bomber, close-support and reconnaissance units. Yet by 1944 they were fully committed to this practice, with the RAF's 2nd Tactical Air Force and USAAF's Ninth Air Force supporting the Normandy Invasion. The Soviet air force had always been primarily an army-support organization, but it was not until 1943 that it was able to make any appreciable impression on its German

Above A Bell AH-1 Huey Cobra of the US Army armed with eight TOW anti-tank missiles, plus a rapid-fire machine gun and grenade launcher in a turret beneath the nose.

ARNHEM 1944

The operation by British airborne troops to secure a bridgehead over the Rhine at Arnhem in September 1944 was part of a wider operation by the 1st Allied Airborne Army. Its objective was to secure crossings of the rivers Maas, Waal and Neder Rijn in order to speed the advance of the Allied armies into Europe. A massive airlift by the USAAF's IXth Troop Carrier Command and RAF Transport Command's Nos 38 and 46 Groups carried the airborne units to their objectives on 17 September. The British 1st Airborne Division was lifted by 519 aircraft, which included RAF Douglas Dakotas and USAAF C-47s, plus RAF Handley Page Halifax, Short Stirling and Armstrong Whitworth Albemarle glider tugs. Some 2800 gliders were involved in the overall operation, most of them

used in the Arnhem landings. They comprised British Horsa and American CG-4A Hadrian troop-carrying gliders, and the British Hamilcar, which could carry jeeps, trailers and stores. Fighter escort and flak suppression was provided by 1200 RAF fighter sorties.

Although the Neder Rijn bridgehead was secured and a second airlift of troops was made on 18 September, the situation at Arnhem rapidly deteriorated. Unexpectedly fierce opposition and the slow advance of the British XXX Corps towards Arnhem by land, forced the airborne troops into a hopeless fight with German troops backed by the artillery and armour that they lacked. Air resupply sorties ran the gauntlet of intense German flak and often the dropping zones were in enemy hands. Communications with the RAF's 2nd Tactical Air Force was poor and so the airborne troops could not obtain satisfactory close air support from the Hawker Typhoon fighter-bombers. On the night of 25/26 September the survivors withdrew across the Neder Rijn at the end of an operation redeemed only by the courage of the men who fought against impossible odds.

Above *Troops of the British 1st Airborne Division unload vehicles and supplies from their Airspeed Horsa gliders in the Arnhem landing zone, September 1944.*

Right *A Short Stirling glider tug is about to lift off with an Airspeed Horsa troop-carrying glider in tow.*

Below right *Paratroopers aboard a Douglas C-47 en route to the drop zone. They carry kit and weapons packed into leg bags to prevent them fouling the parachute harness.*

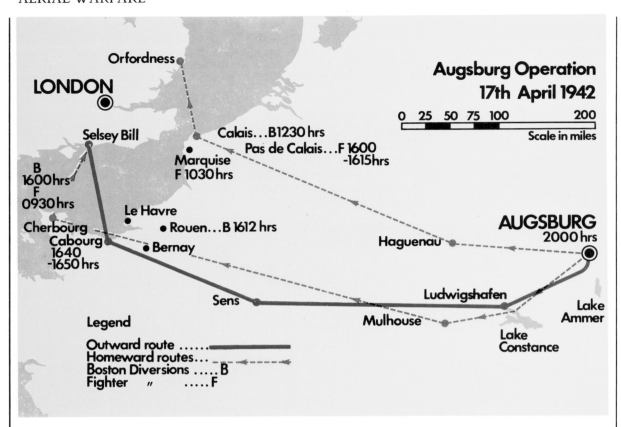

**Augsburg Operation
17th April 1942**

Orfordness

LONDON

Selsey Bill

B
1600 hrs
F
0930 hrs

Calais...B1230 hrs
Pas de Calais...F 1600
-1615 hrs

Marquise
F 1030 hrs

Cherbourg
Cabourg
1640
-1650 hrs

Le Havre
Rouen...B 1612 hrs
Bernay

AUGSBURG
2000 hrs

Haguenau

Sens

Ludwigshafen

Mulhouse

Lake
Ammer

Lake
Constance

0 25 50 75 100   200
Scale in miles

Legend

Outward route ......_____
Homeward routes...   ◄- - -►
Boston Diversions .....B
Fighter   "   .....F

AUGSBURG RAID 1942

On 17 April 1942 a long-distance daylight bombing raid was carried out into the heart of Germany by the RAF's new four-engined Avro Lancaster bombers. Its objective was the MAN factory at Augsburg in Bavaria, which produced diesel engines for U-boats. It was thought that the factory's destruction would severely disrupt U-boat production at a critical phase of the Battle of the Atlantic and so the risks of a 2000km (1250-mile) round-trip over enemy territory were justified.

Twelve Lancasters took part in the raid, flying in two sections of six. The lead section was provided by No 44 Squadron and was led by Squadron Leader J. D. Nettleton, the second was from No 97 Squadron led by Squadron Leader J. S. Sherwood. Flying at low level, the Lancasters crossed the French coast without incident, but near Sens the formation was intercepted by German fighters. At the end of a 15-minute air battle four of the Lancasters had been shot down. The survivors continued towards the target. They bombed

A group photograph showing some of the Lancaster crews who took part in the Augsburg raid. Out of a total of 85 aircrew, 49 failed to return.

Saw Mills

Bronze
Workshops

Main Diesel
Engine Factory

accurately, but three more bombers were lost to flak, including that flown by Squadron Leader Sherwood. Thus only five Lancasters of the 12 that had set out survived. Squadron Leader Nettleton's leadership was recognized by the award of the Victoria Cross.

Reconnaissance photographs showed damage to the MAN factory's assembly shop and other buildings. More detailed assessment after the war revealed that five of the bombs dropped failed to explode. The others did substantial damage, but as five other factories were then producing diesels under licence from MAN the effect on U-boat production was negligible.

BAEDEKER RAIDS
1942

A series of German bomber raids on British cultural centres between April and June 1942 took their name from the famous tourist guides of Karl Baedeker. In a speech to the German people on 26 April Hitler said that as each famous city was destroyed he would cross it off in Baedeker's guides. In the less colourful language of the Fuehrer's operational directive to his bomber commanders, the objectives of the raids were defined as targets with high civilian concentrations. They were terror raids, initiated in reprisal for RAF Bomber Command's incendiary raid on the old Baltic port of Lübeck in March 1942.

German bomber activity over Britain had been at a low level since the night Blitz had petered out in

Above A reconnaissance photograph of Augsburg showing the position of the MAN diesel factory.

Below Dornier Do 217 night bombers of the Luftwaffe's Kampfgeschwader 2 took part in the Baedeker raids, operating from bases in the Netherlands.

the spring of 1941. Many bomber units were then redeployed to the Eastern Front, but Luftflotte 3 in the west controlled the Dornier Do 217s of Kampfgeschwader 2, the Junkers Ju 88s of Kampfgruppe 106 and the Heinkel He 111s of I Gruppe, Kampfgeschwader 100 (the Luftwaffe's pathfinder unit) at the start of the Baedeker offensive. The raids were generally flown at altitudes between 1500m (5000ft) and 3000m (10,000ft), with the relatively fast Do 217s and Ju 88s carrying out most of the sorties. Some of the bombers carried the new ABB 500 incendiary canisters, each containing 140 incendiary bombs which fell in a closely spaced cluster.

The Baedeker raids began on the night of 23/24 April 1942 with an attack on Exeter. The bombing was scattered, due to cloud over the target area, but one of the raiders was intercepted by a Bristol Beaufighter night fighter of No 604 Squadron and shot down. A more accurate raid was made on the same target the following night, with four German bombers falling to the defenders. The Luftwaffe then turned their attention to Bath, causing serious damage, including the destruction of the historic Assembly Rooms. The attack then switched to eastern England, with a raid on Norwich on 27/28 April. York was attacked on the following night and then the bombers returned to Norwich. Then, after seven consecutive night attacks, there was a lull in the German offensive.

The defenders had brought down only ten German bombers during the first week of the Baedeker raids, so clearly more effective defensive measures needed to be taken. Anti-aircraft guns were redeployed to likely targets and intruder aircraft stepped up their nightly patrols over the airfields used by the German bombers. The X-Gerät and Y-Gerät navigation beams used by the raiders were jammed whenever their frequencies could be located and decoy targets were lit in the hope of diverting some of the Luftwaffe's bombs.

On the night of 3/4 May 60 German bombers returned to Exeter and the town was hard hit, with serious damage to the cathedral. There followed raids on Cowes, Norwich and Canterbury. The two attacks on Canterbury, on 31 May/1 June and 2/3 June, were a direct reprisal for Bomber Command's Thousand-Bomber Raid on Cologne. During the month of June it became apparent that the Luftwaffe was switching its attacks back to military targets, although such towns

Below A Bristol Beaufighter of No 29 Squadron. The Beaufighter was the mainstay of the RAF's night defences during the Baedeker raids.

as Ipswich, Norwich and Weston-super-Mare were also hit. Although the Luftwaffe's losses had not been very high, it was realized that the negligible effects of the Baedeker raids on British morale were not worth the effort of mounting them.

BATTLE OF BERLIN 1943–44

In November 1943 the C-in-C of RAF Bomber Command, Air Chief-Marshal Sir Arthur Harris, urged Winston Churchill to authorize an all-out bombing attack on the German capital with the object of knock-

Above Bomber Command aircrew in flying suits and parachute harness before take-off on the evening of 21 January 1944, when Berlin was raided in force.

Left RAF armourers load bombs aboard an Avro Lancaster bomber prior to a night raid. A typical bomb load was a mixture of high explosives and incendiaries.

Below A stick of bombs fall towards Tempelhof airfield, Berlin, during a raid on the city by the bombers of the USAAF Eighth Air Force.

Handley Page Halifaxes and de Havilland Mosquitoes also participated in the battle, but of 9111 sorties despatched to Berlin, 7256 were flown by Lancasters.

Raids continued against Berlin during December and January and on the night of 15/16 February 1944 the battle reached its climax with the heaviest raid of all. A force of 891 bombers was despatched and 806 reached the target, dropping 2685 tonnes (2642 tons) of bombs. Forty-two of the attacking bombers were shot down. Early in March the USAAF joined in the battle, although the American contribution was not significant. This was because, since the heavy losses on the Schweinfurt raid in October 1943, the USAAF daylight bombers had been reluctant to undertake deep penetrations of enemy airspace without fighter cover. It was only when the North American P-51 Mustang long-range fighter became available in sufficient numbers that the USAAF were prepared to fly against Berlin. Even then, a strong fighter escort could not prevent the loss of 69 bombers from a force of 730 which raided the German capital on 6 March. The final raid of the campaign by RAF Bomber Command was somewhat hampered by cloud, which intermittently

ing Germany out of the war. He wrote: 'We can wreck Berlin from end to end if the USAAF will come in on it. It will cost us between 400 and 500 aircraft. It will cost Germany the war.' This claim led to the Battle of Berlin, a series of major operations launched against the German capital between November 1943 and March 1944.

The offensive opened on the night of 18/19 November 1943, when a force of 444 bombers flew to Berlin, while a further 395 were sent against Mannheim. Losses were low on this mission, only nine aircraft failing to return, but cloud obscured the target making bombing difficult. Four nights later, on 22/23 November, a heavier attack was mounted by 764 bombers. The following night a smaller force repeated the attack. As a sortie to Berlin involved a total flight of well over 1600km (1000 miles), the majority of these flights were undertaken by Avro Lancasters, which were Bomber Command's most effective aircraft.

obscured the target markers laid by the Path Finder Force. However, the defenders had no such problems and guns and fighters accounted for 95 RAF bombers, making this the most costly raid of the Battle of Berlin.

By the end of March it was apparent that the damage to Berlin, although very far from being negligible, had not as Harris had anticipated wrecked the city from end to end. Nor had it knocked Germany out of the war. The 16 major raids of the battle had cost Bomber Command 492 aircraft, some 5·4% of the total force despatched. These losses were clearly unacceptably high. Furthermore, Bomber Command's raids on other targets had also led to heavy losses, culminating in the disastrous Nuremberg raid at the end of March, when over a hundred aircraft were destroyed. It seemed that at the end of Harris's Berlin offensive the German night fighters were masters of the night sky over Germany.

BATTLE OF BRITAIN 1940

In the summer of 1940 the Luftwaffe's attempt to gain air superiority over southern Britain was defeated by the squadrons of RAF Fighter Command in the Battle of Britain. It was the first time in history that a decisive major battle had been fought in the air. Following the fall of France in June 1940, the German High Command was faced with the effective anti-tank barrier of the English Channel. Clearly an amphibious assault on the coast of southern England could not succeed without command of the air – and the closing of the Channel to the major warships of the Royal Navy that would follow from this. Therefore it was decided to spearhead the attack on Britain with an all-out air assault.

On the eve of the Battle of Britain the Luftwaffe occupied air bases in France and the Low Countries and also in Norway, enabling it to threaten the RAF's

Above *A Junkers Ju 87B of Stukageschwader 2. Many Stukas were lost during the Battle of Britain.*

Below *Refuelling a Hawker Hurricane Mk I of No 229 Squadron in 1940.*

Below *Luftwaffe ground crew prepare a Heinkel He 111 for a mission. The bomber belongs to Kampfgeschwader 26.*

defences from two directions. Its aircraft strength comprised 1215 bombers, 280 dive-bombers, 755 single-engined fighters, 225 *Zerstörer* (destroyer) twin-engined fighters and 70 reconnaissance aircraft. This force was divided into three major commands: Luftflotte 2 based in the Netherlands, Belgium and north-west France under the command of General Albert Kesselring; Luftflotte 3 on the Channel coast under General Hugo Sperrle; and Luftflotte 5 in Norway commanded by General Hans Juergen Stumpff. The bomber force was made up of twin-engined Heinkel He 111s, Dornier Do 17s and Junkers Ju 88s, all of which had inadequate defensive armament. The Ju 87 Stuka dive-bomber had performed well in the Luftwaffe's early campaigns, but proved to be highly vulnerable to the RAF's fighter defences. The Messerschmitt Bf 110 was intended to fulfil the long-range fighter escort role, but lacked the performance of the RAF single-engined fighters. In this respect the Luftwaffe's Messerschmitt Bf 109E was considerably better, but it lacked the range for extended escort missions over southern England from its bases on the Channel coast of France.

RAF Fighter Command's effective strength comprised 36 squadrons equipped with some 450 Hawker Hurricane and 250 Supermarine Spitfire fighters, plus twin-engined Bristol Blenheims and Boulton Paul Defiant turret-fighters which proved to be unequal to the demands of the daylight air battles. The Spitfire was undoubtedly the best RAF fighter, yet it was the slower Hurricane which bore the brunt of the fighting.

The fighter squadrons were deployed in three groups: No 11 Group under Air Marshal Keith Park covered southern England; No 12 Group was responsible for the Midlands and East Anglia, under the command of Air Marshal Trafford Leigh Mallory; Scotland and the North was the responsibility of Air Vice-Marshal Richard Saul's No 13 Group; and early in the battle No 10 Group was formed under Air Vice-Marshal Quintin Brand to relieve Park of responsibility for south-west England.

Command and control of the British air defences was effected by a highly efficient system, the first of its kind in the world, which was the brainchild of the C-in-C of Fighter Command, Air Marshal Sir Hugh Dowding. Early warning of attack was provided by a chain of coastal radar stations, with the Observer Corps tracking the enemy formations once they had crossed the coast. This information was fed back to control rooms at Command, Group and Sector levels and it was the Sector Controllers who ordered the fighter squadrons into the air and directed them to intercept the enemy. The RAF's outnumbered fighters

July the Luftwaffe lost a total of 216 aircraft (48 of them single-engined fighters), while Fighter Command's losses were 77 aircraft destroyed.

On 11 August a new phase of the battle began, with attacks on south-coast ports and airfields. This was to be the preliminary to *Adler Tag* (Eagle Day), an all-out attack on the fighter airfields in southern England. Yet when it came on 13 August, the *Adler Tag* onslaught was sharply repulsed, with the Luftwaffe losing 45 aircraft destroyed to the RAF's 14 losses. Two days later an attack in the south was timed to coincide with raids on north-east England by Luftflotte 5 flying from Norway. While No 11 Group was hard-pressed to meet numerous raids, the No 13 Group squadrons severely mauled Luftflotte 5 and it never again raided Britain in force. At the end of the day the Luftwaffe had lost 75 aircraft, while 29 RAF fighters had been shot down in air combat and a further 17 aircraft destroyed on the ground.

Despite these losses the Luftwaffe maintained the pressure on Fighter Command and on 24 August stepped up its attack on fighter airfields. The climax of

could thus be used to best effect, with little time and energy wasted on standing patrols.

The advantages of this system were not immediately available to Fighter Command, as the opening phase of the battle took place over coastal convoys beyond its effective area of coverage. Thus the RAF fighters had to mount standing patrols over threatened shipping on the off-chance of effecting an interception. They were further hampered by their outmoded tactics, the RAF at this time operating in 'vic' formations of three aircraft and carrying out preplanned 'Fighting Area Attacks', in contrast to the Luftwaffe fighters which flew in pairs and made use of more fluid attack manoeuvres. During these preliminary skirmishes in

A Supermarine Spitfire Mk I of No 19 Squadron RAF, based at Duxford in Cambridgeshire. A total of 19 squadrons in RAF Fighter Command flew the Spitfire during the Battle of Britain.

this phase of the battle came during the period 30 August to 6 September, during which the RAF lost around 12, the equivalent of a squadron of fighter aircraft, every day. Yet it was the loss of trained and experienced pilots that caused Dowding the greatest anxiety. Respite came on 7 September when the Luftwaffe switched its attack from the fighter airfields onto London. This decision was intended by Goering to be the knockout blow against the tottering defences, yet he had been misled by faulty intelligence into greatly underestimating the condition of RAF Fighter Command. As his bombers pounded the British capital, the RAF fighter squadrons fought back with undiminished ferocity. It was clear by 15 September, on which day

the Luftwaffe lost 62 aircraft to the RAF's 25, that the defenders were still a force to be reckoned with. Consequently the planned invasion of Britain was postponed and ultimately abandoned.

As the Luftwaffe bombers continued their assault on London in the night Blitz, the German fighter force flew a series of high-level sweeps over southern England in the final phase of the battle. A number of Messerschmitt Bf 109s were converted as fighter-bombers, but their raids were of nuisance value only. The RAF found these tactics difficult to counter and in October 1940 the RAF lost 124 Spitfires and Hurricanes in combat to the Luftwaffe's 119 Bf 109s destroyed. Nevertheless, as the final phase of the battle petered out, it was clear that the RAF had won the first decisive victory of the war over the might of the German forces.

Above A captured Messerschmitt Bf 109E in RAF markings. The Bf 109E was the Luftwaffe's standard single-seat fighter during the Battle of Britain.

Below left The Amiot 143 bomber was typical of the obsolescent equipment of the Armée de l' Air in May 1940.

Bottom right The Armée de l'Air's Bloch MB152 fighters were heavily engaged during the Battle of France, being credited with 188 victories over the Luftwaffe.

571 aircraft, but many of these were the unsatisfactory Morane-Saulnier MS406 and Bloch 152 designs. Only 60 of the new Dewoitine D520s had been delivered and the American-supplied Curtiss Hawk 75s, 316 of which were in service, were no match for the German Messerschmitt Bf 109Es. Out of a total force of 400 bombers, nearly half were outmoded types unsuited to modern warfare. The more modern bombers included American Douglas DB-7s and Glenn Martin 167Fs, plus the French-designed LeO 451 of which less than 100 were in service.

On 10 May 1940 the German Luftflotten 2 and 3 possessed 1120 medium bombers, 324 dive-bombers, 248 Messerschmitt Bf 110 *Zerstörer* (destroyer) twin-engined fighters and 1016 Bf 109s. Not only were the French inferior to the Luftwaffe in numbers and quality of aircraft, but they were also quite unprepared to meet the German blitzkrieg tactics. Nor were the RAF forces in France, the Air Component of the British Expeditionary Force and the Advanced Air Striking Force (with a strength of 25 squadrons) any better equipped to stem the German advance. The assault was spearheaded by armoured forces, supported by Junkers Ju 87 dive-bombers and Henschel Hs 123 ground-attack aircraft. Air cover was provided by the Bf 109s, while the medium bombers struck at airfields, communications and supply centres in the rear, and

BATTLE OF FRANCE 1940

The German offensive against France in May 1940 found the Armée de l'Air in the middle of a re-equipment programme. A number of important new warplanes of French design and manufacture were entering service, but were not fully operational, while deliveries of aircraft ordered from the United States had not been completed. The fighter force comprised

Above *Among the RAF aircraft to take part in the Battle of France were the Hawker Hurricane Mk I fighters of No 85 Squadron, which formed part of the Air Component of the BEF.*

Left *The Henschel Hs 126 battlefield reconnaissance aircraft suffered heavy losses during the Battle of France, but nonetheless performed a vital operational role.*

airborne troops were dropped onto key objectives. The Netherlands were quickly overrun, while Belgium held out for 16 days.

The RAF and the Armée de l'Air immediately launched their bombers against the advancing enemy, but losses were heavy and the results poor. On 14 May the bombers shifted their target to the German forces breaking through at Sedan, but flak and fighter defences largely negated their efforts. By 25 May the French had lost over 500 aircraft. There followed the Dunkirk evacuation and the French used this respite from the attentions of the Luftwaffe to regroup their air forces.

On 3 June the Armée de l'Air was again in action, defending the French capital, but the destruction of 18 German aircraft cost them 33 French fighters destroyed. On 5 June the German armies attacked across the Somme and French and British bombers carried out repeated raids on bridges and enemy troop columns. Yet this effort did not prevent a German breakthrough and within eight days the German army had reached the outskirts of Paris. On 10 June Italy entered the war against France, although only minor air battles took place on the Alpine front. By mid-June French resistance had collapsed and an armistice was signed on 22 June.

BERLIN AIRLIFT 1948–49

One of the most successful air resupply operations in the history of military aviation was the Berlin airlift of 1948–9. Soviet interference in the road, rail and waterway communications running from the Western Occupation Zones of Germany into the British, American and French sectors of Berlin began early in

Below *An RAF Short Sunderland flying boat unloads stores on the Havelsee, Berlin, during the Berlin airlift.*

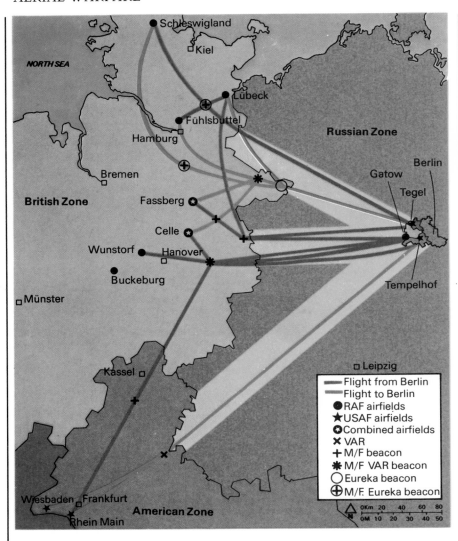

Above *A map showing flight paths and airfields used during the Berlin Airlift.*

equipped with the R5D (the US Navy's designation for the C-54) were included in this force.

The efforts of the USAF's Operation Vittles and the RAF's Operation Plainfare were formally integrated in October 1948, when the Combined Air Lift Task Force was formed under the command of Major-General William Tunner USAF, with Air Commodore J. W. F. Merer RAF as his deputy. The transport aircraft flew through three air corridors, each 32km (20 miles) wide with a ceiling of 3000m (10,000ft), running to Berlin from Frankfurt in the US Zone and from Hannover and Hamburg in the British Zone. At its height the airlift was a 24-hours-a-day, seven-days-a-week operation. The transport aircraft were usually despatched at three-minute intervals and spent 30 minutes on the ground in Berlin during unloading. The main air terminals in the city were Gatow in the British Sector and Tempelhof in the US Sector, although Tegel in the French Sector was also brought into use during the airlift.

RAF Short Sunderland flying boats of Nos 201 and 230 Squadrons flew from Finkenwerder on the River Elbe near Hamburg into the Havelsee in the Spandau suburb of Berlin. Their protection against sea-water corrosion made them especially useful for the transport of salt, which could seriously damage the structure of conventional aircraft. British civil charter aircraft, including Avro Lancastrians and Tudors, Handley Page Haltons and Consolidated Liberators, also parti-

1948. Under normal conditions, some 12,000 tonnes of supplies were brought into Berlin daily to meet the needs of the city's 2¼ million inhabitants. By 24 June the Soviet Union had blocked all surface routes into the city and the Western powers had no alternative but to attempt to keep Berlin supplied by air. The minimum daily load of food and essential supplies was estimated at 4500 tonnes.

The air transport force available at the start of the airlift comprised 102 Douglas C-47s and two Douglas C-54s of the USAF, plus about a dozen RAF Dakotas (the British designation for the Douglas C-47). The C-47s and Dakotas could lift three tonnes of supplies into Berlin on a single sortie and the C-54s ten tonnes. Clearly the existing transport force was inadequate and it was rapidly expanded to meet the emergency. The RAF despatched 54 Dakotas drawn from Nos 38 and 46 Groups and 40 Avro Yorks from No 47 Group to bases in Germany. The American Military Air Transport Service set up an Airlift Task Force and eight squadrons of C-54 transports were flown in from the United States. It was intended to replace all the C-47s by the more efficient C-54s as soon as possible, and a total of 275 of these aircraft were withdrawn from USAF units around the world to take part in the airlift. Two US Navy transport squadrons, VR-6 and VR-8,

cipated in the airlift. Among their special loads was petroleum for motor transport. By October 1948 some 5000 tonnes of supplies were reaching Berlin every day. The airlift continued as a precautionary measure until 30 September 1949, even though the Soviet blockade had been lifted in May. A total of 2,362,000 tonnes (2,325,000 tons) had been delivered, the USAF's share being 1,811,000 tonnes (1,783,000 tons).

THE BLITZ 1940–41

The Luftwaffe night attacks on British cities in 1940–41, known as the Blitz, began as a phase of the Battle of Britain and continued as an offensive in its own right once daylight attacks had proved to be too costly. During August 1940, while day attacks by heavily escorted bombers were mounted against targets in southern England, night raiders roamed over much of the country. For example, on the night of 27/28 August some 200 bombers attacked various targets in the industrial north, the Midlands and East Anglia, while isolated attacks were widespread, ranging from Plymouth in the west to Aberdeen in the north. Since daylight attacks needed to be strongly escorted by single-engined fighters, the Luftwaffe had a surplus of bombers for which no escorts could be provided and

Opposite page, right General Alexander *gives a speech in front of a USAF C-54 Skymaster before its departure from Rhein-Main airfield, Frankfurt, for the last flight of the Berlin Airlift – on 30 September 1949.*

Above *Avro Yorks of RAF Transport Command flew some 230,000 tons of supplies into Berlin, about half the RAF's total during the Airlift.*

Right *The badge of Kampfgruppe 100, the Luftwaffe's pathfinder unit during the Blitz, painted on a Heinkel He 111.*

Above *The Bristol Beaufighter gained its first night victory in November 1940, but few were in service and the RAF's night defences during the Blitz were largely ineffective.*

Left *Luftwaffe bomber crews are briefed for a raid on England in January 1941, when Luftflotten 2 and 3 were operating from France and the Low Countries.*

Opposite page, below *The crew room of the US Navy's Air Transport Squadron VR-6 at Rhein-Main in West Germany on the day the blockade was lifted.*

these were used for night attacks. However, after the defeat of the daylight raiders in September, the Luftwaffe was forced to assign the majority of its bomber force to night attacks during October and November 1940.

The bombers available to the Luftwaffe for its night offensive were the 700 or so Heinkel He 111s, Dornier Do 17s, Do 215s and Junkers Ju 88s which had survived the Battle of Britain. They were divided amongst three major commands, Luftflotte 2 with its HQ at Brussels, Luftflotte 3 at Paris and Luftflotte 5 at Stavanger in

Norway. In order to improve the accuracy of navigation and bomb-aiming by night, the German bombers made use of the Knickebein radio beam system, and a special pathfinder unit, Kampfgruppe 100, was equipped with the more complex X-Gerät and Y-Gerät target-finding systems.

RAF Fighter Command's night-fighter force was poorly equipped to deal with the Luftwaffe at the start of the night Blitz. Six squadrons flew the Bristol Blenheim, fitted with the AI (airborne interception) Mk III radar. This early airborne radar was often temperamental, but even when its operators managed to pick up an enemy bomber the Blenheim had insufficient speed to catch it. The Boulton Paul Defiant turret-fighter, equipping two night-fighter squadrons, was faster, but it could not be fitted with the AI Mk III. Consequently the efforts of the RAF night fighters were largely ineffective and Anti-Aircraft Command's guns and searchlights were no more efficient. The only

brought the Blitz to an end, but the impending campaign against the Soviet Union. In May 1941 most of the Luftwaffe's bombers were ordered east.

BLOODY APRIL 1917

The month of April 1917 saw the heaviest losses of Royal Flying Corps aeroplanes in combat of the war, and has gone down in the history of air warfare as 'Bloody April'. March 1917 saw the strategic withdrawal of German ground forces on the Somme to the strongly fortified Hindenberg Line. While the French prepared to launch the ultimately disastrous Nivelle offensive on Aisne, British forces to the north were to engage the Germans to prevent them reinforcing the threatened sectors. The diversionary offensive was known as the Battle of Arras.

The strong German defences on the ground were matched in the air, although this was not immediately apparent. At the beginning of the Arras offensive in early April, the British air strength was 365 aeroplanes, one-third of them single-seat fighters, while the Germans mustered 195 aeroplanes, of which half were fighters. These figures did not show that the German Army Air Service had an appreciable advantage in the quality of its fighter aircraft. This was demonstrated in the two months before Arras, when the German *Jagdstaffeln* (fighter squadrons, usually abbreviated to *Jastas*) brought down 60 British aircraft for the loss of

defensive success was the efforts of No 80 (Signals) Wing to jam or interfere with the Luftwaffe radio bombing beams.

Although London was the Luftwaffe's main objective, the cities of Coventry, Birmingham, Wolverhampton and Liverpool were also heavily attacked. The bombing was directed in the main against the civilian population, 500 people being killed during the disastrous Coventry raid on the night of 14/15 November. London was set ablaze on the night of 29/30 December, with the fire services attempting to put out 1469 individual fires. However, when military targets could be identified at night they were attacked. The He 111s of III Gruppe, Kampfgeschwader 26 were fitted with Y-Gerät to enable them to bomb such targets as the Rolls-Royce engine factory at Hillingdon.

The night defences improved during the course of the Blitz, with the new Bristol Beaufighter night fighter, fitted with AI Mk IV radar, coming into service in increasing numbers. The first GCI (ground control of interception) radar station, able to direct fighters onto their targets, became operational in January 1941. However, when the Luftwaffe mounted the final attack of the Blitz on London (10/11 May 1941), only 14 of the 541 bombers despatched fell to the defenders. It was not the RAF night fighters that

Above *The aftermath of a night raid on London in 1941. Most of the damage and casualties were suffered by civilian rather than military targets.*

Right *Albatros DIII fighters of von Richthofen's Jasta 11. The Albatros DIII was largely responsible for the RFC's heavy losses in 'Bloody April'.*

Opposite page, below *A Hawker Hurricane fighter-bomber carries out an attack on a bridge on the Tiddim Road in 1944, during operations in support of the fighting at Imphal in India.*

in flying accidents) and 105 pilots and observers became casualties. The new Bristol F2A Fighters of No 48 Squadron RFC fared little better than the older aircraft (largely as a result of faulty tactics), for on 5 April four F2As from a formation of six were shot down. The RFC did enjoy occasional successes in air combat, notably by outstanding aces such as Captain Albert Ball and Captain Billy Bishop. Yet it is significant that both of them flew the French Nieuport 17 and in Ball's case also the new SE5 fighter. Far more successful was the German ace Manfred von Richthofen, who claimed 20 victories during the month.

In May 1917 the situation improved somewhat for the British, as greater numbers of new fighter aircraft began to reach the squadrons in France. The high casualties of Bloody April (1270 British aircraft lost between March and May 1917) were due in the main to inferior equipment. A major contributing factor, however, was Trenchard's insistence on pursuing the offensive at all costs, which gave the Germans the tactical initiative.

BURMA CAMPAIGN 1941–45

In December 1941, when Japan entered World War II, the air defence of Burma consisted of 16 Brewster Buffaloes of No 67 Squadron. They were soon reinforced by 21 Curtiss P-40s of the American Volunteer Group and the Burmese Volunteer Air Force contributed a number of light liaison aircraft. From 23 December onwards, Rangoon came under heavy air attack from Japanese aircraft based in Thailand. Although heavily outnumbered, the defenders fought back until the Japanese ground advance in March 1942 forced them to withdraw northwards. The fighter defences were reinforced early in 1942 by the Hawker Hurricanes of No 135 Squadron. RAF Bristol Blenheim bombers, together with Westland Lysander

only seven of their own fighters. The German success was largely due to the Albatros DIII, which had entered service at the beginning of 1917 and by the spring had fully or partly equipped all 37 *Jastas* at the front. The Albatros DIII had a maximum speed of 175km/h (109mph), service ceiling of 5500m (18,000ft) and endurance of two hours. In contrast the RFC had yet to complete the replacement of its elderly de Havilland DH2 fighter, which had first reached the front in April 1916, with the more modern Sopwith Pup and Bristol F2A Fighter. The DH2's top speed was only 150km/h (93mph), with a service ceiling of 4400m (14,500ft) and endurance of 2 hours 45 minutes. Some RFC squadrons flew the small and agile Nieuport 17, a French design with a top speed of 177km/h (110mph), service ceiling of 5000m (17,000ft) and endurance of 2 hours.

The technically inferior RFC fighters were required to operate offensively over enemy territory, in accordance with the tactical doctrine of the RFC commander in France, Major-General Sir Hugh Trenchard. In addition the prevailing westerly wind was in the Germans' favour, preventing many a damaged British machine from safely regaining its base. Consequently their losses were heavy from the outset. Between 4 and 8 April the British lost 75 aircraft in combat (plus 56

Top The debut of the Bristol Fighter in April 1917 was disastrous, because correct fighting tactics for this two-seat fighter had yet to be worked out.

Above The RFC's BE2e two-seat observation aircraft suffered heavily at the hands of the new German fighter aircraft in the spring of 1917.

army cooperation aircraft of the RAF and Indian Air Force (IAF), also reached Burma at this time. As British and Indian troops retreated north-westwards into India, the five squadrons of No 221 Group RAF did what they could to help the evacuation. Elderly RAF Vickers Valentia transport aircraft, together with commandeered civil airliners and USAAF Boeing B-17 bombers, all flew out civilian refugees and service casualties.

By mid-1942 the Japanese advance had halted on the borders of India and the Allies were beginning to build up their air strength. The US Tenth Air Force was formed in May and supplies of Hurricanes, Blenheims and various American aircraft supplied under the Lend-Lease scheme began to reach the RAF. In October the USAAF's Curtiss P-40s fought off Japanese air attacks on the bases in Assam and at the end of the year the RAF met a series of night attacks directed against Calcutta. The expansion of the Allied air forces continued throughout 1943 and in November of that year they were integrated within Air Command South-East Asia.

Top left The Vultee Vengeance dive-bomber served with Nos 45, 82, 84 and 110 Squadrons RAF in the Burma theatre and proved to be most effective in precision bombing attacks on Japanese positions.

Above left North American P-51 Mustangs of the 1st Air Commando Group USAAF flew in support of Wingate's Chindit forces operating behind Japanese lines in Burma.

Above right These Republic Thunderbolt fighters of the RAF's Third Tactical Air Force operated from Wangjing in Burma in 1944. Eventually 16 RAF squadrons operated this type in the South-East Asia Command.

The planned Allied offensive into Burma was forestalled early in 1944 by the Japanese attack in the Arakan and the siege of Imphal. During this offensive, RAF Douglas Dakotas and USAAF Curtiss C-46 Commandos carried out supply drops to forward units cut off by the Japanese. Close support was provided by Vultee Vengeance dive-bombers and Hurricane fighter-bombers of the RAF and IAF. The transport aircraft also reinforced Imphal by flying-in a complete division and by the end of June the siege was raised.

With the defeat of the Japanese offensive, the Allies were ready to begin the reoccupation of Burma. By this stage of the war, Japanese air activity was only sporadic and the Allies had such modern fighters as the Supermarine Spitfire and Republic Thunderbolt to maintain air superiority. Air resupply continued to be a key feature of the Burma air war and in October 1944 RAF and USAAF transport units were combined in the Combat Cargo Task Force. Heavy bombers – RAF Consolidated Liberators and USAAF Boeing B-29 Superfortresses – pounded Japanese communications behind the front lines and Rangoon was heavily

Above *A Curtiss C-46 Commando of the USAAF Air Transport Command's India-China Wing flies over the snow-capped Himalayas. The type was first used on the Hump route in April 1943.*

Below *An elephant helps workers to load a transport aircraft with petrol drums on an Indian airfield. The C-109 version of the Liberator was specially fitted as a tanker aircraft.*

crossed the mountains between Lashio and Kunming. By late 1941 a total of 13,600 tonnes (13,385 tons) of supplies were passing along this route every month.

With the Burma Road closed, the only means of maintaining a flow of supplies to China was by airlift over the Himalayas. The so-called 'Hump' air route had already been flown by Douglas DC-3s of the Chinese National Aviation Corporation as early as November 1940. However, the USAAF was slow to begin operations over this route. One problem was the lack of suitable airfields in Assam. Even when these had been provided by local labour hacking out dirt strips, they could only handle a limited number of aircraft and became flooded during the monsoon rains. An upsurge in the activity of the Tenth Air Force's Assam–Burma–China Ferry Command came in April 1942, as fuel was lifted to China for Lieutenant-Colonel Doolittle's carrier-borne bombing attack on Tokyo. The impressed civil DC-3s were soon diverted

attacked. Air support was also provided for Wingate's Chindits behind enemy lines – notably by Colonel Philip Cochran's 1st Air Commando, USAAF. By May 1945 the Allies had reoccupied Rangoon and for the remaining months of the war were engaged in mopping up groups of Japanese attemping to fight their way out of Burma.

CHINA AIRLIFT 1942–45

When the Japanese occupied Burma early in 1942 they cut the only overland supply route which the United States could use to ferry supplies to China. With the eastern seaports of China in Japanese hands, since 1938 the Americans had shipped supplies to Rangoon, from where they were carried by truck to China using the Burma Road – little more than a dirt track – which

Left *Boeing B-29 Superfortresses of the Twentieth Air Force flew over the Hump route carrying supplies of fuel and bombs to their own forward airfields in China.*

to the evacuation of Burma, however, and then expected reinforcements were held back for the North African theatre. Consequently supplies reaching China were reduced to a trickle, only 73 tonnes (72 tons) getting through in May 1942.

At the end of the year the situation improved when the USAAF's Air Transport Command became responsible for the China airlift. By the middle of March 1943 a force of 76 Douglas C-47s and 11 Consolidated C-87 Liberators (the transport version of the B-24 bomber) were lifting supplies over the Hump. The operational difficulties were tremendous. Navigation was a problem over the mountains, which were often enveloped in cloud. Storms could come with little warning and strong air currents eddied round the peaks. There was also the ever-present problem of icing, which reduced the aircraft's climb performance as it struggled to clear the peaks. In the spring of 1943 50 new Curtiss C-46 Commandos were supplied for the China airlift and, once the teething troubles of these aircraft were overcome, the monthly supply totals began to rise. In October 1943, 6123 tonnes (6026 tons) were airlifted.

Japanese fighters began to intercept the unarmed transport aircraft in October 1943, but they were countered by flying armed Consolidated B-24 Liberators over the route, while the vulnerable transports flew further to the north. In 1944 the four-engined Douglas C-54 began to operate over the Hump and the Boeing B-29s of the Twentieth Air Force began flying supplies to their advance bases in China. By the end of the year, the monthly supply figure totalled 27,200 tonnes (26,770 tons) and on average 250 transports were available every day. With the reoccupation of Burma, a less hazardous route could be flown over the mountains. When the airlift ended in November 1945, 589,670 tonnes (580,357 tons) of supplies had been lifted over the Hump in one of the most demanding air transport operations in history.

LES CIGOGNES 1916–18

The elite French fighter unit of World War I was Groupe de Chasse No 12, known as *Les Cigognes* because of the stork emblem which their aircraft carried. Originally, Les Cigognes were the pilots of

Left *Capitaine Armand Brocard was the first commander of Les Cigognes and the driving force behind the unit's considerable success.*

Right A group photograph of the pilots of Escadrille N3, the original Cigognes, taken in 1915. Georges Guynemer stands third from the left.

Below This Spad SVII of Escadrille SPA 3, piloted by Henri Vabatell, was forced down behind German lines on 16 August 1917 by fighters of Jagdstaffel 7.

Right When the He 51 biplane fighters of the Condor Legion were replaced in the fighter role by Messerschmitt Bf 109s, the Heinkels were relegated to ground-attack duties. The aircraft illustrated crash-landed after suffering battle damage.

Escadrille N3, commanded by Capitaine Armand Brocard. In February 1917 this unit (redesignated Escadrille SPA 3 on its re-equipment with the Spad SVII) was grouped together with SPA 26, SPA 73 and SPA 103 to form Groupe de Chasse No 12.

Escadrille N3 had begun to make its mark early in 1916. One of its most notable pilots was Georges Guynemer, who had gained eight victories by mid-March. Other successful pilots at this time were Albert Deullin, Alfred Heurtaux and René Dorme. Between March and August Les Cigognes shot down more than 70 enemy aeroplanes. In the summer of 1916 the Escadrille exchanged its Nieuport scouts for Spad SVIIs and over the next six months its pilots brought down 200 enemy aircraft.

With the formation of Groupe de Chasse No 12 in early 1917, the traditions of Les Cigognes were continued, as was the run of combat successes. Each Escadrille used the stork insignia, but it was depicted in different flying attitudes in the emblems of the four units. A fifth Escadrille, SPA 167, was later added to the *groupe*. In April 1917 René Fonck joined SPA 103 and made his name as the greatest French ace of World War I while with France's foremost fighter unit.

CONDOR LEGION 1936–39

The Condor Legion was a German volunteer corps which provided aircraft and crews to assist the Nationalist cause in the Spanish Civil War. Not only did the Legion help in bringing about a Nationalist victory, but it also gained much valuable experience in the conduct of air warfare that was to be exploited by Germany in the early years of World War II. German help to Franco began with the supply of Junkers Ju 52/3m transports and their crews, which were used to ferry troops and ammunition from Morocco to Spain in the crucial early weeks of the conflict.

The Condor Legion, under the command of General Hugo Sperrle, began operations in Spain during November 1936. It consisted of a bomber *Gruppe* (K/88) equipped with Ju52/3m trimotors, a fighter *Gruppe* (J/88) with Heinkel He 51s, a reconnaissance *Staffel* (A/88) flying He 70s and He 46s and a coastal reconnaissance *Staffel* (AS/88) equipped with He 59

less publicized actions against guerrilla forces. Generally the role of the aircraft has been subsidiary to ground operations, as guerrilla forces are best countered by small parties of highly trained troops turning the insurgent's own tactics of raid and ambush against him. However, in such a campaign the aircraft is useful in providing reconnaissance, rapid transportation of forces and rapid fire support in territory which is often inaccessible to artillery.

In Operation Firedog, the successful campaign against Communist terrorists in Malaya, no fewer than 31 different types of aircraft were involved at various times. They were flown by RAF, Royal Navy and Army pilots, and those of the Royal Australian Air Force and Royal New Zealand Air Force. The missions ranged from reconnaissance and leaflet-dropping sorties, through helicopter supply missions into remote jungle clearings, to bombings raids by Avro Lincoln heavy bombers. A total of 375,849 sorties were eventually flown and perhaps the most useful were the supply and casualty evacuation flights in support of jungle patrols. During the Mau Mau rebellion in Kenya (1952–6) armed reconnaissance flights were carried out by Harvard trainers converted to mount machine guns and light bombs. When heavier firepower was needed, Lincoln bombers were detached from the United Kingdom.

France's experience of counter-insurgency warfare, against the Viet Minh in Indochina, was less successful. However, the final defeat at Dien Bien Phu was a conventional battle rather than a guerrilla action. Nonetheless that disaster might have been averted if the French had possessed sufficient transport aircraft to keep their garrison fully supplied. France employed more effective aircraft and tactics in the war in Algeria (1954–62). In 1958 there were 746 aircraft and 97 helicopters supporting the ground forces in North Africa, including many piston-engined aircraft better suited to close-support work in a guerrilla war than the modern jets.

and He 60 floatplanes. The He 51 biplane fighters were found to be completely outclassed by the Soviet Polikarpov I-15 'Chatos' and I-16 'Ratas' flown by the Republicans and consequently were replaced as soon as possible with Messerschmitt Bf 109 monoplanes. Similarly the Ju 52/3ms gave way to He 111s, and Dornier Do 17s were used for reconnaissance. Dive-bombing operations were successfully carried out by small numbers of Ju 87s rushed to Spain for combat evaluation.

When the victorious Condor Legion returned to Germany in May 1939, it had learned valuable lessons in fighter tactics, based on the two-aircraft element of leader and wingman introduced by the rising young fighter pilot Werner Moelders. The Luftwaffe had tested most of the aircraft with which it would begin World War II under operational conditions and had begun to develop the highly effective use of the Ju 87 dive-bomber as flying artillery. Finally, many German airmen had been blooded in combat, for although the Condor Legion's strength was never more than 5000, some 30,000 officers and men had served with the Legion on short assignments.

Top The Luftwaffe used the Spanish Civil War as a testing ground for new equipment. This Heinkel He 111 bomber served with the Condor Legion's Kampfgruppe 88.

Above The introduction of the Messerschmitt Bf 109B into service with the Condor Legion at the end of 1936 redressed the balance in favour of the Nationalist air forces.

COUNTER-INSURGENCY

Aircraft have played an important role in the major counter-insurgency campaigns of the postwar years, notably in French Indochina, Malaya, Algeria, Kenya and Vietnam. They have also participated in numerous

DAMS RAID 1943

The Dams raid of 1943, carried out by the Avro Lancasters of No 617 Squadron, was one of the most meticulously planned operations of World War II. In March 1943 a special squadron was formed under the command of Wing Commander Guy Gibson specifically to attack the German dams which provided the industrial Ruhr with electrical power. They were the Möhne, Eder, Sorpe, Lister and Schwelme dams and a 'bouncing' bomb capable of breaching them had been designed by aeronautical engineer Barnes Wallis. Gibson's No 617 Squadron immediately began practising low flying and the special release technique required for Barnes Wallis's bomb.

On the evening of 16 May, 19 specially modified

Yet in Algeria, as in the later war in Southeast Asia, the enemy won a political victory rather than a military one.

The first American air units to be committed to the Vietnam War were transport, helicopter and light attack units, which assisted the South Vietnamese army in its campaign against the Viet Cong (VC) guerrillas. With the increasing involvement of American combat units, more attention was given to working out new tactics and operational techniques for the guerrilla war. The USAF's counter-insurgency aircraft were grouped into Air Commando Squadrons (later renamed Special Operations Squadrons). Such elderly types as the Douglas C-47, Douglas A-1 Skyraider and armed North American T-28 piston-engined trainers were widely used. More unusual air weapons included the Project Ranch Hand UC-123 Providers which were used to spray the jungle with defoliants, thus denying the VC cover for ambushes. Aircraft were also used for such psychological warfare tasks as leaflet-dropping and broadcasting propaganda messages to the VC. Foward air controllers in Cessna O-1 and O-2 and Rockwell OV-10 aircraft patrolled the countryside in search of VC activities, and the ubiquitous helicopter provided rapid transport and fire support for the troops on the ground.

Top *Fairchild UC-123 Providers spray defoliants over a swathe of forest in South Vietnam to deny cover to the Viet Cong.*

Above *A US Army Bell UH-1B 'Huey' helicopter fires a rocket into suspected Viet Cong positions. Armed UH-1s known as 'Hogs' accompanied the troop-carrying UH-1s which were known as 'Slicks'.*

Right (above and below) *Aerial reconnaissance photographs show the Möhne dam before the raid of 16 May and immediately afterwards, with water flooding through the breach and the level of the lake falling.*

Opposite page, bottom *Curtiss Helldivers are loaded with bombs on a French airfield in Indochina, prior to a sortie against the Viet Minh in April 1954.*

Lancasters took off from Scampton, Lincolnshire, and set course for the Ruhr. Four aircraft of the first wave were assigned the Sorpe dam as their target, but only the formation leader, Flight Lieutenant Joe McCarthy, succeeded in reaching it. In spite of the hazards of mist and the hills surrounding the dam, McCarthy dropped his bomb accurately. The dam wall held, however, and a second attack by Flight Sergeant Brown of the reserve force was no more successful.

Left *Air Marshal Sir Arthur Harris (left) and No 5 Group's commander, Air Vice-Marshal Sir Ralph Cochrane, look on as an intelligence officer debriefs Gibson's crew after the Dams raid.*

In the meantime Gibson led the main formation of nine Lancasters against the Möhne dam, which was breached after five aircraft had attacked. One Lancaster was lost en route to the target and a second crashed in flames near the dam. The three bombers which had still to release their weapons attacked and breached the Eder dam, while a reserve Lancaster attacked the Schwelme dam without breaching it. Thus, despite the long hours of preparation, and the individual heroism of the Dambusters, the operation was only a partial success.

DEFENCE OF DARWIN 1942–43

On 19 February 1942 a Japanese aircraft-carrier force delivered a heavy attack on Darwin in northern Australia, brushing aside the small defending force of five USAAF Curtiss P-40 Warhawks and causing severe bomb damage in the harbour area. Later the same day, land-based Mitsubishi G4M Betty bombers followed up the attack with a raid on Darwin's military airfield. The defence of northern Australia had suddenly become a matter of the utmost urgency.

Two early warning radar stations to cover Darwin were set up in March and additional Warhawk fighters were made available. Only sporadic attacks by Japanese land-based bombers were made in March and April and the defences accounted for 17 bombers and 11 fighters shot down during this period. At the end of May the British government agreed to release three squadrons of Spitfires for the defence of Darwin. These squadrons, comprising Nos 452 and 457 Squadrons of the RAAF and No 54 Squadron RAF, did not reach northern Australia until 1943. They were then formed into No 1 Fighter Wing RAAF under the command of Wing Commander C. R. Caldwell. The wing's first success came on 6 February 1943, when a Mitsubishi Ki-46 Dinah reconnaissance aircraft was shot down.

On 2 March 1943 the Spitfires intercepted a formation of 16 Japanese aircraft, shooting down three of

Below *Ground crew work on a Supermarine Spitfire Mk V of No 1 Fighter Wing, which was based in the Darwin area in 1943.*

Bottom *A Japanese air raid on 25 June 1942 completely gutted this hangar on the Royal Australian Air Force's airfield at Darwin.*

them. Another raid on 15 March led to a fierce dog-fight over Darwin, with seven enemy aircraft being shot down in exchange for four Spitfires lost. The CO of No 452 Squadron, Squadron Leader R. E. Thorold-Smith, was killed in this action. A strong force of 18 Japanese bombers, escorted by 27 fighters, attacked an unoccupied airfield on 2 May, mistaking it for one of the Spitfire bases. This misjudgment was not properly exploited by the defenders, as only one enemy bomber was shot down. Five Japanese fighters were claimed as destroyed in return for five Spitfires lost, but a further eight of the defending fighters had to make forced landings due to engine failure or running out of fuel. A much more decisive engagement was fought on 18 June, with nine bombers and five fighters being shot down by the Spitfires for the loss of only two of their number. It marked the end of serious Japanese raiding and thereafter only sporadic night attacks were made on Darwin.

DEFENCE OF THE REICH 1943–45

The all-out strategic bombing offensive against the German homeland by day and night was formally launched with the Allied Casablanca directive of January 1943. As RAF and USAAF attacks grew in strength during the course of the year, the Luftwaffe was forced to devote more resources to home defence than had hitherto been thought necessary. By March 1944 the Luftwaffe's air defence units were organized into five fighter divisions with a total strength of just over 1000 fighter aircraft. More than half of this total (558 aircraft) comprised single-engined Messerschmitt Bf 109 and Focke Wulf Fw 190 day fighters; there were also

Above *Wrecked Junkers Ju 188 bombers pictured at Leipzig. German aircraft production was one of the targets for Allied strategic bombing.*

Below *A Focke Wulf Fw 190 closes in for the kill on a crippled Boeing B-17, during a USAAF Eighth Air Force raid on Oschersleben in January 1944.*

92 twin-engined day fighters and some 350 single- and twin-engined night fighters. Although this force had to cover all of the Reich and portions of occupied Europe as well, and consequently was spread rather thin, it did have the advantages of good early warning and defence in depth by virtue of the occupied territories which surrounded the homeland.

By the autumn of 1944, however, the Reich's outer defensive perimeter was breached both in Italy and by the Allied invasion of France. USAAF daylight attacks were strongly escorted by long-range fighter aircraft and by night RAF Bomber Command, fully recovered from the débâcle over Nuremburg in March 1944, was back over German targets in strength. It was only at this late stage of the war that Hitler gave top priority to fighter production and to the concentration of the Luftwaffe's fighter force for the defence of the Reich. Overall command of these forces was exercised by General Joseph Schmid, a staff officer lacking in combat experience, but he was ably assisted by two highly experienced combat veterans, Adolf Galland as inspector of day fighters and Werner Streib as inspector of night fighters.

By the end of 1944 some new high-performance aircraft were coming into service, including the Heinkel He 219 night fighter, the Fw 190D piston-engined day fighter, the rocket-powered Me 163 interceptor and the Me 262 jet fighter. Yet the Luftwaffe fighters were consistently outnumbered and their airfields subject to attack by marauding Allied fighters both by day and night. Operation Bodenplatte, the Luftwaffe's New Year's Day fighter offensive, did little to improve the situation. The Allied aircraft destroyed on the ground were soon replaced, while only hastily trained and inexperienced newcomers could take the place of the 200 Luftwaffe fighter pilots lost that day. The seriousness of the situation called for desperate remedies. Rammkommando Elbe was formed to carry out ramming attacks on USAAF bomber formations, but its

DESERT WAR 1940–43

When Italy entered World War II in June 1940 the RAF in Egypt was greatly outnumbered by the Regia Aeronautica. Three squadrons of Gloster Gladiator biplane fighters and five squadrons of Bristol Blenheims were faced by 250 Italian fighters (Fiat CR32 and CR42 biplanes, plus some Macchi MC200 monoplanes) and 200 bombers. However, a series of aggressive fighter sweeps and bomber raids mounted by the outnumbered RAF helped to redress the balance and by the time that the Italians began to advance into Egypt reinforcements had reached the British. In December General Wavell counter-attacked and drove the Italians back into Libya. The ground fighting was accompanied by fierce air combats between RAF Hurricanes and Gladiators and the Italian fighter aircraft. By February 1941 all of Cyrenaica was in British hands.

German air and army reinforcements were rushed to North Africa and in March Rommel began to drive the British back. In the air, the British fighters were outclassed by the Luftwaffe's Messerschmitt Bf 109E and suffered serious losses. The German ascendancy in fighter combat allowed the Luftwaffe to use its Junkers Ju 87 Stuka dive-bombers to good effect. By late April the British were back on the Egyptian border and their 'Battle-axe' offensive in June failed to make progress.

only attempt at a massed attack ended in failure. The Heinkel He 162 jet fighter was to be mass-produced and flown into action by pilots recruited from the Hitler Youth – a plan which predictably came to nothing. Yet it was finally the shortage of the synthetic fuel that the Germans had been forced to manufacture that grounded the remnants of the Luftwaffe fighter force in the closing weeks of the war.

Above These Messerschmitt Bf 110G fighters carry WGr 21 rocket tubes underwing. These weapons were intended to break up the USAAF's bomber formations prior to an attack by single-seat fighters.

Left Bristol Bombay bomber-transport aircraft served in the Western Desert with No 216 Squadron from late 1939 until 1942.

American-supplied Curtiss Tomahawks gave the RAF a better fighter aircraft, but this advantage was quickly countered when the Germans introduced the improved Bf 109F and the Italians the new MC202.

By November 1941 the opposing fighter forces were more evenly matched, although the advantage still lay with the Axis. During the land battles of 1942, the RAF was able not only to engage the enemy

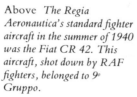

Above The Regia Aeronautica's standard fighter aircraft in the summer of 1940 was the Fiat CR 42. This aircraft, shot down by RAF fighters, belonged to 9° Gruppo.

fighters in the contest for command of the air, but also to help the hard-pressed soldiers with ground-attack sorties. Indeed the newly formed Desert Air Force became adept at army cooperation work, with most tactical fighters being adapted for fighter-bomber duties and the Hurricane Mk IID being used for 'tank-busting'. A welcome reinforcement of USAAF aircraft began to reach North Africa during 1942, including Curtiss P-40 fighters and North American B-25 Mitchell and Consolidated B-24 Liberator bombers. By the autumn of 1942 the balance had tipped and it was henceforth the Luftwaffe that was on the defensive.

The victory at El Alamein and the Allied 'Torch' landings in French Morocco and Algeria marked the beginning of the end for Axis forces in North Africa. As Allied air strength grew the Axis air forces weakened, although the veteran Luftwaffe fighter pilots continued to fight until the final evacuation. During the battle of Tunisia the Luftwaffe attempted to keep the Afrika Korps supplied by air and their trans-

Above left Luftwaffe armourers clean a Messerschmitt Bf 109F's 7·9mm machine guns on a desert airstrip. The Bf 109F carried two 7·9mm machine guns, plus a single 20mm canon.

Top right An RAF Supermarine Spitfire Mk V parked on an airfield in Tunisia. The first Spitfires to reach North Africa arrived in mid-1942.

Above right A Messerschmitt Me 323 six-engined transport aircraft comes under attack from a Martin Marauder while ferrying supplies from Italy to Tunisia in 1943.

port aircraft were decimated by Allied fighter attack. On 13 May 1943 the Axis forces finally capitulated.

DUNKIRK 1940

The evacuation of the British Expeditionary Force from Dunkirk in May/June 1940 presented the RAF with a particularly difficult operation in providing air cover over the embarkation port. Not only were their fighter squadrons outnumbered by the Luftwaffe – 236 RAF fighters were faced with 400 German fighters, 250 dive-bombers and 150 level bombers. They were also operating without the benefit of radar early-warning and the highly efficient command and control system that defended the United Kingdom. Therefore, the fighters could only patrol Dunkirk in the hope of meeting the enemy and it was inevitable that German

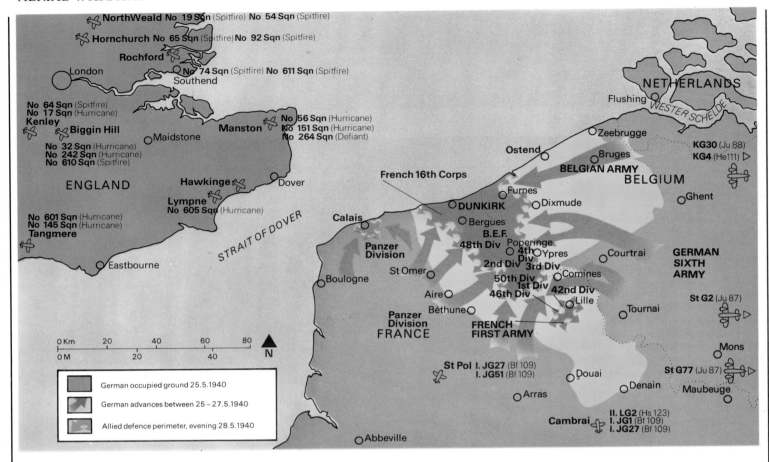

Airfield and division labels on map:

NorthWeald No 19 Sqn (Spitfire) No 54 Sqn (Spitfire)
Hornchurch No 65 Sqn (Spitfire) No 92 Sqn (Spitfire)
Rochford
London No 74 Sqn (Spitfire) No 611 Sqn (Spitfire)
Southend

No 64 Sqn (Spitfire)
No 17 Sqn (Hurricane)
Kenley
Biggin Hill Maidstone Manston No 56 Sqn (Hurricane)
No 32 Sqn (Hurricane) No 151 Sqn (Hurricane)
No 242 Sqn (Hurricane) No 264 Sqn (Defiant)
No 610 Sqn (Spitfire)

ENGLAND Hawkinge Dover
Lympne
No 605 Sqn (Hurricane)

No 601 Sqn (Hurricane)
No 145 Sqn (Hurricane)
Tangmere

Eastbourne

STRAIT OF DOVER

NETHERLANDS
Flushing WESTER SCHELDE

Zeebrugge
Ostend Bruges KG30 (Ju 88)
KG4 (He 111)

French 16th Corps BELGIAN ARMY BELGIUM

Furnes Ghent
DUNKIRK Dixmude
Calais Bergues
B.E.F.
Panzer 48th Div Poperinge
Division 4th Ypres Courtrai GERMAN
2nd Div Div SIXTH
St Omer 3rd Div Comines ARMY
Boulogne 50th Div
1st Div 42nd Div
Aire 46th Div Lille St G2 (Ju 87)
Béthune Tournai
Panzer
Division FRENCH Mons
FRANCE FIRST ARMY
St Pol I. JG27 (Bf 109) Douai St G77 (Ju 87)
I. JG51 (Bf 109) Denain Maubeuge
Arras
Cambrai II. LG2 (Hs 123)
I. JG1 (Bf 109)
Abbeville I. JG27 (Bf 109)

0 Km 20 40 60 80
0 M 20 40
N

German occupied ground 25.5.1940
German advances between 25 – 27.5.1940
Allied defence perimeter, evening 28.5.1940

bombers would get through to bomb the beaches. This was the answer to those embittered soldiers who later asked 'Where was the RAF at Dunkirk?'

The air fighting over the Calais–Dunkirk–Ostend region opened on 25 May with patrols and bomber escort missions by Hurricanes and Spitfires. It was the first time that the Spitfire fighters had gone into action against the Luftwaffe, as hitherto they had been held in reserve in the United Kingdom. On the following day the Spitfires of No 19 Squadron engaged a formation of Junkers Ju 87 Stukas escorted by Messerschmitt

Bf 109Es and shot down six Ju 87s and three of their escort for the loss of two Spitfires. The Boulton Paul Defiant turret-fighter also acquitted itself well on this day, claiming four Heinkel He 111 bombers and two Bf 109Es shot down. The Hurricane pilots of No 145 Squadron were not so fortunate, losing six of their aircraft. The balance sheet for the day totalled 41 German aircraft destroyed, set against 15 RAF fighters lost.

On 28 May cloudy conditions hampered air operations and this weather persisted on the following day, providing concealment for heavy German air raids on

Above The map shows the German advance on Dunkirk in May 1940 and the RAF and Luftwaffe airfields within range of the evacuation beaches.

Left A pall of smoke rises over Dunkirk from burning oil tanks in the town. This reconnaissance photograph shows the craters made by German bombs around the fuel storage depot.

Dunkirk. Five troopships were lost, but the evacuation continued at a tremendous pace. The outnumbered RAF began to suffer heavily, with 31 aircraft lost to the Germans' 21 on 31 May and 37 losses (31 of them fighters) to 29 on the following day. However, on 3 June there came a lull in the fighting as the Luftwaffe regrouped for the offensive against Paris. By the following evening the evacuation had ended. Dunkirk had cost Fighter Command 87 pilots killed or made prisoner-of-war – a loss which it could ill afford. Yet Churchill's claim that the RAF had won a victory over Dunkirk was not simply rhetoric – for all the losses it had inflicted, the Luftwaffe had not prevented the evacuation of the BEF.

Below The Boulton Paul Defiant Mk I turret-fighters of No 264 Squadron RAF were specially successful in combat over Dunkirk on 27 May 1940.

Above right Chesley Peterson was one of the Eagle Squadrons' most successful pilots, rising to command No 71 Squadron RAF and the USAAF's 4th Fighter Group.

Right The Hawker Hurricane Mk I fighters of No 71 Squadron, the first RAF Eagle Squadron, photographed in the spring of 1941 shortly after they became operational.

EAGLE SQUADRONS 1940–42

In September 1940 the first RAF Eagle Squadron, No 71 Squadron RAF, was formed to bring together the growing number of American fighter pilots serv-

ing as volunteers with the RAF. By this time there were already many Americans serving with RAF fighter squadrons, including Pilot Officer A. G. Donahue with No 64 Squadron and Pilot Officers V. C. Keogh, A. Mamedoff and E. Q. Tobin with No 609 Squadron. No 71 Squadron's first CO was an Englishman, Squadron Leader W. M. Churchill, who brought the unit to combat readiness in early 1941.

On 2 July Pilot Officer William Dunn scored No 71 Squadron's first confirmed victory, just beating Pilot Officer 'Gus' Daymond to the honour. Another successful Eagle pilot was Chesley Peterson, who became CO of the squadron in November 1941.

In May 1941 a second Eagle Squadron – No 121 Squadron – was formed. It first went into action in August and at the end of the year joined the North

Weald Wing. No 133 Squadron became the third Eagle Squadron in July 1941, and joined the Biggin Hill Wing in the following May. It took part in the great air battle over Dieppe in August 1942, but in a disastrous escort mission over Brittany the following month the Squadron lost 11 out of 12 brand-new Spitfire Mk IXs. This proved to be the Eagles' swansong, as in late September the squadrons were transferred to the USAAF to become the 4th Fighter Group.

EASTERN FRONT 1941–45

On 22 June 1941 Hitler launched the German armed forces on an invasion of the Soviet Union. The Luftwaffe's strength at the opening of the campaign comprised 680 fighters, 765 medium bombers, 317

Above *A wrecked Tupolev SB-2 bomber on the Eastern Front in 1941.*

dive-bombers, nearly 500 reconnaissance aircraft and 180 transports. The force was in the main well-equipped and combat-tested in the German offensives of 1939–40. The Soviet air force deployed some 9300 combat aircraft in the western USSR, according to German intelligence estimates. However, they were for the most part obsolescent machines, with few of

Above *The Polikarpov I-153 biplane fighter still served in substantial numbers in 1941.*

Below *This Messerschmitt Bf 109E-4/B fighter-bomber served with II Gruppe of Schlachtgeschwader 1 on the Eastern Front.*

the newer types such as MiG-1 and MiG-3 fighters or Petlyakov Pe-2 bombers in service. The Polikarpov I-153 biplane fighters and I–16 monoplanes were no match for the Luftwaffe's Messerschmitt Bf 109Es and Bf 109Fs. Similarly, the bomber force's Tupolev SB-2s and Ilyushin DB-3s were outmoded designs with little hope of operating effectively against the German air defences.

The Soviet air force was completely unprepared for the German assault and many aircraft were caught by the Luftwaffe lined up on their forward airfields. Under such conditions the Germans quickly established air superiority and on the first day of the offensive alone they claimed more than 1800 enemy aircraft destroyed. As Soviet air opposition along the front weakened, the Luftwaffe switched part of its bomber force to atttacks on Moscow and the Soviet fighter force used some of its best aircraft and pilots for the capital's defence. In general the Soviet airman was totally outclassed in training and in the quality of his equipment by his opponents, yet he continued to fight against daunting odds with the stubborn courage born of patriotism. By early August 1941 more than 4000 Soviet aircraft had been destroyed and it was not uncommon for the Luftwaffe fighter force to destroy 100 enemy aircraft in a single day.

As the German armies advanced into the Soviet Union, the Soviet fighters concentrated on the air defence of the major cities of Leningrad, Moscow, Stalingrad and Kiev. It was in defence of Moscow that the major battles were fought and as the Russian winter brought the German armies to a halt in December, the Soviet forces counter-attacked. Paratroop forces were dropped behind German lines in an attempt to encircle German forces, but the operation was not a success and airborne operations were little used during the remainder of the war. However, a substantial pocket of German troops was encircled by ground forces at Demyansk and Luftwaffe transport aircraft flying-in supplies were badly mauled by Soviet fighters and anti-aircraft guns before the German troops were relieved.

Early in 1942 the Germans halted the Soviet counter-offensive and stalemate ensued for the remaining winter months. The respite was used by the Soviet Union to reorganize her air forces into air armies. An air army typically comprised some 300 aircraft (although, particularly later in the war, they could be much stronger). Each air army supported an army group on the ground and was made up of air divisions specializing in the fighter, ground-attack or bomber roles. Another innovation of this period was the institution of elite guards air regiments, which usually

Above The Henschel Hs 129 anti-tank aircraft, armed with a 75mm cannon, proved to be especially effective against Soviet heavy tanks and it played a notable part in the Battle of Kursk in July 1943.

Below The two-seat Ilyushin Il-2m3 was one of the most effective Soviet ground attack aircraft, having especially good armour protection for its crew.

flew the most up-to-date aircraft. Although in general the quality of Soviet aircraft and pilot training remained inferior to that of the Luftwaffe, the situation did improve in 1942. Lend-Lease supplies of Allied aircraft, such as the Hawker Hurricane and Bell P-39 Airacobra fighters, began to reach the Soviet air regiments (eventually some 20,000 Lend-Lease aircraft were despatched). Furthermore by early 1942 the Soviet Union's own aircraft industry was producing around 1000 aircraft per month.

In the spring of 1942 the German army resumed its offensive and although Moscow and Leningrad held out, in the south the Germans occupied the Crimea and large areas of the Caucasus, before their advance halted at Stalingrad. The Soviet air force was husbanding its resources for a second winter counter-offensive and so made little impression on the advancing Germans. However, the Ilyushin Il-2 Shturmoviks and Polikarpov Po-2 biplane bombers used for night nuisance raids caused the Germans some damage. In November 1942 the Soviet armies launched their counter-offensive at Stalingrad and the German 6th Army was encircled. The Luftwaffe's attempt to keep this force supplied by air proved to be a costly failure and 488 transport aircraft were lost during Soviet fighter attacks and bombing of the transports' airfields. Early in February the 6th Army surrendered.

The decisive event of 1943 on the Eastern Front was the great tank battle of Kursk. The German offensive was expected by the Soviet commanders, who had assembled a force of more than 2500 aircraft to take part in this trial of strength. The fighting began on 5 July and the Luftwaffe fighter arm soon demonstrated that it was far from being a spent force, claiming 432 victories on that day alone. However, the Luftwaffe began to be worn down by the sheer numbers of Soviet aircraft thrown against it. The Soviet armies successfully counter-attacked and were well supported by Il-2 ground-attack aircraft. By November they had reoccupied Kiev and in the spring of 1944 Soviet forces began the reconquest of the Crimea.

The Soviet air force rapidly expanded during 1944 from a strength of some 8500 aircraft at the beginning

ELECTRONIC COUNTER-MEASURES

The increasing use of radar and radio aids to direct and control offensive air operations during World War II led to the widespread use of electronic counter-measures (ECM) in that conflict. Attempts at radio and radar jamming and deception were met with electronic counter-countermeasures (ECCM) and thus began the thrust and counterthrust of electronic warfare which has been a feature of air operations ever since. The earliest use of ECM techniques was by the RAF against the Luftwaffe's *Knickebein* (and later X-Gerät and Y-Gerät) radio beam bombing and navigation aids during the night Blitz of 1940–1. As well as attempting to jam these beams, the RAF's No 80 (Signals) Wing used deception tactics against radio navigation beacons and on several occasions Luftwaffe aircraft were tricked into landing in Britain by this means.

As the RAF's night-bomber offensive gathered strength, ECM tactics were increasingly employed against the German defences. One of the most effective ECM devices was found to be strips of radar-reflective foil, codenamed Window. (It remains in use to this day in modified form, but is now more usually referred

of the year to 15,500 in January 1945. This expansion took place despite the high attrition rate (estimated at 2700 aircraft per month) which the Soviets suffered during the last phase of the war. During this period the Soviet armies had pushed the Germans back to their own borders and for the final assault on Berlin the ground troops were supported by 7500 aircraft drawn from four air armies. The Luftwaffe, which by this time was hopelessly outnumbered, fought on until the end.

Above The Lavochkin La-5, which entered Soviet service later in 1942, was a rugged, all-wooden fighter with especially good performance at low and medium altitudes.

Below The Avro Canada CF-100 Canucks of No 414 Squadron, Canadian Armed Forces, were used to fly ECM missions on training exercises.

to by its American name, Chaff.) Window was first used during Bomber Command's raid on Hamburg on the night of 24/25 July 1943. The attacking bombers dropped 92 million strips of Window, effectively blinding the German radars. As a result the night defence was totally disorientated and the target was devastated. Countermeasures were swiftly introduced, however, notably the Luftwaffe's *Wilde Sau* (Wild Boar) tactics. These made use of large numbers of free-hunting fighters operating against the RAF bomber stream without radar control from the ground. The Luftwaffe too was adept at ECM and one of its cleverest devices (codenamed Flensburg) enabled a night fighter to home onto the RAF bombers' Monica tail-warning radar. Thus a device intended to protect the bomber was neatly exploited to effect its destruction.

During the conflict in Southeast Asia (1965–72), American warplanes operating over North Vietnam made extensive use of ECM against the North Vietnamese defences. Specialized ECM escort aircraft (such as the USAF's Douglas EB-66 Destroyer and the US Navy's Grumman EA-6B Prowler) accompanied strike forces and additional jamming was provided by ECM pods fitted to the tactical fighters. Often chaff clouds would be sown over a target to confuse the defence radars and every aircraft had a radar warning receiver to alert the crew to the presence of enemy radar-directed defences. Specialized defence suppression aircraft, codenamed Wild Weasels, would attack surface-to-air missiles and anti-aircraft gun sites,

Top The US Navy's standard electronic warfare aircraft is the Grumman EA-6B Prowler.

Above A Martin EB-57E used by the US until early 1982 for training in dealing with ECM jamming.

Below Air defence of the Falklands task force was provided by Sea Harriers of the Fleet Air Arm, here armed with Sidewinder missiles.

and anti-radiation missiles were developed, which would home onto the source of a radar emission. Electronic warfare continues to play an important part in present-day air forces' training for war.

FALKLANDS CONFLICT 1982

Argentina's occupation of the Falkland Islands at the beginning of April 1982 led to a large-scale military operation by Britain to reoccupy the territory. The difficulties of mounting an amphibious assault at a distance of over 12,000km (8000 miles) from the home base were immense and were compounded by the severe weather of a South Atlantic winter. However, a naval task force of over 100 ships was assembled and sailed southwards. The air defence for this force was provided by the BAe Sea Harriers of Nos 800, 801, and 899 Squadrons Fleet Air Arm, later supplemented

As the ships of the task force steamed into the South Atlantic RAF Lockheed Hercules and BAe VC10 transport aircraft flew personnel and supplies into Wideawake airfield on Ascension Island, midway between Britain and the Falklands. It was from this base that RAF Hawker Siddeley Vulcan bombers mounted five attacks on the Falklands between 1 May and 12 June. Refuelled en route by Victor tankers, the bombers atacked the Port Stanley airfield and Argentine radars. Another important support mission flown from Ascension was the maritime patrol sorties carried out by No 18 Group's BAe Nimrods, which also required in-flight refuelling. Among the hasty modifications to RAF aircraft made necessary by the Falklands conflict was the fitting of refuelling probes to Hercules and Nimrod aircraft and the conversion of a number of Vulcans and Hercules as tanker aircraft.

by further Sea Harriers of the specially formed No 809 Squadron. The Fleet Air Arm also provided a force of shipborne helicopters, including Sikorsky Sea King, Westland Lynx and Wessex types, which could perform anti-submarine, anti-surface ship, troop transport and resupply missions.

The Argentine air force and naval air arm was equipped with some 200 combat aircraft and helicopters, including some 40 Dassault Mirage III fighters (or similar Mirage 5 and Israel Aircraft Industries Dagger fighters), over 60 McDonnell Douglas A-4 Skyhawk attack aircraft, five BAe Canberra bombers and the same number of Dassault Super Etendard naval strike aircraft armed with the sea-skimming Exocet anti-shipping missile. The Mach 2 Mirages had a considerably better performance than the Mach 0.97 Sea Harriers, but this advantage could not be properly exploited over the Falklands as the Mirages were operating at extreme range from their bases in Argentina. Only lower performance attack aircraft such as the turboprop FMA Pucará and the naval Aermacchi MB339 operated from airfields on the Falklands.

Above A Mirage III of the Argentine Air Force. The most effective Argentine combat aircraft during the Falklands conflict were Mirage IIIs and the similar Israel Aircraft Industry's Daggers.

Right A Royal Navy frigate comes under attack from a Mirage III fighter-bomber during the landings at San Carlos Water.

Below Army Air Corps Scout helicopter, fitted with a casualty pannier. Army Air Corps, RAF and Fleet Air Arm helicopters were an invaluable aid to mobility over the difficult terrain of the Falklands.

As the naval task force began operations against the Argentine forces in the Falklands at the beginning of May, the Royal Navy ships came under increasingly heavy air attack. Sea Harriers flew combat air patrols to intercept the attackers and also attacked Argentine forces ashore. On 4 May the Argentine naval air arm scored a significant success when an Exocet missile launched from a Super Etendard sank the destroyer HMS *Sheffield*. This loss highlighted the task force's lack of an airborne early warning aircraft, which would have given the Sea Harriers sufficient warning of attack to allow them to intercept. However, shipborne and helicopter-mounted electronic countermeasures were employed against Exocets with some success, although the container ship *Atlantic Conveyor* was also sunk by these missiles on 25 May. Bomb and rocket attacks by Skyhawk and Dagger aircraft sunk the frigates HMS *Ardent* and HMS *Antelope*, and the destroyer HMS *Coventry*. These attacks were pressed home with great courage in the face of intense fire from

anti-aircraft guns and surface-to-air missiles (SAMs). Over 40 victories were claimed by British SAMs and the Sea Harrier accounted for a further 20 enemy aircraft. After 8 June heavy losses and bad weather restricted Argentine bombing missions, although sporadic attacks continued until the final surrender on 14 June.

Once British forces were ashore at San Carlos on 21 May they were supported by RAF Harrier GR Mk 3s, operating from HMS *Hermes* and HMS *Invincible* until a shore base could be established on 5 June. Fleet Air Arm Wessex and Sea King helicopters were used to lift troops and supplies, supplementing the efforts of the sole RAF Boeing-Vertol Chinook to survive the loss of the *Atlantic Conveyor*. Aérospatiale

Above RAF Victor K Mk 2 tanker aircraft parked on Wideawake Airfield, Ascension Island, during the Falklands conflict.

Below An RAF Hercules transport aircraft refuels from a Hercules tanker aircraft over the South Atlantic. Hercules aircraft were hastily converted for inflight refuelling.

Gazelle helicopters of the Royal Marine and Army Air Corps performed scouting, liaison, casualty evacuation and artillery spotting missions. Scout helicopters armed with SS-11 anti-tank missiles took a more active role, attacking Argentine field fortifications. When Argentine forces on the Falklands finally surrendered on 14 June, the British forces had lost six Sea Harriers, four Harriers and 23 helicopters, the majority of them in accidents rather than to enemy action. Surprisingly, in view of the Sea Harrier's claim of 20 enemy aircraft destroyed in the air, none of the Harrier or Sea Harrier losses occurred in air combat. The establishment of such air superiority by the British was a major factor in their victory in the South Atlantic conflict.

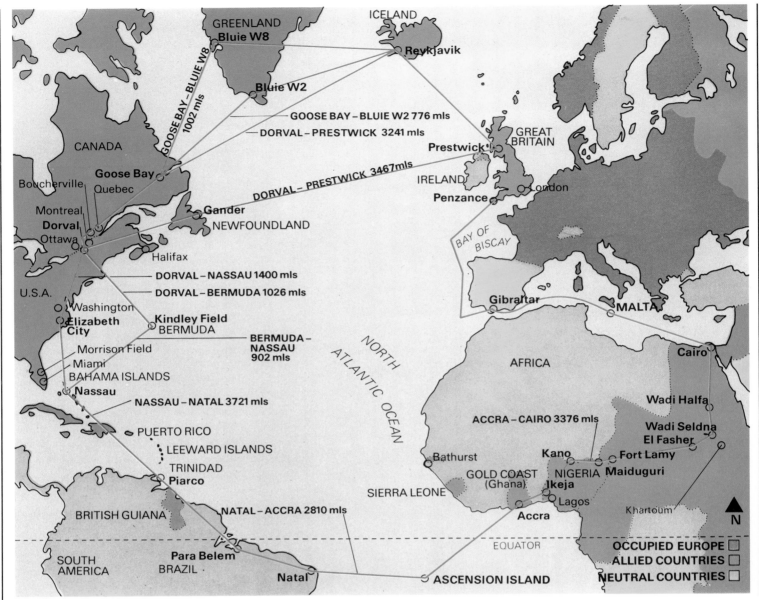

Above *A map illustrating the ferry routes flown across the North and South Atlantic by Allied ferry pilots in World War II.*

Opposite top *During World War II Consolidated Liberators of the RAF Return Ferry Service operated between the United Kingdom and Canada, carrying ferry aircrew and priority passengers.*

Opposite centre *New Spitfire Mk IXs await collection by ferry pilots at the Castle Bromwich factory.*

Right *Ferry pilots of the Air Transport Auxiliary prepare to board the Avro Anson air taxi that will fly them from their base to the aircraft factory.*

FERRY OPERATIONS

The delivery of military aircraft from their factories or storage depots to the operational units in the field was often most efficiently carried out by ferrying. This avoided the complicated and time-consuming process of disassembling the machine, packing it and then reassembling it on arrival. During World War I ferrying was the usual method of transferring replacement aircraft to the Royal Flying Corps in France. The machines were flown either by regular ferry pilots, or by pilots returning to France after a period of home leave. Aircraft Acceptance Parks would receive new aircraft and they would then be ferried to the Aircraft Depots at St Omer and Candas in France.

This method of distribution was continued during World War II, although the distances involved were

often considerably greater than the flight across the English Channel. Within the United Kingdom, ferrying was carried out by the Air Transport Auxiliary, which employed men and women pilots who were ineligible for service with the RAF. At its peak strength in 1944 the ATA comprised 658 pilots, over 100 flight engineers and some 3000 ground staff. Ferry pools were set up at 14 airfields from which the pilots operated a delivery service of aircraft from factories to maintenance or storage units. Between the outbreak of war and November 1945 the ATA made 308,567 ferry flights.

When Italy's entry into World War II threatened to close the Mediterranean to Allied convoys in June 1940, a ferry route was opened from Takoradi in the Gold Coast (now Ghana) to Egypt. American-supplied aircraft were flown from the United States to South America and from there across the South Atlantic, staging through Ascension Island, to destinations in Africa and the Middle East. Lend-Lease aircraft for the Soviet Union were ferried to Abadan in Iran, or to Ladd Field in Alaska, where Soviet ferry pilots took them over. Perhaps the most demanding ferry route was that over the North Atlantic, opened in November 1940 by the Atlantic Ferry Organization (later to be absorbed by RAF Ferry Command). These flights were made from Goose Bay, Newfoundland, via Greenland and Iceland, to Prestwick in Scotland. The longer-range aircraft, such as the Consolidated B-24 Liberator, flew direct from Dorval, Quebec, to Prestwick. In 1943 the USAAF began flying single-engined fighters across the North Atlantic. The Ferrying Division of the USAAF's Air Transport Command also operated over the Pacific, opening a route to Australia later in 1941.

FIGHTER TACTICS

Fighter tactics originated in 1915, with the development of such specialized fighter aircraft as the British de Havilland DH2 and the German Fokker Eindecker. At first fighter pilots operated alone, hunting out two-seater observation aircraft which they were then able to despatch with relative ease, thanks to their superior performance and the advantages of a fixed forward-firing machine gun armament. The German ace Max Immelmann introduced a refinement into the tactics of air combat with his Immelmann turn. He would dive onto a victim, open fire, then pull up and execute a half-roll off the top of a loop – thus positioning his fighter for a diving attack from the opposite direction.

Another German air ace and fighter tactician, Oswald Boelcke, was responsible for the formation of specialized fighter squadrons. The first of these *Jagdstaffeln* (*Jastas*) were formed in the summer of 1916 and thereafter air combats involved formations rather than individual aircraft. Boelcke's protégé, Manfred von Richthofen, increased the size of such formations when

Above *The Fokker Eindecker was the first really successful fighter aircraft in history, and its pilots, notably Oswald Boelcke and Max Immelmann, laid the foundations of the science of air fighting.*

Left *An Albatros Scout makes use of the cover provided by the sun's glare in launching his attack on a Bristol F2B Fighter (foreground).*

he grouped together four *Jastas* to form Jagdegeschwader I in June 1917. The French followed suit, with the formation of *groupes de chasse*, but Britain only grouped fighter squadrons together on an *ad hoc* basis.

Certain basic rules of air fighting emerged from World War I. The advantages of suprise and superior height when making an attack, the need for accurate gunnery, preferably at close range, and the necessity of operating as a team and maintaining a good look-out throughout a patrol were all important factors in the outcome of a combat. So too, quite obviously, was the quality of the aircraft flown and its pilot's training and experience.

At the beginning of World War II the RAF still flew the V-shaped 'vic' formation of three fighters inherited from World War I and made use of ponderous attack sequences worked out in pre-war air exercises against

unescorted bombers. Not so the Germans, who had the great advantage of recent combat experience during the Spanish Civil War. They flew in a four-aircraft *Schwarm*, made up of two-aircraft sections of leader and wingman. The leader did the fighting, while his wingman covered his vulnerable tail. The RAF was quick to see the advantage of the four-aircraft formation, which allowed a good all-round look-out to be kept, and adopted it itself as the 'finger four' formation.

The higher speeds of jet fighters has tended to reduce the size of formations, although the two-aircraft element of leader and wingman remains valid to this day. In the air fighting over North Vietnam between USAF and US Navy McDonnell Douglas F-4 Phantoms and North Vietnamese MiG-17s, MiG-19s, and MiG-21s, various manoeuvres were used in combat for the first

Right *These Messerschmitt Bf 109Gs illustrate the basic fighting formation of leader and wingman, evolved by the Luftwaffe in the Spanish Civil War and still in use today.*

Below *Italian air force Fiat G91Y fighters fly in tactical formation, with each aircraft able to cover the blind spots of the others.*

Bottom *The Avro 504s prepare to take off from the parade ground at Belfort prior to the Friedrichshafen raid.*

time. One example is the scissors, in which each aircraft rolls around the other seeking to reach its vulnerable 'six o'clock' position. Air-to-air missiles enable the modern fighter to knock down its opponent before the two can close in a dogfight. However, the need to identify the target positively as hostile often means that jet fighters must close to visual range.

FRIEDRICHS-HAFEN RAID 1914

In November 1914 three Avro 504s of the Royal Naval Air Service bombed the airship sheds at Friedrichshafen on Lake Constance in one of the earliest bombing raids in the history of air warfare. The Admiralty, which was responsible for the air defence of the United Kingdom at that time, decided to attack the German airships at their bases and thus remove a threat to the British homeland. Lieutenant Noel Pemberton-Billing

RNVR was ordered to Belgium to prepare the attack on Friedrichshafen. He secured the use of the parade ground at Belfort as a landing ground and then planned the 200km (125-mile) flight to the target.

On 13 November four Avro 504s arrived at Belfort together with their pilots and ground crew. Bad weather then intervened, but on 21 November the aircraft were prepared for take-off and each loaded with four 9kg (20lb) Hales bombs. Squadron Commander E. F. Briggs was the first to take off, followed at five-minute intervals by Flight Commander J. T. Babbington and Flight Lieutenant Sidney Sippe. The fourth aircraft had to abandon the mission. Briggs succeeded in releasing his bombs over the target, but was wounded by ground-fire, forced to land and became a prisoner-of-war. Babbington too was forced down after his attack, but not until he had reached friendly territory. Only Sippe landed safely back at Belfort. Damage to the airship sheds was slight, although the Germans were sufficiently alarmed to increase the base's anti-aircraft defences.

GREECE 1940–41

In October 1940 Italy launched an assault on Greece, operating from bases in Albania which she had occupied in April 1939. The attack was supported by some 190 aircraft, the bulk of them Fiat CR32, CR42 and G50 fighters, but including a force of 50 Savoia Marchetti SM79 and Fiat BR20 bombers. Opposed to the Regia Aeronautica were four Greek fighter squadrons equipped with 36 PZL P-24F and 9 Bloch

MB151 fighters, three bomber squadrons flying the Bristol Blenheim and four army support squadrons with Henschel Hs 126s, Breguet 19s and Potez 25s.

The Greeks defended their airspace bravely and in November they were reinforced by three RAF Bristol Blenheim squadrons (Nos 30, 84 and 211) and the Gloster Gladiators of Nos 33 and 80 Squadrons RAF. Further Gladiators were supplied to equip a Greek squadron. Poor weather hampered air operations throughout the winter months, but the RAF Gladiator squadrons saw action in November and December, claiming 29 victories during this period for the loss of five British fighters. The Blenheims too had suffered casualties, five aircraft being lost. Air activity intensified during February, with fighter sweeps and bombing raids over Albania. By this time the first Hawker Hurricanes had reached Greece and these went into action on 20 February. On that day British and Greek fighters claimed 20 enemy aircraft destroyed for no loss to themselves. On 28 February the RAF fighter

explosion caused extensive damage to the port. The German army's advance into Greece was rapid and on 19 April the surviving RAF aircraft were withdrawn to the Athens area. British aircraft losses had been heavy and the Greek air force had been virtually wiped out. On 20 April a big air battle was fought over Athens between Luftwaffe Ju 88s, Messerschmitt Bf 110s and Bf 109s and the 15 remaining RAF Hurricanes. Five RAF pilots were shot down, including the South African ace Pat Pattle, in return for 14 enemy aircraft destroyed. Within a week the surviving aircraft were withdrawn to Crete, where they made a last stubborn stand against the German airborne assault in May.

HIROSHIMA 1945

The atomic bomb developed in the United States under Project Manhattan was first used against the Japanese city of Hiroshima in August 1945. The first bomb, known as 'Little Boy', weighed some 4535kg (10,000lb) and so only the Boeing B-29 Superfortress was capable of carrying it from the US air bases in the Mariana Islands to the Japanese homeland. As construction of the weapon proceeded during the summer of 1944, a B-29 unit was selected for special training in its delivery. This was the 393rd Bomb Squadron, which was separated from its parent 504th Bomb Group and moved to Wendover Air Force Base, Utah. Under the command of Colonel Paul W. Tibbets, an Eighth Air Force veteran, the unit's B-29s began training flights which involved the dropping of a 4535kg (10,000lb) practice bomb from a height of 9,150m (30,000ft). The crews, who did not at this stage know the nature of their mission, were told to practise a sharp diving turn away from the target after bomb release, so that they would be 8km (5 miles) away from the bomb when it detonated.

squadrons, reinforced by No 112 Squadron's Gladiators, accounted for no fewer than 27 Italian aircraft for the loss of only one Gladiator, whose pilot parachuted to safety.

In March 1941 the situation altered dramatically, with Germany's entry into the Balkans War. Supporting the German army as it entered Bulgaria were the 1200 warplanes of Luftflotte 4. In April they were used ruthlessly in a series of devastating bombing raids against Belgrade and at the same time German troops attacked Greece from their bases in Bulgaria. On 6 April the Junkers Ju 88s of III Gruppe, Kampfgeschwader 30, led by Hauptmann Hajo Herrmann, bombed an ammunition ship in Piraeus harbour and its

Above *RAF pilots pictured during the Greek campaign. RAF Hurricane and Gladiator fighters and Blenheim bombers were heavily engaged in the defence of Greece.*

Below *Hauptmann Hajo Herrmann, pictured (right) in the cockpit of his Junkers Ju 88A, led the attack on Piraeus harbour on 6 April 1941 which devastated the port.*

Above *The atomic bombing of Hiroshima and Nagasaki was carried out by B-29 Superfortresses of the 509th Composite Group. Enola Gay (illustrated) made the Hiroshima attack.*

Left *The atomic bomb 'Little Boy' devastated some 13sq. km (5sq. miles) of Hiroshima when it detonated over the city on 6 August 1945.*

In December 1944 the 509th Composite Group was activated under Tibbet's command for the Hiroshima mission. The group had its own transport unit, the Douglas C-54–equipped 320th Troop Carrier Squadron, and in April 1945 it moved to North Field, Tinian, in the Marianas. In July the B-29s began to practise their atom bomb delivery tactics, using conventional bombs, over Japanese targets. All was ready for the attack on Hiroshima by 6 August and Tibbet's B-29 *Enola Gay* loaded with 'Little Boy' took off at 0245 hours, preceded by three B-29s which would report on the weather along the route. The target was reached at 0815 hours and the bomb detonated at a height of 580m (1900ft) above the ground. The explosion, equivalent to that of 20,000 tonnes of TNT, caused 129,000 casualties. Yet, despite this devastation, Japan showed no signs of surrendering. Consequently a second bomb, known as 'Fat Man', was released over Nagasaki on 9 August by Major Charles Sweeney's B-29 *Bock's Car*. The 95,000 casualties caused by this second weapon finally led Japan to capitulate.

INDEPENDENT FORCE RAF 1918

In May 1918 the British Air Ministry decided to form a bombing force to attack German industrial and population centres and the Independent Force, RAF, came into existence under the command of Major-General Sir Hugh Trenchard in the following month. It was by no means the first attempt to carry out strategic bombing raids on Germany. It was realized early in the war that the sources of the enemy's military power would provide as fruitful a target for bomber aircraft as his forces in the field. However, the equipment available to attack such targets was woefully inadequate. Only isolated raids on strategic targets were made in 1914–15, with negligible effect. In the spring of 1916 the RNAS formed No 3 Wing, which carried out bombing raids on German industrial towns in cooperation with French bombers. In June 1917, however, the demands of the army for air support led to No 3 Wing's disbandment.

In the autumn of 1917 the Royal Flying Corps formed No 41 Wing for strategic bombing, and in the following year it was expanded into the five-squadron strong VIII Brigade RFC. It was this brigade, operating from bases in eastern France, that formed the basis for the Independent Force, and four additional bomber squadrons were added to its strength in August. The

force met with heavy opposition from German anti-aircraft guns and interceptor aircraft during its raids in daylight against such targets as Cologne, Mannheim, Coblenz and Stuttgart. A squadron of Sopwith Camel fighters was assigned to the force in September, but this aircraft lacked the range to escort the bombers throughout their missions. Consequently losses were heavy.

Handley Page O/100 and O/400 heavy bombers operated by night, as did the elderly FE2bs of No 100

Right A map showing the Independent Force's area of operations.

Far right DH 4 bombers of No 55 Squadron made the Royal Flying Corps' first raid on Mannheim in December 1917.

Below Handley Page O/400 bombers of the Independent Force dropped some 350 tons of bombs on targets in Germany during the last two months of World War I.

Squadron. The heaviest monthly bomb-load delivered by an Independent Force squadron was the 38 tons dropped by the Handley Pages of No 216 Squadron in September 1918. Although the scale of such attacks was minuscule in comparison with the great bomber offensives of World War II and results of individual raids were often disappointing, the efforts of the Independent Force were not totally in vain. German

morale suffered from attacks on the homeland and guns and fighter aircraft were diverted from the front to provide defences. The intensity with which the Independent Force's raids were contested is shown by the casualties suffered. In more than 500 raids, 458 aircraft were lost in action or in accidents and 439 aircrew were killed, injured or taken prisoner.

Above   The DH9A two-seat day bombers of No 110 Squadron joined the Independent Force in September 1918 and flew their first bombing raid against Metz on the 14th of that month.

INTRUDER OPERATIONS

Intruder operations is the name given to the tactic whereby aircraft penetrate enemy airspace in search of targets of opportunity, rather than pre-briefed objectives. In World War II RAF Fighter Command made extensive use of this type of operation to harass German forces in occupied Europe. As early as 1940, Bristol Blenheim night fighters were despatched to patrol over enemy airfields in France in the hope of destroying returning bombers. By the following year the first

Right   No 23 Squadron RAF operated DH Mosquito Mk II intruders from Malta, flying intruder sorties over Sicily and the Italian mainland.

Left   The Douglas Boston Mk III night intruder aircraft of No 418 Squadron RCAF operated from March 1942 until March 1943, when the squadron re-equipped with DH Mosquitoes.

specialized night intruder unit, No 23 Squadron, was flying Douglas Havocs in this role. The Luftwaffe too was operating at night over British airfields, using the Junkers Ju 88s of I Gruppe, Nachtjagdgeschwader 1. However, on the orders of Hitler, who failed to see the value of night intruder operations, these missions had ceased by the time Bomber Command's night offensive was gathering strength. Consequently, an excellent opportunity of attacking the RAF bombers was neglected.

Intruder operations by day were generally carried out by pairs of RAF fighters operating at low level in cloudy conditions. These 'Rhubarb' operations began in early 1941 and usually attacked transport targets such as military trucks and locomotives. Luftwaffe fighter-bombers carried out hit-and-run raids

on the south coast of England in 1943, more as a gesture of reprisal for raids on Germany than with serious military intent. At the same time RAF intruder operations expanded with the introduction of day and night 'Ranger' sorties, flown by de Havilland Mosquitoes, Bristol Beaufighters and North American Mustangs. These covered much of occupied Europe and forced the Luftwaffe to keep widespread fighter defences.

As the Allied bomber offensives gathered weight in 1944, intruder raids were mounted on enemy airfields to hamper the defence effort. Beaufighter and Mosquito night fighters sought out enemy night-fighter airfields as part of No 100 Group's bomber support operations. Similarly, USAAF P-51 Mustangs and Republic P-47 Thunderbolts covered the day fighters' airfields in free-ranging sweeps intended to bring the Luftwaffe to battle wherever it could be found.

On the Eastern Front the Soviet air force was adept at night raiding behind enemy lines, using obsolete

The specialized night intruder version of the English Electric Canberra, the B (I) Mk 8, entered RAF service in 1956.

Polikarpov Po-2 and R-5 biplanes for these missions. So successful were they that the Luftwaffe followed suit and formed their own *Nachtschlachtgruppe* equipped with elderly biplanes. During the Korean War the Po-2 was again in action and these 'Bedcheck Charlies' caused the Americans serious problems until Vought F4U Corsair night fighters were despatched to Korea to deal with them. In Vietnam the Douglas AC-47, Fairchild AC-119 and Lockheed AC-130 gunships operating over the Ho Chin Minh Trail at night were the nearest equivalent to the earlier intruder aircraft and their operations.

fought on with undiminished vigour. The Salerno landings were attacked by Focke Wulf Fw 190 fighter-bombers, while Dornier Do 217s armed with the Hs 293 missile attacked offshore shipping. Initially fighter defence over the beachhead was supplied by Fleet Air Arm Supermarine Seafires until RAF fighter units could be established ashore. One notable German success came on 10 September, when the Italian battle-ship *Roma* on its way to surrender at Malta was sunk by Fritz-X guided bombs dropped by the Do 217s of III Gruppe, Kampfgeschwader 100.

As the Allied soldiers began the hard fight to drive

Italian Reggiane Re 2001 fighters serving with the 358ᵃ Squadriglia, 2° Gruppo of the Regia Aeronautica, based on Sicily.

ITALY 1943–45

In August 1943 the Allies were poised for the invasion of Italy and a tactical air force of some 100 squadrons of fighters, bombers and reconnaissance aircraft was deployed in readiness on the airfields of Sicily, Malta and North Africa. An additional force of 32 squadrons of strategic bombers was already in action against targets in southern Italy. The defending Axis forces comprised six *Gruppen* of Luftwaffe fighters, plus fighter-bombers, medium bombers and reconnais-sance aircraft, and the weakened and demoralized units of the Regia Aeronautica with about 100 aircraft in southern Italy. On 3 September Allied forces crossed the Straits of Messina and five days later an armistice was signed by the Italians. The Germans, however,

Left *Republic P-47D Thunderbolt fighter-bombers of the USAAF Twelfth Air Force's 27th Fighter Group fly over the Apennine Mountains.*

Below *An RAF Douglas Dakota transport of No 267 Squadron flies over the Adriatic. Dakotas of the Balkan Air Force supported partisan forces in Yugoslavia.*

fighting took place over the beachhead as Axis aircraft, including fighter aircraft of the new Republica Sociale Italiana (formed in 1943 in northern Italy to continue the fight alongside Germany), attacked shipping and ground forces. Stubborn German resistance at Anzio and at Monte Cassino stalled the Allied advance until May, and Rome finally fell on 5 June. Meanwhile the Allied air forces had launched Operation Strangle, directed against the road and rail communications used to supply the German army. Many of these fighter-bomber and medium-bomber sorties were launched from airfields in Corsica.

In August 1944 the Allied advance was halted by the German Gothic Line defences, which were unsuccessfully attacked the following month. The invasion of southern France had temporarily drained air units from Italy during August and September. However,

the German army from Italy, Allied fighter-bombers of the Desert Air Force instituted cab-rank patrols, so that aircraft were always available in the air to be directed onto a ground target with the minimum of delay. USAAF Lockheed P-38 Lightning, Republic P-47 Thunderbolt and North American P-51 Mustang fighters accompanied the bombers of the Fifteenth Air Force on raids as far afield as Austria, Hungary and Bulgaria. In January 1944 some 850 aircraft were assembled to support the Anzio landings and heavy air

Below *In September 1943 German commandos landed by DFS 230 glider on the Gran Sasso to rescue Mussolini from his mountain-top prison.*

interdiction continued throughout the winter and as air opposition was then virtually nonexistent, all fighter units were assigned to fighter-bomber duties. The breakthrough of the Gothic Line defences came in the spring and on 2 May 1945 all Axis units in Italy surrendered unconditionally.

KABUL AIRLIFT 1928–29

One of the earliest successful airlift operations was the evacuation of British residents from Kabul in Afghanistan during the winter of 1928–9. This operation became necessary when a revolt against the Afghan king Amanullah threatened to involve British diplomats and other residents in the bloodshed. The British envoy therefore requested that the RAF evacuate the endangered civilians by air, using the Afghan airfield at Sherpur. The nearest available transport aircraft were the Vickers Victorias of No 70 Squadron in Iraq. They were immediately despatched to India, but in the meantime the evacuation was begun using the two-seat de Havilland DH9A bombers of Nos 27 and 60 Squadrons. The first Victoria sortie to Kabul was flown on 23 December and two days later a Handley Page Hinaidi transport joined the airlift.

Right *The officers and airmen of No 70 Squadron RAF are inspected by the Viceroy of India and Sir Geoffrey Salmond, the AOC, three days after the Kabul airlift ended.*

Below *Victoria twin-engined transports are escorted by Wapiti two-seaters over the Indian Northwest Frontier during the Kabul evacuation.*

All women and children had been flown to safety by 1 January. Two weeks later the Afghan rebellion reached its climax and the king was overthrown and replaced by his brother. Nevertheless, the British envoy, Sir Francis Humphrys, judged that the evacuation should continue. For the next four weeks the transport aircraft continued their flights, despite the handicap of severe winter weather. The last day of the airlift was 25 February, when Humphrys himself was flown to safety. In all 586 people had been evacuated in the course of 84 flights. Despite the appalling weather conditions and the inhospitable terrain beneath the route, not one casualty had been suffered during the operation.

Left *Crews receive their final briefing for a kamikaze sortie. In the background is an Ohka suicide aircraft, fitted into the bomb-bay of a Mitsubishi G4M Betty.*

KAMIKAZE OPERATIONS 1944–45

In October 1944 an American invasion force steamed into Leyte Gulf to begin the reoccupation of the Philippines. The Japanese prepared to defend the islands with all the resources at their command and most desperate amongst their defensive measures was the kamikaze suicide attack. *Kamikaze* (Divine Wind) was the name given to the storms that had scattered the Mongol invasion fleets off the Japanese coast in the 13th century. It was hoped that the 20th-century kamikazes would have a similar effect on the United States fleet. The opening kamikaze attack on 25 October 1944 launched by bomb-carrying Mitsubishi A6M Zero fighters of the 201st Kokutai (Naval Air Corps), succeeded in sinking the escort carrier *St Lo* and badly damaging three others. The Japanese were convinced that kamikaze attacks were a success, yet in order to sink two escort carriers, three destroyers and 11 other vessels during the Philippines invasion, they sacrificed the lives of 480 airmen.

During the invasion of Iwo Jima and Okinawa early in 1945, the kamikazes were again in action. On 6 April no fewer than 198 kamikaze aircraft were launched against the Okinawa invasion fleet. They sank only two destroyers and two smaller ships. However, damage from kamikaze attacks was often severe, although in this respect the British carriers of the Royal

Left *A bomb-laden Mitsubishi A6M Zero taxies out to begin a kamikaze mission.*

Navy's Pacific Fleet were well protected by their armoured decks. In the period between 7 April and 15 August alone, the kamikaze pilots of four air fleets carried out 1979 suicide missions. The Ohka rocket-powered suicide aircraft, more than 800 of which were built, first appeared over Okinawa, but its successes were few. The tremendous sacrifice of the Japanese pilots in the end had little effect on the United States' inexorable advance on Japan.

KOREAN WAR
1950–53

When the North Korean army attacked across the 38th parallel into South Korea on 25 June 1950 it met with little initial opposition. The South Korean troops were lightly armed and the air force little more than a training organization. Yet help was at hand from the aircraft of the USAF's Fifth Air Force based in Japan. On 27 June patrolling North American F-82 Twin Mustang fighters encountered North Korean Lavochkin La-7 and Yakovlev Yak-9 fighters, destroying three of them for no loss. The following day attacks began on advancing North Korean troops by Douglas B-26 Invaders, F-82s and Lockheed F-80 Shooting Stars. The air attacks then switched to North Korean airfields and the enemy air force was soon virtually eliminated. Yet in the South the enemy continued to advance. President Truman decided to commit American troops and on 1 July the Douglas C-54s of the 374th Wing began to fly the 24th Infantry Division into Pusan.

Later in July the United Nations appealed to members to provide forces to repel the invasion and among

Above left A kamikaze pictured seconds before impact into the side of the battleship USS Maine.

Above A Lockheed F-80 Shooting Star pulls away from a ground target. F-80s were generally used for close air support and interdiction missions over Korea.

Below Boeing B-29 Superfortresses attacked strategic targets and enemy communications during the Korean War.

those to respond was Australia, which committed the RAAF's No 77 Squadron flying North American P-51 Mustangs and later Gloster Meteor F Mk 8s. South Africa assigned No 2 Squadron SAAF, also flying Mustangs, to Korea, and this unit later flew the North American F-86F Sabre. Britain's main contribution to the air war were the Fleet Air Arm's Supermarine Seafires, Hawker Sea Furies and Fairey Fireflies, which operated from the aircraft carriers HMS *Glory*, HMS *Ocean*, HMS *Theseus* and HMS *Triumph*. RAF Short Sunderland squadrons carried out coastal patrols and Austers flew artillery spotting and liaison missions for the army.

Throughout July the advancing North Korean army was subjected to heavy air attack, mostly from F-80 jets flying from bases in Japan. However, this aircraft lacked endurance and could only remain over the

target area for some 15 minutes. Piston-engined B-26s and P-51s were more efficient in this respect and over 140 P-51D Mustangs were withdrawn from Air National Guard units in the United States for service in Korea. As the crucial battle for Pusan approached, US Navy carrier aircraft – Vought F4U Corsairs and Douglas AD Skyraiders – began to operate over Korea. Close air support missions were directed by battlefield controllers flying Stinson L-5 light observation aircraft and these were later replaced by faster T-6s. US marine Corps F4U Corsairs also entered combat at this time, flying from shore bases or from the carriers *Sicily* and *Badoeng Strait*.

In mid-August saturation bombing raids by Boeing B-29s were made against Communist troop concentrations and the campaign against road and rail communications intensified. All these measures had their effect and in September the UN troops counter-attacked with devastating results. The North Korean army was virtually annihilated, Fifth Air Force fighter-bombers alone killing 8000 Communist troops within a five-day period. The UN troops advanced into North Korea, but then the entry of Communist China into the war altered the situation dramatically. General Lin Piao's 18 divisions broke the UN forces and sent them streaming southwards in a disorderly retreat. As in the

Above F-86Fs of the 8th Fighter-Bomber Wing. F-86 Sabres operated in the air-superiority and latterly ground-attack roles in Korea.

Right In April 1951 US Navy Douglas Skyraiders of Attack Squadron VA-195 succeeded in breaking the Hwachon Dam in North Korea, using aerial torpedoes.

Below A Sikorsky HU3S-1, used for aircrew rescue. Korea saw the first widespread use of the helicopter in warfare.

opening phase of the war, only air power could slow the enemy's headlong advance and allow ground defences to be organized. By mid-December the enemy had lost some 33,000 troops to air attacks and by the end of January their advance had been halted.

In the meantime the Communist MiG-15 fighter had appeared in combat, outclassing the USAF's F-80 Shooting Star. Consequently the F-86A Sabre-equipped 4th Fighter Interceptor Wing (FIW) was rushed to Korea. Sabre and MiG-15 first met in combat on 17 December and the first of more than 790 MiG-15s to fall to the Sabres' guns went down under the fire of Lieutenant-Colonel Bruce Hinton. The 4th FIW was joined by the Sabre-equipped 51st FIW, commanded by World War II ace Francis Gabreski, in December 1951. The interdiction campaign against enemy supply routes continued throughout the war and it involved B-29 four-engined bombers, B-26 medium bombers and land- and carrier-based fighter-bombers. The Chinese and North Koreans became adept at concealing supply dumps and rapidly repairing damage to roads and railways. In March 1952 attacks were concentrated on the railways, however, and by the end of May they had achieved 20,000 cuts in the North Korean rail network. On 27 July 1953 the Communist forces finally acknowledged defeat and an armistice was signed.

LAFAYETTE ESCADRILLE 1916–17

Although the United States did not enter World War I until April 1917, many American citizens served with the British and French air services before this date. Only in France were these volunteers grouped into a special unit: the Escadrille Américaine, later known as the Lafayette Escadrille. The unit came into being on 20 April 1916, flying Nieuport 11 fighters (later changed for Nieuport 17s) under the command of a French officer, Capitaine Georges Thenault. The unit's first victory came on 18 May 1916, when Kiffin Rockwell shot down an LVG two-seater when on patrol over the Vosges.

neutrality. The unit soon also changed its Nieuport fighters for the new Spad SVII. Its score then rose to 28 victories, 17 of these due to the skill of Raoul Lufbery. In 1917 the Lafayette Escadrille became the US Army Air Service's 103rd Aero Squadron.

LEAFLET RAIDS

The dropping of propaganda leaflets from aircraft became one of the chief instruments of psychological warfare during World War I. The means of delivery ranged from aeroplanes to small unmanned balloons and the leaflets themselves could be aimed at a specific audience – for example Austria-Hungary offered a large reward to any Italian pilot defecting with his aeroplane – or simply at the general demoralization of the enemy. After the Armistice the practice of leaflet-dropping was continued by RAF air control squadrons in Iraq. Government proclamations were dropped over rebel territory and warnings issued of impending bombing raids.

At the outset of World War II RAF Bomber Command was specifically forbidden to bomb any target in Germany that might result in civilian deaths, for fear of provoking reprisals against British and French cities. Therefore most of the early RAF bomber sorties over the Reich were simply leaflet raids, or 'Nickelling' as it was codenamed. In all, 4086 wartime sorties by Bomber Command were purely for leaflet-dropping, an activity derided by critics as merely augmenting German stocks of toilet paper. Many bombers later in the war carried bundles of leaflets in addition to their bombloads. In August 1943 the Allies introduced a clever variation in the propaganda war by dropping forged ration cards into Germany. Clearly if these had got into widespread circulation they would have totally disrupted the German food supply system and

On the day after Rockwell's victory the Escadrille moved to the Verdun Sector of the front, where it soon became involved in heavy fighting. Bert Hall scored the unit's second victory on 23 May, but the following month Victor Chapman became the Escadrille's first fatal casualty. In September during a bomber escort mission from Luxeuil, Kiffin Rockwell crashed to his death. However, by October the American pilots had scored 17 victories, with five of them credited to the rising star Raoul Lufbery. In December 1916 the Escadrille Américaine was renamed the Escadrille Lafayette to quieten criticisms of a breach of American

Top French and American pilots of the Escadrille Américaine in July 1916.

Above Raoul Lufbery stands by the cockpit of his Nieuport. The highest-scoring ace of the Lafayette Escadrille, he was killed in combat in May 1918.

Below Propaganda leaflets are loaded aboard an A W Whitley bomber of No 102 Squadron RAF early in World War II.

Above *A Lockheed C-130A Hercules of the 374th Tactical Airlift Wing carries out a leaflet drop over South Vietnam in October 1969.*

Left *The navigator of an RAF Whitley bomber dropping leaflets through the aircraft's flare chute. When released the leaflets scatter in the Whitley's slipstream.*

onto Japanese cities warning the inhabitants of impending bomber raids. In postwar counter-insurgency operations in Malaya, South Vietnam and Rhodesia, leaflets have continued to be used by government forces in the battle for the 'hearts and minds' of the people .

the Germans therefore imposed stringent penalties on those found using the forgeries.

The widespread use of propaganda leaflets by the Allies is illustrated by the statistics for March 1944. A total of nearly 56 million leaflets were dropped and these were directed not only at the German enemy, but also to French, Belgian, Dutch, Danish and Norwegian allies in occupied Europe. In 1945 Boeing B-29s of the USAAF's 21st Air Force dropped leaflets

Below *A German propaganda leaflet dropped to French troops garrisoning the Maginot Line early in World War II.*

LIBYA 1911–12

The first campaign in which military aeroplanes were employed was the war between Italy and Turkey in Libya in 1911–12. An Air Flotilla of the Italian army, consisting of nine aeroplanes, 11 pilots and 30 mechanics, was despatched by sea to Tripoli in October 1911. On their arrival the aeroplanes were uncrated and assembled, the first being ready for action

on the Tanguira Oasis on 1 November 1911. By February 1912 the early hand-held bombs had been replaced by a bomb cell fitted to each machine which could release up to ten bombs individually or in salvoes. Opposition to the Italian aeroplanes was confined to ground-fire, but the only fatal casualty among the Italian airmen was the result of a flying accident rather than enemy action. By the end of the conflict the aeroplane had been convincingly demonstrated as a weapon of war.

MALTA 1940–42

The island of Malta occupies a strategically important position in the central Mediterranean, which allows forces based there to dominate the sea routes from Italy to North Africa – hence the bitterly fought battles for control of Malta in World War II. At the time of Italy's entry into the war, the island had three airfields, at Hal Far, Luqa and Takali, plus a seaplane base at Kalafrana, but the four fighter squadrons authorized for its defence had yet to be deployed there. A makeshift defence force was hastily assembled, using Fleet Air Arm Gloster Sea Gladiators piloted by RAF staff officers. Fortunately the early attacks of the Regia Aeronautica on Malta were ineffective and the Sea Gladiators succeeded in holding their own until Hawker Hurricanes arrived on the island later in June. The story of the three Malta Sea Gladiators, *Faith*, *Hope* and *Charity*, although it has a factual basis, is largely an invention of the wartime propaganda machine.

At this time Malta's offensive air strength consisted of six Fairey Swordfish of No 830 Squadron FAA and

within a week. On 23 October a Blériot XI monoplane, piloted by Capitano Carlos Piazza, the Air Flotilla's commander, made a reconnaissance flight over advancing Turkish forces. This was the first sortie by a military aeroplane in wartime.

Further reconnaissance flights followed and the Air Flotilla's military usefulness was increased by using the aeroplanes to observe artillery fire and to correct the gunners' aim by dropping them messages. On the initiative of Capitano Piazza, one of the Blériots was fitted with a plate camera for aerial photography. In November a second air unit was despatched from Italy and this established itself at Benghazi. Its commander, Capitano Marengo, distinguished himself in May 1912 by making the first night reconnaissance flight. His only night-flying aid was a torch attached to his flying helmet.

The great innovation of the Libyan Campaign was aerial bombing, which was first tried during a raid

Above This Maurice Farman biplane nosed over in a landing accident during operations in Libya. The Italo-Turkish War of 1911–12 saw the first use of aeroplanes in warfare.

Below left A Blériot XI of the Italian Air Flotilla at Tobruk in Libya.

Below A Supermarine Spitfire Mk V is serviced by RAF and Army personnel in its sandbagged revetment on Malta. Spitfires first reached Malta in April 1942.

the Short Sunderland flying boats of Nos 228 and 230 Squadrons. Later in the year this force was strengthened by the Martin Maryland reconnaissance aircraft of No 431 Flight and the Vickers Wellingtons of No 148 Squadron. Yet it was the defensive forces that required the greatest attention. No 261 Squadron was formed on the island in early August 1940, but an attempted reinforcement in May ended in disaster when eight out of the 12 Hurricanes flown off the carrier HMS *Argus* failed to arrive.

In January 1941 the Malta defences came under attack from the bombers and fighters of the Luftwaffe's Fliegerkorps X, newly installed in Sicily. Continuous pressure on the island's defences (still only a single fighter squadron) and its supply ships brought Malta near to defeat in April, but the following month supply convoys fought their way through and a second Hurricane squadron – No 185 – joined in the defence. During the latter part of 1941, the Malta-based bomber aircraft and naval forces seriously interfered with Axis supply convoys to North Africa. This led to a renewed all-out air offensive against the island early in 1942. In April the hard-pressed Hurricanes were joined by 47 Spitfire Mk Vs flown from the American carrier USS *Wasp* and in May a further 62 Spitfires from USS *Wasp* and HMS *Eagle*. Further heavy air attacks were launched by the Luftwaffe and Regia Aeronautica in July and August, but by this time the defending fighter force had expanded to 260 aircraft. The raiders were badly mauled and Malta's epic defence, which had earned the island the award of the George Cross, had finally reached a triumphant conclusion.

Above *The Junkers Ju 87R long-range dive bomber operated against Malta and the island's supply convoys from the Luftwaffe's bases on Sicily.*

Below left *This Macchi C202 fighter of the Regia Aeronautica's 51° Stormo was brought down over Malta in August 1942.*

Bottom left *In late 1940 the Luftwaffe's Fliegerkorps X was deployed to Sicily to begin an all-out blitz on Malta. Its principal bomber was the Junkers Ju 88A.*

Below right *Flt Lt D. Turley-George (left) and second pilot Flt Off C. Fenwick with their Sea Hurricane catapult fighter aboard the SS Empire Tide.*

MERCHANT SHIP FIGHTER UNIT 1941–43

As losses to British shipping grew to alarming proportions in late 1940, urgent measures were taken to defeat the threats to Britain's ocean lifelines. The main enemy was of course the U-boat, but surface raiders and long-range maritime reconnaissance aircraft were also taking their toll of merchant shipping. The Luftwaffe's Focke Wulf Fw 200 Condors, operating from bases in France and Norway, were particularly difficult to counter, due to the shortage of aircraft carriers for escort. Accordingly, it was proposed that a number of merchant ships be modified to carry a Hawker Hurricane fighter on a catapult. The fighter could be launched when a Condor was picked up on radar and at the end of the sortie the pilot could take to his parachute and be picked up by the convoy.

Early catapult fighters were manned by the Fleet

Air Arm, but in May 1941 the RAF formed the Merchant Ship Fighter Unit at Speke, near Liverpool, for this duty. The first success went to the naval catapult ship HMS *Maplin* on 3 August 1941, when Lieutenant R. Everett's Sea Hurricane brought down a Condor. The catapult-armed merchantmen (or CAM-ships) continued in use until July 1943, when they were superseded by merchant aircraft carriers (MAC-ships). Although operational launchings were very few, most of them resulted in a 'kill'. Nevertheless, the CAM-ships had plugged a gap in the convoys' air defence at a time when nothing but this hazardous expedient was available.

Above left A Sea Hurricane 1A is lowered onto a CAM-ship's catapult. The first 50 aircraft of this type were converted from standard RAF Hurricane Mk I fighters.

Above An MSFU Hurricane is catapulted from its parent ship.

Below A Short 184 floatplane of the Royal Naval Air Service detonates an enemy mine by gunfire.

MINE WARFARE

The sowing of sea mines from the air had been considered both by the Germans and British in World War I, but had proved to be impracticable with the aircraft of the day. However, aeroplanes, airships and kite balloons were all widely used for mine-spotting duties during the war. At the beginning of World War II the Germans had developed an effective magnetic mine, which was dropped by Heinkel He 59 floatplanes and later He 111 and Dornier Do 17 bombers

Above *Heinkel He 115 floatplanes of the Luftwaffe were responsible for laying magnetic mines in British coastal waters early in World War II.*

Left *The Handley Page Hampden bombers of No 5 Group Bomber Command pioneered the RAF's sea mining campaign against Germany in the spring of 1940.*

Below *A Consolidated Catalina flying boat of No 43 Squadron Royal Australian Air Force prepares to make a minelaying sortie from Darwin in May 1945.*

in the North Sea and Thames Estuary. These weapons caught the British by surprise and in three months they sank a total of around 250,000 tonnes of shipping. In November 1939 a mine was dropped in error onto the mudflats of Shoeburyness and a bomb disposal team was able to unravel its secrets. One countermeasure introduced by the RAF was the Vickers Wellington DWI, which was fitted with a generator and magnetic coil of sufficient power to detonate a mine when the aircraft flew over it.

The British too put the magnetic mine into production and mining sorties, codenamed 'Gardening', were flown by Fleet Air Arm Fairey Swordfish, Bristol Beauforts of RAF Coastal Command and Bomber Command Wellingtons and Handley Page Hampdens early in the war. Later the four-engined 'heavies' took on the task. One notable successful mining campaign was directed against the River Danube. It was calculated that one vessel was sunk for every 50 mines sown and examination of German records after the war indicated that these mines had sunk a total of 1050 Axis warships and merchant vessels. Mining took place on a smaller scale in the Pacific theatre, but in March 1945 the Marianas-based Boeing B-29s began to mine Japanese coastal waters. A total of 21,389 mines were dropped and they sank or damaged 83 vessels.

Since World War II magnetic mines of increasing sophistication have been produced and new types of acoustic and pressure mines have come into service. Towards the end of the Vietnam War, in May 1972, Grumman A-6 Intruders of the US Navy mined the North Vietnamese harbours, the most important of which was Haiphong. So effective was this operation that the Americans themselves had to clear the minefields following the ceasefire agreement with the North Vietnamese in January 1973. The minesweeping

Germans, with their useful pre-war experience of Zeppelin designs, preferred the rigid airship.

Two of the most important developments in naval aviation during World War I were the evolution of long-range patrol flying boats and the invention of the aircraft carrier. Early in the war the Royal Naval Air Service purchased two Curtiss America flying boats from the United States. These were followed by more than 60 Curtiss H4 flying boats, but although these aircraft had sufficient range for naval patrol work their unseaworthy hulls limited their usefulness as operational aircraft. This shortcoming was overcome by Squadron Commander John Porte, who designed a more efficient hull form which was married to the Curtiss design to produce the Felixstowe F.1. A scaled-up Porte hull was then produced for the larger and more efficient Curtiss H12 design, resulting in the highly successful Felixstowe F.2. This flying boat was

force included Sikorsky CH-53A Sea Stallion helicopters, which were used to tow a hydrofoil minesweeping 'sled' through the water. A similar minesweeping operation to clear the Suez Canal took place in 1974, when the US Navy made use of the improved Sikorsky RH-53D minesweeping helicopter.

NAVAL AVIATION

The earliest naval aircraft were intended for overwater reconnaissance and at the outbreak of World War I in August 1914 the Royal Naval Air Service had 52 seaplanes and seven non-rigid airships on strength, while the German navy had one rigid airship and 36 seaplanes. Airships were found to be particularly useful for naval scouting, as they had sufficient endurance for long oversea reconnaissance flights, unlike the seaplanes. However, the range of the seaplane could be extended by operating it from seaplane carriers accompanying the fleet, an expedient tried with some success by both the British and French. The

Above The United States Navy employed minesweeping Sikorsky RH-53D helicopters to clear the Suez Canal of mines and unexploded ordnance in the aftermath of the Yom Kippur War.

Above right A Blackburn Dart of the Fleet Air Arm releases a torpedo during training exercises in the Mediterranean in the 1920s.

the first truly effective long-range patrol aircraft of this type and was used with considerable success in North Sea patrols during 1917–18.

The development of the aircraft carrier followed from the extensive use of seaplane carriers by the Royal Navy, including HMS *Ark Royal*'s participation in the Dardanelles Campaign and HMS *Engadine*'s inconclusive part in the Battle of Jutland. As well as providing air reconnaissance naval aircraft could be used to attack enemy shipping and shore installations. The first sinking of a ship by an aircraft's torpedo took place in August 1915, when Flight Commander C. Edmonds' Short 184 seaplane attacked a Turkish merchantman. Later, in 1916, seaplanes from three carriers had demonstrated the aircraft's shore-attack potential by bombing the German airship sheds at Cuxhaven. As naval aircraft developed, the air defence of warships at sea became an important requirement. This was initially met by operating high-performance landplanes, such as the Sopwith Pup and later the Sopwith Camel, from platforms carried above the gun turrets of capital ships.

The development of a true aircraft carrier, which would allow all these naval aviation roles to be carried

bombers often came near to denying the waters around the island fortress of Malta to allied warships and merchantmen. Another hard battle between shore-based anti-shipping forces and supply convoys was fought in the Arctic Ocean, as the Royal Navy battled to maintain a flow of Lend-Lease supplies to the Soviet port of Murmansk.

The Pacific War opened on 7 December 1941 with one of the most devastating carrier air strikes in the history of warfare, the Japanese attack on the US Pacific Fleet at Pearl Harbor in the Hawaiian Islands. A force of less than 450 naval aircraft, operating from six carriers, succeeded in sinking four battleships and severely damaging the remaining four, as well as knocking out 164 American aircraft on the ground. On 10 December Japanese navy Mitsubishi G3M Nell

out by a single warship, was clearly a logical outcome of the Royal Navy's experience in World War I. Such a ship, HMS *Furious*, was in commission at the end of the war. She was not an entirely satisfactory design, as her two flying decks were divided by the formidable barrier of her funnel and superstructure. A more satisfactory layout was the flush deck fitted to HMS *Argus*, and *Furious* was later modified to this layout. The inter-war years saw the build-up of carrier forces in Britain, the United States and Japan. This development was unwittingly stimulated by the Washington Naval Treaty of 1921 which imposed reductions on battleship and cruiser construction but was less concerned with the latest capital ship. Indeed the effectiveness of bombers against battleships was at this time a matter of bitter controversy, especially in the United States where General Billy Mitchell's demonstration air attacks on former German warships had failed to convince the admirals.

In World War II the aircraft carrier played a decisive role in the battles of the Pacific War, but its impact on the fighting in Europe was less dramatic. Nonetheless, carrier aircraft inflicted a serious defeat on the Italian fleet at Taranto in November 1940. Shore-based aircraft too proved their worth in the naval war. Long-range-patrol Consolidated Liberators provided vital coverage of the mid-Atlantic air gap, one of the most successful anti-U-boat measures of the Battle of the Atlantic. In the Mediterranean Italian and German

Top During the inter-war years, long range overwater patrols were undertaken by flying boats, such as this Naval Aircraft Factory PN-9 of the US Navy.

Above A Grumman F6F Hellcat of Fighter Squadron VF-9, serving aboard USS Yorktown in late 1943. The US Navy's Hellcat was the most successful carrier fighter of World War II.

Below A Fairey Swordfish biplane landing aboard its parent aircraft carrier. These aircraft served with front-line units of the Fleet Air Arm throughout World War I.

land-based bombers, flying from Saigon in Indochina (now Vietnam), sank the powerful British warships HMS *Repulse* and HMS *Prince of Wales* off the coast of Malaya. The Japanese successes were incomplete, however, for the US Navy's aircraft carriers had escaped the carnage at Pearl Harbor, and at the Battles of Coral Sea and Midway (May/June 1942) they exacted their revenge. These remarkable naval battles were fought largely by carrier aircraft and the main fleets were never within sight of each other. They set the pattern for much of the war that was to follow, with US carrier forces supporting an island-hopping campaign that drew ever nearer to the Japanese homeland. The Japanese navy never fully recovered from the loss at Midway of four carriers and the skilled personnel of their air groups. Its subsequent decline in naval air strength culminated in the Battle of the Philippine Sea on 19 June 1944, popularly known as the 'Great Marianas Turkey Shoot'. In this single action, US Navy fighter pilots destroyed 402 Japanese aircraft for the loss of only 30 of their own. The only riposte that the Japanese naval airmen could produce was the ultimately self-defeating expedient of kamikaze suicide attacks.

Since World War II the United States has maintained the most powerful carrier forces afloat, latterly including the massive nuclear-powered carriers of which USS *Enterprise* (1961) was the prototype. Yet if no other naval power has equalled the US Navy's carrier forces, few are totally without naval aircraft, as the versatile helicopter can operate from platforms aboard vessels as small as frigates and destroyers. The

took place when the defending aircraft's patrol crossed the track of an airship. Not only was the interception perforce left to chance, but the subsequent combat was also fraught with uncertainties. The BE2c aircraft which the defenders flew were unable to match the airships' rate of ascent and until effective explosive and incendiary bullets became available, the defenders' only offensive weapons were bombs and Rankin explosive darts. Yet despite these shortcomings the defenders scored a number of successes. On the night of 2/3 September 1916 Lieutenant W. Leefe Robinson brought down the Schutte-Lanz airship SL17 at Cuffley in Hertfordshire. During the next Zeppelin raid on the night of 23/24 September two airships fell to defending fighters and by the end of the year the defences had mastered the airship menace. In 1916 there were 22 Zeppelin raids over Britain, but this fell to seven raids in 1917 and only four in the final year of the war.

A new threat faced Britain's air defences in 1917: the long-range bomber. Gotha and Giant bombers flying at night required interceptors of far better performance than the lumbering BE2c to bring them to combat. Accordingly a night-fighter version of the Sopwith Camel was developed and issued to the home defence squadrons. The commander of the London Air Defence Area, Major-General E. B. Ashmore, evolved an impressive system of anti-aircraft gun belts, fighter patrol lines, searchlights and observers to cover the British capital and he linked all its ground elements to his headquarters by land line. Yet by the time Ashmore's preparations were complete in September 1918 the German night raiders had been switched to attacking targets of immediate value to the army commanders in France. Therefore the British air defences were not fully tested in combat. It is clear, however, that there were two major weaknesses in night-fighting techniques, the lack of ground-to-air communication to guide the night fighters onto the raiders, and the lack of an efficient early-warning system to alert the defences.

These deficiencies in night air defence were to be made good in World War II – indeed reliable ground-to-air communication was introduced soon after the end of World War I. The means of directing the night fighter onto its victim had to await the development of specialized radars. The Chain Home radars which

V/STOL (vertical/short take-off and landing) BAe Sea Harrier and to some extent the less flexible Soviet Yakovlev Yak-36MP Forger mark the beginning of a new era in naval aviation. These aircraft can operate from the small flight decks of helicopter carriers (such as the British HMS *Invincible*, the Soviet *Kiev* and the USS *Iwo Jima*) and yet they can hold their own against aircraft operating from super carriers or runways ashore. The Fleet Air Arm's Sea Harriers demonstrated this in action against the Argentine Air Force during the Falklands War. For the loss of six Sea Harriers (none of them in air-to-air combat) 20 Argentine aircraft were destroyed. However, naval V/STOL aircraft have yet to match the performance attainable by carrier aircraft. For example, whereas the Sea Harrier's maximum level speed is Mach 0.97, that of the US Navy's Grumman F-14 Tomcat is Mach 2.4. The US Navy is at present working on the long-term development of supersonic V/STOL aircraft for operation at sea and such aircraft may well be the standard naval fighters of the 21st century.

Top *A US Navy Grumman F9F Panther landing aboard USS* Bon Homme Richard *during operations off Korea in 1951.*

Above *A McDonnell Douglas F-4J Phantom of the US Navy is brought to a stop by the crash barrier aboard USS* America, *during combat operations off Vietnam in 1970.*

Below *In the early years of World War II many night-fighter units were equipped with single-seat day fighters, such as this Hawker Hurricane Mk IIC of No 87 Squadron RAF.*

NIGHT FIGHTING

Night fighting began in World War I at a time when none of the scientific aids to interception in darkness were available. The first night combats were hit-or-miss affairs between the Royal Flying Corps home defence squadrons and marauding Zeppelins and only

Left *The most widely used German night fighter of World War II was the radar-equipped Messerschmitt Bf 110. A Bf 110G-4 is pictured in the markings of NJG 3.*

provided RAF Fighter Command's day fighters with early warning of enemy attack were of little use to the night fighters. What they required was a ground radar with 360-degree coverage overland, which could be used to plot the course of enemy raiders and to direct the night fighter into a position where it could take over the interception. The first GCI (ground control of interception) radar became operational at the beginning of 1941. When used in conjunction with the night fighters' own AI (airborne interception) radar it provided the theoretical answer to the problem of night interception. Yet it was not until both radars and night fighters had considerably improved in performance and controllers and aircrew had gained practical experience of the new interception procedures that the British night defences became truly efficient. This state of affairs had been reached early in 1943, when the Mosquito NF Mk XII fitted with AI Mk VIII centimetric radar became operational. When the Luftwaffe bombers launched Operation Steinbock, the 'Little Blitz' of January–May 1944, more than 300 bombers were lost to the defences, representing some 60 per cent of the attacking force.

The German night air defence system was slow to develop in World War II. In July 1940 Goering had ordered Colonel Joseph Kammhuber to establish a night-fighter force, but this initially comprised only some 35 aircraft (none of them radar-equipped), plus early-warning radars and searchlights on the ground to assist in bringing about interceptions. By September 1942 this force had expanded to meet the increasing weight of attack of the RAF night bombers and numbered some 350 fighter aircraft, most of them radar-equipped Messerschmitt Bf 110s. They were controlled, under the Himmelbett system, by a chain of ground radars running from Denmark to the Swiss border. This force took an ever increasing toll of RAF raiders, but on 25/26 July 1943, during a massive raid on Hamburg, the RAF totally disrupted the German night-fighter control system with the introduction of Window. These strips of metallized foil created false radar returns on the German radar screens.

The Luftwaffe evolved two different tactics to deal with Window. One involved the direction of single-seat and night fighters to the target, where they could use the light from flares and burning buildings to pick out the bombers without needing to use radar. The alternative was to direct the night fighters to the position where the concentrations of Window were strongest, which would of course bring them into contact with the bomber stream. These measures were

Below *The RAF's most effective specialized night fighter was the DH Mosquito, which became operational early in 1942. A Mosquito NF Mk II is illustrated.*

Bottom *The cockpit of a DH Mosquito night fighter, showing the navigator's radar scope and associated controls on the right.*

fairly effective, but represented only stop-gap solutions to the problem, which was more satisfactorily solved by the introduction of the SN-2 night-fighter radar. This radar worked on a frequency not yet jammed by Window and as it came into service early in 1944 RAF bomber losses rose sharply. The German night fighters scored their greatest success of the war on the night of 30 March, when 94 bombers out of a force of 781 attacking Nuremberg were shot down. The Luftwaffe had developed a number of noteworthy night-fighter aids, including the Naxos device which homed onto the RAF H2S bombing radar emissions, the Flensburg which homed onto the Monica tail-warning radar and an upward-firing twin-cannon armament, codenamed *Schräge Musik* (Jazz Music). By the end of the war the Luftwaffe had introduced the first operational jet night fighter, a two-seat variant of the Messerschmitt Me 262.

It was not until after World War II that the first British and American jet night fighters appeared. The RAF operated Gloster Meteors and de Havilland Venoms, while the USAF flew the Lockheed F-94 Starfire and Northrop F-89 Scorpion. The American fighters pioneered automatic, collision-course engagements, in which a salvo of air-to-air rockets was fired on instructions from a weapons-aiming computer. By the 1960s the specialized night fighter had given way to the all-weather fighter, which was able to operate

Left One of the Luftwaffe's most successful night-fighter pilots was Prince Heinrich zu Sayn-Wittgenstein, pictured (centre) by the tail of his Junkers Ju 88C night fighter.

Below The Luftwaffe's Heinkel He 219 night fighter proved to be a match for the RAF's fast and manoeuvrable DH Mosquito when it went into service in mid-1943. A captured example is pictured in British markings.

both by day and night. Consequently, present-day air defence forces have no night-fighter units as such, but operate all their interceptors by day or night according to the need.

NORMANDY INVASION 1944

One of the largest air operations of World War II was mounted in support of the Allied invasion of Europe in June 1944. The air forces directly involved comprised the US Ninth Air Force and the RAF's Second Tactical Air Force, which were made up of medium bombers, and fighter and reconnaissance squadrons. RAF Bomber Command and the USAAF's Eighth Air Force also added their weight to the assault and a total

Right RAF armourers load 20mm cannon shells into the wing of a rocket-armed Hawker Typhoon, which served with the Second Tactical Air Force's No 226 Squadron.

Below left A Republic P-47D Thunderbolt fighter-bomber of the USAAF Ninth Air Force's 373rd Fighter Group flies over Mont St Michel in Normandy shortly after D-Day.

Bottom right This DH Mosquito PR Mk XVI photo reconnaissance aircraft is marked with the alternating black and white stripes which were applied to all tactical aircraft prior to D-Day.

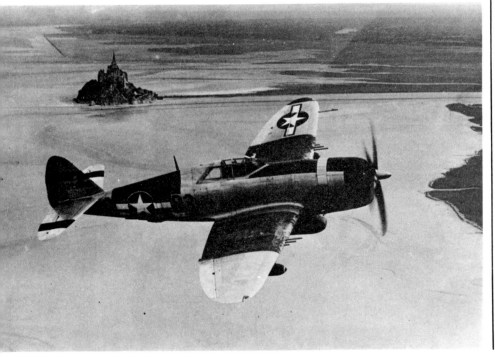

inland Allied fighters carried out sweeps over the Luftwaffe's airfields to prevent German aircraft from contesting the landings. The flanks of the invasion beaches were to be seized by airborne assault, and a force of USAAF Douglas C-47s and RAF Dakotas, together with Waco CG-4A Hadrian and Airspeed Horsa gliders, carried the airborne troops to their dropping zones. This part of the assault was successfully accomplished and the German defences generally taken by surprise. Widespread deception measures, including the creation of a phantom invasion fleet by air-dropped Window and the releasing of dummy parachutists, were carried out by RAF Bomber Command. RAF Coastal Command patrolled the seaward flanks of the invasion fleet to prevent interference from U-boats and E-boats. Once the warships were in position offshore, their bombardment was directed from Supermarine Seafires and Spitfires of the Air Spotting Pool, manned by RAF, Fleet Air Arm and US Navy pilots.

The Luftwaffe's reaction to the landings was a feeble one. Allied intelligence assessed the strength of Luftflotte 3 in France as 800 aircraft and believed that 600 of these would go into action on D-Day. In fact only

force of some 10,000 aircraft was committed to Operation Overlord. Preparations for the landings included extensive photographic reconnaissance of the beaches and invasion area, the bombing of coastal radar stations to minimize warning of the invasion fleet's approach, and attacks on coastal defences, military garrisons and the French railway system. In order to make identification of friendly aircraft as easy as possible all Allied tactical aircraft were painted with alternating black and white bands on wings and fuselage on the eve of Overlord. Furthermore fighter cover over the invasion armada was to be flown exclusively by the distinctive twin-boom Lockheed P-38 Lightning to further ease recognition problems.

The invasion began early on the morning of 6 June with bombing attacks on coastal fortifications, while

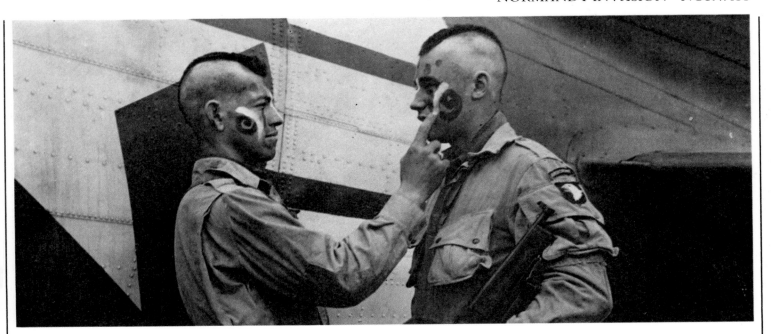

100 sorties were flown by German aircraft before nightfall on 6 June, although bombers and torpedo-bombers attacked the Allied shipping under cover of darkness.

During the evening airborne troops were reinforced and supplies were dropped into the beachhead area by Dakota transports. However, the latter operation, code-named Rob Roy, did not go according to plan. The Dakota transports were mistaken for German bombers and engaged by the anti-aircraft guns. Six of them were shot down and most of the supplies were lost. Yet this fiasco was not typical of the D-Day air operations and most of the 14,674 sorties flown that day achieved their objectives.

NORWAY 1940

In April 1940 the Luftwaffe prepared to launch a surprise attack on the Scandinavian countries of Denmark and Norway. A force of some 300 bombers, 40 dive-bombers, 100 fighters and nearly 500 transport aircraft was assembled. On 9 April both countries were attacked simultaneously, and, after fighter attacks and paratroop assaults on their airfields, the Danes capitulated within a day. The Norwegian attack was not to succeed so quickly. Oslo's Fornebu airfield and Stavanger/Sola were strafed by Messerschmitt Bf 110s as a prelude to airborne landings, Gloster Gladiator fighters of the Norwegian air force fought back, but with little success. Only a few Fokker CV reconnaissance aircraft survived the initial onslaught to continue to fight from bases in northern Norway. Meanwhile, British aircraft intervened, with Handley Page Hampden and Vickers Wellington bombers going into action on the night of 9/10 April. The following day Blackburn Skua dive-bombers attacked and sank the German cruiser *Königsberg*, but it was an isolated success.

The Norwegian army determined to defend the north of the country for as long as possible. Kristiansund and Vaernes airfield near Trondheim were in German hands, so the British were forced to rely on their aircraft carriers. HMS *Furious*, HMS *Ark Royal*

Above Paratroops of the 101st Airborne Division don their warpaint before boarding a C-47 Skytrain transport aircraft on D-Day.

Left An RAF Gloster Gladiator and Fleet Air Arm Blackburn Skua (background) are camouflaged against air attack on a Norwegian airfield.

Left *Two of No 263 Squadron's Gloster Gladiators were burned out following a German air attack on Lake Lesjaskog.*

and HMS *Glorious* were committed to the campaign and Allied troops were landed in the Narvik and Trondheim areas. So desperate was the need for fighter cover that the Gladiators of No 263 Squadron RAF were flown off *Glorious* to operate from the frozen waters of Lake Lesjaskog. Yet German air attack soon made this temporary air base unusable. The Allies were forced to evacuate the Trondheim area and concentrate their efforts on holding Narvik. No 263 Squadron was again ordered to provide air defence and it was joined by the Hawker Hurricane equipped No 46 Squadron. The defensive patrols of these fighter squadrons were assisted by bomber attacks on German-held airfields mounted from Britain.

The Narvik position was soon judged to be unten-

able and Allied forces evacuated the port on 7 June. The surviving Gladiators and Hurricanes were flown out to land on the carrier *Glorious* for evacuation. The Hurricanes were not equipped with deck landing equipment and the successful recovery of all ten fighters aboard the carrier was a considerable feat of airmanship. Ironically, however, all these aircraft and many of their pilots were lost the following day when *Glorious* was intercepted and sunk by the battlecruisers *Scharnhorst* and *Gneisenau*. Fewer than 50 men survived. The final act of the Norwegian campaign was an attack on the *Scharnhorst* and *Gneisenau* by Fleet Air Arm Skua dive-bombers flying from *Ark Royal* on 13 June. The battlecruisers escaped damage, but eight of the naval aircraft were lost.

Below *Heinkel He 111 bombers of III Gruppe Kampfgeschwader 26 operated from the snow-covered airfield at Trondheim during the Norwegian campaign.*

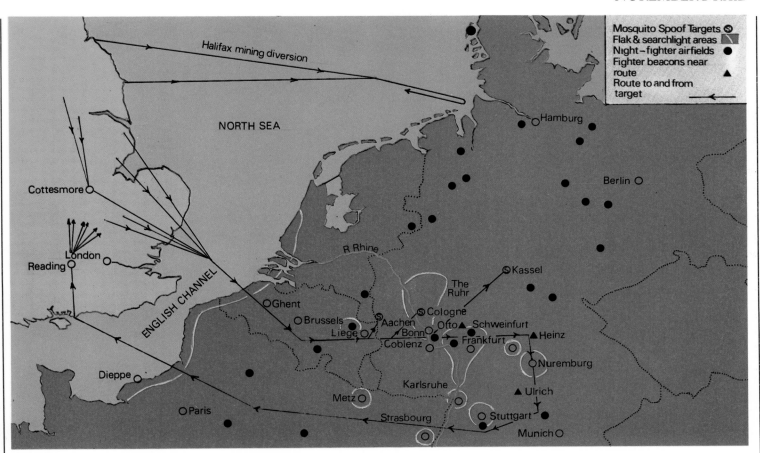

Mosquito Spoof Targets ⊙
Flak & searchlight areas ◨
Night-fighter airfields ●
Fighter beacons near route ▲
Route to and from target ⟵

NUREMBERG RAID 1944

On the night of 30 March 1944 RAF Bomber Command despatched a force of nearly 800 bombers against the city of Nuremberg in southern Germany. In contrast to the Command's normal route planning which favoured a zig-zag course to the target in order to keep the defenders guessing as to the objective, the Nuremberg raiders were briefed to fly a long approach leg to their target. Nor would the Nuremberg raid be accompanied by the usual effective diversionary attacks and feints which Bomber Command generally mounted in order to mislead the German night-fighter controllers. Minelaying sorties in the Heligoland Bight and Mosquito attacks on the Ruhr and Holland were easily identified as diversions. Thus the stage was set for the RAF's most costly bombing raid of World War II.

Even the weather conspired against Bomber Command, as the bombers met unexpected winds which scattered their compact stream, and conspicuous contrails formed at a lower level than usual. As the raiders passed Aachen the Luftwaffe's night fighters pounced on the bomber stream in ever increasing numbers. Moonlight made the task easy and their controllers soon realized that the target was Nuremberg. When the target was reached the bombers found it obscured

Top *A map showing the route followed by the Nuremberg raiders on the night of 30 March 1944.*

Above *An Avro Lancaster Mk II of No 408 Squadron RCAF takes off from its base at Linton-on-Ouse, Yorkshire. This unit despatched 12 aircraft on the Nuremberg raid and lost one to a night fighter.*

Left *The scene in a bomber station's briefing room as crews are briefed for the Nuremberg raid.*

by cloud, and, as the pathfinder aircraft were over 40 minutes late, hundreds of aircraft were forced to circle the target area waiting for their aiming point to be marked. The Luftwaffe night fighters were quick to exploit Bomber Command's mistakes and a total of 94 RAF aircraft failed to return. A further 12 were destroyed on returning to base and 59 were damaged. Following these heavy losses Bomber Command switched its efforts to attacks on French targets in preparation for the Normandy invasion.

OPERATION BODENPLATTE 1945

The Luftwaffe's last major offensive of World War II, Operation Bodenplatte, was mounted on New Year's Day 1945 against the airfields of the Allied tactical air forces. The operation was originally planned as a massive attack against the bombers of the Eighth Air Force attacking the German homeland, but by December 1944 when detailed planning of the operation began, its objective had changed to the Allied tactical airfields in the Netherlands, Belgium and north-eastern France. A force of ten *Jagdgeschwader* would make a simultaneous assault on 16 target airfields. As the opening of the German Ardennes offensive on the ground coincided with a period of atrocious flying weather, there was no question of coordinating the two attacks. Yet it was feared by the airmen that the land offensive had compromised their plans for a surprise attack.

In fact Operation Bodenplatte caught Allied intelligence completely unawares, as it was generally assumed that the Luftwaffe was incapable of mounting a large-scale operation. Secrecy was maintained during the Luftwaffe fighters' take-off, assembly and approach to the targets by flying at low level and keeping strict radio silence. The routes flown by the fighters were carefully planned, and ground markers helped with navigation over friendly territory, while a Junkers Ju 88 night fighter carrying a navigator led each formation. Briefing on the target airfields was assisted by recent reconnaissance photographs — and by the fact that the Luftwaffe itself had operated from them only months before.

The attacking force, in total some 1000 fighters, was divided into three main groups. In the north the fighters of JG 1, JG 3, JG 6, JG 26, JG 27, and JG 77 raided the forward airfields in the Netherlands and those in northern Belgium. In the centre, formations drawn from JG 2, JG 4, and JG 11 flew to the southerly Belgian airfields of Asch, Saint Trond and Le Culot. In the south, JG 53 flew from airfields in the Stuttgart region to attack the French airfield at Metz-Frescaty.

Although the Luftwaffe achieved surprise over the Allied airfields, they themselves suffered heavy losses.

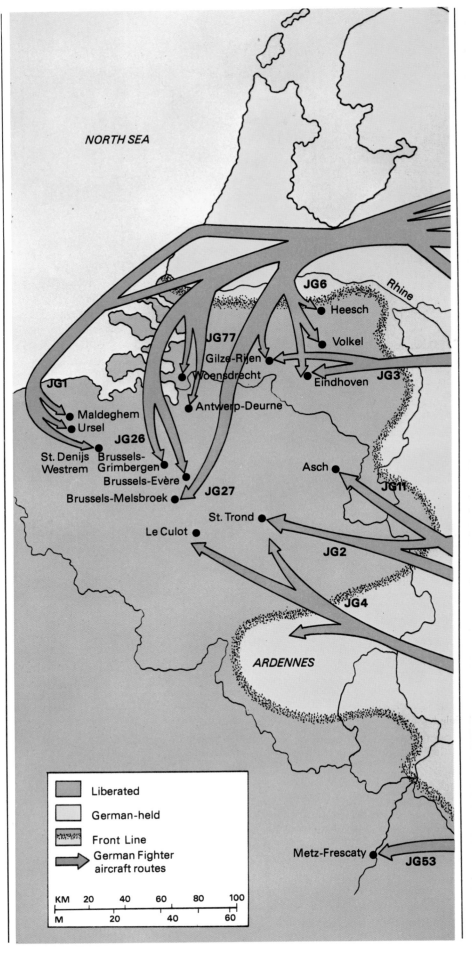

Oahu. The specially reinforced air groups of the Japanese carriers *Akagi, Kaga, Hiryu, Soryu, Shokaku* and *Zuikaku* launched 183 dive-bombers, torpedo-bombers and escorting fighters at 0600 hours in the first wave of the attack, which was led by Commander Mitsuo Fuchida. It was followed 75 minutes later by a second wave of 167 carrier aircraft. Complete surprise was achieved, as there had been no declaration of war and the Americans were following a peacetime Sunday routine. Four battleships were sunk and another four badly damaged, while ashore Oahu's five military airfields were strafed and bombed and some 160 aircraft were destroyed. Yet, unprepared as they were, the defenders fought back with vigour and 29 Japanese aircraft were brought down, 13 of them during air combats with the few American fighter aircraft that managed to get airborne.

As the Japanese carriers withdrew across the Pacific, the American-held Wake Island came under attack from the Japanese base at Kwajalein in the Marshall Islands. A single US Marine Corps squadron of Grumman F4F Wildcat fighters took part in the island's 16-day defence, inflicting heavy losses on the enemy before it was finally overwhelmed. On a much larger scale, the USAAF was fighting desperately to repulse the Japanese invasion of the Philippines. The islands' Boeing B-17 bomber force was soon wiped out and the Curtiss P-40 and Seversky P-35 fighters were hard-pressed in defence. Even the newly formed Philippines air force, flying obsolete Boeing P-26 fighters, was flung into the fray, but the defenders were consistently outnumbered and outperformed by the Japanese fighters and in May 1942 the remaining American forces surrendered.

The British defence of Malaya fared no better. The greatest blow came on 10 December, when Japanese Mitsubishi G3M Nell bombers flying from Indochina attacked and sank the warships HMS *Repulse* and HMS *Prince of Wales*. The Brewster Buffalo fighters flown by RAF, RAAF and RNZAF squadrons in defence of

Three Focke Wulf Fw 190s were lost early in the operation to German flak gunners, who had not been informed of the plan and assumed that any large formation of aircraft would be Allied. Some interceptions were made by Allied aircraft purely by chance. For example, the Messerschmitt Bf 109s of III Gruppe, JG 53 were pounced on by USAAF Republic P-47 Thunderbolts before they could reach their target and nine German fighters were shot down. Once their targets were reached, however, the Luftwaffe fighter pilots found only light anti-aircraft defences and Evère and Eindhoven were very hard hit.

The Luftwaffe's New Year's Day attack accounted for about 500 Allied aircraft destroyed. Most of these were tactical fighters and reconnaissance aircraft of the RAF's 2nd Tactical Air Force. Few Allied aircrew were killed, however, and the German victory was a hollow one, because more than 200 fighters and their pilots failed to return. The Luftwaffe was never again to mount an offensive on the scale of Operation Bodenplatte.

Top *A Messerschmitt Bf 109 (foreground) and Focke Wulf Fw 190s. These two fighters were the main participants in Operation Bodenplatte.*

Above *A Polish RAF pilot poses with the wreckage of an Fw 190 shot down by his Spitfire on 1 January 1945.*

Below *During the air strike on Pearl Harbor eight American battleships were sunk or damaged.*

PACIFIC WAR 1941–45

The war between the United States and Japan began on 7 December 1941 with a massive carrier air strike by the Japanese navy against the US Pacific Fleet's main base at Pearl Harbor, on the Hawaiian island of

Malaya proved to be no match for the Japanese Naka-jima Ki-43 Oscar fighters. The air defences of Sumatra and Java were no better, as the Netherlands East Indies Army Air Corps also relied on the Buffalo fighter. As these islands were occupied by the Japanese, the threat to Australia became serious. The air defence of Darwin relied only on a handful of USAAF P-40s at this time.

One advantage that the Allies did have was that the US Navy's aircraft carriers had so far escaped damage by the enemy. The USS *Yorktown*, USS *Enterprise* and USS *Lexington* were able to relieve the pressure on Australia at a critical time. *Lexington*'s air group raided the Japanese-held island of Rabaul, diverting the Japanese bombers away from Darwin and onto the carrier. One of *Lexington*'s fighter pilots, Lieutenant 'Butch' O'Hare of Squadron VF-3 accounted for five

Top *The highly manoeuvrable Japanese Mitsubishi A6M Zero fighter dominated the skies over the Pacific, before Allied fighter pilots evolved suitable tactics to master it.*

Above *Although armed with a heavy-calibre cannon, the USAAF's Bell P-39 Airacobra was no match for the agile Japanese fighters.*

Below left *The Nakajima B5N Kate torpedo-bomber took part in the Japanese attack on Pearl Harbor.*

clashed in the Battle of the Coral Sea. USS *Lexington* and USS *Yorktown* faced the Japanese fleet carriers *Shokaku* and *Zuikaku*, backed by the light carrier *Shoho*. It was the *Shoho* that became the first casualty of the battle, Douglas SBD Dauntless dive-bombers and TBD Devastator torpedo-bombers sending her to the bottom on 8 May. The following day the Japanese retaliated by seriously damaging the *Lexington*, which later sank. However, both Japanese fleet carriers and their air groups had been badly mauled and were unable to take part in the decisive Battle of Midway.

The Japanese navy's master strategist, Admiral Isoroku Yamamoto, intended to bring the US fleet to battle and to destroy it. The main operation against Midway Island and a diversionary feint towards the Aleutian Islands involved a force of five fleet carriers and three light carriers (one of each being despatched to the Aleutians). Against this the US Navy assembled the carriers *Enterprise*, *Yorktown* and *Hornet*, plus a Marine Aircraft Group and USAAF bomber units on Midway Island. The action opened on 3 June and on the following day US Navy carrier aircraft, at considerable loss to themselves, succeeded in sinking the four Japanese fleet carriers. *Yorktown* was so badly damaged that she had to be abandoned and sunk, yet the American victory was indisputable. The tide of Japanese conquest had finally been turned.

The Japanese Aleutian operation achieved little, although garrisons were established on Kiska and Attu islands. After these setbacks in the North and Central Pacific regions, the Japanese then pushed southwards into the Solomon Islands, threatening American communications with Australia. Key to the Solomons group was the island of Guadalcanal, which the Japanese occupied and on which they began building an airfield. In early August the Americans pushed an invasion force ashore and captured the airfield, which they named Henderson Field. US Marine infantry ashore were faced with a bitterly fought contest for

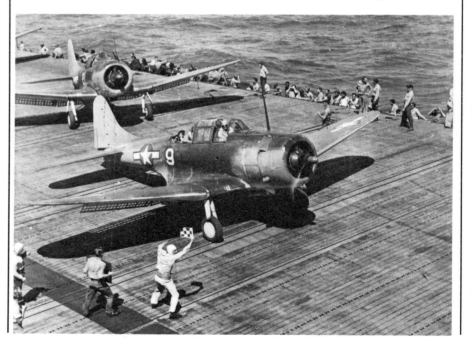

Japanese bombers in a single combat, becoming the first US Navy ace of the war and winning the Medal of Honor. USS *Hornet* had also gone onto the offensive by launching Lieutenant-Colonel Doolittle's 16 North American B-25 Mitchells in a morale-boosting raid on Tokyo. Yet these were comparatively small-scale successes. A more testing trial of strength came in early May 1942 when Japanese and US Navy carrier forces

solidate their position on Guadalcanal. Meanwhile new carriers were leaving the American shipyards and fresh air groups were being trained, while by contrast Japanese naval air power was wasting away.

In New Guinea General George Kenney's US Fifth Air Force, assisted by squadrons of the RAAF, had succeeded in mastering the opposing air forces by early 1943. The Fifth Air Force was to produce the two top-scoring American fighter pilots of the war – Dick Bong and Tommy McGuire. In the Solomons, the Japanese evacuated their remaining troops from Guadalcanal in February 1943 and Marine fighter strength in this area was greatly boosted by the arrival of Vought F4U Corsair fighters. Yet it was the USAAF that carried out the most successful fighter mission of early 1943, when on 18 April 16 Lockheed P-38s ambushed the Mitsubishi G4M Betty carrying Admiral Yamamoto on a tour of inspection and sent it crashing into the jungle.

By September 1943 new Essex-class carriers were ready for combat, carrying air groups of 100 aeroplanes. The Grumman Wildcat, Douglas Dauntless

Below *Vought F4U Corsair fighter-bombers of the US Marine Corps operating from an airstrip in the Solomon Islands.*

control of the island, while in the air Marine Grumman F4F Hellcats and USAAF Bell P-400 Airacobras fought off Japanese bombing attacks. On 24 August US Navy aircraft sank the carrier *Ryujo* off Guadalcanal, but enemy submarines damaged USS *Saratoga* and sank USS *Wasp*. This left USS *Hornet* as the sole American carrier at sea in the Pacific. Yamamoto determined to exploit this weakness and despatched three fleet carriers and a light carrier to the South Pacific. However, by the time that battle was joined on 27 October, USS *Enterprise* had reinforced the *Hornet*. The Battle of Santa Cruz resulted in a stalemate, with the loss of the *Hornet* and damage to *Enterprise* offset by severe damage to two Japanese carriers and the mauling of the Japanese air groups. The action gave the Americans breathing space to con-

Left *A North American B-25 Mitchell bomber of the USAAF's Fifth Air Force attacks Japanese shipping in Hansa Bay, New Guinea.*

Opposite page, bottom right *The US Navy's Douglas SBD Dauntless dive-bomber served throughout the Pacific War and achieved particular success at the crucial Battle of Midway in 1942.*

Left *The Consolidated B-24 Liberators of the 380th Bomb Group, Fifth Air Force, operated from Darwin in northern Australia in 1943.*

and Devastator aircraft of the early war years then began to give way to Grumman F6F Hellcats, TBM Avengers and Curtiss SB2C Helldivers. The new carrier forces began a series of strikes in the Central Pacific, attacking the Japanese garrisons on Marcus Island, Makin, Tarawa and Wake Island. As American forces in the Solomons prepared to occupy Bougainville in October, units of the Fast Carrier Task Force supported the landings and kept pressure on Japanese forces in the Marshall Islands, Rabaul and New Britain. In the new year the carriers, under the command of Admiral Marc Mitscher, covered the occupation of Truk atoll in the Central Pacific.

In the Southwest Pacific the Japanese were finally pushed out of New Guinea during 1944. By June Mitscher's carriers were in the Central Pacific, providing air cover for the assault on the Marianas. This operation provoked a counter-thrust by Japanese carrier forces. The Battle of the Philippine Sea not only resulted in the loss of three more of Japan's precious carriers, but US Navy fighters decimated the enemy air groups, accounting for 402 Japanese aircraft destroyed in an air action that became known as 'the Marianas Turkey Shoot'. The way was then open to occupy the islands of Saipan, Guam and Tinian, which were quickly developed as bases for the Boeing B-29 Superfortresses. In November 1944 the first B-29 raid was flown from the Marianas against the Japanese homeland – the target being Tokyo. The offensive was slow to build up momentum, yet by the spring of 1945 the raids began to achieve results. Japan's cities were especially vulnerable to incendiary attack and in all 65 of them were devastated by fire raids. In the final five months of the war 141,230 tonnes (139,000 tons) of bombs were dropped by the B-29s over Japan.

In October 1944 the Americans were poised for the invasion of the Philippines. The Japanese reaction was fierce and the Battle of Leyte Gulf was the last major action between the American and Japanese fleets. Four Japanese carriers went to the bottom for the loss of the American light carrier *Princetown*. By this time the US fleet had to deal with an increasing number of kamikaze suicide attacks. The wooden-decked carriers were especially vulnerable to the kamikazes and however efficient the combat air patrols of F6F Hell-

cats, a number of suicide pilots generally broke through to complete their grisly mission. Kamikaze attacks continued during the assaults on Iwo Jima and Okinawa, yet their results, though often spectacular, could not affect the outcome of the war at this late stage. It seemed that the Pacific War must end with a full-scale assault on the Japanese home islands. Yet the atomic bombs dropped on Hiroshima and Nagasaki in August 1945 entirely altered the strategic picture and forced the Japanese surrender.

Above *Boeing B-29 Superfortress bombers began raids on the Japanese home islands in 1944, operating from bases in China and the Marianas.*

PATH FINDER FORCE 1942–44

RAF Bomber Command's Path Finder Force was an elite corps in the RAF during World War II. Its crews were highly experienced and skilled in the complexities of night-bombing operations, and were respon-

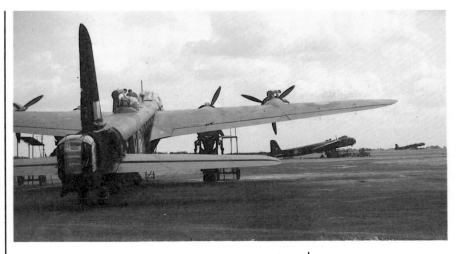

sible for finding and marking targets for the aircraft of the Main Force to bomb. Hence wearing the gilt cagle PFF badge denoted a level of expertise and courage above the average. The idea of a special target-marking force was forcefully promoted by Group Captain Sydney Bufton, Deputy Director of Bomber Operations at the Air Ministry. In spite of the reluctance of Sir Arthur Harris, the C-in-C of Bomber Command, to deprive the squadrons of their best aircrew to form such a force, the go-ahead was given in August 1942. The PFF was commanded by Group Captain Donald Bennett, an expert in navigation, and initially comprised Nos 7, 35, 83, 109 and 156 Squadrons.

The prime justification for forming the PFF was of course the poor record of ordinary bomber crews in finding their targets. The Gee radio-beam navigation aid had helped in this respect, but it had a limited range, and by the summer of 1942 it was being jammed by the Germans. Consequently when the PFF led its first raid to Flensburg on the night of 18/19 August it was not surprising that the raid was a failure. However,

Above Short Stirling bombers of No 7 Squadron joined with the Path Finder Force in 1942 and took part in the first pathfinder operation – a raid on Flensburg on 18/19 August.

Below left One of the first Path Finder Force units was No 35 Squadron, which operated Handley Page Halifax bombers from Graveley in Huntingdonshire.

a new and highly accurate navigation aid, known as Oboe, was soon to enter service. Oboe was in many ways suited to the PFF concept since only one bomber could use the system at a time and it was therefore best used for target marking. When fitted to de Havilland Mosquitoes of the PFF, Oboe produced excellent results, although it too could only be used over a relatively limited range. Any target lying beyond the Ruhr (which marked the effective range of Oboe until ground stations could be set up on the Continent) had to be found using the H2S ground-mapping radar or more conventional navigation techniques.

By the end of 1942 the PFF had succeeded in convincing Bomber Command of its value. When the Battle of the Ruhr opened in March 1943, the pathfinders were able to use Oboe-equipped Mosquitoes and achieved very accurate results. This was in spite of the industrial haze which shrouded the region and had previously defeated attempts at pinpoint bombing. Hamburg was the next major target for Bomber Command and the PFF's success was repeated using H2S, which was especially effective as a port target produced clear radar returns. Neither bombing aid was of use against Berlin, however, and many of the raids launched against the German capital early in 1944 went astray. These failures were compounded by the defeat over Nuremberg on the night of 31 March/1 April 1944.

At the time of the Nuremberg raid the PFF (by this time Bomber Command's No 8 Group) comprised seven Avro Lancaster squadrons, three Mosquito bomber squadrons, two Oboe-Mosquito squadrons and a Mosquito meteorological flight. The target-marking techniques employed by the pathfinders involved the dropping of target indicator bombs to provide a visual aiming point for the Main Force bombers. If the weather over the target was clear, flares were dropped first to illuminate the target for the marker aircraft. In overcast conditions the target was marked blind, if necessary using sky markers (pyrotechnics attached to a parachute) which would ignite above the cloud layer. After Nuremberg, Bomber Command was restricted to targets in occupied France which were well within Oboe range. Another result of that débâcle was that the PFF lost its monopoly of target marking, and No 5 Group began to mark its own targets. However, the PFF remained an important part of the RAF's night-bomber force and when heavy raids deep into Germany resumed in the autumn of 1944 the pathfinders' skills were again put to good use.

Right Target markers can be seen glowing on the ground in this photograph taken during a Bomber Command raid on Pforzheim on the night of 23/24 February 1945.

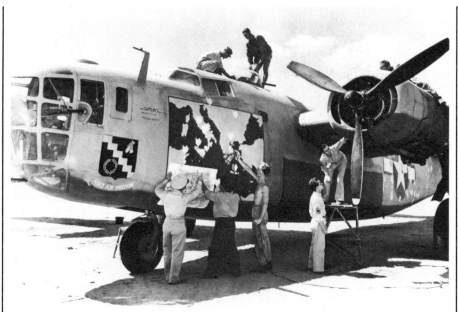

The following year a massed raid by some 200 B-24s was planned. It was decided to fly in daylight, in order to make navigation easier, but to confuse the defences the bombers would operate at very low level. On 1 August preparations were complete and the B-24s of five USAAF bomb groups took off from bases in Libya and set course for the target. The defenders put up a wall of flak around the refineries and 33 American bombers were shot down. A further eight were lost to enemy fighters and other causes raised the total loss to 52 bombers, with a further 58 damaged. The results of the bombing, while less than the planners' sanguine expectation of 90 per cent destruction, were nonetheless very damaging. In the spring of 1944 Allied bombers based in Italy began a series of attacks on Ploesti, 19 raids being flown by the USAAF between April and August. The RAF too made a number of night raids during the period, at the end of which the advancing Soviet armies occupied the area, thus effectively denying further supplies to Germany.

PLOESTI RAIDS 1942–44

Above This Consolidated B-24D Liberator of the Ninth Air Force's 98th Bomb Group took part in the first Ploesti mission.

POLAND 1939

The Romanian oilfields at Ploesti, a sprawling complex of refineries, offered the Allies a tempting target for air attack, as by 1942 they were supplying 60 per cent of Germany's natural oil. Yet the target lay deep in the Balkans, beyond the range of most Allied bombers, and its defenders would get ample warning of any attack. Nevertheless, the USAAF launched the first attack on the refineries on the night of 11/12 June 1942, using Consolidated B-24 Liberators based in Egypt and carrying a reduced bomb-load. The target was approached in darkness and the 13 bombers reached Ploesti by dawn. There was cloud over the target, however, and little damage resulted from the attack.

Below left USAAF reconnaissance photographs, showing bomb damage inflicted on Ploesti's Romana Americana oil refinery, the third-largest in Romania.

Below Fighter pilots of No 113 (Owl) Squadron stand by a camouflaged PZL P-11. This unit took part in the defence of Warsaw.

When the German armies, spearheaded by seven Panzer divisions, began their invasion of Poland on 1 September 1939 they were supported by a force of some 1500 aircraft. The Luftwaffe had deployed 219 Junkers Ju 87 Stuka dive-bombers, 648 Heinkel He 111, Dornier Do 17 and Junkers Ju 86 medium bombers and 30 ground-attack Henschel Hs 123 bi-planes for the attack in the east. The fighter force comprised 210 single-engined Messerschmitt Bf 109s and twin-engined Bf 110s. In general the German air force was well-equipped and highly trained, only the Hs 123 and Ju 86 being obsolescent aircraft at this time. In contrast, the Polish air force was generally poorly equipped, as it had been unable to obtain supplies of modern

Left *Luftwaffe personnel examine a damaged PZL P-11. The standard fighter of the Polish air force, it was completely outclassed by the German Messerschmitt Bf 109.*

Below *The PZL P-23 Karas light-bomber and reconnaissance aircraft equipped 12 Polish squadrons in September 1939.*

fighters from the West and the indigenous aircraft industry was slow to produce modern warplanes. The operational units fielded some 400 aircraft on 1 September 1939, comprising 159 PZL P-11 and P-7 fighters, 118 PZL P-23 Karas light bombers, only 36 of the new twin-engined monoplane P-37 Los bombers and various obsolescent bombers and reconnaissance types. The fighters in particular were outclassed by their opponents and the new PZL P-50 Jastreb fighter was not yet in production.

German operations over Poland began as early as July 1939 with incursions by high-flying Do 17 reconnaissance aircraft, which the P-11 fighters had neither the speed nor the altitude performance to intercept. Once the assault got under way, the advancing ground forces were supported by Hs 126 short-range reconnaissance aircraft and Ju 87 Stukas, while the medium bombers attacked Polish airfields. Although a number of Polish aircraft were destroyed on the ground, most of them moved from their peacetime bases to dispersed temporary airstrips from which they continued the unequal fight. By 3 September 46 Polish fighters had been destroyed in the air and on the ground, while Luftwaffe aircraft losses were 55 aircraft destroyed.

The city of Warsaw was heavily attacked by German bombers from the outset and some 60 bombing

raids were mounted against the Polish capital over a three-week period. The outnumbered Polish fighters were forced to divide their efforts between attempting to defend Warsaw and providing some air support to the hard-pressed armies. Although individual pilots fought with great skill and heroism, their efforts were doomed to failure from the outset. The Karas light bombers were thrown against the German Panzer columns, but their losses to flak and fighters was very high. By 12 September the Polish air force was reduced to some 50 fighters and a similar number of bomber and reconnaissance aircraft. The Luftwaffe continued to suffer losses, however, and more than 150 German aircraft had been destroyed at the end of two weeks' fighting. Yet the resistance of the Polish air force could not halt the inexorable advance of the German armies and on 17 September the Soviet armies attacked across Poland's frontiers in the east. Warsaw managed to hold out for a further ten days, but with the fall of the capital organized Polish resistance virtually collapsed. Isolated groups fought on until 4 October, when the German and Soviet occupation was complete. More than 100 operational and training aircraft escaped across the Carpathians to Romania, and Polish aircrew continued to fight with the Allied air forces. German aircraft losses totalled 285 machines, 67 of which were single-engined fighters. The virtual annihilation of the Polish air force had not been achieved without cost.

RADAR

Since its invention in the late 1930s, radar has assumed an increasingly important role in virtually every aspect of air warfare. The first operational radar system was RAF Fighter Command's Chain Home early-warning radar stations, 18 of which were in service by the outbreak of World War II. With a detection range against high-flying aeroplanes of about 160km (100 miles), these radars provided much-needed early warning of air attack. The invention of radar, known initially by the cover-name RDF (radio direction-finding), is credited to Sir Robert Watson-Watt. Yet German scientists were also working along the same lines and

Below *The British Chain Home early-warning radar network was a key weapon in fighting the Battle of Britain.*

also be used to detect surface targets and its earliest application in this role was the RAF's ASV (air-to-surface vessel) Mk I, which became operational early in 1940 and in developed forms was to play an important part in the battle against the U-boats. RAF Bomber Command's principal radar aid during World War II was the H2S ground-mapping radar, which first appeared in January 1943. Although H2S was effective over areas where coastlines, rivers or lakes provided a sharp contrast to the land, over built-up areas or countryside the radar picture was less distinctive. Modern attack radars are considerably improved in this respect.

The greatest new postwar development in military radars is the AEW (airborne early warning) set, which can cover a far greater area of sky than a ground-based sensor and is also far more effective against low-flying

in 1939 the Luftwaffe had a chain of eight Freya early-warning radars covering the approaches to the North Sea coast of Germany.

The next step in the development of ground-based radars was the production of the British GCI (ground control of interception) set, which became operational early in 1941. This radar had a rotary scanner to give 360-degree coverage. Consequently both a raiding aircraft and an intercepting fighter would appear on the controller's screen and he could use this information to direct the interception. This development was especially significant for night fighting, but was used increasingly for all interceptions. The modern air defence radar operates on much the same principle, although such systems as the American SAGE (semi-automatic ground environment) and NADGE (NATO air defence ground environment) used computer processing to speed up interchange of information.

Airborne radar systems for locating targets was the next development, with AI (airborne interception) sets for night fighters being accorded priority in development. The British AI Mk III radar was fitted to Blenheim night fighters during the Blitz and thereafter became increasingly widely used. The Luftwaffe was slower to develop an airborne radar for night fighters, and the first Lichtenstein sets did not reach the night-fighter squadrons until early 1942. Airborne radar can

Top left The AI Mk VIII radar fitted in the nose of this DH Mosquito Mk XII night fighter made use of a dish-shaped scanner fitted beneath the radome.

Above left This Junkers Ju 88 is fitted with FuG 200 Hohentwiel search radar for maritime reconnaissance work.

Above The Panavia Tornado strike aircraft of the RAF is fitted with an advanced terrain-following radar, which enables it to follow the contours of the ground while flying at low level.

aircraft. However, all applications of radar have greatly increased in efficiency, thanks to the application of modern high technology. To quote but one revealing example, the AWG-9 system fitted to the US Navy's Grumman F-14 fleet defence fighter has a maximum effective range of 210km (130 miles), can track 17 targets simultaneously and can engage up to six at once. From the BMEWS (ballistic missile early warning system) which keeps an eye on space, to the Panavia Tornado's automatic terrain-following, radar systems have proliferated and their significance today is as great as ever before.

RECONNAISSANCE

The earliest aerial reconnaissance vehicles were observation balloons, first used in battle by the armies of Revolutionary France late in the eighteenth century. Aerial photography was used for military purposes during the American Civil War at the siege of Richmond, Virginia, in 1862. Therefore with the invention of the aeroplane early in the twentieth century it is not surprising that this too was adapted for military reconnaissance. Reconnaissance aeroplanes were used during the Italian War in Libya (1911–12) and had become an established

Between the wars military photographic reconnaissance was in general neglected, although aerial mapping surveys of various little-known regions were undertaken. In the late 1930s the Luftwaffe was technically well-equipped for photo reconnaissance, but interpretation of photographs and dissemination of the resulting intelligence was a serious weakness of the German system. In Britain the RAF's resources were generally poor and it was left to a civilian, Sidney Cotton, to obtain clandestine photographs of German installations flying a Lockheed 12A civil-registered airliner. Cotton's work was taken over by the Air Ministry in September 1939 and his organization formed the basis for the later Photographic Reconnaissance Unit (PRU).

One of the most successful wartime reconnaissance

part of the armies of the great powers by the outbreak of World War I in August 1914. Aerial reconnaissance photographs were particularly useful in mapping the enemy's trench systems, and Haig's attack on Neuve-Chapelle in March 1915 was planned using such photographs. Typical of the reconnaissance cameras of this time was the Royal Flying Corps' P-7 camera, which was fitted with an 18-plate magazine and could obtain excellent results from an altitude of 4300m (14,000ft).

Hand-in-hand with the development of aerial photographic techniques came the skills of photographic interpretation. The increasing use of aerial reconnaissance had led to the camouflaging of important military installations, but careful and expert scrutiny of a print could reveal much that was not immediately apparent. Tell-tale signs such as the shadows cast by camouflaged equipment, or well-worn tracks converging on a concealed headquarters or dump, could lead the interpreter to discover a hitherto unsuspected enemy offensive in the making. Various new techniques aided scientific photo interpretation. For example, pairs of prints viewed through a stereoscope gave a three-dimensional effect unobtainable from a single print, thus throwing building and geographical features into relief and making the interpreter's task easier. Photo mosaics covering a wide area with a series of overlapping pictures also helped to ensure that no important intelligence indications were overlooked.

Above The pilot of an RFC BE 12 is briefed prior to carrying out a photographic reconnaissance mission.

Right RAF photographic interpreters pinpoint the location of aerial photographs by means of a map.

Below A Luftwaffe Junkers Ju 88D reconnaissance aircraft of Fernaufklärungsgruppe 122, serving on the Eastern Front in the winter of 1942–3.

aircraft was the RAF's Supermarine Spitfire PR variants, which were completely unarmed and relied on their altitude and speed to keep them out of trouble on sorties that took them over virtually all of Germany and occupied Europe. Operating from such British airfields as Benson, St Eval, Wick and Leuchars, they were later joined by the equally successful twin-engined de Havilland Mosquito. Their tasks included the provision of photographs of potential targets for RAF Bomber Command and then coverage after a raid to enable bomb damage to be assessed. The PRU also covered objectives of interest to the army and navy and specialized tactical reconnaissance squadrons were formed exclusively for army cooperative work. One of the greatest PR coups of the war was the discovery of a V1 flying bomb under test at Peenemünde at the end of 1943. The USAAF joined in this effort later in the war with modified PR versions of their North American Mustang and Lockheed Lightning fighters.

The Spitfire and Mosquito PR variants remained in RAF service until the mid-1950s, by which time jet-engined Gloster Meteor and English Electric Canberra reconnaissance aircraft were in service. The Canberra PR Mk 9 was an extended-wing version of the standard bomber design, capable of high-altitude photography. An even better altitude perfomance was obtained from the RB-57F version of the American-built B-57 Canberra. During the Cold War between

the Soviet Union and the NATO powers in the West clandestine reconnaissance flights were carried out over Soviet and Chinese territory in order to obtain information on their armed forces and military potential. Most notorious of the aircraft employed on such missions was the Lockheed U-2, a glider-like high-flying reconnaissance aircraft. In May 1960 a U-2 was shot down by a Soviet surface-to-air missile while flying at an altitude of 21,000m (68,000ft) over Sverdlovsk, thus provoking an international incident. Reconnaissance satellites which could obtain similar intelligence were soon brought into service and thus the hazardous overflights of Soviet territory ended. Nonetheless, developed versions of the U-2 remain in USAF service, as does the later Mach 3 Lockheed SR-71 Blackbird, which has a ceiling of more than 24,500 (80,000ft).

While these exotic aircraft were developed for strategic reconnaissance, tactical reconnaissance missions were flown by such types as the USAF's Republic RF-84 Thunderflash and Douglas RF-101 Voodoo, both conversions of standard tactical fighter types. Reconnaissance Voodoos saw action with the USAF in Southeast Asia, flying reconnaissance missions over North Vietnam until superseded by the RF-4C version of the McDonnell Douglas Phantom. An important new development of the Vietnam War was the reconnaissance drone, which was launched from a Lockheed DC-130 Hercules mother plane, flew a preprogrammed mission (generally over a heavily defended area) and parachuted down in friendly territory to be

recovered together with its precious films. As well as conventional photography, modern reconnaissance aircraft make use of infra-red and radar imagery, while specialized ELINT (electronic intelligence) aircraft can gather an electronic order of battle by monitoring enemy radio and radar emissions, thereby locating the positions of main forces and headquarters.

SCHWEINFURT RAIDS 1943

The USAAF's Eighth Air Force was formed in Britain with the object of carrying out daylight strategic bombing raids on Germany. It was believed that the defensive firepower of the bombers alone would be sufficient to defend their massed formations from fighter attack. However, this doctrine could not be put to the test until the summer of 1943, when the Eighth Air Force had sufficient bombers on strength to fly missions deep into Germany. The German aircraft industry was a primary target and the ball-bearing works at Schweinfurt in southern Germany was identified as a key production centre. Accordingly a force of 230 Boeing B-17s was despatched against this target on 17 August 1943, losing 36 of their number to the German defences. Although the target was hit the damage was by no means crippling and a later mission was planned.

The second Schweinfurt mission was flown on 14 October 1943 by a force of 420 B-17s and Consolidated

Above *The B-17 Flying Fortresses of the Eighth Air Force relied on tight box formations and mutual support from the bombers' defensive fire to penetrate the German defences during the Schweinfurt Raid.*

Below *USAAF armourers collect spent 0·5in machine-gun cartridges from a B-17 after a raid on Germany. The bombers' gunners claimed 288 victories on 14 October 1943.*

B-24 Liberators, but the latter were turned back by bad weather. Despite heavy opposition, the B-17s succeeded in seriously damaging the target. However, the formations had been under heavy attack as soon as their short-range fighter escort had withdrawn and losses were cripplingly high. In all 60 bombers had fallen to the defences, a further five had crashed in England and over 100 were damaged. The American gunners claimed 288 fighters shot down, a wildly exaggerated figure as actual Luftwaffe losses were some 50 fighters. Ball-bearing production at Schweinfurt fell by 50 per cent and it took the Germans six months to repair the damage fully. However, the Eighth Air Force's losses were far too high to be sustained over a long campaign. Consequently it was decided to build up a long-range fighter escort force and, when the Eighth Air Force resumed deep penetration raids, the bombers were accompanied by North American P-51 Mustang fighters.

SHIPPING STRIKES

The earliest anti-shipping weapons carried by aeroplanes were bombs and torpedoes and it was the latter weapon that was considered to be the more effective. The first successful air torpedo attack was carried out in 1915 by Flight Commander C. H. Edmonds, flying

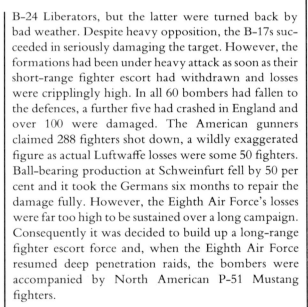

a Short 184 seaplane from HMS *Ben-my-Chree*, when he sank a Turkish merchantman in the Dardanelles. The British continued to develop torpedo-carrying aircraft and in 1918 the carrier HMS *Argus* embarked a full squadron of single-seat Sopwith Cuckoo torpedo aircraft. In the United States the potential of the bomb was demonstrated in 1921 when Martin NBS-1 bombers of the US Army Air Service sank the former German battleship *Ostfriesland* in a much-publicized demonstration. Thereafter the inter-war development of anti-shipping aircraft followed the parallel lines of bomb and torpedo carrier. In Britain the Fleet Air Arm (a branch of the RAF until 1937) flew such Blackburn types as the Dart, Ripon, Baffin and Shark biplanes. By the outbreak of war the FAA was equipped with the Blackburn Skua dive-bomber and Fairey Swordfish torpedo-bomber. Ashore RAF Coastal Command began the replacement of Vickers Vildebeest torpedo biplanes with the twin-engined Bristol Beaufort torpedo-bomber monoplanes, and bomb-carrying Lockheed Hudsons were purchased from the United States.

The US Navy had done much to develop the shipborne dive-bomber with such inter-war aeroplanes as the Curtiss F8C Helldiver and F11C Goshawk biplanes. By 1941 the main American carrier-borne anti-shipping aircraft were the Douglas TBD Devastator torpedo-bomber and SBD Dauntless dive-bomber, both of them single-engined monoplanes. The USAAF's Boeing B-17 also had an anti-shipping role, as it had originally been intended for the coastal defence of the North American continent. On the other side of the Pacific the Japanese were proceeding

on similar lines, with the Nakajima B5N Kate torpedo-bomber and Aichi D3A Val dive-bomber in service aboard the carriers, backed up by Mitsubishi G3M Nell and G4M Betty land-based naval bombers.

The RAF and FAA enjoyed little success in anti-shipping operations in the early years of World War II, although there were some notable exceptions to the general rule. For example FAA Skua dive-bombers sank the German cruiser *Königsberg* during the Norwegian Campaign and the FAA's Fairey Swordfish crippled the Italian fleet at Taranto in November 1940. Yet when the German battlecruisers *Scharnhorst* and *Gneisenau* made their Channel Dash from Brest in February 1942 the combined resources of the RAF and FAA did not achieve a single bomb or torpedo hit. Had it not been for the efforts of the minelaying aircraft, the German ships would have escaped unscathed. The situation improved in November 1942 with the formation of the RAF's first Bristol Beaufighter strike wing. Early operations combined torpedo-armed Beaufighters with bomb-armed aircraft. The Beau-

Above *The Douglas TBD Devastator was the US Navy's carrier-based torpedo-bomber at the start of the Pacific War, but the type suffered heavy losses in action.*

Left *A Heinkel He 111 bomber is loaded with practice torpedoes. This aircraft operated against the British Arctic convoys in 1942.*

Below *Junkers Ju 88A bombers operated against British convoys in the Mediterranean, this aircraft serving with I Gruppe Kampfgeschwader 77 in Sicily.*

fighter's built-in armament of four 20mm cannon was also useful for flak suppression. However, the real breakthrough came with the introduction of the rocket-armed Beaufighters, armed with eight 27kg (60lb) rocket projectiles. These aircraft were less vulnerable to flak than the torpedo-armed 'Torbeaus' because they did not have to hold a steady course at low level in order to launch their weapons.

German anti-shipping operations were often carried out by Junkers Ju 88 and Heinkel He 111 medium bombers, although the latter was adapted as a torpedo-bomber. An especially successful anti-shipping aircraft in the early war years was the Focke Wulf Fw 200 Condor four-engined maritime patrol aircraft, although as the anti-aircraft armament of merchantmen increased the Condor's successes diminished.

Left *Bristol Beaufighters armed with rocket projectiles and cannon proved to be a formidable anti-shipping weapon in the hands of the RAF Strike Wings.*

and tactically skilled personnel by making an audacious attack which, if successful, would neutralize Arab air power at the outset of the conflict.

The initial attack was planned for 0745 hours Israeli time because by then the Egyptian air force's dawn air patrols would have landed and the state of readiness of fighter aircraft on the ground would have been relaxed. Furthermore, as Cairo time was an hour behind Israel's, it was hoped that the attack would find many senior officers on their way to their headquarters, making a prompt Egyptian reaction to the initial air attacks very difficult. Egypt's forward airfields in Sinai were the objectives of Dassault Mystères and Ouragans flying direct from their bases. The targets in the Canal

From 1943 onwards the Germans began to use Fritz-X guided bombs and HS 293 glider bombs against shipping. Another successful Axis aircraft was the Savoia Marchetti SM79 torpedo-bomber of the Regia Aeronautica, which was widely used in the Mediterranean.

In the Pacific the great carrier battles provided the dominant theme of the naval air war, with the US Navy replacing the Devastator and Dauntless with the new Grumman TBM Avenger and Curtiss SB2C Helldiver later in the war. However, shore-based anti-shipping strikes often proved to be highly successful and the operations of the USAAF Fifth Air Force's Douglas A-20 and North American B-25 Mitchell bombers were especially noteworthy. The Japanese kamikaze attacks of 1944–5 are perhaps most interesting in that they provided a foretaste of the problems of defending naval ships against guided missiles – for the suicide aircraft was virtually a missile with human guidance.

In 1982 the Falklands conflict in the South Atlantic showed that missile-armed naval strike aircraft pose a formidable threat to shipping. Exocet-armed Dassault Super Etendards of the Argentine navy sank the destroyer HMS *Sheffield* and the container-ship *Atlantic Conveyor*. The Soviet Union's Tupolev Tu-26 Backfire bomber and the US Navy's Harpoon-armed Grumman A-6 Intruders and Lockheed P-3 Orions may achieve even more spectacular successes in a future naval conflict.

SIX-DAY WAR 1967

On 5 June 1967 the Israeli air force opened hostilities against her Arab neighbours with an air attack which has become a classic example of tactical suprise. Its primary target was the Egyptian air force and the intention was to catch it on its airfields and to wipe out its aircraft on the ground. With a strength of some 350 aircraft, the Israeli air force was vastly outnumbered by her Arab enemies, who could muster a total of 800 combat aircraft with Egypt alone contributing 450 warplanes. Consequently it made sense for Israel to exploit her qualitative advantages in highly motivated

Top *One of the most unusual anti-shipping aircraft of World War II was the DH Mosquito Mk XVII, which was armed with a nose-mounted 57mm cannon.*

Above *MiG-17s of the Egyptian air force flew a number of ground-attack missions during the Six-Day War.*

Zone and Nile Delta were the objectives of Israel's newly acquired Dassault Mirage III fighters and the older Super Mystères. They were approached from the north-west by the Israeli fighters, which had swept out over the Mediterranean at low level and then swung in over the Egyptian coast in an unexpected direction to evade detection.

The first priority of the attacking force was to put the enemy runways out of commission. A specially developed runway cratering bomb was used and a number of them were fitted with delayed-action fuses to hamper the work of runway repair. Meanwhile the grounded Egyptian warplanes were at the mercy of the Israeli aircraft, which attacked in relays of four over a period of some two hours. By the end of this time the Egyptian air force had virtually ceased to exist as a coherent fighting force. Attacking with fragmentation bombs, rockets and cannon, the Israeli fighter-

on Jordan, Syria and Iraq. With Arab air power neutralized, the Israeli air force concentrated on the support of ground forces. The wholesale destruction of Egyptian armour and other vehicles retreating through the Mitla Pass in Sinai was especially impressive. Helicopter assaults on enemy rear areas were also mounted to good effect. At the end of six days of fighting Israel was in possession of the Sinai peninsula, Jerusalem, the west bank of the Jordan and in Syria had established positions on the commanding Golan Heights. These tremendous gains were made possible by the early achievement of air superiority by the Israeli air force.

Left The burnt-out remains of three Egyptian MiG-21s which were caught lined up in the open on their airfield by the initial Israeli air attack.

SPANISH CIVIL WAR 1936–39

When civil war broke out in Spain in July 1936, the Spanish air force was equipped with mostly outdated combat aircraft. The main fighter type was the Nieuport-Delage NiD 52 sesquiplane, supplied by France. The same country had provided the 60 or so Breguet 19 reconnaissance bombers then in service and Britain's contribution was 20 Vickers Vildebeest

Below Republican fighter pilots stand beside a Polikarpov I-15, more than 500 of which were supplied by the Soviet Union during the Spanish Civil War. They were flown by Soviet air force volunteers and Soviet-trained Spaniards.

bombers found it difficult to miss the warplanes neatly parked in rows. By the end of the day Israeli claims totalled 240 enemy aircraft destroyed.

The pattern of the initial attack was varied in two areas. In Sinai the airfields of El Arish and Jebel Libni were spared the destruction of their runways. This was because the Israelis were confident that their ground forces could quickly overrun them and thereafter the Israeli air force could put them to good use. In southern Egypt the airfields of Luxor and Ras Banas were beyond the range of fighter-bombers and they became the target of twin-engined Sud Aviation Vautour bombers. Few air-to-air combats took place, although in one clash between 16 Mirages and 20 MiG-21s over Abu Sueir four of the Arab fighters were destroyed for no Israeli loss.

Egypt's allies came under attack later on 5 June and 68 enemy aircraft were claimed destroyed in attacks

Left *The Republicans acquired combat aircraft from many sources. These Letov S-231 fighters came from Czechoslovakia.*

torpedo-bombers, plus three Hawker Fury biplane fighters. In the main, these aircraft remained in government hands with the Republican air force, but many experienced pilots were attracted to the Nationalist cause. The first large-scale air operation of the war was the ferrying of General Franco's Nationalist troops from Morocco to southern Spain. The airlift was begun by a handful of Douglas DC-2 and Fokker Trimotor airliners, but these were quickly joined by German Junkers Ju 52/3m military transports.

In August further aid reached the Nationalists from Germany, including Heinkel He 51 fighters and instructors. Italy despatched Savoia Marchetti SM81 trimotor bombers and Fiat CR32 fighters, together with volunteer aircrew to fly them. The first combat of the war was fought on 23 July between Nationalist and Republican NiD 52s, the former emerging victorious. Yet substantial aid was now reaching the Republicans, in the form of French-supplied bombers and fighters and volunteer pilots from many countries. As Nationalist forces advanced on Madrid, their air force was strengthened by further Italian and German aircraft and German pilots were beginning to fly in combat as well as providing instruction.

Opposition to the Nationalists stiffened in October 1936 with the arrival of Soviet aircraft and volunteers to assist the Republicans. Tupolev SB-2 monoplane bombers could often outrun the Nationalist fighters, and the Polikarpov I-15 and especially the I-16 fighters proved to be very effective in combat. By December the Republicans had achieved a measure of ascendancy in the air and the advance on Madrid had come to a halt. The Nationalists' German and Italian allies responded by forming the Condor Legion and Aviazione Legionaria respectively, to formalize their air assistance to Franco's forces. Both were aware of the pressing need for newer warplanes to combat the Soviet types and over the next three months the Germans introduced the Heinkel He 111 and Dornier Do 17 bombers and the Messerschmitt Bf 109B

fighter, while the Italian contribution was the Savoia Marchetti SM79 bomber. Heavy ground fighting on the Madrid front in February 1937 was accompanied by intense air combat. Yet the result was a stalemate and attention shifted northwards to the Basque region at the end of March. It was during this campaign that the notorious bombing of Guernica by the German Condor Legion occurred.

In May 1937 the Republicans launched a diversionary offensive at Guadalajara in an unsuccessful attempt to relieve the pressure on the northern region. Nationalist air forces were quickly switched south, however, and the Republicans were halted. A similar attack at Brunete in July was also defeated. By the summer of 1937 fresh supplies of aircraft, mostly of Soviet design, had reached the Republicans and Spanish pilots trained in the USSR were available in increasing numbers. Therefore when a third Republican offensive was launched at Belchite in late August, their air force outnumbered the Nationalists by 470 aircraft to 350. Yet by this time Franco was victorious in the north and could concentrate his forces in central Spain.

With increasing numbers of Messerschmitt Bf 109 fighters becoming available, the Nationalists had an aircraft that could effectively deal with the I-16 and

Above *This Republican Tupolev SB-2 bomber was captured by Nationalist forces. When the SB-2 first appeared over Spain, no Nationalist fighters were fast enough to intercept it.*

*Among the warplanes supplied
by Germany to the Nationalist
air force was this Heinkel
He 70 light reconnaissance
bomber, which is pictured in
the markings adopted after the
end of the war.*

SB-2. Late in 1937 the Italians introduced their new Fiat BR20 bomber into combat and the Germans began to test the Junkers Ju 87A dive-bomber under operational conditions. The strengthened Nationalists opened an offensive in Aragon in March 1938 and by the middle of April had reached the coast, cutting Republican Spain in half. Heinkel He 51s and Italian Meridionali Ro 37bis light bombers provided especially effective close support for ground forces. During the summer of 1938 the Republicans' Soviet volunteer pilots began to return to the USSR, leaving the relatively inexperienced Spanish Republican airmen to continue the struggle. A major offensive by the Republicans on the Ebro Front in July was defeated and losses in the air were particularly heavy.

In January 1939 the Nationalists occupied Barcelona and the civil war entered its final phase. An infusion of new equipment from Germany and Italy included the Bf 109E and Fiat G50 fighters. Yet the result of the fighting was then beyond doubt. The Nationalist forces were concentrated for the advance on Madrid, which fell in late March, bringing the war to an end.

Spain had been used as a testing ground for the aircraft of the Soviet Union, Italy and Germany. It was there that the Luftwaffe formulated its new fighter tac-tics and concepts of close air support for ground forces, which were to be put to good use in the opening campaigns of World War II.

SPECIAL DUTIES

The use of aircraft in clandestine missions to support intelligence operations or Resistance activity began in World War I. From 1915 until the end of the war the Aviation Militaire made regular agent-dropping flights behind enemy lines. As the landing requirements of the aeroplanes of the day were modest, it was comparatively easy to find a suitable field in which to land and drop off the agent. These conditions were not always available and in May 1918 Major W. G. Barker of the RAF (later to win the Victoria Cross) dropped an agent by parachute over the Italian Front.

In World War II after the German occupation of France and the Low Countries a special RAF unit was formed to infiltrate agents of the Special Operations Executive and MI6 into enemy territory. No 419 (Special Duties) Flight was equipped with the Westland

Above *A pilot of No 148 Squadron RAF stands by his Westland Lysander. This squadron operated behind enemy lines in Italy, Albania, Greece and Yugoslavia.*

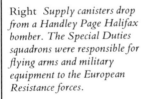

Right *Supply canisters drop from a Handley Page Halifax bomber. The Special Duties squadrons were responsible for flying arms and military equipment to the European Resistance forces.*

Lysander, an army cooperation aircraft with excellent short take-off and landing characteristics, and was initially based at North Weald in Essex. With the increase of subversive activity, the unit was expanded to squadron strength, becoming No 138 Squadron and moving to Newmarket in Suffolk. Early in 1942 a second Special Duties unit, No 161 Squadron, was formed at Newmarket and both units later moved to Tempsford in Bedfordshire. Flights were made to such distant destinations as Czechoslovakia, Poland and Yugoslavia, with Armstrong Whitworth Whitleys,

Short Stirlings and Handley Page Halifaxes making the longer-range supply and agent drops, while Lysanders operated into western Europe to land and collect agents.

In 1943 the demand for clandestine transport increased to such an extent that Lockheed Hudson aircraft were pressed into service for pick-up work. They were later joined by Douglas C-47 transports, while American Consolidated B-24 Liberators flew supply- and agent-dropping missions. After the Normandy invasion Boeing B-17 bombers were diverted from

their usual bomber duties to drop arms to the Maquis (French underground Resistance). In the Mediterranean both USAAF and RAF special duties units kept Yugoslav and later Italian partisans supplied. Great efforts were made by all these Allied units to fly supplies into Poland after the Warsaw Uprising in August 1944, but their efforts were in vain.

In the Far East RAF Liberators and Consolidated Catalinas operated from Ceylon to maintain agent networks in Malaya. Rather surprisingly the B-24 Liberator was also used by the Luftwaffe on clandestine missions, along with similarly captured B-17 Flying Fortresses. These aircraft were repainted in German markings and were operated by Kampfgeschwader 200. German aircraft used on clandestine operations included the Arado Ar 232B, which flew an assassination squad into the Moscow area in 1944 in an abortive attempt to assassinate Stalin. The modern successors to the wartime special duties units are the USAF Special Operations Squadrons, which fly such types as the Lockheed MC-130E Hercules and Sikorsky CH-53 helicopter in support of US Army Special Forces troops.

Above *This Consolidated Liberator of No 1585 (Polish) flight, based in Italy, flew supplies into Warsaw during the Home Army's uprising in August 1944.*

Right *The Luftwaffe transports carried wounded German troops to safety on the return flights from the Stalingrad pocket.*

Below *Junkers Ju 52/3m transport aircraft operated in severe winter weather during their vain attempt to keep the Stalingrad garrison supplied with arms and other supplies.*

STALINGRAD AIRLIFT 1942–43

In November 1942 the German Sixth Army became encircled by Soviet troops at Stalingrad and the task of supplying these beleaguered forces fell to the Luftwaffe. Reichsmarschall Hermann Goering undertook to airlift 500 tonnes of supplies into Stalingrad every day. Yet the air transport forces immediately available on the southern sector of the Eastern Front were clearly inadequate for this task, comprising less than 100 Junkers Ju 52/3m trimotors. During the first two days of the siege only 65 tons of supplies were flown in. Within a week the transport force was reinforced; double the number of Ju 52/3ms were made available and converted Heinkel He 111 and Junkers Ju 86

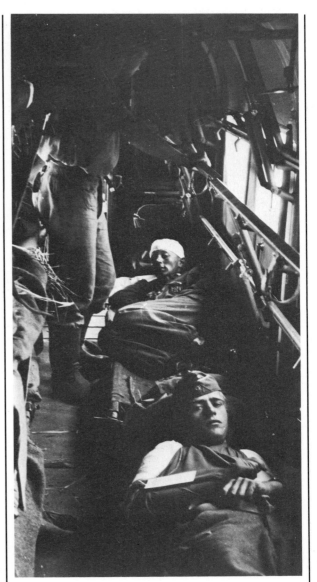

bombers were also pressed into service. By the beginning of December over 100 tonnes a day were being flown into the Stalingrad pocket. Yet winter weather and Soviet fighter aircraft took their toll of the transports.

At the end of December advancing Russian forces overran the transports' forward airfields, thus lengthening the distance to be flown on the supply missions. In order to reduce losses to enemy fighters the transports were flown in formations escorted by Luftwaffe fighters and some aircraft operated at night. On their return flights the aircraft evacuated wounded troops. Further reinforcements of the transport fleet included Focke Wulf Fw 200 Condors, He 177s and Ju 90s. However the defensive perimeter at Stalingrad was shrinking under Soviet attack. Pitomnik airfield was overrun in mid-January and the remaining airfield at Gumrak was heavily shelled. Further supplies were delivered by parachute, but at the end of the month the Sixth Army formally surrendered. During the siege, which had lasted ten week, the Luftwaffe had delivered less than 20,000 tonnes of supplies and had lost some 470 aircraft in the process.

STRATEGIC BOMBING

The central idea of strategic bombing is that an attack on the sources of an enemy's military power – his industry, sources of energy and raw materials – will lead to his defeat as surely as a direct offensive against his armed forces. During World War I various desultory strategic bombing campaigns were mounted by both sides. The Zeppelin and Gotha raids on Britain and the RAF's Independent Force raids into Germany were all attempts to strike at the sources of enemy power, yet none was prosecuted with sufficient vigour to bring about any decision. Indeed with the means available at that time it is highly unlikely that any positive results could have been obtained. However, if the raids of World War I did little material damage, what they did appear to show was that an attack on the civilian population centres, by undermining the population's will to resist, may have the same result as the widespread destruction of manufacturing capacity.

It was during the inter-war years that many highly ambitious theories of strategic bombing were for-

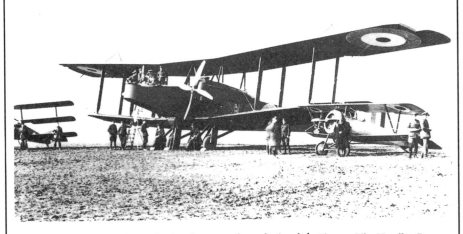

mulated, often based on the inadequate data derived from assessment of the World War I strategic bombing experiments. The ideas of the influential Italian theorist Giulio Douhet, propounded in *The Command of the Air* (1921) are in many ways typical. Douhet believed that the correct use of air power was in offensive action against the bases of the enemy air force. Once this was destroyed the enemy could be forced to surrender in a short time by a direct attack on the morale of the

Above *The Handley Page O/100 long-range bomber of World War I dwarfs the Nieuport Scout (right) and Fokker Triplane beside it.*

Below *A German Gotha GV is loaded with 100kg and 50kg bombs during World War I.*

civilian populated. Although this was popularly dubbed 'Douhet's theory of frightfulness', the Italian believed his proposals to be essentially humane, in that the issue of a conflict fought according to his ideas would be decided within a matter of days and thus the years of wasteful bloodletting experienced during World War I would be avoided.

The notion that 'the bomber would always get through', as stated by the British prime minister, Stanley Baldwin, in 1932 was a belief inherited from Marshal of the RAF Lord Trenchard who had retired after a ten-year period as Chief of the Air Staff in 1929. It was based on the mistaken belief that the bomber aircraft was that philosophers' stone of the military planner: a weapon against which there is no defence. Misconceptions about the nature of the strategic bomber did not end here. On the eve of the war it was calculated that a German bomber force of 1600 aircraft could inflict 600,000 deaths during a six-month campaign. In fact during the period of heavy German bombing between August 1940 and May 1941 a total of 43,000 civilians were killed. These losses were of course far from being negligible, but they did not begin to approach the catastrophic casualty figures predicted, and the effect on civilian morale was a hardening of resolve rather than the anticipated collapse.

Above High-explosive bombs used by the RAF in World War II.

Below A Handley Page Halifax Mk II is loaded with bombs prior to a night raid.

Bottom An Avro Lancaster of No 617 Squadron releases a 22,000lb Grand Slam bomb.

The fallacies of pre-war strategic bombing theory were thoroughly exposed during the German offensives of the Battle of Britain and the Blitz in 1940–41. Inadequacies of equipment soon became apparent as RAF Bomber Command attempted to strike back at Germany. It was learned during the first month of the war that unescorted bombers were an easy prey for the Luftwaffe's fighters and that turret-mounted defensive armament gave little protection. Consequently in the spring of 1940 the RAF bombers began night attacks on Germany. It was soon realized, however, that the bombers lacked the navigation aids to find and bomb precise targets, such as individual factories, in darkness. As a result of this shortcoming RAF Bomber Command adopted the 'area bombing' policy which took whole towns or large areas of cities as the aiming point. With the development of such navigation aids as Gee and Oboe and the H2S ground-mapping radar, the RAF's night-bombing accuracy increased. The development of pathfinding techniques also helped to bring the general skill of the bomber force up to the level of its most experienced members. In July 1943 Bomber Command raided Hamburg in force, inflicting 50,000 casualties.

Such results could not be obtained consistently, however, and Bomber Command's attacks in the early months of 1944, notably the series of raids on the German capital that became known as the Battle of Berlin, resulted in a heavy loss of bombers to flak and the German night-fighter force. Following the unacceptably high casualties at Nuremberg at the end of March 1944, the bomber force was switched to targets in western Germany, the Low Countries and France as part of the preparations for D-Day. By this time the night bombers were capable of great precision in night attacks, as shown by raids on French railway centres which generally avoided heavy civilian casualties. By August 1944 raids deep into Germany could be resumed as the German night-fighter force was weakened by shortage of fuel and the loss of forward bases and early-warning radar in France. Escorted by night fighters and electronic countermeasures (ECM) jamming aircraft of No 100 Group, Bomber Command was in a position to attack such key targets as

A formation of USAAF Boeing B-17 Flying Fortresses of the Eighth Air Force's 452nd Bomb Group. A typical bomb load for a B-17 operating over Germany was only some 4000lb.

A Soviet Myasishchev Mya-4 jet bomber is intercepted by an RAF English Electric Lightning fighter over the North Sea, during the 1960s.

justified when the Eighth Air Force began long-range missions deep into Germany. By the time of the Schweinfurt raid in October 1943, bomber losses had reached unacceptably high levels. Yet the USAAF was reluctant to abandon its daylight offensive, not least because bombing accuracy using the Norden bombsight was generally very high.

The answer to the problem of bomber protection lay in the provision of fighter escort for the bomber boxes throughout the mission. The North American P-51B Mustang escort fighter which became available early in 1944 had sufficient range to accompany the bombers to virtually any target in enemy-occupied Europe. Consequently the American fighters were able to bring the Luftwaffe to combat and establish a degree of air superiority which allowed the bombers to operate virtually at will over Germany. More than 11,000 enemy aircraft were claimed as destroyed by the Eighth Air Force's fighter groups during its escort missions and fighter sweeps in support of the bombers. The bombers themselves contributed to the Luftwaffe's defeat, not only by luring their fighters into battle, but by the precision attacks on German oil refineries and synthetic oil plants which began in earnest in February 1944. From late 1943 the Eighth Air Force's attacks were supplemented by raids mounted by the Fifteenth Air Force from bases in Italy. By the end of the war attacks on oil and communications targets had virtually crippled German industry, but it was only during the final year of the bombing campaign that decisive results were achieved.

Strategic air operations against Japan were clearly beyond the capabilities of the Boeing B-17 Flying Fortresses and Consolidated B-24 Liberator bombers used by the USAAF in Europe, and not until the 2500km

centres of synthetic oil production. This course was urged on its C-in-C, Sir Arthur Harris, by the Air Staff, but Harris was reluctant to abandon his policy of area attacks. Consequently the final months of the bomber offensive saw both precision attacks such as that which sank the battleship *Tirpitz*, and area attacks, including the devastation of Dresden.

The American approach to strategic bombing was quite different from the British. The USAAF's Eighth Air Force began operations against Germany in August 1942, flying by day from bases in eastern England. The American commanders were convinced that their tactics of high-flying box formations of bombers, which relied on the mutually supporting defensive fire of the heavily armed bombers for protection, would succeed in penetrating enemy airspace. The RAF's commanders warned the Americans that losses to enemy fighters would be heavy and their forebodings were

Tu-4 (an unlicensed copy of the B-29). The medium-range Tu-16 jet bomber appeared in 1955 and was joined by long-range turboprop-powered Tu-20 and jet-powered Myasishchev Mya-4 bombers. With the increase in intercontinental ballistic missile forces in 1960, the strategic bomber lost its pre-eminent position in the nuclear arsenals of the superpowers. However, both the United States and the Soviet Union retain substantial manned bomber forces. New aircraft such as the USAF's Rockwell B-1B and the Soviet Blackjack will ensure that strategic bombers remain in service until the end of this century and quite possibly beyond.

(1600-mile) range Boeing B-29 Superfortresses became available in the late summer of 1943 could they be contemplated. The early B-29 raids on the Japanese homeland were mounted by the Twentieth Air Force from airfields in China, but as all supplies of bombs and fuel had to be flown over the Hump air route from India, the logistics problems of such operations were formidable. However, the American invasion of the Mariana Islands in June–August 1944 provided more suitable B-29 bases and by November the bombers based there were ready for operations against Japan. In contrast to USAAF tactics in Europe, it was decided to employ area attacks on Japanese cities, using incendiaries rather than high-explosive bombs. Such raids were flown by night and at low level and devastating fires destroyed large portions of the major Japanese cities. The B-29s also carried out precision attacks on the Japanese aircraft industry and mined offshore waters extensively. The Twentieth Air Force's campaign succeeded in severely disrupting the Japanese economy, as well as totally dislocating normal civilian life in the cities. However, the extent to which this contributed to Japan's final surrender is difficult to assess, because it was clearly the atomic bombing of Hiroshima and Nagasaki which was the immediate cause of the Japanese collapse.

The invention of atomic weapons (and the later immensely more powerful thermonuclear bombs) transformed the role of strategic bombardment into that of deterrence. In March 1946 the USAAF formed Strategic Air Command (SAC) as a nuclear-armed air striking force capable of attacking targets anywhere in the world. At that time, however, few nuclear weapons had been manufactured and only the B-29 was available to lift them. The situation improved with the introduction of the massive ten-engined Convair B-36 bomber in 1948 and with the advent of the swept-wing Boeing B-47 Stratojet in 1951. However, it was not until SAC began to re-equip with the Boeing B-52 Stratofortress in the late 1950s that the United States had a strategic nuclear bomber of truly global range.

Following the first Soviet atomic bomb test in 1949, the Soviet Union began to build up its own strategic nuclear bombing force, equipped with the Tupolev

Above A Boeing B-52G Stratofortress of the USAF's Strategic Air Command carries a pair of Hound Dog, nuclear-armed missiles underwing.

Below The Fairey Swordfish attack on Taranto was met by a barrage of anti-aircraft fire, but only two of the attacking aircraft were lost.

TARANTO 1940

In the autumn of 1940 the Royal Navy was seriously outnumbered by the Italian Fleet in the Mediterranean and yet the Italians were unwilling to risk a battle at sea. The British commander Admiral Sir Andrew Cunningham determined to break this stalemate by carrying out a torpedo-bomber strike on the enemy fleet in its harbour at Taranto. As originally planned the operation was to have taken place on 21 October – Trafalgar Day – and the Fairey Swordfish of Nos 813, 815, 819, and 824 Squadrons Fleet Air Arm were to fly from the carriers HMS *Eagle* and HMS *Illustrious*. However, *Eagle* was unable to take part in the operation due to bomb damage, and some of her aircraft and crews transferred to *Illustrious*. Then fire broke out aboard *Illustrious* and so the attack was postponed until 11 November.

On 10 November a preliminary reconnaissance was flown over Taranto by a Martin Maryland from Malta, piloted by Pilot Officer Adrian Warburton. His photographs showed five battleships in the port and that night they were joined by a sixth. On the evening of 11 November *Illustrious* launched two waves of Swordfish armed with torpedoes, bombs and flares for

Whitworth Whitleys and Handley Page Hampdens, plus some of the newer Short Stirlings, HP Halifaxes, Avro Manchesters and Lancasters. They dropped a total of 1478 tonnes (1,455 tons) of bombs onto the target, a third of which were incendiaries. Damage was heavy, with 240 hectares (600 acres) of the city completely gutted. A total of 486 people were killed and many thousands made homeless. The raid represented Bomber Command's greatest victory of the war up to that date, especially as losses had been acceptable, only 40 bombers failing to return. The Cologne raid was followed by two further Thousand-Bomber raids, on Essen (1/2 June 1942) and Bremen (25/26 June), but poor weather prevented the previous success from being repeated. Nonetheless, Operation Millennium had achieved its object by giving Bomber Command's prestige a much-needed boost.

target illumination. The first wave of 12 Swordfish was led by Lieutenant-Commander K. Williamson and the second of nine aircraft by Lieutenant-Commander J. Hale. They sank the battleship *Littorio* at her moorings and badly damaged the *Cavour* and *Duilio*, while a cruiser and destroyer were also damaged. Only two aircraft failed to return, Williamson and his crew being shot down and made prisoners-of-war. At a single stroke the balance of naval power in the Mediterranean had been dramatically altered.

THOUSAND-BOMBER RAIDS 1942

When Air Marshal Arthur Harris was appointed C-in-C of RAF Bomber Command in February 1942 he determined to mount an attack by a thousand bombers on a German city at the earliest opportunity. Such an attack, he reasoned, would still the voices of Bomber Command's critics and help him to obtain the resources needed for an expansion of the night-bomber force. On the face of it, the attack was an impossibility, because the average number of bombers operational on any one night at this time was only some 300. However, by ensuring that all front-line bombers were serviceable and by using aircraft drawn from the Operational Training Units, Coastal Command and Flying Training Command, Harris was able to amass sufficient numbers.

The target selected for the aptly named Operation Millennium was Cologne and on the evening of 30 May 1942 a force of 1046 bombers was despatched against this city. It was planned that the attack should be concentrated within 90 minutes and, despite thick cloud encountered en route to the target, the bombers' timing was reasonably accurate. The bulk of the force was made up of Vickers Wellingtons, Armstrong

Right *Only a handful of four-engined heavy bombers, such as these Short Stirlings, were in Bomber Command service at the time of the Thousand-Bomber raid on Cologne.*

Below *The burnt-out wreck of a Vickers Wellington bomber that fell to the German defences. Losses on Operation Millennium were fairly light, as only 40 out of 1046 bombers failed to return.*

destroying the Zeppelins L54 and L60 inside it. The second formation bombed a smaller shed, and all six Camels escaped undamaged, despite meeting anti-aircraft fire over the target. Dickson and Smart regained the *Furious* and ditched alongside an escort vessel – the carrier's 90m (300ft) flight deck was only suitable for take-offs. Yeulett ran out of fuel over the sea, was forced down and drowned. The remaining three aircraft ended their flight in neutral Denmark.

TONDERN RAID 1918

In July 1918 Sopwith Camels from the aircraft carrier HMS *Furious* caried out the first carrier strike operation in the history of air warfare when they bombed the German airship sheds at Tondern on the North Sea coast of Germany.

Eight Sopwith 2F1 Camels were embarked aboard *Furious* in June 1918, but the first attempt to mount the Tondern raid was thwarted by bad weather. By 19 July conditions had improved and *Furious* and her escorts were positioned 130km (80 miles) from the target. Seven Camels were flown off for the raid, each carrying two 23kg (50lb) bombs. The first wave of three aircraft was flown by Captain W. Jackson, Captain W. Dickson and Lieutenant N. Williams. The second formation followed after an interval of ten minutes, and comprised the Camels of Captain B. Smart, Captain T. Thyne, Lieutenant S. Dawson and Lieutenant W. Yeulett.

Before the target was reached Thyne's aircraft suffered engine failure and he was forced to ditch in the sea. Jackson's three aircraft dive-bombed the target from a height of 900m (3000ft) and scored direct hits on a large airship shed, which burst into flames

Top left The large airship shed at Tondern ablaze following the Camels' attack.

Top right Sopwith 2F1 Ship's Camels parked on the forward flight deck of HMS Furious. *Seven aircraft of this type carried out the air attack on the Tondern airship sheds.*

Above The aircraft carrier HMS Furious.

Below One of the most successful training aircraft of World War I was the Avro 504K, and later versions remained in use throughout the inter-war years.

TRAINING

In the early days of military aviation pilot training was generally a neglected branch of the flying services. In Britain a prospective military pilot's initial flying training was undertaken at his own expense at a civilian flying school. Once he had gained the Royal Aero Club's pilot certificate, he would then obtain the cost of his training from the government. His military flying training took place at the Central Flying School at Upavon in Wiltshire, a joint army and navy training establishment which flew such standard military types as the BE2. However, with the outbreak of World War I the demand for pilots forced the Royal Flying Corps and Royal Naval Air Service to set up their own training organizations. By the end of 1915 the RFC alone had established 18 reserve squadrons to train

replacement pilots for the squadrons in France. The standards of instruction were generally poor, largely because no systematic training programme had been worked out. This deficiency was made good by Major Robert Smith-Barry, who was appointed to command No 1 Reserve Squadron at Gosport, Hampshire, in January 1917. The Gosport system taught the pupil how to handle his aircraft in all flight conditions, including such potentially dangerous manoeuvres as stalls and spins. So successful was this method that the School of Special Flying was established at Gosport to teach the RFC's instructors the Smith-Barry system.

Although after the Armistice of November 1918 the Royal Air Force was dramatically reduced to a small peacetime establishment, flying training played an important part in the service's activities. Because the front-line strength was so small, Air Marshal Sir Hugh Trenchard, Chief of the Air Staff, was determined that the RAF should be capable of a rapid expansion if the

Above left *The German Bücker Bü 131 Jungmann trainer of the 1930s was noted for its fine aerobatic qualities. This example served with the Spanish Nationalist air force.*

Above right *An Avro Anson Mk I trainer, serving in Canada during World War II.*

Below *The Avro Tutor succeeded the venerable Avro 504N in service with the RAF's flying training schools in the early 1930s.*

Bottom *The DH Tiger Moth was the most famous RAF training aircraft of World War II. This example served with the Fleet Air Arm as late as the 1960s.*

need arose. Consequently the training organization was carefully planned, with a number of flying training schools for new pilots (one of them in Egypt to take advantage of the good flying weather) and the Central Flying School to train instructors and maintain training standards. One important innovation of the period was blind-flying instruction, with the pupil's cockpit covered by a hood so that he had to rely on instruments alone. This method was first practised at the Central Flying School, by then located at Wittering in Northamptonshire, in 1930.

The late 1930s saw a considerable expansion of flying training activity. In order to supplement the efforts of the RAF's own flying training organization, elementary flying instruction was given to aircrew of the RAF Volunteer Reserve at civilian-run flying schools. However, the real breakthrough in flying training was the establishment of the British Commonwealth Air Training Plan in 1939. This allowed RAF aircrew to train in the peaceful skies of Australia, Canada, New Zealand, South Africa and Rhodesia. Basic flying training was carried out on the de Havilland Tiger Moth or Miles Magister, the pupil then progressing to the Miles Master and ending his training on North American Harvard single-engined or Airspeed Oxford twin-engined advanced trainers. The ubiquitous Avro Anson was used both for pilot training and to instruct other aircrew members such as navigators and air gunners. By the end of the war the Commonwealth training scheme had produced 131,552 aircrew, 49,707 of them pilots.

The USAAF's training syllabus was broadly similar to that of the RAF and indeed many RAF pilots trained at British flying training schools in the United States. Primary instruction was on the Stearman PT-17 or Fairchild PT-19, basic flying training followed on the Vultee BT-13 and advanced trainers included the North American AT-6 single-engined trainer (which in the RAF was known as the Harvard) or the Cessna AT-17 twin. Between July 1939 and August 1945 USAAF Flying Training Command produced 193,444 pilots. Once an RAF pilot had qualified, his training was completed at an Operational Training Unit. The USAAF too adopted this system and also operated Replacement Training Units.

At the beginning of World War II the Luftwaffe operated a smoothly run and efficient flying training organization. However, as the war progressed the need for replacement pilots to be rushed through training and the acute shortage of aviation fuel from 1944

onwards eroded the German training organization to a point in February 1945 where it had virtually ceased to exist. At its peak of efficiency, the Luftwaffe training organization provided the pupil pilot with a period of theoretical ground instruction, before he progressed to elementary flying training on such types as the Focke Wulf Fw 44 or Bücker Bü 131. Basic training was carried out on the Arado Ar 66 or Gotha 145, followed by advanced instruction on the Heinkel He 51, Arado Ar 65 or twin-engined Fw 58. Pilots destined for

Above *The Lockheed T-33, based on the design of the F-80 Shooting Star fighter, was one of the earliest jet trainers. As well as serving with the USAF for over 30 years, it was widely exported.*

Left *The British Aerospace Hawk T Mk I serves with the RAF both as an advanced trainer and as a weapons and tactics trainer. It also has a secondary air defence role.*

bomber or reconnaissance units received an additional period of instruction flying obsolescent bomber aircraft and blind-flying training. German pilots ended their training at an operational training (*Ergänzung*) unit before posting to a front-line *Staffel*. By early 1944, with the gradual disintegration of the German pilot training organization, Luftwaffe pilots were going into action with only 160 hours of training behind them. This was less than half the hours flown by newly qualified Allied pilots.

After World War II flying organizations had to adapt to the widespread introduction of jet aircraft. In 1955 the RAF began an experimental 'all-through' jet training course, with pupils commencing basic instruction on the Jet Provost T Mk 1 and progressing to the de Havilland Vampire T Mk 11 advanced trainer. By the end of the decade the flying training schools had standardized this system. However, it was found that a short period of instruction on piston-engined trainers was desirable, simply to establish the pupil pilot's basic flying aptitude. Consequently the present-day RAF pilot begins his training on the Chipmunk T Mk 10 or University Air Squadron Bulldog T Mk 1. Basic training is on the Jet Provost T Mk 3A and T Mk 5A and advanced training (for fast jet pilots) follows on No 4 Flying Training School's Hawker Siddeley Hawk T Mk 1. After a course in tactics and weapons, the RAF pilot then finishes his training at an Operational Conversion Unit.

The USAF's flying training organization is used by many foreign nations, including several NATO members, to train their military pilots. It comprises seven Flying Wings (one of which specializes in instructor training) all of which fly both the Cessna T-37 basic trainer and the Northrop T-38 supersonic advanced trainer. After initial grading, flying the piston-engined Cessna T-41A, the trainee flies some 90 hours on the T-37 and a further 120 hours on the T-38. USAF Air Training Command's output of qualified pilots is some 3000 each year. A recent trend in flying training has been the introduction of a turboprop basic trainer, such as the Pilatus PC-7, and the RAF's next basic trainer could be such a machine. However, the USAF has ignored this development and its new basic trainer will be the turbofan-powered Fairchild T-46A.

TRANSPORT

Air transport operations were slow to develop, primarily because the load-carrying capabilities of early aircraft were limited. The first purpose-built transport aircraft to serve in the RAF was the Vickers Vernon, which fulfilled the dual bomber-transport role and served with Nos 45 and 70 Squadrons in the Middle East from 1921. Among the tasks undertaken by these aircraft were troop reinforcement, casualty evacuation and carrying mail along the route established from Baghdad in Iraq to Cairo in Egypt. In 1926 the Vernon was replaced by the Victoria and this in turn gave way to the Valentia, which soldiered on until the early years of World War II. One of the most important developments in air transport of the inter-war years was the Soviet Union's establishment of airborne forces in the early 1930. On manoeuvres Soviet paratroops dropped from Tupolev TB-3 four-engined bombers to secure landing zones, into which further aircraft flew light tanks and artillery. By 1938 the Soviet army had formed four airborne brigades, each a thousand men strong.

It was the Luftwaffe, however, rather than the Soviet air force that was to exploit the full potential of airborne operations in the early campaigns of World War II. The Junkers Ju 52/3m was the standard transport aircraft flown by the Luftwaffe. It could carry 12 paratroops or 18 standard infantrymen and could also be used to tow the DFS 230 troop-carrying gliders. Over 500 Ju 52/3m transports were in Luftwaffe service in September 1939 and they supported airborne assaults in the Polish Campaign and during the assault in the west. The costly victory gained during the invasion of Crete in May 1941 resulted in the virtual elimination of the German airborne forces and the Luftwaffe's transport force suffered crippling losses during the Stalingrad airlift operations in the winter of 1942/3. Thereafter, despite the introduction of such technically advanced transport aircraft as the Messerschmitt Me 323 and Junkers Ju 90, the Luftwaffe's

airlift capability steadily declined. The losses suffered during the final phase of the campaign in Tunisia in the spring of 1943 finally eliminated the Luftwaffe's transport organization as an effective military force.

In Britain air transport units in the early war years were equipped with a miscellaneous collection of impressed civil air transports and such military types as the Bristol Bombay, Handley Page Harrow and Lockheed Hudson. The airborne forces were initially supported by Armstrong Whitworth Whitley bombers converted into paratroop transports and glider tugs. This unsatisfactory state of affairs was only remedied when substantial numbers of American Douglas C-47 transports (known to the RAF as Dakotas) were supplied under the Lend-Lease scheme.

Above *The Vickers Victoria bomber-transport served with the RAF, mainly in the Middle East, during the inter-war years.*

Left *The Douglas C-47, known as the Dakota in RAF service, was the most famous military transport aircraft of World War II. This example served with the USAAF during the war.*

and the Naval Air Transport Service into the Military Air Transport Service (MATS) in June 1948. During the 1950s MATS established a worldwide chain of air routes, as well as responding to specific contingency operations such as the war in Korea. The wartime C-47 and C-54 transport aircraft were supplemented by newer types such as the Douglas C-118 and Lockheed C-121 based on the civil DC-6 and Constellation airliners. Cargo transport capacity was greatly increased with the introduction of the Douglas C-124 Globemaster II into service, as this could lift a 45,000kg (100,000lb) payload.

Great demands were made on the USAF's transport force in the 1960s by the war in Southeast Asia. Tactical transport operations within South Vietnam were flown by elderly C-47s and Fairchild C-123 Providers during the early years of the war. However, the more modern Lockheed C-130 Hercules was committed in increasing numbers in the mid-1960s and by 1968 15 Hercules squadrons were supporting the war. During the siege of the Marine Corps outpost at Khe Sanh in the first four months of 1968 more than 12,000 tonnes of supplies were flown into the garrison. American forces also required a massive strategic airlift of men and material from the United States. This was flown by the regular squadrons of MAC (Military Airlift Command, as MATS had been retitled), supplemented by units of the Air National Guard, the Air Force Reserve and civil airlines. In the course of the war MAC replaced its piston-engined Douglas C-124 and turbo-

The first deliveries were made in mid-1942, but it was not until early 1944 that the Dakota was in widespread service. Eventually 33 RAF squadrons were equipped with Dakotas for medium-range transport tasks, while long-range flights were undertaken by American Douglas C-54 and British Avro York four-engined transports. RAF Transport Command was formed in March 1943 and by the end of the war it controlled six subordinate groups and operated nearly 100 staging posts scattered all over the world.

The USAAF's air transport operations were coordinated by Air Transport Command, although numerous troop carrier and combat cargo groups operated with the numbered tactical air forces. For example the Ninth Air Force at peak strength controlled 15 troop carrier groups, the majority of them operating the C-47, but others flying the Curtiss C-46 Commando and Consolidated C-109 Liberator. The Hump airlift from India to China was probably Air Transport Command's greatest single operation of World War II, but transport aircraft supported American forces in every theatre of war. At peak strength in August 1945, Air Transport Command controlled 3705 aircraft, divided between eight overseas divisions and one in the United States. The smaller Naval Air Transport Service had a strength of 431 aircraft.

The Berlin airlift of 1948–9 emphasized the importance of military air transport in postwar operations. The USAF was particularly well organized in this respect, as it had amalgamated Air Transport Command

Top The Messerschmitt Me 323 six-engined transport aircraft, converted from a cargo glider, could lift such loads as trucks, or up to 120 troops.

Centre A Junkers Ju 90 transport with its ramp extended for loading. The ramp could also be lowered in flight for para-dropping.

Above An RAF Hercules C Mk 1 of the Air Transport Wing at Lyneham, Wiltshire. The four-turboprop Lockheed C-130 Hercules is the most widely used tactical transport aircraft in the world.

prop C-133 Cargomaster transports with the turbofan-powered Lockheed C-141 Starlifter and Lockheed C-5A Galaxy. The new aircraft not only offered increased capacity, but could substantially reduce the time taken to fly from the United States to the combat theatre.

The current strategic transport force of USAF Military Airlift Command is equipped with the C-5A and the C-141, while the standard tactical transport remains the C-130 Hercules. The Hercules has been exported to many countries and now forms the mainstay of the RAF's air transport force. The Soviet air force's Military Transport Aviation is equipped with the Ilyushin Il-76 and Antonov An-22 long-range transports, while the much older An-12 turboprop-powered tactical transport is also widely used. Such

forces permit the rapid deployment of troops to virtually any part of the world and NATO's reinforcement plans depend on the establishment of an 'air bridge' over the Atlantic in time of crisis.

VIETNAM WAR 1962–73

American involvement in South Vietnam's guerrilla war against Viet Cong (VC) insurgents began in the early 1960s, with the supply of aircraft and combat advisers. At the end of 1961 US Army Vertol CH-21 helicopters and their crews were ferried to Saigon aboard the former escort carrier *Card* and by September 1964 more than 400 US Army aircraft were deployed in Vietnam in support of the ARVN (Army of the Republic of Vietnam). Similar helicopter airlift support was provided by US Marine Corps Squadron

Above The USAF's Lockheed C-5A Galaxy provides the American forces with long-range airlift for heavy and bulky items of military equipment.

Opposite page, top The armed attack helicopter, such as this Bell AH-1J, was the most notable innovation of the Vietnam War.

Below left A Douglas A-1E skyraider of the USAF's 1st Air Commando Wing drops a phosporus bomb on a Viet Cong position in 1966.

Below right The door gunner of a Bell UH-1 'Huey' helicopter keeps watch for enemy activity in the Mekong Delta. This helicopter served with the US Navy's Light Helicopter Attack Squadron HAL-3.

HMM 362 ('Archie's Angels') whose Sikorsky CH-34s began operations from the former Japanese airfield at Soc Trang in April 1962. At the same time USAF instructors were training South Vietnamese pilots to operate the piston-engined North American T-28D counter-insurgency aircraft and often flying in combat with them. The South Vietnamese Air Force (VNAF) suffered from an acute shortage of trained pilots and so 30 USAF pilots (known as the 'Dirty Thirty') were assigned to the two VNAF Douglas C-47 transport squadrons in 1962.

The nature of American involvement changed radically following the Tonkin Gulf incident of 1964, when North Vietnamese torpedo boats attacked US destroyers on patrol in international waters off the Vietnamese coast. Retaliatory air strikes were mounted against North Vietnamese naval bases from the carriers USS *Ticonderoga* ad *Constellation*. Congress authorized President Lyndon Johnson to take 'all necesary measures' to deter further aggression. Early in 1965 a VC attack on Pleiku airbase and nearby Camp Holloway killed eight American servicemen. Operation Flaming Dart, a series of air attacks on North Vietnam, was the president's response. In March 1965 a force of 3500 US Marines landed at Da Nang and by 1968 the number of American troops in South Vietnam had risen to 510,000.

An air campaign, codenamed Rolling Thunder, was initiated against targets in the North, although the strike aircraft were subjected to numerous restrictions and all targets had to be approved in advance by the Department of Defense in Washington. USAF aircraft operated against North Vietnam from bases in Thailand and in the South, while US Navy carriers launched their air strikes from Yankee Station in the Gulf of Tonkin. At first North Vietnamese resistance was confined to anti-aircraft fire, but then Soviet-supplied SA-2 surface-to-air missiles (SAMs) were deployed.

Because of the target restrictions imposed on the strike aircraft operating against North Vietnam and the frequent bombing halts (the longest lasting from November 1968 until March 1972), it became necessary to attack munitions and other supplies intended for the VC when they were in transit, rather than at source. The main supply route to the South was the network of jungle tracks running through southern Laos, which were known as the Ho Chi Minh Trail. Because of the threat of US air attack, movement along the trail took place mostly at night and so special tactics had to be developed by the American interdiction aircraft. A series of seismic and acoustic sensors were sown along the trail by aircraft and these transmitted indications of enemy movement to a central

However, it was not until one of these missiles shot down a USAF McDonnell Douglas RF-4C reconnaissance aircraft that attacks on the SAM sites were authorized. North Vietnamese interceptors were also encountered and on 17 June 1965 a McDonnell Douglas F-4 Phantom from US Navy Squadron VF-21 destroyed a MiG-17 in combat, the first American air combat victory of the war.

In South Vietnam the Bell UH-1 'Huey' troop-carrying helicopter became one of the key weapons of the war. Air Mobile troops were flown into action aboard these helicopters, each of which carried an infantry squad. It was found that the helicopters were vulnerable to VC ambush as they approached or left their landing zones and so troop-carrying UH-1 'Slicks' were escorted by armed UH-1 'Hogs'. The need for helicopter fire support eventually led to the development of the Bell AH-1 Cobra gunship helicopter, which first went into action in Vietnam in 1967. American ground forces were also able to call on close air support from the fighter-bombers of the USAF and at the peak of American involvement in the war an

Above *An F-4J Phantom of the US Navy's Fighter Squadron VF-96 landing on USS* Constellation.

control centre. Attacks were then mounted by fighter-bombers, the more specialized Martin B-57G intruder aircraft, or fixed-wing gunships. The latter were Douglas C-47, Fairchild C-119 and Lockheed C-130 Hercules transport aircraft modified to fire a broadside armament of cannon and rapid-fire machine guns.

In 1968 the VC mounted a nationwide offensive in South Vietnam timed to coincide with the Tet (lunar new year) celebrations on 31 January. At the same time North Vietnamese regular units laid siege to the Marine Corps outpost at Khe Sanh. Air resupply missions carried out under heavy fire and a massive air support operation by fighter-bombers helped the Marine garrison at Khe Sanh to hold on for the first four months of 1968 until they were relieved. Similar hard fighting quelled the VC's Tet offensive, but in the United States there was increasing disillusionment with the war. Consequently the newly elected president, Richard Nixon, announced that he would wind down American troop involvement, while strengthening the South Vietnamese armed forces. This process of 'Vietnamization' saw the strengthening of the VNAF to a force of 700 aircraft, with deliveries of sufficient Northrop F-5A and F-5E fighters to equip eight squadrons, plus Cessna A-37 and Douglas A-1 attack aircraft.

In 1969 Nixon authorized clandestine B-52 attacks on North Vietnamese sanctuary areas in Cambodia, followed by incursions of ground troops into Cambodia and Laos in 1970 and 1971. However, it was clear

average of 800 such sorties were flown every day. The most widely used close air support aircraft was the North American F-100 Super Sabre, but when heavier firepower was needed the USAF's giant Boeing B-52 bombers flew 'Arc Light' sorties from their bases in Guam and in Thailand. A single B-52D could lift a total of 108 bombs of 340kg (750lb) in a single mission.

Above *Two of the USAF's leading aces of the war, pilot Captain Steve Ritchie (left) and weapons systems officer Captain Chuck Debellvue, flew F-4 Phantoms from Udorn in Thailand.*

that without American support the ARVN forces were no match for the combined forces of the North Vietnamese Army and Viet Cong (NVA/VC). The failure of Vietnamization allowed the North Vietnamese to mount a full-scale invasion of the northern provinces of South Vietnam in the spring of 1972. American air power was immediately thrown into the battle. US Navy Grumman A-6 Intruders mined the sea ports of North Vietnam, massive air strikes were flown against targets in the North (Operation Linebacker) and tactical fighter-bombers, fixed-wing gunships and B-52s pounded the NVA forces in the South. By June the NVA/VC advance had been halted and, although the northernmost provinces of South Vietnam had been overrun, it appeared that the Paris peace talks would bear fruit. However, towards the end of the year the situation deteriorated, the North Vietnamese withdrew from the Paris negotiations and it seemed that their assault on the South would recommence. The American response was rapid and effective. During the 11-day Linebacker II campaign in December 1972 North Vietnam, including the capital Hanoi, was pounded by USAF and US Navy bombers, including the massive B-52. Fifteen B-52s fell to the defences,

Above A bomb-laden F-4 Phantom of the USAF breaks away from a Boeing KC-135A tanker aircraft, after a refuelling rendezvous en route to a target in North Vietnam.

Right A V1 flying bomb shortly after launching. This pilotless aircraft was powered by a pulse-jet and carried an 850kg high-explosive warhead.

but at the end the North Vietnamese returned to the Paris talks and a ceasefire was negotiated.

Peace for the Republic of Vietnam lasted until the North Vietnamese invasion of April 1975, which brought all of Vietnam under the control of the Hanoi regime. The final American air action in Vietnam was the helicopter evacuation of personnel from the Saigon embassy to the Seventh Fleet lying offshore.

V–WEAPONS

The German V-weapons (*Vergeltungswaffen*, or reprisal weapons) comprised the Fieseler Fi 103 flying bomb, or V1, and the A-4 rocket (V2), both of which were under development at Peenemünde on the Baltic coast during the early war years. British intelligence gained its first indications of this work in a document known as the Oslo report, apparently written by a well-placed German sympathetic to the Allied cause, which was delivered to the British embassy in Norway in November 1939. In 1942–3 more definite information on the work being carried out at Peenemünde was gained from photographic reconnaissance sorties and reports from agents. Accordingly it was decided to bomb the experimental station and on the night of 17/18 August 1943 a force of nearly 600 bombers raided Peenemünde. At a cost of 41 RAF aircraft lost, they destroyed many production drawings and killed over 100 German technicians including a number of key personnel, putting the V-weapons programme back at least two months.

Later in 1943 the construction of V1 launch sites in France was detected by photographic reconnaissance

and air attacks on these targets, codenamed 'Noball', began on 20 December. The aircraft involved included RAF Spitfire dive-bombers, Martin B-26 Marauder medium bombers of the USAAF's Ninth Air Force and both RAF and American heavy bombers. Between April and June 1944 RAF Bomber Command devoted 13 per cent of its overall effort to attacks on V1 storage and launching sites. Although Oberst M. Wachtel's Flak Regiment 155(W) was scheduled to commence operations with the V1 late in 1943, it was not until

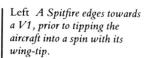

a fighter could send a V1 crashing out of control by tipping its wingtip under that of the flying bomb. This avoided the risk of the fighter being destroyed in the explosion of the V1's 850kg (1870lb) warhead if it were shot down by cannon-fire. Additional squadrons of Mk IX and Mk XII Spitfires, Hawker Typhoons and de Havilland Mosquito night fighters joined in the campaign, but their best efforts could only account for about half of the V1s launched. The remainder caused terrible damage and by mid-July had killed some 4000 civilians.

Hill and Pile decided to redeploy their defences, a courageous decision in the middle of a battle, but it paid dividends. The AA guns, firing shells fitted with the new proximity fuse, were deployed to the coast, while the fighters were allocated inland patrol lines. Soon the guns were destroying more V1s than the fighters, even though the latter now included RAF North American P-51 Mustangs and the first Gloster Meteor jet fighters. The efforts of the defenders, continued bombing attacks on launching sites and the advance of the Allied armies in France finally defeated the V1. Of the approximately 9000 launched, of which many went astray, fighters had accounted for 1900, AA guns for 1560 and the balloon barrage for 278. Heinkel He 111 bombers directed air-launched V1s against Britain between September 1944 and January 1945 and night fighters had some successes against them.

The first V2 rockets were launched in September 1944. They had a 975kg (2145lb) warhead and reached a speed of 5580km/h (3467mph) in flight. As they could not be intercepted, the only defence against them was to bomb the launching sites. They were inaccurate weapons, however, only about 1100 landing in Britain, and the damage they inflicted was not catastrophic. By March 1945 the battle of the V-weapons had ended.

a week after D-Day that the first V1s were launched against Britain. Furthermore the attack was on a far smaller scale than the launch rate of 1000 flying bombs a day originally envisaged.

Defence against the V1 was the responsibility of Air Marshal Sir Roderick Hill, the commander of Air Defence of Great Britain, and General Sir Frederick Pile, C-in-C of Anti-Aircraft Command. Hill's fighters found it difficult to intercept the 640km/h (400mph) V1 and even the high-performance Spitfire Mk XIVs and Hawker Tempest Mk Vs allocated this duty had to be stripped of armour and given a highly polished finish to achieve extra speed. It was found that

WINTER WAR 1939–40

The Winter War of 1939–40 between the Soviet Union and Finland arose out of Soviet demands for bases on Finnish territory. The Finns were adamant in their refusal. Consequently negotiations were broken off and on 30 November the Soviet armies launched an all-out attack into the Finnish province of Karelia. On the ground 30 Soviet divisions were opposed by ten Finnish divisions. This imbalance of forces was even greater in the air, as the Finnish air force with 145 aircraft faced nearly 700 Soviet aircraft operating in support of the armies, while a further 200 Soviet bombers were based across the Gulf of Finland in Estonia. The two Finnish fighter squadrons flew the Fokker D XXI monoplane, with a handful of older Bristol Bulldog Mk IVA biplanes remaining in service. Two bomber squadrons were equipped with Bristol Blenheim Mk Is, three army cooperation squadrons flew Fokker C X and C VE biplanes, while a naval reconnaissance unit flew Blackburn Ripon and Junkers K43 floatplanes. The Soviet air armies were equipped with Antonov TB-3 heavy bombers, Ilyushin DB-3 and Tupolev SB-2 twin-engined bombers and

Top *During the Winter War a total of eight Soviet Polikarpov 1-153s were captured after forced landings and they were impressed into service by the Finnish air force.*

Above *Bristol Blenheim Mk I bombers were supplied to Finland by Britain during the Winter War.*

Left *This Soviet Ilyushin DB-3 bomber was brought down by the Finnish fighter defences. Although heavily outnumbered the Finnish fighter pilots destroyed many enemy aircraft.*

Polikarpov R-5 reconnaissance aircraft. At the outset of hostilities the Soviet fighter regiments generally flew the Polikarpov I-15bis biplanes.

Estonian-based bombers made heavy raids on Helsinki and other towns in southern Finland from the first day of the war. On 1 December Finnish fighters shot down ten Soviet bombers for the loss of one Fokker D XXI and one Bulldog, at which point severe winter weather brought air operations to a standstill for three weeks. The Finnish defences of the Mannerheim Line halted the Soviet advance south of Lake Ladoga, but further north Soviet troops made some progress at the cost of heavy losses. The Soviet fighter regiments were reinforced by Polikarpov I-16 monoplanes in mid-December, but the Finnish Fokker

D XXIs retained their ascendancy. By the end of the year they had shot down 50 enemy aircraft, including eight I-16s. In the new year, while the Finnish army counter-attacked, the air force was reinforced by aid from abroad. A Swedish volunteer unit flying Hawker Hart light bombers and Gloster Gladiator fighters arrived on 11 January and Sweden also supplied the Finnish air force with aircraft. From Britain came Gloster Gauntlet and Gladiator fighters and Bristol Blenheim bombers, the French supplied Morane-Saulnier MS406 fighters, and Fiat G50 fighters ordered from Italy before the war also began to arrive. On 6 January a formation of eight Ilyushin DB-3 bombers was intercepted by two Fokker D XXIs and all the bombers were shot down.

Early in February the Soviet armies attacked the Mannerheim Line in force and their sledgehammer tactics began to take effect. In the air, the Finnish fighter squadrons used their new Gladiators, MS406s and Fiat G50s to good effect, while Blenheims and Fokker C Xs flew ground-attack missions. In general the Finnish pilots were inflicting far heavier casualties on the Soviet air forces than they were suffering. However, on 29 February a large formation of I-16s surprised a Finnish fighter flight just after take-off and five Gladiators and one Fokker D XXI were shot down. The Soviet air armies had been reinforced to bring them up to a strength of 2000 aircraft by the end of February and in early March the advancing ground forces were nearing Viipuri. Although the town was held, the Finns were forced to recognize the hopelessness of their position and on 13 March 1940 an armistice was signed which gave up large areas in Karelia and northern Finland to the Soviet Union.

YOM KIPPUR WAR 1973

In contrast to the opening days of the Six-Day War of 1967, the Yom Kippur War of October 1973 began with an Arab assault across the Suez Canal which caught the Israelis almost totally unprepared. In the air, the Soviet-equipped Egyptian and Syrian air forces outnumber the Israeli air force by about two-to-one. The Arab air forces' combat equipment included 260 MiG-21s (a highly manoeuvrable Mach 2 fighter aircraft well suited to the air superiority mission) and 175 Sukhoi Su-7s, a fighter-bomber with an excellent low-level performance. The Israelis' most modern equipment comprised US-supplied McDonnell Douglas F-4 Phantom multi-role fighters and the same company's A-4 Skyhawk light attack aircraft, with about 150 each in service. The older French-supplied Dassault Mirage IIICJs and an Israeli copy, the IAI Nesher, were also in service in some numbers.

Below The most effective warplane in Israeli service in 1973 was the F-4E Phantom multi-role fighter.

Centre Potez Magister trainers were flown in the light-attack role by Israeli reservist pilots during the Yom Kippur War.

Bottom An Egyptian Sukhoi Su-7 fighter-bomber lights up its afterburner in an attempt to escape from an Israeli air force Mirage IIICJ interceptor.

The Egyptian assault, coordinated with a Syrian and Iraqi attack, opened on 6 October, which was Yom Kippur – the Day of Atonement – in the Jewish religious calendar. The Israelis had received little warning and had not fully mobilized their forces. The Egyptians therefore were able to cross the Suez Canal in strength and breach the fortifications of the Bar Lev Line. Their armies were well equipped with anti-aircraft defences, comprising both AA artillery and surface-to-air missiles (SAMs) and these took a heavy toll of Israeli aircraft. It was only when American-supplied electronic countermeasures equipment and Shrike radar-homing missiles were brought into use against these ground-

based air defences that Israeli aircraft losses fell to acceptable limits.

The Israelis in their turn were inflicting heavy losses on the Egyptian air force and on 7 October alone more than 30 fighter-bombers were destroyed while attempting to attack Israeli air bases. By 10 October the Israeli army had held the Egyptian advance into Sinai, but the air force was making little impression on the AA and SAM defences deployed within the bridgehead. Two days later, with total aircraft losses approaching 100, the Israelis appealed to the United States for resupply, claiming that they only had sufficient stocks of munitions for four more days of fighting. The United States responded with an airlift of arms and munitions, which was complicated by the refusal of many European states (under pressure from oil-rich Arab nations) to grant them landing rights. However, by staging through the Azores, the transport aircraft were able to fly-in the much-needed munitions. Replacement warplanes followed by the same route, some of them withdrawn from front-line units of the US armed forces to meet the emergency.

On 14 October a massive tank battle was fought in Sinai, with the Egyptians committing reserve armour forces from the west bank of the Canal. Two days later Israeli forces exploited this weakening of the defences by crossing the Canal and establishing a bridgehead on the Egyptian side. They were provided with strong air cover, which fought off Egyptian air-force attacks, and many of the Egyptian's front-line airfields were overrun by Israeli troops. In the north heavy fighting with Syrian forces in the Golan Heights also ended with an Israeli advance, heliborne commandos being used to assault Mount Hermon on 21 October. On the following day the Arab government recognized their military defeat and a ceasefire was signed, which effectively marked the end of hostilities.

3

AEROPLANE MANUFACTURERS

AÉROSPATIALE

The French Aérospatiale Company was formed by the amalgamation of the nationalized Nord Aviation and Sud Aviation concerns in 1970. Nord Aviation dates back to 1937, when the Société Nationale de Constructions Aéronautiques du Nord was created from the privately owned CAMS, Potez, Amiot and ANF-Mureaux companies. The most significant of Nord's pre-war designs was the Potez 63 series of twin-engined, multi-role warplanes. During the German occupation of France, Nord produced Dornier Do 24 flying boats and Messerschmitt Bf 108 and Me 208 communications aircraft for the Luftwaffe. The two Messerschmitt types remained in production after the war as the Nord Pingouin (Bf 108), Ramier and Noralpha (Me 208).

The most significant Nord design was the N2501 Noratlas twin-engined tactical transport aircraft, which first flew in 1949. The Armée de l'Air received 200 of these, some of which remain in service in the early 1980s, and the West German Luftwaffe was another large-scale operator of the type. It was used in combat, often as a paratroop transport, by the French at Suez in 1956 and in the Algerian War, as well as by the Israeli Air Force (which operated 30 Noratlases). Its successor, the C160 Transall (Transporter Allianz), was built in collaboration with the

HFB and VFW companies of West Germany and 175 of the initial production version were produced for the Armée de l'Air and Luftwaffe. The Transall was put back into production in the early 1980s to fulfil a French requirement for a further 25 aircraft. On the civil side Nord produced the N262 Frégate twin-turboprop airliner, which carried 26 passengers over short-haul routes.

Sud Aviation was formed in 1957 from the pre-war SNCASO (Société Nationale de Constructions Aéronautiques du Sud-Ouest) and from SNCASE (Société Nationale de Constructions Aéronautiques du Sud-Est). Sud-Ouest was responsible for the first French jet aircraft to fly, the SO 6000 Triton of 1946. In 1952 the twin-jet SO 4050 Vautour medium bomber made its maiden flight and the type was produced for the Armée de l'Air in attack, bomber and all-weather fighter versions. It served as a nuclear-armed bomber with the Forces Aériennes Stratégiques and a number of Vautours exported to Israel saw action in the Six-Day War of 1967.

The Caravelle, a twin-jet medium-range airliner, first flew in 1955, entering airline service with Air France in 1959. It was the first aircraft of its type to have tail-mounted engines, an innovation that was to be followed by many later airliner designs. The Caravelle remained in production until 1974 and a total of 280 were built. The even more innovative Concorde supersonic airliner of 1969, designed and built in

Left A Vautour IIN of the 92ᵉ Escadre de Bombardement. This was a two-seat all-weather fighter, 70 of which served with the Armée de l'Air.

Below The Nord 2501 Noratlas tactical transport entered service with the Armée de l'Air in 1953. This example served with the 64ᵉ Escadre de Transport.

Top *Air France was the first operator of the Sud Caravelle, which began to operate on the Paris, Rome and Istanbul route in May 1959.*

Above *An Alouette III helicopter of the Aéronavale's Escadrille 22S, based at Lanvéoc-Poulmic in Brittany, which carries out search and rescue duties.*

Below *The twin-turbofan Airbus wide-bodied airliner has won orders from many of the world's major operators.*

Below right *The Dauphin helicopter is the intended successor of the highly popular Alouette III.*

collaboration with the British Aircraft Corporation, failed to match this commercial success. However, the Sud subsidiary company SOCATA produced Europe's most successful light aircraft, the Rallye (inherited from Morane-Saulnier), over 4000 of which were built.

Aérospatiale's involvement with rotorcraft can be traced back to the early post-war years, when Sud-Est employed Professor Heinrich Focke as a designer. The two-seat Djinn of 1953 was produced by Sud-Ouest for the French Army and for civil operators, with a total of 178 built. The Alouette II of 1955, powered by a turboshaft rather than a piston engine, was further developed into the highly successful Alouette III. With accommodation for a pilot and six passengers, the Alouette III found favour with both civil and military operators and stayed in production for over twenty years. Helicopter development continued with the

Super Frelon, which served in the anti-submarine role with France's Aéronavale and as a troop transport with the Israeli and South African air forces. In 1967 Sud Aviation signed an agreement with Westland in the United Kingdom to cover production of three helicopter types for the French and British armed forces. The aircraft involved were the Lynx, Puma and Gazelle, the latter two being French designs. The Gazelle is a lightweight scout helicopter with accommodation for up to five people and it can be armed with Hot or Tow anti-tank missiles, a 20mm cannon or rocket pods. Rocket-armed Gazelles saw action with the Army Air Corps and Royal Marines in the Falkland Islands in 1982. The twin-turbine Puma is an assault transport helicopter, with accommodation for up to 20 troops. In its more powerful Super Puma version it is capable of carrying two Exocet anti-shipping missiles and these weapons have been used by Iraqi Super Pumas in the war with Iran.

The AS 350 Ecureuil five/six-seat helicopter is a civil machine in much the same class as the military Gazelle. It first flew in 1974 and production deliveries began four years later. The larger Dauphin, built in both single- and twin-turboshaft versions, is intended as a successor to the Alouette III. Following its first flight in 1972, Aérospatiale secured an important export order for the type from the US Coast Guard which will operate 90 in the air/sea rescue role. In the early 1980s the piston-engined Epsilon primary trainer was in production for the Armée de l'Air, which has a requirement for 150 of these aircraft. Civil work centred on production of the wide-bodied, short-haul Airbus, in collaboration with West Germany and the United Kingdom.

11 scouts by the Allies. Germany's answer was the Albatros DI biplane fighter, fitted with a powerful 160hp Mercedes DIII engine and armed with twin 7·92mm Spandau machine guns. At the beginning of 1917 the much-improved Albatros DIII, first of the 'V-Strutters', appeared and it was this fighter that so dominated the Allies in 'Bloody April', 1917. The later Albatros DV and DVa versions offered no great improvements over the DIII, although large numbers were in service in 1917–18.

ALBATROS

The two-seat reconnaissance aircraft and single-seat fighters produced by the Albatros Werke in Germany during World War I were among the most successful aircraft of the army air service. The Albatros BI, designed by Ernst Heinkel, equipped the Feld Flieger Abteilung at the outbreak of war. Powered by either a Mercedes DI of 100hp or a DII of 120hp, they carried a pilot and an observer seated ahead of him. No defensive armament was carried apart from the observer's rifle. In the summer of 1915 the Albatros B-types (BI, BII and BIII variants were produced) gave way to the armed C-type two-seater. The Albatros CI was fitted with a Parabellum machine gun for use by the observer, whose cockpit was moved behind the pilot's in this version. The Albatros CI became something of a maid-of-all-work, being used for photographic and visual reconnaissance, artillery observation and light bombing. Among the improvements introduced on the Albatros CIII which appeared later in 1915, was a forward-firing gun for the pilot. The next Albatros C-type was the CV of 1916, an entirely new design, and further developments took the series up to the CXII of 1918.

By the summer of 1916 the success enjoyed by the Fokker Eindecker fighters was waning with the introduction of the de Havilland DH2 and Nieuport

Top left The Albatros DIII was a highly successful fighter aircraft in the spring of 1917.

Top right A captured Albatros C-type of the Austro-Hungarian air service.

Above The Albatros BII reconnaissance two-seater first appeared in 1914.

Below The An-2 utility transport biplane first appeared in 1947 and remains in widespread use today. This An-2ZA meteorological variant has an observer's cockpit mounted forward of the tailplane.

ANTONOV

The Soviet aircraft designer Oleg Antonov began his career with a series of successful gliders in the late 1920s and 1930s. He joined the Yakovlev design bureau after the closure of the Moscow Glider Factory in 1938 and his work included producing a copy of the German Fieseler Storch short take-off liaison aircraft. In World War II he designed the A-7 troop transport glider, which was used to supply partisan forces behind enemy lines. He also worked on the design of the Yak-3 and Yak-9 piston-engined fighters and the Yak-15 jet fighter.

In 1946 Antonov formed his own design bureau and one of its earliest aircraft, the An-2, has proved to be the most widely used light transport aircraft in the Soviet Union. A robust single-engined biplane, the An-2 has good short take-off and landing characteristics and can accommodate up to 12 passengers. About 5000 An-2s were built up to 1960 and many remain

in service today. Antonov's next successful design was the An-12, which entered service with the Soviet air force in 1959 and rapidly became the standard Soviet tactical transport aircraft. Powered by four turboprops, it has a range of 3400km (2100 miles) with a 10,000kg (22,000lb) payload. The heavy-lift An-22, which first flew in 1965, can carry a 45,400kg (100,000lb) payload over 10,900km (6800 miles). Some 100 An-22s were built and until the Lockheed C-5A appeared in 1968 it was the world's largest aircraft.

The An-24 twin-turboprop airliner entered service with Aeroflot in 1962 and carries up to 40 passengers over medium-haul routes. It has been developed into the An-26 military freighter, with a rear-fuselage cargo door. The An-30 is a photographic survey version of the An-24, while the An-32 has more powerful engines for operations in high temperatures from high-altitude airfields.

ARADO

The Arado company of Warnemünde in north Germany was noted for successful floatplane and trainer designs and it manufactured the first jet bomber to see operational service anywhere in the world. Formed in 1925, the company's early designs were undistinguished. However, the Ar 66 of 1932 was adopted as the Luftwaffe's primary trainer and more than 6000 were built. The Luftwaffe also operated the Ar 68 biplane fighter in some numbers during the late 1930s,

Top left   The twin-turboprop An-24 of 1959 was used extensively in civil and military service by the countries of the Warsaw Pact. This example serves with the Bulgarian air force.

Above   The An-12 four-turboprop military transport is the Soviet equivalent of the USAF's Lockheed C-130 Hercules. It has been widely exported, this example serving with the Iraqi air force.

Top right   The Arado Ar 196 floatplane served aboard the German navy's major warships and also equipped many coast defence flights. The Ar 196 A-3 pictured was the main production version.

Right   The Arado AR 234 twin-jet bomber was the first aircraft of its type, entering service with the Luftwaffe in 1944.

but by the outbreak of war the aircraft had been relegated to second-line duties. The Ar 95 was a biplane fitted with either a wheeled or float undercarriage, which saw service in small numbers with the Luftwaffe and several foreign air arms.

Arado's most successful trainer was the Ar 96, a low-wing monoplane fitted with a retractable undercarriage, which served with the German pilot training units and fighter pilot schools. Produced by Letov in Czechoslovakia and SIPA in France, as well as by the parent company, some 11,500 had been built by the end of the war. The Arado Ar 196 twin-float maritime reconnaissance aircraft was also widely used. It served with shore-based coastal reconnaissance units in the Baltic, North Sea, Bay of Biscay, Mediterranean and Black Sea and also aboard the major German warships. The twin-jet Ar 234 Blitz bomber and reconnaissance aircraft first flew in June 1943 and reached operational units in the following year. Among the missions flown by Ar 234s were reconnaissance flights over Britain and the bombing of the Remagen bridge over the Rhine.

ARMSTRONG WHITWORTH

The British engineering firm of Armstrong Whitworth produced two successful reconnaissance aircraft in World War I, the FK3 and FK8, both designed by the Dutchman Frederick Koolhoven. They also produced non-rigid and rigid airships, including the R33, which was based on the Zeppelin L33. In the inter-war years the company built the Siskin III fighter for the

RAF, the first RAF aircraft to have an all-metal air-frame. It also supplied the RAF with Atlas army co-operation two-seaters, some of which were modified as advanced training aircraft. On the civil side, Armstrong Whitworth designed the Argosy, Atalanta and Ensign airliners for Imperial Airways.

The most famous of the company's aircraft was the Whitley twin-engined monoplane bomber, which first flew in 1936. Although already obsolescent by the outbreak of World War II, the Whitley soldiered on with RAF Bomber Command until 1942. It also served as a parachute transport and glider tug with the air-borne forces and with Coastal Command as a maritime patrol aircraft. The twin-engined Albemarle bomber

of 1940 never served in its intended role, but it did operate as a glider tug and transport for airborne forces. Albemarles took part in the major airborne assaults on Sicily in July 1943, Normandy in June 1944 and Arnhem in September 1944. After the war the company produced the twin-boom Agosy civil freighter. This was not a success, however, although more than 50 of the military version served with the RAF. In 1963 the company became part of the Hawker Siddeley group.

Below The Avro 504K was one of the most widely used British training aeroplanes of World War I. This example is preserved in flying condition by the Shuttleworth Trust at Old Warden in Bedfordshire.

Above left An RAF Atlas army cooperation biplane with its message pick-up hook extended. The Armstrong Whitworth Atlas was in RAF service between 1927 and 1935.

Left Intended for service as a medium bomber, the Albemarle was used operationally as a glider tug and paratroop transport.

Below left After their retirement from Bomber Command in 1942, Whitleys served on as glider tugs for the airborne forces. The aircraft pictured has been converted for this role and carries underwing supply canisters.

Below Production of the Anson ended in 1952 with the Anson T Mk 21 navigation trainer.

AVRO

The Avro company formed by aviation pioneer A. V. Roe before World War I proved to be one of the most successful in British aviation. The Avro 504 of 1914 was an immediate success in the war, flying armed reconnaissance and bombing missions, and in its Avro 504J and K versions serving as an important training aircraft. Production of the 504 continued in the 1920s, as the Avro 504N trainer for the RAF, and the last of these was delivered in 1933. The 504's successor was the Avro Tutor, which entered service in 1933 and remained in service until 1939. Military aircraft built by Avro in the inter-war years included the RAF's Alder-shot bomber and the Bison spotter-reconnaissance aircraft of the Fleet Air Arm. The Avian two-seat sports biplane enjoyed considerable popularity with private pilots.

Although it is primarily remembered as a training aircraft, the Avro Anson in fact first entered RAF service with Coastal Command's maritime reconnais-sance squadrons and it also formed the initial equip-ment of a number of bomber squadrons hastily brought into being during the RAF expansion of the late 1930s. Coastal Command's Ansons served on into the early years of World War II and an Anson of No 500 Squadron made the first attack on a U-boat on 5 September 1939. The same squadron was heavily

tion calling for a twin-engined bomber to replace the Vickers Wellington. This resulted in the Avro Manchester, which first flew in 1939 and entered RAF service in the following year. The Manchester was powered by two Rolls-Royce Vulture engines, which proved to be highly unreliable powerplants. Engine failures were frequent, often resulting in the loss of aircraft, and engine defects often grounded Manchesters for weeks on end. Consequently, it was with relief that Bomber Command flew its last Manchester sortie in June 1942 and the type was withdrawn from service.

Although the problems with the Manchester were

engaged in the Dunkirk fighting, when the Anson's standard armament of one fixed and one turret-mounted 0·303in machine gun was supplemented by a 20mm cannon on some aircraft. Yet it was as a trainer that the aircraft performed its most notable services during World War II. When the British Commonwealth Air Training Plan was introduced, the Anson became one of its standard trainers, and thousands were produced both in the United Kingdom and in Canada. Apart from pilot training, the Anson provided a flying classroom for navigators, bomb aimers and air gunners. Another vital if unglamorous role it undertook was that of air taxi for the Air Transport Auxiliary's ferry pilots. The last Anson to be produced for the RAF was a T Mk 21 delivered in 1952. In all 10,996 Ansons were built, including 2883 manufactured in Canada.

In 1936, during the expansion of the RAF before the outbreak of war, the Air Ministry issued a specifica-

Top *An Avro Manchester of No 207 Squadron. The forerunner of the Lancaster, the Manchester proved to be a failure.*

Above right *This Avro Lancaster B Mk III served with No 619 Squadron of RAF Bomber Command. By the spring of 1945 over 1000 Lancasters were available for operations every day.*

Above left *The RAF's last Lancasters were retired from service with Coastal Command at St Mawgan in Cornwall in October 1956.*

Below *A Lincoln B Mk II in the colour scheme adopted for operations in the Far East.*

considerable, there were no basic faults in the design other than the temperamental engines. This was proved with the appearance of the Manchester Mk III which was similar to the earlier aircraft, but had extended wings and was powered by four Rolls-Royce Merlins. Renamed the Lancaster it was to become the most effective bomber aircraft in RAF service during World War II and one of the classic warplanes of aviation history. The prototype first flew on 9 January 1941 and production examples entered service with No 44 Squadron at Waddington in Lincolnshire at the end of that year. Carrying a crew of seven, the Lancaster could lift a bomb load of 5500kg (12,000lb) over a range of 2780km (1730 miles). Defensive armament comprised pairs of 0·303in machine guns in powered nose and dorsal turrets, while a tail turret housed four 0·303in weapons. Maximum speed was 462km/h (287mph) at 3500m (11,500ft) and service ceiling was 7500m (24,500ft).

The Lancaster's first notable operation was the daylight raid on Augsburg on 17 April 1942, but the greater number of Lancaster sorties were flown at night. Lancasters took part in the Thousand Bomber Raids of May–June 1942 and all the major Bomber Command campaigns thereafter, including the battles of the Ruhr, Hamburg and Berlin. By the end of World War II Lancasters had flown a total of 156,192 operational sorties, the majority of them bombing missions, but also including sea minelaying and anti-submarine patrols. The Lancaster's most famous exploit of World War II was undoubtedly the Dams raid of May 1943, but No 617 Squadron (the Dambusters) made many other notable attacks, including the sinking of the battleship *Tirpitz* with 5500kg (12,000lb) Tallboy bombs on 12 November 1944.

The Rolls-Royce-Merlin-powered Lancaster Mk I was joined on operations at the end of 1942 by the near-identical Mk III, which differed in having American Packard-built Merlin engines. The Lancaster Mk II, powered by Bristol Hercules radial engines, was produced as an insurance against the supply of Merlins drying up. In the event this fear proved to be unfounded and consequently only 300 Lancaster Mk IIs were built. Two other marks of Lancaster saw wartime service: the Mk VI with more powerful Merlin engines and the Canadian-built Mk X. A total of 7377 Lancasters of all versions were produced, all

but 430 of them built in the United Kingdom. At peak strength 58 squadrons flew the Lancaster. After World War II they quickly disappeared from RAF Bomber Command's squadrons, but the type served on in photographic survey and maritime reconnaissance roles until its retirement in October 1956.

The Lancaster's postwar successor with Bomber Command was the Avro Lincoln, an extensively modified 'Super Lancaster' powered by four Rolls-Royce Griffon engines. The Lincoln entered service in August 1945, eventually equipping 23 RAF bomber squadrons, and it was finally withdrawn in the mid-1950s. During this period it saw action in the counter-insurgency conflicts in Malaya and Kenya. Two transport versions of the Lancaster served with the RAF in the immediate postwar years. The Lancastrian was a straightforward transport conversion, which carried up to 13 passengers. The York made use of an entirely new fuselage, which could accommodate 24 passengers. Seven RAF York squadrons took part in the Berlin airlift in 1947–8.

Below (upper) *An Avro Shackleton MR Mk 2 of No 224 Squadron, RAF Coastal Command flies an overwater patrol.*

Below (lower) *A Vulcan B Mk 2 of No 101 Squadron. The RAF retired its Vulcan B Mk 2s from the bombing role in 1982, No 101 Squadron being one of the last units to operate the type.*

Below *The success of the Beech Aircraft Company was founded on sales of the Model 17 Staggerwing in the 1930s.*

The last in the line of Lancaster descendants was the Avro Shackleton maritime reconnaissance aircraft, which first flew in March 1949. It began to replace Coastal Command's Lancasters in 1951 and eventually three main versions were produced, which equipped 15 Coastal Command squadrons. These were finally replaced by Hawker Siddeley Nimrods in 1972. However, a single squadron of Shackletons (No 8 Squadron) equipped with the airborne early warning Mk 2 version, remained in RAF service in the AEW role until the early 1980s. A number of Shackletons also remain operational with No 35 Squadron of the South African Air Force. Other Avro designs that saw limited service were the Athena trainer and the Tudor civil airliner.

Avro's most important project of the 1950s was the Vulcan bomber. This aircraft, together with the Vickers Valiant and Handley Page Victor, formed the V-Force – Britain's nuclear deterrent between 1956 and 1968. The delta-wing Vulcan was produced in two marks and served with nine RAF bomber squadrons. In 1982, on the eve of its retirement from operational service, the Vulcan saw action for the first time – in the Falklands conflict.

BEECH

The Beech Aircraft Company, noted for its light aircraft and executive transports, was formed by Walter H. Beech at Wichita in Kansas in 1932. It first success was the Model 17, a five-seat cabin biplane with the wings set at a negative stagger (with the upper wing set behind the lower), giving the aircraft its popular nickname of 'Staggerwing'. There followed in 1935 the twin-engined Model 18 executive transport, which could seat up to eight passengers in considerable comfort. This aircraft was adapted for military use in World War II as the USAAF's AT-7 and AT-11 trainers and the C-45 light transport. It was also operated by the US Navy as the JRB transport and SNB trainer, and several hundred flew with the RAF and the

built. In the following year the Model 99 Commuter airliner was introduced. This twin-turbine, 17-seat aircraft was intended to fly the routes set up by third-level operators to feed passengers into the major cities from outlying districts. Also in 1966, Beech passed an important milestone when its 25,000th aircraft (a King Air) came off the production line. Since that time the company has continued to produce a range of light planes ranging from the single-engined Bonanza (some 10,000 of which have been built) to the larger King Air and Model 99 turboprop-powered 'twins'.

BELL

The Bell Aircraft corporation was formed at Buffalo, New York, in 1935 and its first aircraft design was the YFM-1 Airacuda, a twin-engined escort fighter armed with two 37mm cannon. This radical design did not progress beyond the service test stage, but it was quickly followed by the equally unconventional P-39 Airacobra single-seat fighter. The XP-39 prototype first flew in August 1939 and it was powered by an Allison V-1710 engine buried in the fuselage behind the pilot's cockpit, which drove a nose-mounted propeller through an extension shaft. Unusually for an aircraft of the period, it was fitted with a tricycle rather than a tailwheel undercarriage. Armament comprised a 37mm cannon and twin 0·5in machine guns mounted

Fleet Air Arm, the British versions being named Expediter. Eventually some 9000 Model 18s were built.

After the war Beech produced two new light aircraft of note: the V-tailed Bonanza and the Twin Bonanza. Success with these designs led to the twin-engined Model 95 Travel Air (later developed into the Baron) and the single-engined Debonair. A military trainer, the T-34A Mentor, was produced in the 1950s and in its turboprop-powered T-34C form it remains in production today. The piston-engined Musketeer, although primarily a civil light aircraft, has also achieved some success as a military trainer. For the executive private aircraft owner there was the twin-engined Queen Air and the later twin-turbine King Air.

By 1965 there were 15 different Beech models in production and more than 8000 Bonanzas had been

Top The twin-engined Beech Model 18 found favour with both civil and military operators and over 9000 examples were built between 1935 and 1969.

Above The Beech Model 35 Bonanza has been built with both the distinctive 'butterfly' tail-unit illustrated and with a more conventional empennage.

Right The Bell P-39Q Airacobra had an armament of two 0·5in machine guns mounted underwing, as well as a 37mm cannon and twin-machine guns in the nose.

in the fuselage, plus four wing-mounted 0·3in machine guns in the P-39D model. Despite its many advanced features, the P-39 was not a great success in air-to-air combat, although it was to perform well as a ground-attack fighter. It served in action with the USAAF in the Southwest Pacific and Alaska and many newly formed fighter groups trained on the Airacobra in the United States. It was widely exported, serving with the RAF (briefly, and with only one squadron), the Soviet air force, the French air force and the Italian Co-Belligerent air force (those elements of the Regia Aeronautica who elected to fight with the Allies after 1943). Total Airacobra production was 9558 and over half of these were despatched to the Soviet Union.

The P-63 Kingcobra which first flew in December 1942 was a refined version of the Airacobra with a low-

Left Aimed at the executive transport market, the turboprop-powered Beech Super King Air can carry up to 15 passengers at a speed of 530km/h (330mph).

drag 'laminar flow' wing. Over 3000 were built and they served as gunnery trainers with the USAAF and front-line equipment with the Soviet air force. There followed the P-59, which saw little military service but which was noteworthy because it was the first American jet aircraft. Named the Airacomet, it first flew on 1 October 1942 and was powered by two General Electric J31 turbojets (based on the Whittle W2B engine). Although it saw no operational service during World War II, 50 production P-59s were flown by the USAAF as fighter trainers.

Bell's most important aircraft of the immediate post-war years was the experimental rocket-powered XS-1, which on 14 October 1947 became the first aircraft to exceed the speed of sound (Mach 1) in level flight. This experimental work was continued in 1949–52 with the X-1A and X-1B rocket aircraft, and led to

the swept-wing Bell X-2, which reached a speed of 3057km/h (1900mph) in July 1956. The company was also working on helicopter designs and in December 1945 the Model 47 appeared. This was one of the most successful rotary-winged aircraft in aviation history, remaining in production in the United States until 1962. It was widely exported in both civil and military versions and was manufactured under licence in Britain, Italy and Japan. Production of the Bell 47 totalled some 6000 aircraft.

An even greater success was in prospect, for in 1955 the company designed a troop-carrying helicopter for

Above left The Bell P-59A Airacomet was the United States' first jet aircraft and more than 60 were produced as advanced training aircraft.

Left The Bell UH-1, nicknamed the 'Huey', formed the backbone of the US Army's helicopter force in South Vietnam and it remains in service during the mid-1980s.

Top right The Bell OH-58 Kiowa is the US Army's version of the highly successful Jet Ranger civil helicopter. Its primary role is that of an airborne scout.

Above right The Bell AH-1 gunship helicopter was produced for service in Vietnam. An AH-1J Sea Cobra is pictured in service with the US Marine Corps.

the US Army, the UH-1 (nicknamed the 'Huey'), which was the most widely used helicopter ever produced. Capable of carrying a squad of troops, the Huey became the army's workhorse of the Vietnam War. It was exported all over the world and progressively improved versions have greatly extended its payload, range and reliability. An important offshoot of the Huey programme was the AH-1 'Hueycobra' helicopter gunship, a specialized armed helicopter making use of the UH-1's powerplant and transmission married to a new sharklike fuselage seating a pilot and gunner in tandem. Now under development by Bell is the XV-15 tilt-rotor V/STOL aircraft. This may well be ordered into production for the US armed forces in preference to a conventional helicopter, to meet the JVX requirement (Department of Defense's project designation) for the three armed services.

BLACKBURN

The company founded by the British aviation pioneer Robert Blackburn before World War I was chiefly noted for its naval and maritime reconnaissance aircraft. The twin-engined Blackburn Kangaroo of 1918 was one of the earliest specialized anti-submarine patrol aeroplanes and several Kangaroos were converted

Right *A float-equipped Blackburn Shark naval spotter aircraft flies over the battleship* HMS Nelson *during naval manoeuvres in the late 1930s.*

Below *The Blackburn Roc turret fighter was not an operational success, although the type did see service in World War II.*

Below right *A Blackburn Beverley C Mk 1 transport painted in the camouflage finish first adopted by No 84 Squadron in the RAF Middle East Command during the 1960s.*

Below *A Buccaneer S Mk 2 aircraft of No 12 Squadron RAF, which serves in the anti-shipping role.*

air, and four Iris IIIs were produced for the RAF, followed by a similar number of Perth flying boats.

Blackburn continued to specialize in naval aircraft with the Ripon torpedo-bomber of 1926 giving way to the Baffin in 1932. There followed the Shark of 1933 and four years later the first naval monoplane, the Skua dive-bomber. The Skua was the first British aeroplane to shoot down a German aircraft in World War II, and during the Norwegian Campaign Skuas dive-bombed and sank the cruiser *Königsberg*. The Roc turret-fighter, developed from the Skua, was not very successful and the Botha land-based reconnaissance/torpedo-bomber was an unmitigated failure. Consequently Blackburn's main contribution to the war effort in World War II was the licence production of

to civil airliners after the Armistice. The company produced the Dart single-seat shipboard torpedo-bomber for the Fleet Air Arm and the oddly named Blackburn Blackburn fleet-spotter aircraft for the same service. In 1924 the Bluebird trainer appeared, which like the later Blackburn B-2 was notable for providing side-by-side seating for trainee and instructor, rather than the then more usual tandem seating arrangement. In 1926 the three-engined Iris flying boat first took to the

other company's aircraft and the modification of American naval warplanes to meet British requirements. One postwar success was the Beverley C Mk 1 transport, 47 of which were built for the RAF, serving from 1956 until 1968. Another was the twin-jet NA.39 naval strike aircraft, soon to be named the Buccaneer, which first flew in April 1958. It was to be the last Blackburn aircraft as in 1963 the company became part of Hawker Siddeley Aviation.

Left *The Boeing P-12E of 1931 was the most widely used of the P-12 series fighter biplanes and remained in service with the US Army Air Corps until replaced by the Boeing P-26 in 1935.*

BOEING

Today the name of Boeing is virtually synonymous with the airliner and with the strategic bomber, but William E. Boeing's first aircraft was a twin-float seaplane which first flew in 1916. In the following year he offered his Model C floatplane training aircraft to the US Navy, which placed an order for 50. On the strength of this contract the Boeing Airplane Company was established at Seattle, Washington, a major aircraft manufacturer by the standards of the day.

At the end of World War I the United States had yet to produce a successful fighter aircraft, but in 1919 the Thomas-Morse Company produced its MB-3 fighter, or in the parlance of the day 'pursuit airplane'. This first effective American-built fighter was built under licence by Boeing, which received a contract for 200 MB-3As in 1920. Good though the MB-3 was, Boeing set out to produce a better aircraft. Accordingly the Model 15 was designed and built as a private venture, using company funds. The design immediately found favour with the US Army Air Service, which ordered two prototypes, designated XPW-9s, in 1923. Among the aircraft's advanced features was its 435hp Curtiss D-12 in-line engine and its welded steel-tube fuselage structure (pioneered by the Dutchman Anthony Fokker).

The PW-9 fighter, as the production examples became, laid the foundations of Boeing's postwar prosperity. Production orders from the army totalled nearly 100 aircraft, and the navy also bought the fighter as the Boeing FB. It was the latter service which encouraged development of the next Boeing fighter model, when it decreed that all its future aircraft would have radial, air-cooled engines. The company responded with its F2B and F3B fighters, powered by the 425hp Pratt & Whitney R-1340 Wasp radial. The first F2Bs were delivered in 1928 and served as fighter-bombers aboard the carrier USS *Saratoga*.

Below *The Boeing P-26, nicknamed the Peashooter, was the first monoplane fighter to serve with the US Army Air Corps. A few saw action against the Japanese in China and in the Philippines.*

monoplane, and the Boeing company produced one of the earliest and most successful of the inter-war monoplane fighters. This was the Boeing Model 248, officially designated P-26 by the US Army Air Corps, but universally known by the affectionate nickname of 'the Peashooter'. Its tubby, well-rounded fuselage was of all-metal monocoque construction, but the wings were externally braced rather than cantilever. This is somewhat surprising as such advanced internally braced wing structures had already been used by Boeing in the B-9 prototype bomber. Power was provided by a 500hp Pratt & Whitney R-1340 radial, giving a maximum speed of 376km/h (234mph). Among the Peashooter's less advanced features were its fixed undercarriage and open cockpit, but perhaps its greatest shortcoming was the woefully inadequate armament of only two 0·5in machine guns. Yet despite these features the P-26 gave American fighter pilots their first experience of an all-metal monoplane pursuit aircraft and it was well liked by the men who flew it.

If Boeing enjoyed considerable and deserved good fortune with its fighters, then it was less lucky in selling other advanced aircraft designs. Its B-9 bomber, which first flew in 1931, was an advanced twin-engined all-metal monoplane, but army orders went instead to the rival Martin B-10. Similarly, the Model 247 airliner

The F2B and F3B series were essentially straightforward adaptations of the PW-9/FB fitted with the Wasp radial engine. The F4B model which followed was an entirely new design, but retained the Wasp powerplant. This machine was designed entirely on the company's initiative, yet the risk paid off and the F4B (army designation P-12) became one of the most successful biplane fighters of the early 1930s. The navy's F4B differed from the army's P-12 only in the addition of such naval equipment as the arrester hook. Production of this fighter model totalled 586 aircraft, the later variants (P-12Es and F4B-3s) having a metal-skinned monocoque (load-bearing) fuselage instead of the fabric-covered structure of the earlier models. The first such modification, the company-funded Boeing Model 218, was the first American-designed fighter to see combat. Sold to China, it was flown in defence of Soochow by the mercenary pilot Robert Short against the Japanese in 1932. Unfortunately the Model 218 was shot down and Short was killed, but it is believed that he shot down one or two of his enemies.

During the 1930s the biplane fighter which had first appeared in World War I gradually gave place to the

lost out to the Douglas DC series and only 75 Model 247s were built. Another commercial venture was the Model 314A four-engined flying boat, which could operate a transatlantic route. However, with international tension growing daily in the Europe of the late 1930s, it was with military rather than civil designs that the Boeing company's immediate future lay.

Boeing's Model 299 four-engined bomber, which was to become the B-17 Flying Fortress, first flew in July 1935. Despite the crash of the prototype, which was due to aircrew error rather than to a fault in design or manufacture, the US Army Air Corps ordered a batch of them for service testing. Orders for the first production version followed in 1937 and by the time production ended 12,731 Flying Fortresses had been

produced for air/sea rescue (carrying a lifeboat beneath the fuselage), for photographic reconnaissance, electronic countermeasures, and as a heavily armed bomber-escort. At the end of World War II the B-17 quickly disappeared from front-line service, partly because so many Fortresses had been lost in combat, but primarily due to the appearance of an advanced new bomber, the Boeing B-29 Superfortress.

The B-29 represented a tremendous advance over previous bomber designs. It incorporated pressurized crew compartments which allowed the crew to function in comfort at altitudes of 9150m (30,000ft) or more. The bomber's defensive armament included four remote-controlled barbettes, each mounting two 0·5in machine guns. Powered by four 2200hp Wright Double Cyclones fitted with turbo-superchargers, the B-29 had a range of over 6400km (4000 miles) and could lift a maximum bomb load of 9100kg (20,000lb). The Superfortress first went into action in June 1944 and when airfields in the Marianas became available later that year, highly effective raids were launched against the Japanese homeland. Night raids using incendiary bombs rather than high explosives were especially damaging and in one attack on Tokyo more than 80,000 people were killed and 100,000 injured. These were higher casualties than those produced by the Hiroshima and Nagasaki atomic bombs with which B-29s brought the war against Japan to an end. The Superfortress remained in service until the mid-1950s, constituting the mainstay of the newly formed Strategic Air Command (SAC) in 1946 and operating against targets in North Korea during the Korean War in 1950–53. An improved and re-engined variant, designated B-50, was produced in 1947 and this served both as a strategic bomber and as a tanker aircraft for in-flight refuelling.

Even at the time of the B-29's combat debut it was clear that the days of the piston-engined bomber were numbered. Accordingly, Boeing began work on the design of a jet-engined successor to the Superfortress. After many vicissitudes this aircraft eventually emerged as the B-47 Stratojet, a six-engine swept-wing bomber which first flew in December 1947. With the opening of the Cold War in the early 1950s, funds became available for the production of more than 2000 Stratojets. The bomber's 6400km (4000-mile) range was insufficient for intercontinental missions and so for most of the 1950s nuclear-armed B-47s stood on alert at forward bases in North Africa, Spain and the United Kingdom, ready to fly their war mission against the Soviet Union at an instant's notice.

A jet bomber with truly intercontinental range, the eight-engined Boeing B-52 Stratofortress, entered service with SAC in 1955. The B-52's 16,000km (10,000-mile) unrefuelled range could be yet further extended by in-flight refuelling, giving the bomber a truly global reach. This capability was convincingly demonstrated in January 1957, when three Stratofortresses made a non-stop around-the-world flight, remaining airborne for over 45 hours. A total of 744 B-52s were built and the later B-52G and H models

built. With the Consolidated Liberator it bore the brunt of USAAF strategic bombing operations throughout World War II, serving in all theatres of war. B-17s dropped nearly half a million US tons of bombs on targets in Europe alone, a greater tonnage than any other American bomber aircraft. Yet this record was only achieved at a price and some 5000 B-17s were destroyed on combat missions.

Above A USAF Strategic Air Command Boeing B-52F releases its bomb load during operations over South Vietnam in the 1960s. This model could carry 12,260kg (27,000lb) of high-explosive bombs in the weapons bay, plus a further 4080kg (9000lb) underwing.

In the course of its development the B-17 grew from the 10,000kg (22,000lb) empty weight of the prototype to the B-17G's 16,300kg (36,000lb). Defensive armament was increased from the early bomber's five 0·3in machine guns in hand-held positions to the 13 0·5in guns of the B-17G, which was fitted with power-operated gun turrets. Although the B-17's bomb-load was fairly small in comparison with contemporary bombers, the G-model could carry 2700kg (6000lb) of bombs over a range of 3200km (2000 miles). As a combat aircraft it was well liked by its crews, being easy to fly and to hold in formation, and it could absorb a considerable amount of battle damage and still return to base. Although primarily used as a bomber throughout its service life, variants of the Fortress were

Above The USAF's KC-135A Stratotanker (illustrated) and the Boeing 707 airliner both stemmed from the Boeing 367-80, which made its first flight in July 1954.

Above *The first airline to order the twin-jet Boeing 737 in 1965 was the West German carrier Lufthansa, which operates the type on domestic and European services.*

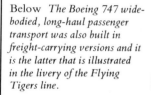

Below *The Boeing 747 wide-bodied, long-haul passenger transport was also built in freight-carrying versions and it is the latter that is illustrated in the livery of the Flying Tigers line.*

are expected to remain in service with SAC until the end of the present century. In the Vietnam War B-52s based in Thailand and on Guam took part in many bombing raids over South Vietnam and during the short but intense Linebacker II operation in December 1972 they successfully operated against heavily defended targets in the North.

Since the early 1950s SAC's bomber operations have depended upon support from tanker aircraft. Among the most successful of these have been the KC-97 derivative of Boeing's Stratocruiser airliner, and the KC-135 Stratotanker, a close relative of the Boeing 707 airliner. The piston-engined Stratocruiser offered a hitherto unprecedented degree of passenger comfort, with sleeping berths, private compartments and cocktail lounge, as well as the then unusual amenities of adjustable armchair seats, wide aisles, air conditioning and soundproofing. However, as with bomber aircraft, the future lay with jet propulsion. Boeing's Type 367-80, which first flew in July 1954, was developed into both the military Stratotanker and the civil 707. The Boeing 707 has probably contributed more to civil aviation than any other aircraft, pioneering long-range jet air travel over most of the world's air routes. It first operated with Pan American over the North Atlantic route in 1958 and thereafter has served both as a passenger carrier and freight transport. One of the latest members of the 707 family is the E-3A Sentry AWACS aircraft, a military airborne radar and control system.

The success of the Boeing 707 was reinforced with the development of the 727 medium-range airliner. This tri-jet first entered service with Eastern Airlines in 1964 and in its developed versions can carry 189 passengers over a distance of 4000km (2500 miles). It has proved to be one of the most successful postwar airliners. In 1967 the short-haul Boeing 737 twin-jet appeared. This offered six-abreast seating for its 75–100 passengers, in contrast to its narrow-fuselage competitors such as the BAC One-Eleven and Douglas DC-9. The 737 first went into service with the German airline Lufthansa in 1968 and has been purchased by airlines all over the world. Its particularly strong features are its high utilization rates (due to easy unloading and maintenance, good fuel capacity etc.) and its ability to operate in extremes of climate.

Boeing was at the forefront of the next revolution in civil air transport operations with the first flight of its 747 wide-bodied jet in February 1969. This massive airliner can carry 360 passengers over a 9700km (6000-mile) route. Among its major operators are Pan American, Japan Airlines and British Airways. A freighter version, with an upward swinging nose to facilitate loading, can lift up to 110 tonnes. The future of Boeing's commercial transports rests with the Boeing 757 and 767 turbofan designs which are intended to meet the air transport needs of the 1990s.

BOULTON PAUL

In World War I the Norwich woodworking company of Boulton and Paul began the manufacture of aeroplanes, building the Royal Aircraft Factory's FE2bs, Sopwith Camels and Sopwith Snipes. In 1917 the aircraft designer John North joined the firm, producing the Bobolink fighter, the P6 research aircraft and the Bourges twin-engined bomber, none of which progressed beyond the prototype stage. In the inter-war years there followed the Atlantic (intended to compete for the *Daily Mail* prize for a transatlantic flight, which was won by Alcock and Brown in a Vickers Vimy), the Bodmin and the Bugle. Then in 1928 the firm's twin-engined Sidestrand bomber entered service with the RAF, albeit in limited numbers, for only one squadron (No 101 Squadron based at Bircham Newton in Norfolk and Andover in Hampshire) flew the

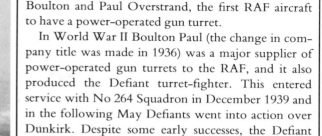

Above *The Boulton and Paul Overstrand bomber, pictured in service with No 101 Squadron, was the first RAF bomber to feature a power-operated gun turret.*

type. The Sidestrand was replaced in 1934 with the Boulton and Paul Overstrand, the first RAF aircraft to have a power-operated gun turret.

In World War II Boulton Paul (the change in company title was made in 1936) was a major supplier of power-operated gun turrets to the RAF, and it also produced the Defiant turret-fighter. This entered service with No 264 Squadron in December 1939 and in the following May Defiants went into action over Dunkirk. Despite some early successes, the Defiant proved to be totally unsuited to daylight operations and was relegated to the night-fighter role. They were finally retired from front-line service in 1942. After World War II Boulton Paul produced the Balliol trainer for the RAF and Fleet Air Arm, 162 being built. Its last aircraft, the P.111 and P.120, were delta-wing research aeroplanes. The company remains in aviation, however, as part of the Dowty Group, producing powered flight control systems.

BREGUET

The first aircraft built by the brothers Louis and Jacques Breguet was the Gyroplan helicopter of 1906. Although the machine succeeded in lifting off the ground during tests the following year, it was in no sense a practical flying machine. Louis Breguet then turned to producding aeroplanes and in 1911 the Société des Avions Louis Breguet was formed. During World War I Breguet cooperated with the tyre manufacturer Michelin to produce the Breguet-Michelin series of pusher-engined bombers. In 1916 he turned to a tractor layout in designing the Bre 14 bomber/reconnaissance

Below right *The Breguet 14 two-seater bomber and reconnaissance aircraft was one of the best French warplanes to serve during the later years of World War I.*

Above left *During World War II the Boulton Paul company produced power-operated gun turrets for the RAF. This example is fitted to their own Defiant two-seat fighter aircraft.*

Left *The Boulton Paul Balliol advanced trainer entered service with the RAF in 1952 and it was also produced for the Fleet Air Arm as the Sea Balliol.*

aircraft. This was one of the most successful World War I aeroplanes, equipping both French and American squadrons in 1917–18. It remained in production until 1926, by which time well over 8000 had been built.

The classic Breguet 14 was followed into production by the Bre 19, another two-seat bomber/reconnaissance aircraft, which saw widespread service in the inter-war years. One of the most famous Bre 19s, named *Point d'Interrogation* (Question Mark) made the first Paris-to-New York crossing of the North Atlantic in September 1930. In the following year the company

began production of a version of the Short Calcutta flying boat and from this was developed the much larger Bizerte, over 30 of which were built for the Aéronavale between 1935 and 1940.

With the approach of World War II, Breguet went into production with the Bre 690 series of twin-engined monoplane attack aircraft. However, as the company had refused to participate in the nationalization of the French aircraft industry at this time, official approval for its new design was tardy. Consequently, fewer than 150 reached front-line units before the French collapse in June 1940. In the 1930s Breguet had also resumed his work on the helicopter, designing and building the promising Gyroplan Laboratoire in collaboration with René Dorand. However, with the enforced interruption of his work during the German occupation of France, Breguet was overtaken by the American pioneers.

In 1940–44 the Breguet factories at Villacoublay and Bayonne produced German aircraft for the Luftwaffe. After the war, work resumed on Breguet's own designs, including the massive, four-engined Br 763 Deux

Above left The Bre 19 Point d'Interrogation, *used by Costes and Bellonte to make the first east-to-west Atlantic flight, is today preserved in the Musée de l'Air in Paris.*

Left The Bre 693 *twin-engined attack aircraft was only available in limited numbers during the Battle of France in 1940. The example illustrated was in Vichy service.*

Above right The twin-turboprop Breguet Atlantic anti-submarine aircraft was intended to replace the Lockheed P-2 Neptune in NATO service, but only France, West Germany and the Netherlands operate the type.*

Below The Aéronavale's standard shipboard anti-submarine aircraft since 1959 has been the Breguet Br 1050 Alizé, which has a crew of three and is powered by a Rolls-Royce Dart turboprop.*

Ponts transport (the Bre abbreviation was changed to Br during the war). There followed the Br 1050 Alizé (Trade Wind) a shipboard anti-submarine warfare (ASW) aircraft powered by a Rolls-Royce Dart turboprop. The Alizé entered service in 1959 and it remains in use with France's Aéronavale and the Indian navy. In 1958 Breguet won a design competition for a land-based ASW patrol aircraft to succeed the Lockheed P-2 Neptune in NATO service. Although the Br 1150 Atlantic did not become a standard NATO aircraft as was intended, it served with the Aéronavale, the West German, Italian and Dutch navies, as well as with Pakistan. An updated Atlantic Nouvelle Génération is in prospect for the late 1980s.

In 1955 Louis Breguet died and within little more than a decade his company lost its independence when Dassault assumed leadership of the private sector of the French aerospace industry. However, Breguet was to take part in two important collaborative ventures, sharing the production of both the Anglo-French Jaguar strike aircraft and the Franco-German Alpha Jet strike trainer.

BRISTOL

The Bristol aircraft company was formed in 1910 as the British and Colonial Aeroplane Company Ltd and, although its products were generally known as Bristol aircraft, it was not until 1920 that the firm became officially titled the Bristol Aeroplane Company. The Boxkite of 1910 was its first successful design and by 1914 some 200 aircraft of various types had left the company's Filton works. Early in World War I the company's chief designer Frank Barnwell produced the Bristol Scout, which served with the Royal Flying Corps and Royal Naval Air Service in 1915–16. In September 1916 the prototype F2A made its first flight, and this aircraft was to be developed into the F2B Bristol Fighter, an outstandingly successful two-seat fighter aircraft. Over 3000 were built by the end of the war and the type remained in RAF service in the army cooperation and training roles until 1932.

In 1920 the company acquired the Cosmos engineering firm which built aero engines and soon the name

Left RFC mechanics rig the wings of a Bristol F2B Fighter.

Below The pilot climbs aboard a Bristol Bulldog Mk IIa fighter, serving with No 23 Squadron, one of ten front-line RAF units to operate the type between 1929 and 1937.

By the outbreak of war around a thousand Blenheim Mk Is were in RAF service, plus nearly 200 of the improved Blenheim Mk IV. They operated primarily as daylight bombers and as night fighters. The first RAF aircraft to cross the German frontier in World War II was a Blenheim Mk IV of No 139 Squadron,

Bristol was to be as famous for its engines as for its aeroplanes. Yet it was not until 1928 that Bristol gained a substantial contract for its aircraft. In that year the RAF adopted the Bulldog as its standard fighter. Eventually ten RAF fighter squadrons flew the Bulldog and it was exported to various foreign air forces. It even saw limited combat service in 1939 with the Finnish air force during the opening stages of the Finns' Winter War with the Soviet Union. In 1935 the Bombay high-wing monoplane first flew and it was ordered for the RAF as a bomber-transport. This work was subcontracted to the Short company as Bristol's Filton works was fully employed in producing the RAF's new Blenheim bomber.

Deliveries of the Blenheim, a twin-engined monoplane, began to RAF bomber squadrons in 1937.

Above right Rocket-armed Bristol Beaufighters proved to be a potent anti-shipping weapon, and were also used against targets ashore. This example was serving in the Mediterranean theatre in 1944.

Below The Bristol Blenheim Mk 1 entered RAF service in 1937 and over 1000 were in service at the outbreak of World War II.

and a Blenheim Mk IF night fighter made the first AI radar-assisted interception of an enemy aircraft in July 1940. Nevertheless Blenheims suffered heavier losses than any other RAF aircraft type in World War II, largely because they had to fight against heavy odds in the early battles. Blenheims served in every theatre in which the RAF was engaged and remained in front-line service until 1943.

In October 1938 the prototype of the Beaufort torpedo-bomber first flew and this type entered RAF service at the end of the following year. It flew anti-shipping strike missions with the RAF over the North Sea, English Channel and Mediterranean and also served in the conventional bombing role with the Royal Australian Air Force in the Far East. RAF Beauforts were superseded by their stablemate the Beaufighter in 1943. This fast, twin-engined fighter first entered service in 1940, but priority in re-equipment was given to the RAF night-fighter squadrons with which the Beaufighter served with distinction. It later served with the RAF as a long-range day fighter and anti-shipping strike aircraft in Europe, the Middle East and the Far East. It was built under licence in Australia and operated with the RAAF in the Southwest Pacific. A successor to the Beaufighter, the Brigand, served with the RAF in Malaya after World War II in operations against the Communists.

Immediately after the war Bristol began designing the Freighter twin-engined transport, some 200 of

Above *The Bristol Britannia turboprop-powered airliner entered service with British Overseas Airways Corporation in 1957.*

Left *The Bristol Sycamore was the first British-designed helicopter to enter RAF service, undertaking the air/sea rescue and personnel transport roles.*

173 helicopter took to the air. This was developed into the RAF's Belvedere, but by the time it entered service in 1961 it had become the Westland Belvedere. In 1960 the Bristol company became part of the British Aircraft Corporation. It was under the auspices of the new organization that Filton's ambitious supersonic transport project was brought to fruition with the production of the Anglo-French Concorde.

BRITISH AEROSPACE

Below *The Panavia Tornado is being produced for the air forces of the United Kingdom, West Germany and Italy, as symbolized by the roundel on this aircraft's tail fin.*

In April 1977 BAC and Hawker Siddeley were merged to form British Aerospace, a publicly owned corporation. Much of the new company's business involved the further development of designs inherited from the earlier concerns, such as BAC's One-Eleven, and Jaguar and Hawker Siddeley's HS 125 and Harrier.

which were built. They served as car ferries from Britain to the Continent with Silver City Airways and a number were used as military transport aircraft by the air forces of New Zealand and Pakistan. An altogether more ambitious transport aircraft project was the Brabazon transatlantic airliner, which flew in prototype form in 1949 but never entered airline service. A more successful airliner design was the four-turboprop Britannia, which began scheduled services with BOAC in 1957. Its safety record was outstanding as not a single passenger was killed or injured when flying on a BOAC Britannia. A total of 85 were built, including 20 for the RAF, which flew with Nos 99 and 511 Squadrons from Lyneham in Wiltshire.

In 1945 Bristol formed a helicopter department at Weston-super-Mare in Somerset and before this was taken over by Westland in 1960 two successful designs were produced. The first was the Sycamore, a piston-engined helicopter which made its maiden flight in 1947. A total of 178 were built for civil and military operations and it was the first British helicopter to serve with the RAF. In 1952 the twin-engined Bristol

However, several important new designs have been developed primarily under the auspices of BAe. Undoubtedly the most significant of these is the Tornado multi-role strike aircraft and interceptor, which is an international collaborative venture, involving Britain, West Germany and Italy. The tri-national Panavia company is to produce a total of 809 Tornadoes, 385 for Britain, 324 for West Germany and 100 for Italy. Most of these will be the Interdictor/Strike variant, with an unrivalled performance at low

Below *The British Aerospace Hawk T Mk 1 serves with the RAF both as an advanced trainer and for tactics and weapons instruction. A Hawk of No 4 Flying Training School is pictured.*

altitudes, but 165 of the RAF's order will be the specialized Air Defence version. The Tornado prototype first flew in August 1974 and by 1983 the aircraft was in service with all three participating nations.

The BAe Hawk military trainer has proved to be a versatile and reliable aircraft. The RAF has a total of 175 on order to fulfil the advanced training and weapons training roles, with a number of aircraft modified to carry out a secondary air defence mission. The most notable export order has come from the US Navy, which has selected the Hawk to replace its North American/Rockwell T-2 Buckeye advanced trainer. The BAe 146 fan-jet, short-haul airliner first flew in 1981 and was certified for commercial operations two years later.

BRITISH AIRCRAFT CORPORATION

The British Aircraft Corporation was formed in 1960 and took over the aircraft manufacturing interests of Vickers, the Bristol Aeroplane Company, English Electric and Hunting. While continuing the manufacture of existing designs such as the Lightning and Canberra, it also developed a range of new military and commercial aircraft. BAC's first military venture was the Strikemaster, a development of the Hunting Jet Provost, intended to fulfil the dual training and light attack roles with small air forces. It was produced in parallel with the BAC 145 pressurized trainer, which

entered RAF service as the Jet Provost T Mk 5. Among the Strikemaster's customers were New Zealand, Singapore, Ecuador, Saudi Arabia and various other Middle East nations.

A more ambitious warplane project, produced in collaboration with Dassault-Breguet in France, was the Jaguar low-level strike aircraft. A joint company, SEPECAT, was formed to manage the project, which involved manufacture of components in both France and Britain and final assembly of Jaguars in each country. A two-seat version was designed, originally as an advanced trainer, but it proved to be too expensive to use in this role and so only a small number were built for operational conversion and continuation training. RAF Jaguars serve with RAF Germany and No 38 Group in RAF Strike Command in the low-level strike and attack roles, with a number being converted for tactical reconnaissance duties. France and Britain each ordered 200 Jaguars and export orders were received from Ecuador, India, Nigeria and Oman.

On the civil side, BAC inherited the VC10 airliner design from Vickers. This four-engined long-range civil transport first flew in June 1962 and entered

Above *BAC Strikemaster Mk 88 light-attack aircraft are operated by No 14 Squadron of the Royal New Zealand Air Force, which ordered 16 Strikemasters in the early 1970s.*

service with BOAC two years later. This airline ordered both Standard and Super VC10s, the latter with a stretched fuselage to increase passenger capacity. A total of 54 VC10s were built, including orders from Gulf Air and East African Airways. The RAF ordered 14 VC10 C Mk 1 transports, a hybrid version incorporating features of both the Standard and Super VC10. No 10 Squadron RAF continues to operate

Right *An RAF BAC Jaguar GR Mk 1 demonstrates its ability to operate from a roadway, taking off with an underwing bomb load and using full afterburner.*

Top *The RAF's VC10 C Mk 1 strategic transports are operated by No 10 Squadron, based at Brize Norton in Oxfordshire.*

Above *This BAC One-Eleven short-haul airliner serves with the Sultan of Oman's air force.*

Below *A British Airways' Concorde in landing and take-off configuration, with the droop nose lowered.*

these aircraft from Brize Norton in Oxfordshire and in the 1980s many of the civil airliners are being converted as tanker aircraft for RAF service.

The most ambitious civil project undertaken by BAC was undoubtedly the Concorde supersonic air transport, produced in partnership with Aérospatiale of France. An elegant delta-wing aircraft, powered by four Rolls-Royce Olympus turbojets, Concorde can carry 100 passengers at a cruising speed of Mach 2 over transatlantic routes. Although a masterpiece of modern technology, Concorde has failed to find widespread approval amongst airline operators. The French and

British national airlines, Air France and British Airways, began scheduled Concorde operations in January 1976. A greater commercial success was achieved with the BAC One-Eleven series of twin-turbofan airliners. As well as achieving healthy orders from British independent operators, such as British United Airways, the One-Eleven sold well in the United States. It has proved to be an adaptable design and a second production line for One-Elevens was opened in Romania in 1982. By that time BAC had disappeared into the larger company British Aerospace.

CAPRONI

The first Caproni aircraft took to the air in May 1910 and by the time that Italy entered World War I in 1915 Gianni Caproni was well-established as an aircraft designer. His greatest contribution to the war effort was the development of a series of highly efficient trimotor bombers, which were capable of taking the war over the Alps and into the Austro-Hungarian Empire's homeland. The Ca 3 trimotor not only served with the Corpo Aeronautica Militare in Italy, but was built under licence in France by Esnault-Pelterie and operated against German targets on the Western Front with the Aviation Militaire. Although not capable of lifting a great bomb load (the Ca 3 carried 200kg/440lb of bombs), the bombers operated over long ranges and on the Italian Alpine Front had to cross one of the most formidable land barriers in Europe.

In the years following World War I the Caproni firm turned to the investigation of all-metal airframe construction and in 1924 produced the Ca 64 mono-

was the Ca 100, which served as a primary and refresher training aircraft with the Regia Aeronautica. In addition to some 600 military trainers, the Ca 100 was produced for flying clubs and private owners. Another workhorse of the Regia Aeronautica was the Ca 133, a high-wing trimotor, built to replace the Ca 101. It carried out light bombing, reconnaissance, transport and casualty evacuation roles, serving in Italy, North Africa, East Africa and the Balkans. The Ca 309 Ghibli twin-engined, low-wing monoplane performed essentially the same utility roles in colonial territories. It was followed by the Ca 310, an unsuccessful design that was relegated to training and light transport duties. The series continued with the Ca 311, which operated in the observation and reconnaissance roles, and the Ca 313, which was ordered by both the British and French although none was in fact delivered. The last of the series was the Ca 314 and this operated during World War II in light attack and torpedo-bombing roles.

Caproni ceased production after World War II. Probably the last of the firm's designs to be used in combat were the Ca 135 medium bombers operated by the Hungarian air force on the Eastern Front.

plane fighter using this technique. The amazing Ca 60, an eight-engined flying boat having three sets of tri-plane wings, also appeared at this time. Against all probabilities it succeeded in flying twice, although its second attempt ended in a crash. The Ca 73 twin-engined bomber of 1924 enjoyed great success and its derivatives equipped Regia Aeronautica bomber units from 1926 until 1934. A number of these aircraft took part in the pacification of dissident tribes in Italy's North African possessions and so in the late 1920s Caproni began design work on a series of warplanes intended specifically for this role. The Ca 97 was widely used in the Italian colonial territories and the Ca 101 was 'blooded' during the conquest of Abyssinia in 1935–6. The last of this series, the Ca 111, operated as a light bomber, reconnaissance and transport aircraft and many remained in service during World War II.

Italy's equivalent of the de Havilland Moth series

Above *The best-known Caproni aeroplane of World War I was the Ca 3 trimotor.*

Below *A Caproni Ca 309S ambulance aircraft of the Italian Regia Aeronautica. Most of the 243 built from 1936 to 1943 served in the colonial policing role.*

Bottom left *A line-up of Caproni Ca 311 reconnaissance bombers of the Regia Aeronautica's 119ª Squadriglia.*

Bottom right *Cessna's first postwar light aircraft was the Model 140 of 1946, which was of all-metal construction and carried a pilot and one passenger.*

CESSNA

The name of Cessna has become virtually synonymous with the privately owned light plane. Clyde Cessna first began series production of light aircraft at Wichita, Kansas, in 1927 with the Model A. Over 70 of these high-wing monoplanes were built and they were followed by the four-seat DC Model. Then came the Depression, which forced Cessna to switch production to rudimentary training gliders. This cutback in operation did not prevent the Cessna directors from closing the factory in 1931. Three years later it was reopened and began production of the successful Airmaster series. With the approach of war, the Cessna company concentrated on building the twin-engined Bobcat trainer, over 5000 of which were produced. Variously designated AT-8, AT-17 and (in Royal Canadian Air Force service) Crane Mk I, they provided advanced instruction for pilots destined to fly multi-engined bomber and transport aircraft.

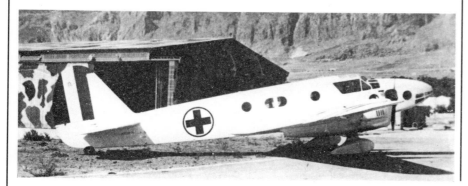

Anticipating a postwar boom in private flying, Cessna went into production with the Model 120/140 series in 1946. The company succeeded in selling 7076 of these and a further 1094 of the more powerful 190/195 series, despite fierce competition from such manufacturers as Piper, Stinson, Taylorcraft and Aeronca. In 1950 it puts its experience of light aircraft construction to good use in designing a two-seat liaison and observation aircraft for the US army. The L-19 Bird Dog (redesignated O-1 in 1962) served in both the Korean and Vietnam Wars and was exported to many foreign armed forces.

In 1953 Cessna launched the Model 180, which has since been used as a light utility transport by bush pilots in many undeveloped areas of the world. The Model 180 and its developments the Skywagon, Stationair and Super Skywagon can be fitted with wheel, float, amphibious or ski landing gear to suit varied terrains and operating conditions. Also in 1953 there appeared the Cessna 310 twin-engined lightplane, which proved to be popular with the business pilot. Over 5000 of this model have been built, including 195 for the USAF. Another important military order was for the T-37 two-seat primary jet trainer, which entered

Top *The Cessna 172 Skyhawk was promoted as 'the world's most popular airplane' and some 26,000 have been built.*

Above centre *The USAF*

operates the Cessna Super Skymaster in the forward air control role as the O-2.

Above *The Model 411 was Cessna's first executive-class twin aeroplane. It can carry six*

passengers in comfort and was first introduced in 1964.

Below *The Cessna T-37 has been the USAF's standard basic jet trainer since the late 1950s.*

service with USAF Air Training Command in 1957. The design was later modified as a light attack aircraft, designated A-37B Dragonfly, and this version was used in combat by the USAF and South Vietnamese air force in Southeast Asia.

The most popular Cessna light aircraft, the Model 172, first appeared in 1955 and some 26,000 have since been built. Its success has been closely matched by that of the 182 and 150 Models. The Model 336 Skymaster of 1961 and the later Model 338 Super Skymaster were something of a departure from the standard Cessna single-engined, high-wing monoplane formula. The radical feature of the design was the powerplant installation, with one engine installed as a tractor in the nose and the other in the aft fuselage as a pusher. A military variant, the O-2, was extensively used in Southeast Asia as a forward air control aircraft. In 1964 Cessna entered the business twin-engine aircraft market with its Model 411 and this has led to the much more ambitious Citation twin-jet executive transport.

CONSOLIDATED

Most famous for its B-24 Liberator of World War II, the Consolidated Aircraft Corporation was formed at Buffalo, New York, by Reuben Fleet in 1923. It achieved early success with a series of primary training aircraft produced for the US Army Air Corps and US Navy. The PT-1 trainer of 1923 was successively refined as the PT-3 and PT-11, while the O-17 was another variant produced for the National Guard. The navy's NY series of trainers were similar, except that

some were fitted with floats for seaplane training. In 1931 the US Navy ordered from Consolidated a small number of P2Y patrol flying boats of sesquiplane design (with a lower wing of much less span than the upper), and two years later followed up with an order for the PBY monoplane. This twin-engined high-wing patrol aircraft (known by the RAF as the Catalina) was produced in both flying boat and amphibian versions and became one of the most famous maritime patrol aircraft of World War II. It served with US Navy, RAF and Royal Canadian Air Force squadrons during the Battle of the Atlantic and

also saw extensive use in the Pacific. A total of 3290 were built in the United States and Canada, with a few hundred more of the GST copy being produced in Soviet aircraft factories.

In December 1941 the four-engined XB-24 Liberator prototype first flew. This bomber was produced in greater numbers (18,188) than any other American warplane of World War II and it saw widespread service in both the European and Pacific theatres. It served as a strategic bomber with the USAAF's Eighth and Fifteenth Air Forces operating against Germany, and as a patrol aircraft it exercised a decisive influence on the Battle of the Atlantic. It served as a cargo and fuel transport with the USAAF (designated C-87 and C-109 respectively), and as a patrol bomber (designated PB4Y) with the US Navy. The navy's PB4Y-2 Privateer was an extensively modified variant, fitted with a large single fin and rudder in place of the Liberator's distinctive twin fin and rudder assembly. Other Consolidated designs which saw limited wartime service were the Navy's Coronado four-engine patrol flying boat and the USAAF's B-32 Dominator long-range bomber.

Immediately after World War II, Convair, as the company had become in 1943, turned to the design of civil airliners. Its twin-engined Model 240 entered airline service in 1948 and 176 civil models were ordered, plus 364 military T-29s. The stretched Convair 340 of 1951 also sold both to civil operators and the US services. Convair ended production of the series with the Model 440 Metropolitan, but various turboprop conversions were later made to existing aircraft. Meanwhile in 1947 Convair had begun production of the massive B-36 long-range bomber for the USAF's Strategic Air Command (SAC). Powered by six piston engines installed as pushers, plus four auxiliary turbojets on later aircraft, the B-36 at an all-up weight of 126,000kg (278,000lb) was then the heaviest aircraft ever to fly. Another Convair aircraft with a claim to fame was the Model 990 four-jet airliner, which until the advent of Concorde was the world's fastest civil transport aircraft.

The F-102 Delta Dart interceptor entered service with USAF Air Defense Command in 1955 and its successor the F-106 Delta Dagger has defended the North American continent from 1959 up to the present day. The Convair bomber tradition ended with the B-58 Hustler, a Mach 2 strategic bomber, which entered

Above centre A PBY-5A Consolidated Catalina of the Royal Danish Air Force after retirement in the 1970s.

Above A Consolidated B-24D Liberator of the USAAF

Fifth Air Force's 380th Bomb Group undergoes servicing at its base at Darwin, Northern Australia, in June 1943.

Below The prototype Convair XB-36, which made

its first flight on 8 August 1946.

Top right The Convair Model 440 twin piston-engined airliner first flew in 1955. This is one of six which operated with Finnair.

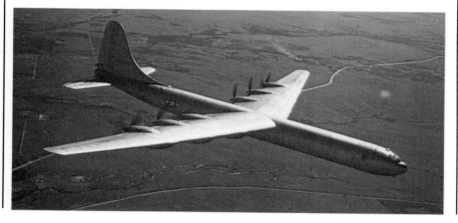

service with SAC in 1960. Its service life spanned only a decade and by the time of its retirement its manufacturer had become known as General Dynamics.

CURTISS

The American aviation pioneer Glenn Curtiss built his first aeroplane, the June Bug, in 1908, and the following year he formed the first American aircraft manufacturing company in partnership with A. M. Herring. In 1909 he took his Golden Flyer to the great aviation gathering at Reims in France, where he gained several awards including the Prix de la Vitesse. In an attempt to interest the US Navy in his aircraft, Curtiss arranged for one of his machines to take off from a platform on the USS *Birmingham*. Piloted by Eugene Ely, a Golden Flyer successfully carried out this demonstration on 14 November 1910 – the first time it had ever been accomplished – and the navy ordered two aeroplanes.

Another pioneering achievement by Curtiss was the construction of the first flying boat, which took to the air on 10 January 1912. The machine was developed into the Model F, which was ordered by the US Navy

Top *This underside view of the USAF's Convair B-58 Hustler clearly shows the jettisonable pod which carried fuel and nuclear weapons.*

Above *A Convair F-106A Delta Dart of the USAF's 84th Fighter Interceptor Squadron.*

Below *The Curtiss NC-4 flying boat was the first aeroplane to fly across the Atlantic Ocean in May 1919.*

and remained in service until 1918. Curtiss went on to develop the America flying boat, which was intended to compete for the *Daily Mail*'s prize for the first air crossing of the Atlantic. However, World War I intervened and Curtiss instead sold his flying boats to the Royal Naval Air Service. Another notable World War I aeroplane, the Curtiss JN-1 trainer, affectionately nicknamed the 'Jenny', had its first flight in 1914. More than 8000 Jennies were eventually built, training Royal Flying Corps and Royal Naval Air Service airmen in Britain and Canada as well as the vast majority of US Army Air Service pilots. The Jenny also had the distinction of becoming the first American military aeroplane to fly a war mission, during operations against Mexican bandits in 1916. Curtiss continued his flying-boat development work with the H-12 Large America of 1916, which was operated by both the US Navy and RNAS. It was joined in late 1917 by the H-16, which had a more efficient and seaworthy hull than its predecessors.

At the end of World War I Curtiss turned again to his plans for a transatlantic flight. The aeroplanes that he wished to use were four trimotor flying boats, NC-1 to NC-4, which he had built for US Navy anti-submarine operations. The navy fell in with his plans and three of these aircraft left Newfoundland on 16 May 1919 bound for the Azores. Only NC-4 commanded by Lieutenant-Commander Arthur Read completed the flight and carried on to arrive at Plymouth on the last day of May. Although overshadowed by Alcock and Brown's later non-stop flight, this was the first crossing of the Atlantic by air. It was at this time that Glenn Curtiss retired from active participation in the running of the company that bore his name. However, the concern continued to prosper, building a series of successful high-speed racing aircraft which won both the Pulitzer Race in the United States in 1922 and the Schneider Trophy contest in Britain in the following year. In 1925 a Curtiss floatplane repeated its success in the Schneider Trophy, but failed to secure a third win in 1926, which would have secured the trophy permanently for the United States.

Much of the success of the Curtiss racers was due to the performance of the company's D-12 in-line engine and this powerplant was also fitted to the P-1 fighter of 1925. It was to be the first in a long line

of successful Curtiss Hawk fighters, which included the P-6 Hawk series of 1927–32 and culminated in the P-23, the last biplane fighter to be ordered by the US Army Air Corps. The Curtiss O-1 Falcon of 1925 led to an equally successful run of military observation air-

Below The US Navy's version of the Army Air Service's Curtiss P-1 was designated F6C-1. This one served with the Marine Corps.

craft. Other important military aircraft contracts at this period included the F8C Helldiver, which pioneered dive-bombing missions with the navy, and F9C Sparrowhawk fighters, which were carried aboard the airships *Akron* and *Macon*. The Sparrowhawks often flew without undercarriages during operations from the airships, hooking on to trapezes lowered from the parent craft. The Condor transport of 1933 flew both with civil operators, including American Airways and Eastern Airlines, and with the US Army Air Corps.

By the mid-1930s it was clear that the age of the biplane fighter aircraft had passed. Accordingly the next

Above left Chinese ground crew work on a Curtiss P-40 of the USAAF's 23rd Fighter Group.

Above right The Curtiss C-46 entered service with the USAAF in 1942. This example served with the Chinese Nationalist air force.

Below The Curtiss Jenny was an important training aeroplane of World War I.

Curtiss fighter for the USAAC, the Model 75 or P-36, was a low-wing monoplane. The first P-36s were delivered in 1938, but saw little action with American fighter squadrons in World War II. However, Curtiss Hawk 75s exported to France were heavily engaged in combat in May–June 1940, Dutch Hawk 75s contested the Japanese invasion of Java and Sumatra, and the RAF's version, known as the Mohawk, operated from India against the Japanese in 1942–3. If the P-36 saw little combat with the USAAF, its developed version, the P-40 Warhawk, was to bear the brunt of the United States' early fighter battles. The P-40 was powered by an in-line Allison Vl710 engine in place of the P-36's radial, but otherwise the two aircraft were very similar. Nearly 14,000 P-40s were built in World War II and they served with virtually all the Allied air forces.

The Curtiss C-46 Commando transport was built in substantial numbers (over 3000) for the USAAF and

proved to be second only to the Douglas C-47 in reliability and usefulness. The Commandos' greatest achievement was their participation in the 'Hump' airlift from India to China. Another Curtiss aircraft produced in quantity during the war was the SB2C Helldiver, 7200 of which were built. A carrier-borne dive-bomber intended to replace the redoubtable Dauntless, the Helldiver was not a great success in US Navy service. It was perhaps a disappointing end to the long line of distinguished aeroplanes to carry the name of Glenn Curtiss.

DASSAULT

The Dassault company, famous for the Mirage series of French warplanes, traces its origins back to the pre-war Bloch company. Its founder, Marcel Bloch, was responsible for the Bloch MB200, MB210 and MB131 twin-engined bombers of the 1930s. He also produced the Bloch MB150 fighter series, which fought in the Battle of France, and the high-speed MB175 bomber which was just coming into service at the time of the French collapse in June 1940. During World War II Bloch refused to collaborate with the Germans and so

service with the Armée de l'Air in 1951 and 350 were built. Export versions served with the Israeli air force and with the Indian air force, who named the aircraft Toofani. In 1954 the first Mystère IIA was delivered to the Armée de l'Air. This was a development of the Ouragan with a swept rather than a straight wing and it was powered by a Rolls-Royce Tay. A batch of 150 Mystère IIAs was built before the improved Mystère IVA became available in 1955. The Armée de l'Air bought 241 of these and export customers were Israel and India. The last fighter in this line of development was the Super Mystère B2, which was the first European aircraft to exceed Mach 1 in level flight. A total of 175 were built in 1957–9 and 24 of these were

was sent to Buchenwald concentration camp, from which he was fortunate to emerge alive in 1945. When he had recovered from the rigours of his imprisonment, he set about reforming his aircraft company in 1946. It was then that he changed his name and that of his firm to Dassault (the cover-name adopted by his brother in the Resistance).

The Dassault company began work on a jet fighter, which was to emerge in 1949 as the Ouragan (Hurricane), and a twin-engined light transport and trainer, the MD315 Flamant. The Flamant first flew in 1947 and some 300 were built for the Armée de l'Air and Aéronavale, the last of them being retired in the early 1980s. The Ouragan, a rugged fighter-bomber powered by the Rolls-Royce Nene engine, entered

Top *The Dassault Ouragan proved to be a rugged and straightforward jet fighter.*

Above centre *A Dassault Super Mystère B2 fighter of the Armée de l'Air's 12ᵉ*

Escadre de Chasse in the colours of the Nato 'Tiger Meet' competition of 1977.

Above *The Mirage IIIE tactical fighter entered service with the Armée de l'Air in*

1964. *This example carries the Cigognes emblem of the EC1/2 fighter wing.*

Below *The Mirage IVA strategic bomber serves with the Armée de l'Air.*

supplied to Israel, where the type saw action during the Six-Day War in 1967.

In 1960 Dassault began deliveries of the Atar-powered Etendard shipboard strike fighter to the Aéronavale. They were built in two versions, the Etendard IVM for attack and the Etendard IVP for reconnaissance. At peak deployment they equipped four *flotilles* aboard the carriers *Clemenceau* and *Foch*. In 1978 the Super Etendard, a development with a more powerful Atar turbojet and improved avionics, entered French service. The small numbers exported to the Argentine navy achieved fame during the Falklands conflict of 1982, using Exocet missiles to sink the destroyer HMS *Sheffield* and the container ship *Atlantic Conveyor*.

In 1956 the prototype Mirage III Mach 2 tailless delta first flew, and production Mirage IIIC interceptors entered service with the Armée de l'Air in 1960. The Mirage III proved to be an adaptable design, serving with the Armée de l'Air in the air superiority, reconnaissance and attack roles, as well as for air defence. The Mirage III also found favour with export customers and has seen action in the Middle East wars with both Israeli and Arab air forces, with the Pakistani air force against India and with Argentina against Britain. A simplified attack version, the Mirage 5, was originally developed for Israel. However, the Israeli air force's aircraft were impounded by the French in 1970 and entered service instead with the Armée de l'Air. Further improvements on the basic design led to the Mirage 50 and the recently launched Mirage IIING

(Nouvelle Génération). In total some 1400 of the family have been built.

The Mirage IV strategic bomber is in effect a scaled-up Mirage III, powered by two Atar 9B turbojets. Each armed with a 50-kiloton free-fall nuclear weapon, the Mirage IVs of France's Force de Frappe became fully operational in 1968. On the other hand, unlike previous members of the Mirage family, the Mirage F1 Mach 2·2 interceptor is a tailed swept-wing aircraft rather than a tailless delta. Entering service with the Armée de l'Air in 1974, some 700 examples have been built. Some of those for export are intended for the attack mission, and France has developed the recon-naissance Mirage F1CR to replace her ageing Mirage

IIIR aircraft. Latest members of the Mirage family, the Mirage 2000 and 4000, have returned to a tailless delta configuration. The former has been ordered by the Armée de l'Air as an air superiority and strike fighter and is due to enter service in 1984.

Above *The Mirage F1 fighter is the Armée de l'Air's standard interceptor aircraft of the mid-1980s and over 500 of them have been built for France and for export.*

Left *The Dassault Super Etendard naval strike fighter entered service with the Aéronavale in 1978 and has been exported in small numbers to Argentina and Iraq.*

DE HAVILLAND

Geoffrey de Havilland joined the design staff of the Royal Aircraft Factory at Farnborough before World War I, where he was responsible for the design of the widely used BE2 biplane. However, on the eve of war in June 1914 he left the government aircraft factory to join the Aircraft Manufacturing Co. (Airco) at Hendon as chief designer. His DH1A two-seat pusher biplane saw only limited service with the Royal Flying Corps, but the DH2 pusher fighter became one of that service's most important aeroplanes in 1915–16. It was the DH2 that helped to end the 'Fokker Scourge' when flown by such pilots as Major Lanoe Hawker and the young Flight Sergeant James McCudden. The other important de Havilland designs of World War I were bombers. The DH4 of 1916 eventually equipped 12 British squadrons in France and was also produced in quantity in the United States. The DH9 was a failure, due to the unreliability of its Puma engine, and losses during operations were heavy. However, this short-

coming was overcome with the introduction of the Liberty-engined DH9A of 1918. Indeed so successful was this design that it remained in RAF service throughout the 1920s.

Geoffrey de Havilland's greatest contribution to British aviation in the inter-war years was the Moth family of light aircraft intended for the private owner. The DH60 Moth of 1925 was ordered for government-sponsored flying clubs and the RAF. It was produced both in Britain and abroad in the United States, Canada, Australia and South Africa. The de Havilland Canada company founded at this time later prospered

Below *The de Havilland DH2 single-seater fighter was one of the Allied aeroplanes which succeeded in ending the 'Fokker Scourge' in 1916. This DH2 served with No 24 Squadron RFC at Bertangles in France.*

with such postwar designs of its own as the Chipmunk, Otter, Caribou and Beaver. The next member of the Moth family replaced the original aircraft's Cirrus engine with the new Gipsy powerplant produced by de Havilland itself. Amy Johnson's *Jason* was perhaps the most famous of the Gipsy Moths. In 1928 the DH60 began to be built with a metal structure in place of wood, while the Moth Major and Moth Trainers had improved powerplants. A greater departure from the Moth formula came with the DH80A Puss Moth with its enclosed cabin and the similar Hawk and Leopard Moths. Undoubtedly the most famous of the family was the DH82 Tiger Moth, a superb military basic trainer which served throughout World War II with the RAF and Empire training schools. Total production was some 8800.

Other notable civil aircraft designs of the inter-war

Above *The DH9 bomber of 1917 proved to be a failure in service due to the unreliability of its Siddeley Puma engine.*

Left *Three members of the famous DH Moth family of light aircraft fly in formation. In the lead is a DH60G Gipsy Moth, with a DH60X Hermes Moth (background) and a DH80A Puss Moth.*

Below *A DH91 Albatross airliner of Imperial Airways at Croydon Airport in the late 1930s, with a Handley Page HP42 in the background.*

years deserve mention: the DH Dragon and Dragon Rapide small airliners, the DH Comet racers and the four-engined monoplane Albatross, which entered service with Imperial Airways in 1938. However, with the approach of war the de Havilland company turned its attention to military aircraft and produced the twin-engined Mosquito. Nicknamed the 'Wooden Wonder', the Mosquito was largely of wooden construction thus conserving scarce strategic materials and allowing woodworking firms to be brought into its manufacture. Originally intended as a fast daylight bomber which would rely on its speed for protection, the Mosquito's operational roles proliferated. It first went into action in the summer of 1941 as a photo reconnaissance aircraft, then became both a day and night bomber, night fighter and anti-shipping strike aircraft, and in all of these duties it excelled. Mosquito bombers of the Pathfinders' Light Night Striking Force dropped 1800kg (4000lb) 'cookies' (high-blast bombs) on Berlin. Mosquito fighter-bombers carried out daylight pinpoint raids on Gestapo headquarters and Mosquito night fighters destroyed over 500 V1 flying bombs in two months. One of the classic warplanes of aviation history, when production ended in 1950 7781 Mosquitoes had been built.

The Mosquito fighter's postwar successor was the twin-engined Hornet, the RAF's last piston-engined

Right The DH Mosquito was one of the most versatile combat aircraft of World War II. These Mosquito B Mk IVs were day bombers serving with No 139 Squadron RAF.

Below right The Fleet Air Arm's DH Sea Hornet F Mk 20, which entered service in 1947, was based on the RAF's Hornet F Mk 3. Only one first-line FAA squadron was fully equipped with this Sea Hornet variant.

Below The first RAF fighter unit to fly the DH Vampire F Mk 1 was No 247 Squadron, which received its first aircraft in April 1946. Eventually eight squadrons flew this mark of Vampire.

Bottom The ultimate version of the DH Comet jet airliner was the Comet 4C. The example pictured was operated by the Royal Aircraft Establishment as a flying laboratory.

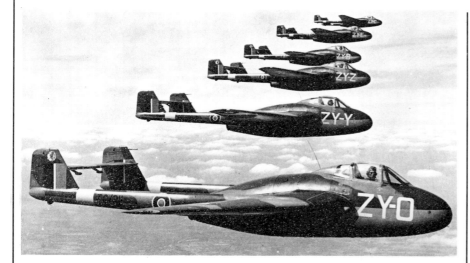

fighter, which served with four squadrons in Fighter Command, three in the Far East, and as the Sea Hornet day-fighter, night-fighter and photographic reconnaissance versions with the Fleet Air Arm. In 1943 de Havilland entered the jet age, when the prototype of its Vampire fighter first flew. Production Vampires entered RAF service in April 1945 and undertook the day-fighter role until they were retired in 1956. Two-seat versions served both as night fighters and as jet trainers and the Vampire's successor, the Venom, was produced as a day fighter, night fighter and shipboard naval fighter. Both types were widely exported and Swiss air force Venoms remained in service until 1982.

In the immediate postwar years de Havilland again turned its attention to the civil aviation market and in 1949 the Comet first took to the air. The world's first commercial jet liner, its introduction into service was marred by a series of mysterious accidents. The problem was eventually identified as metal fatigue in the structure of the pressure cabin and the fault was rectified. In 1958 the Comet began scheduled transatlantic services with BOAC. It also flew with BEA and some foreign civil operators, although its export potential was seriously diminished by the appearance of the rival Boeing 707 in 1958. Comets also formed the equipment of No 216 Squadron of RAF Transport Command, the world's first military jet transport squadron. In 1963 the de Havilland company became part of Hawker Siddeley Aviation in the series of mergers which saw the disappearance of many famous names from the British aircraft industry.

DEWOITINE

In 1920 the young Emile Dewoitine established his own aircraft manufacturing company and in the following year his D1 fighter appeared. Fitted with the high parasol wing characteristic of all the early Dewoitine fighters, it saw limited service with the Aéronavale and abroad. Further export successes followed with the D9 going to Switzerland, Yugoslavia and Italy, the D12 and D21 to Argentina and the D19 and D27 to Switzerland. In 1929 Dewoitine began work on the D33 long-range aircraft intended for a 10,000km (6200-mile) non-stop record flight. However, two attempts to achieve this record both ended in crashes. With the D500 low-wing monoplane fighter of 1932, Dewoitine at last obtained a substantial production contract from the Armée de l'Air. The D500 entered service in 1935 and by 1938 most French fighter squadrons flew this aircraft or the similar cannon-armed D-501. In 1933 the Dewoitine D332 Emeraude

civil airliner first flew and its derivative the D338 served with Air France until after World War II. However, Dewoitine was primarily a fighter designer and both his D37 and D510 served the Armée de l'Air in this role before World War II.

In 1938 the D520 made its first flight and by the outbreak of war Dewoitine had received orders for over 700. Yet deliveries of this high-performance fighter were slow and in May 1940 only 50 were in front-line service with the Armée de l'Air. Consequently, although these aircraft acquitted themselves well and gained 77 aerial victories, they had little effect on the outcome of the air battle for France. However, the Vichy regime maintained four *groupes de chasse* and two Aéronavale *escadrilles* equipped with the D520, and the French ace Pierre Le Gloan scored most of his victories while flying Dewoitine's last service fighter.

DORNIER

Claudius Dornier began his design career in 1910 with the Zeppelin company, working on airships and on a number of experimental flying boat designs during World War I. His first real success was the Wal

(Whale) flying boat of 1922, which was to remain in production until well into the 1930s. It found favour not only with many airlines, but also as a military aircraft with the air arms of Portugal, the Netherlands and later Germany. The monstrous 12-engined Do X of 1929 was less successful, for although it was designed to carry 150 passengers in considerable comfort, its early technical problems were never satisfactorily resolved. There followed the more conventional Do 18, Do 24 and Do 26 flying boats, all of which saw service with the Luftwaffe. Indeed the Do 24, which was originally built for the Netherlands, became the most important German air/sea rescue aircraft of World War II.

With the increase in clandestine military aviation

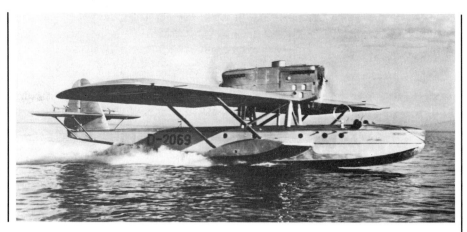

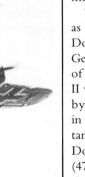

activities in Germany in the 1930s (in contravention of the Treaty of Versailles), Dornier turned his attention to the building of bomber aircraft. The Do 11 of 1932 was flown under the cover of Lufthansa's airline operations, as were the early Do 17s which were classed as mailplanes. However, by 1937 the re-emergence of the Luftwaffe was no longer a secret and the Do 17 went into combat with the Condor Legion in Spain, operating in both bomber and reconnaissance roles. In 1939 the Do 17's elegant lines, which had led to its nickname 'the flying pencil', were marred by the installation of an enlarged, bulbous nose section on the Do 17Z variant. While this modification did nothing to enhance the aircraft's appearance, it did improve crew comfort and efficiency. On the outbreak of war, the Luftwaffe had 470 Do 17 bombers on strength, plus 280 Do 17 reconnaissance aircraft. They took part in the Luftwaffe's early campaigns of 1939–40, but by

mid-1941 most had been withdrawn from service.

The improved Do 215 and Do 217 types were built as both bombers and night fighters. A total of 1730 Do 217s were built and this type employed the early German guided missiles in action during 1943–4. One of the most remarkable German fighters of World War II was the Do 335 Pfeil (Arrow), which was powered by two Daimler Benz DB603E engines, one installed in the nose and the other as a pusher in the tail. This tandem arrangement was highly efficient and the Do 335 achieved a maximum speed of 760km/h (470mph). It was planned to put the Pfeil into production, but the war ended before it reached the front-line fighter units.

The Dornier Company did not disappear after World War II and in the mid-1950s the Do 27 light transport went into production in West Germany. The

Above The Dornier Wal flying boat of 1922 was the first Dornier design to go into production and was widely used by both civil and military operators in the inter-war years.

Left The Dornier Do 217K-2 variant was specifically modified as a launch aircraft for the Fritz X radio-guided air-to-surface missile and it became operational in 1943.

Left The Dornier Do17Z bomber began to equip Luftwaffe units in the spring of 1939. Do 17Zs participated in all the campaigns of 1939–40, but they had been withdrawn from front-line service by mid-1941 when the assault on the Soviet Union was launched.

Below Dornier resumed aircraft manufacture after World War II and was responsible for the Luftwaffe's Alpha Jet light-attack aircraft, built in collaboration with Dassault-Breguet of France.

early design work on this aircraft had been carried out in Spain and the Spanish air force was among those to place orders for it. Small quantities were ordered by a number of African states, while Belgium, Sweden and Switzerland in Europe were also customers. The newly reformed Luftwaffe was the largest customer with an order for 428. The twin-engined Do 28 Skyservant also served in large numbers with the Luftwaffe (125 were ordered) and has been exported to civil and military customers. A vertical take-off transport, the Do 31, first flown in 1967, did not progress beyond the prototype stage, but Dornier's Alpha Jet light strike aircraft, built in collaboration with France, is in service with three Luftwaffe fighter-bomber wings.

DOUGLAS

The first aeroplane built by Donald Douglas was the Cloudster civil biplane in 1920, and it was with commercial transport aircraft that the company he founded in Los Angeles, California, was to achieve its greatest successes. Yet ironically the Cloudster could not compete with the mass of war surplus aeroplanes flooding the civil market after World War I and it was as a naval torpedo-bomber, the DT-2, that the basic Cloudster design went into production. The same design was also adapted for use by the US Army Air Service as the Douglas World Cruiser and in 1924 a flight of these aircraft undertook the first flight around the world. There followed orders from the US Army Air Service for the O-2 observation aircraft, another Cloudster derivative. They were built in many versions and led to the O-25, O-32 and O-38 of the 1930s. Other military aeroplanes built by Douglas in the inter-war years were the BT-1 and BT-2 trainers, related to the O-2 and O-32. The C-1 transport series was yet another offshoot of the O-2 family.

A new venture for the Douglas company was the Dolphin twin-engined flying boat of 1931, which served with four branches of the US services – the Army Air Corps, Navy, Marine Corps and Coast Guard. Other twin-engined aircraft of this period were

Top A DC-2 of Swissair. The DC-2 twin-engined civil airliner entered airline service in 1934 and achieved immediate popularity.

Above A Douglas C-47 of the Royal Danish Air Force. Over 10,000 C-47s were built during World War II and the type remains in service to this day.

Below In 1924 a flight of Douglas World Cruisers crewed by pilots of the US Army Air Service completed a flight around the world, covering 45,000km (28,000 miles), in 175 days.

the B-7 bomber and the navy's T2D patrol aircraft. This experience led to the design of an important new commercial airliner. The DC-1 of 1933 was a low-wing, twin-engined monoplane of all-metal, stressed-skin construction, which could carry 14 passengers over a range of 1600km (1000 miles). It was in effect the prototype of the DC-3 commercial and military transport, which was to become the most famous aeroplane of its kind in the world. The DC-1 and improved DC-2 went into airline service with TWA in 1933-4. Another early customer, the Dutch airline KLM, entered one of its DC-2s in the 1934 England to Australia air race. The airliner won the handicap section and was placed second overall to Scott and Black's de Havilland Comet – a specially designed racing aircraft. Total production of the DC-2 was 220 machines.

In 1935 American Airlines asked Douglas to develop an airliner that would provide sleeping accommodation for 14 passengers on coast-to-coast flights across the United States. Design work on the Douglas Sleeper Transport began in 1935 and at the end of the year it made its first flight. Compared with the DC-2 it had a wider fuselage, more powerful engines and a redesigned wing. In 1936 the first DST was delivered to American Airlines, and it was the day-passenger version of this aeroplane, with accommodation for 21 passengers, that was to achieve fame as the DC-3. Total sales of this airliner stood at 448 by the outbreak of World War II, but it was military production that was to boost this figure to well over 10,000. As well as the basic C-47 Skytrain for the USAAF, the type was supplied to the RAF as the Dakota and pirated versions

line use in 1942. The SBD Dauntless dive-bomber, which entered service in 1939, was far more successful for the US Navy. Derived from the Northrop BT-1 of 1935, it was developed under the auspices of Douglas after Northrop was taken over in 1937. Nearly 6000 were built and it remained in front-line service throughout World War II, chiefly with US Navy and Marine Corps squadrons, although the USAAF and Royal New Zealand Air Force also operated the type.

The Douglas DB-7 bomber of 1938 attracted early interest in Europe, with order from the Armée de l'Air and later from the RAF. Named Boston in RAF service, the aeroplane served as a daylight bomber, night fighter and night intruder. USAAF bomber and night-fighter versions, designated A-20 and P-70 respectively, were active in the Pacific theatre, the bombers also serving in Europe and North Africa, and over 3000 were supplied to the Soviet Union under the Lend-Lease scheme. A much-refined development of the A-20, the A-26 Invader, first flew in 1942. Although it did not reach front-line units until late in 1944, it performed outstandingly well in its few months of combat with the USAAF in Italy and France. The Korean War (1950–53) provided a better opportunity for the A-26 (confusingly redesignated B-26 by this time) to demonstrate its worth, and it carried out most of the night interdiction missions flown against the North. Its last experience of combat came with the Vietnam War, when Invaders (redesignated yet again as A-26As) operated with the 609th Special Operations Squadron against the Ho Chi Minh Trail in 1966–9.

The Douglas expertise in the design of transport aircraft was again convincingly demonstrated with the DC-4. This was a four-engined aeroplane fitted with a tricycle undercarriage and able to accommodate 42 passengers. Although orders had been received from the civil operators American Airlines and United Airlines, the United States' entry into World War II meant that the DC-4 was diverted to military use. As the C-54 Skymaster, over 1000 served with the USAAF's Air Transport Command, operating on long-distance routes in the Pacific and European theatres of war. At the end of hostilities, several hundred C-54s passed to civil operators and Douglas continued production of DC-4s until 1946. The DC-6 was a developed version of the DC-4, with more powerful engines, a pressurized cabin and accommodation for 58 passengers. Further development produced the DC-6A, DC-6B and the C-118 military transport. The DC-7, powered by four turbo-compound engines, was capable of non-stop coast-to-coast flights across the United States and in its ultimate DC-7C version could carry 100 passengers. Douglas produced a total of 2284 of its four-engined transports and they made an immensely important contribution to the re-establishment of civil air routes after World War II.

Another notable achievement by the Douglas company in the late 1940s was the Skyrocket research aircraft of 1948, which was the first aeroplane to exceed

were built in Japan as the Showa L2D Tabby and in the Soviet Union as the Lisunov Li-2. After the war, C-47s were acquired by airlines and air forces in virtually every part of the world. In the 1960s the design found a new lease of life in Vietnam in the AC-47 'Spooky' gunship, and, while by no means as common as it was in the 1950s and 1960s, nonetheless many remain in use today.

In 1935 a bomber version of the DC-2 was flown, and it served with both the USAAF as the B-18 and with the Royal Canadian Air Force as the Digby. The Douglas TBD Devastator torpedo-bomber also appeared in that year and 129 were built for the US Navy. The Devastator took part in the early naval air battles of the Pacific War, but suffered heavy losses (notably at Midway) and was withdrawn from front-

Top The Douglas A-20 attack bomber served with the USAAF in World War II, and the RAF also operated the type as the Havoc night fighter and Boston bomber.

Above Bulky items of equipment could be accommodated in the Douglas C-124 Globemaster's capacious freight hold. Loading was effected through clamshell doors beneath the aircraft's nose.

Below The triple-fin tail assembly of the DC-4 prototype was replaced by a more conventional single unit on production aircraft.

Top *An AEW radar-equipped AD-5Q Douglas Skyraider. Piston-engined Skyraider attack aircraft entered US Navy service in 1945 and remained in use for over a quarter of a century.*

Above *The Douglas A-4 Skyhawk saw action with the US Navy over Vietnam and with the Israeli air force in the Middle East wars. An A-4M of the US Marine Corps is pictured.*

Below *A 'stretched' DC-9 Series 50 with seating for 139 passengers. The DC-9 twin-turbofan airliner of 1965 has proved to be a considerable success for Douglas.*

a speed of Mach 2 in level flight. More prosaic Douglas aeroplanes included the Globemaster and Cargomaster military transports and the AD-1 Skyraider attack aircraft, all of which were to have long and useful working lives. The original C-74 Globemaster, 14 of which were built, was developed into the C-124 Globemaster II, a large four-engined transport with clamshell loading doors in the nose, which could lift such outsize loads as ballistic missiles or up to 220 troops. Over 400 were produced in 1950–55 and they served with the USAF's Military Air Transport Service until replaced in the late 1960s by Lockheed C-141 and C-5 jet transports. The turboprop-powered C-133 Cargomaster of 1960 had an even greater payload and 50 were built for the USAF.

The AD-1 Skyraider was a shipboard, piston-engined attack aircraft which entered US Navy service in 1946. It fought with distinction during the Korean

War and airborne early warning and electronic warfare versions were also produced. Redesignated A-1 Skyraider in 1962, it fought throughout the Vietnam War with the USAF and South Vietnamese air force, as well as seeing action with the navy, and a total of 3180 were built. Another important naval aircraft was the twin-jet A3D Skywarrior, a carrier-based nuclear-armed bomber. A similar aircraft ordered for the USAF was designated B-66 Destroyer. The Skyraider's successor was the outstandingly successful A-4 Skyhawk, a single-engined light jet attack aircraft which entered US Navy service in 1956. Another stalwart of the Vietnam War, it has also been used in combat by the Israeli air force.

Yet for all the Douglas company's military successes, its civil transports have attracted the greatest acclaim. The four-jet DC-8 of 1958 was not produced in the same numbers as the rival Boeing 707, but nonetheless was a substantial commercial success. The twin-jet DC-9, in contrast, was a fast-selling trend-setter, which first appeared in 1965 and remains in production. Powered by two tail-mounted JT8D turbofans, the original DC-9 could seat up to 90 passengers, but the design has since been stretched to increase its passenger load. The DC-10 wide-bodied, long-haul jet transport first entered airline service in 1971, and a military version, the KC-10A Extender, has been produced as a dual-purpose transport and tanker aircraft. In 1967 Douglas merged with McDonnell to form the McDonnell Douglas Corporation, and the later products of the St Louis, Missouri, plant are dealt with under the McDonnell entry.

ENGLISH ELECTRIC

The English Electric company is best known for its jet warplane designs of the postwar years, but its first aeroplanes were produced in the firm's early years following World War I. The company was formed in 1918 by the amalgamation of five engineering firms, one of which had produced flying boats for the Admiralty during the war. This work continued and resulted in the Kingston flying boat, six of which were built, tested and modified between 1924 and 1926. The company also produced the Wren ultra-light aircraft, which was offered for sale at £350, but when no orders were forthcoming English Electric's interest in aviation languished.

With the approach of World War II English Electric re-entered the aviation industry and by the end of that conflict it had built 770 Handley Page Hampden and 2145 HP Halifax bombers under sub-contract from the parent company. Between 1945 and 1950 English Electric built the de Havilland Vampire fighter under a similar arrangement. By this time English Electric had acquired their own design staff and in 1945 they began

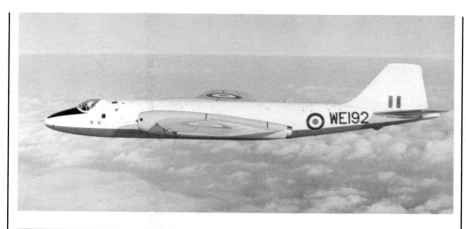

work on a jet bomber to succeed the Avro Lincoln. This emerged in 1949 as the Canberra, the RAF's first jet bomber and one of the most successful postwar British aeroplanes. A total of 1376 Canberras were built in 22 separate variants.

In 1954 the P1A experimental aircraft was flown and this design was developed into the Lightning interceptor, the first British aircraft to exceed Mach 2 (twice the speed of sound). This fighter entered RAF service in 1960 and although it had been largely replaced by the McDonnell Douglas Phantom by 1977, two Lightning squadrons are expected to remain in service until the mid-1980s. A total of 338 Lightnings were built, including export versions for Saudi Arabia and Kuwait. English Electric's last design (undertaken jointly with Vickers) was the ill-fated TSR-2, a Mach 2 bomber intended to replace the Canberra, which was cancelled by the Labour government in 1965. By that time English Electric had been absorbed by the British Aircraft Corporation which was formed in 1960.

FAIRCHILD

In 1924 Sherman Fairchild formed the Fairchild Aviation Corporation to build light utility transport aeroplanes. His Model 24 of 1930, a three-seat high-wing transport built in six different versions, proved to be extremely popular. However, early sales were slow and Fairchild diversified with a five-seat Model 45 intended for the wealthy private owner, and the Model

Top A Canberra T Mk 4 trainer. The English Electric Canberra was the first jet bomber to serve with the RAF, entering service with No 101 Squadron in 1951.

Above A pair of English Electric Lightning F Mk 6 interceptors over Malta during deployment from the United Kingdom. They belong to No 5 Squadron RAF.

Below The very popular Fairchild Model 24 high-wing cabin monoplane could accommodate the pilot and two passengers. The RAF version illustrated was known as the Argus during World War II.

91 amphibian transport, both of which sold in modest numbers. In 1929 a Canadian subsidiary had been established and in 1930 this produced the Model 71. It was a high-wing, seven-seat transport of rugged construction, ideally suited to the spartan conditions of the Canadian north and other undeveloped regions. It was succeeded by the ten-seat Model 82 and both these models had interchangeable wheel, float or ski undercarriages.

In 1939 Fairchild produced a two-seat monoplane trainer, which was bought by the US Army Air Corps as the PT-19 in 1940. It remained in production until 1944, by which time 7260 had been built. The T-23 was fitted with a radial engine in place of the Ranger in-line powerplant of the PT-19, but was otherwise similar. As the Cornell, the PT-19 served with the Royal Canadian Air Force and the type was manufactured in Canada. The outbreak of war also boosted sales of the Model 24, which was sold to the RAF as the Argus and to the USAAF as the UC-61. Fairchild manufactured the AT-13, AT-14 and AT-21 twin-engined trainers for the USAAF in 1942–4.

Perhaps Fairchild's most important project of World War II was the C-82 tactical troop and cargo transporter named the Packet. It first flew in September 1944, but the end of the war meant that USAAF orders were cut back to a mere 220. However, the Packet's layout, with its large cargo hold and the tailplane carried on twin booms, was further developed in the C-119 which entered USAF service in 1949. More than 1000 C-119s were built and they served with the USAF in the Korean War and in Vietnam. The AC-119 gunship variant was developed for the latter conflict, with a side-firing armament of 7·62mm and 20mm rapid-fire weapons. C-119s were exported to Belgium, Italy, India and South Vietnam and the Indians fitted an auxiliary turbojet to their aircraft to boost its performance in high temperatures and at altitude. This expedient was also adopted by the USAF, its C-119K being fitted with two underwing auxiliary turbojets. The C-123 Provider transport, a contemporary of the C-119, was built by Fairchild in 1954–8, although the original design was by Chase Aircraft. Only some 300 were built for the USAF, but the type served throughout the Vietnam War and was also supplied to South Vietnam and Thailand.

FAIREY

In 1956 Fairchild acquired a licence to build the Fokker F27 Friendship and ten years later a similar agreement was made with Pilatus of Switzerland to build the Turbo-Porter. Fairchild also manufactured small numbers of the Hiller-designed FH-1100 helicopter in the 1960s. However, its greatest postwar success came in 1973 with a USAF order for the A-10A Thunderbolt II. This is a specialized anti-armour attack aircraft, powered by twin turbofans and armed with a massive 30mm rapid-fire cannon. Total production of the A-10A will be 733, all for the USAF, which has also ordered Fairchild's T-46 basic jet trainer for delivery in the late 1980s.

Top *A Fairchild AC-119K gunship in South Vietnam.*

Above *This Fairchild C-82 Packet was operated as a civil freighter by TWA and has an auxiliary turbojet mounted atop the fuselage.*

Below *The Fairchild C-123K Provider has underwing-mounted General Electric J85 turbojets.*

Bottom *A Fairchild A-10A Thunderbolt II – popularly known as the Warthog.*

The Fairey Aviation Company was founded in 1915 by C. R. Fairey at Hayes in Middlesex. Its first products were Short 827 seaplanes and Sopwith 1½-Strutters. There followed in 1917 an original Fairey design, the F2 three-seat bomber, but this did not progress beyond the prototype stage. However, the next Fairey design, the Campania seaplane, was taken up by the Royal Naval Air Service and 62 were built. The Fairey Hamble Baby also went into production, although this was an adaptation of an existing Sopwith aeroplane rather than an original design. Also in World War I there appeared the N10 experimental seaplane, which was the forerunner of the well-known Fairey III series. The first of these to see action was the IIIB, which was used for mine-spotting, and the IIIC operated in north Russia against the Bolsheviks in 1919.

The Fairey IIID first flew in 1920 and this versatile and dependable aeroplane was produced for the RAF in both land and seaplane forms. In all 227 were built and Portuguese navy Fairey IIIDs completed a crossing of the South Atlantic in 1922, although two aircraft were lost en route. Other notable flights included one around Australia by a Fairey IIID of the Royal Australian Air Force in 1924 and an RAF flight from Cairo to Cape Town and back in 1926. The Fleet Air Arm's Fairey Flycatcher had its first flight in 1922 and this manoeuvrable single-seat fighter served aboard all the Royal Navy's aircraft carriers in the period 1923–32. The Fawn light bomber did not, however, enjoy such a long career with the RAF and only three squadrons flew the type. A much more effective aircraft in this class, the Fox, appeared in 1925. Powered by a Curtiss D12 in-line engine, it could out-perform all contemporary fighters. Yet despite this success only one RAF squadron flew the Fox – No 12 Squadron, whose motto 'Leads the Field' dates from this period. (Foxes were, however, built in Belgium for the Armée de l'Air Belge.) More substantial orders were received for the Fairey IIIF general-purpose biplane, 622 of which were built. They served with both the Fleet Air Arm (FAA) and land-based RAF squadrons and could be fitted with wheel or float undercarriages. A further

Left *The Fairey Fox two-seat day bomber entered RAF service in 1926. Powered by a Curtiss D12 inline engine, it could outpace all contemporary fighter aircraft.*

Below *The Fairey IIID general purpose biplane of 1920 was produced in both landplane and floatplane versions, serving with the RAF and Fleet Air Arm.*

World War II the lean years were ending. The Fairey Battle three-seat light bomber of 1936 was the first type to be ordered from Fairey in substantial numbers. Ultimately a total of 2203 were built, including 18 manufactured under licence by Avions Fairey in Belgium. By the outbreak of war about 1000 Battles were in RAF service, but the bomber performed badly in combat during the Battle of France and was withdrawn from front-line service in 1940. A far more successful warplane was the Swordfish biplane torpedo-bomber of 1934, which served with distinction throughout World War II. Swordfish attacked the Italian Fleet at Taranto in 1940, took part in the hunting of the *Bismarck*, and operated from escort carriers in the Atlantic in 1944. Perhaps most notably it outlasted its intended successor, the Fairey Albacore, in FAA service. The Albacore biplane entered service in 1940, seeing action at the Battle of Matapan in March 1941, but was retired in 1944. The little-known Seafox reconnaissance floatplane operated as a spotter aircraft from naval warships early in the war, one taking part in the Battle of the River Plate. A more widely used Fairey aeroplane of the early war years was the Fulmar two-seat fighter, which served with 14 FAA squadrons between 1940 and 1942.

Fairey's preoccupation with naval aircraft continued in the later war years with the Barracuda torpedo- and dive-bomber, which first went into action in 1943. It was not, however, a great success, unlike the Firefly two-seat fighter which appeared in action the following year. Fireflies served with the FAA until 1956, seeing considerable combat service in the Korean War. After World War II the Firefly was adapted for anti-submarine duties and eventually some 1700 were built for the FAA. In 1949 a new naval aircraft, the Gannet, appeared, and it served from 1950 until 1979 in the anti-submarine and airborne early warning roles. One

development of the design, with the IIIF's Napier Lion in-line engine replaced by a Jaguar air-cooled radial, was known as the Seal in FAA service and as the Gordon with the RAF's land-based squadrons. A special record-breaking aircraft, the Fairey Long Range Monoplane, set a new world distance record in 1931.

In 1934 Fairey received an order for 14 Hendon monoplane night bombers, but with the approach of

Below *Perhaps the most famous of all Fleet Air Arm aircraft, the Fairey Swordfish served throughout World War II in many roles, notably that of carrier-based torpedo bomber.*

Above *Turboprop-powered Fairey Gannets served with the Fleet Air Arm from 1955 until 1979, primarily in the anti-submarine and AEW roles. The aircraft pictured is a Gannet T Mk 5 trainer.*

of the last aeroplanes to be built by Fairey, before the company ended aircraft design and manufacture in 1960, was the Fairey Delta 2. This aircraft established a new world air speed record in 1956, and later, as the BAC 221, carried out aerodynamic research for the Concorde project.

FARMAN

The Farman brothers are best known for their pioneering work in France before World War I. In 1909 Henry Farman (as an Englishman living in France he also used the spelling Henri) set up an aeroplane factory at Mourmelon and began building biplanes based on the designs of the Voisin brothers. Farman improved the

basic design to such a degree that they came second only to the Blériot monoplanes in popularity. Meanwhile Henry Farman's brother Maurice had designed his own pusher biplane and set up a rival factory at Mallet. The separate designs were designated HF for Henry Farman and MF for his brother. The MF 7 and MF 11 biplanes were used in great numbers by the Aviation Militaire and Royal Flying Corps early in World War I both for observation and training duties. The HF 20, 22, 23, and 27 were also built in quantity at this time, the last-mentioned type having a steel tube airframe rather than the then conventional wooden structure.

In 1915 the Farman brothers combined their two concerns and their first joint venture was the F 40, which was generally used as a night bomber and equipped 47 *escadrilles* of the Aviation Militaire. The only other Farman design to see service in World War I was the F 50 biplane bomber, which was used in small numbers by the French and American air arms. In September 1918 the Farman FF 60 flew for the first time, and this twin-engined biplane was the prototype of the Goliath series of bombers and airliners which were widely used in the 1920s. In French military service they saw action in Morocco in 1924–6 and were exported to Poland, Belgium and Japan. The airliners were fitted with a modified fuselage, which provided accommodation for 12 passengers. In 1924 the F 140 Super Goliath appeared, but only six were built, while two years earlier the David – a two-seat sports aircraft – had made its first flight.

The F 160 and F 168 series, which first appeared in 1928, were a follow-on to the Goliath bombers, and included the F 162 floatplane for the Aéronavale. Another successful design of this period was the F 430 five-seat light civil transport. When the Armée de l'Air called for a multi-role combat aeroplane in 1930, Farman responded with the twin-engined, high-wing F 420. A more specialized four-engined bomber, the

F 220, appeared in 1933 and led to the F 221 troop carrier (ten produced) and F 222 bomber (35 produced). On the outbreak of World War II these massive and ungainly machines formed the backbone of the Armée de l'Air's night-bombing force. During the 'phoney war' they carried out leaflet raids to targets as far distant as Czechoslovakia, while in May 1940 they began bombing Germany. Losses were light, the 15ᵉ Escadre which operated the type reporting only one aircraft destroyed in a crash-landing. The last in the line of Far-

Above *The Maurice Farman MF7 of 1913 operated as an observation aeroplane in French and British service early in World War I.*

Left *An adaptation of the Goliath twin-engined bomber, the F60 airliner could accommodate twelve passengers in an enclosed cabin while the pilot occupied an open cockpit.*

man bombers was the F 223, which was built in both military and civil mailplane versions. It was one of the latter, impressed into service with the Armée de l'Air, which made history on the night of 7/8 June 1940 when it became the first Allied aircraft to bomb Berlin. By this time the Farman brothers' firm had been nationalized by government decree, becoming part of the Société Nationale de Constructions Aéronautiques de Centre.

FIAT

Fiat (Fabbrica Italiana Automobile Torino) was formed in 1899 and first began the manufacture of aeroplanes in 1914, when it built a Maurice Farman biplane. Under the name Società Italiana Aviazione (changed to Fiat Aviazione in 1918) the firm produced the SIA 7B reconnaissance two-seater in 1917 (572 were built) and followed it with the SIA 9B bomber of 1918 (62 built). In 1918 the Fiat R2, based on the SIA 9 design, made its first flight, and 129 were built, remaining in Italian military service until 1925. Following the establishment of the Regia Aeronautica as an independent air arm in 1923, Fiat produced 150 BR1 biplane bombers for the new service. The CR1 fighter of 1925 was an inverted sesquiplane (with the upper wing of lesser span than the lower) and 109 were built. It was the first of a long line of famous fighters designed for Fiat by Celestino Rosatelli. Yet bomber development was not neglected and in 1925 the improved BR2 and its R22 reconnaissance derivative appeared.

Rosatelli's next fighter, the CR20, entered service with the Regia Aeronautica in 1927 and a total of 518 were built. The type was exported to Austria, Hungary, Lithuania and Paraguay, and took part in Italy's

invasion of Abyssinia in the ground-attack role. It was succeeded by the CR30 of 1932, which went into service with the air forces of Austria, China and Paraguay, as well as Italy's. Yet Rosatelli was dissatisfied with its performance and in 1933 produced the redesigned CR32. It proved to be a superbly manoeuvrable aeroplane and over 1000 were built for the Regia Aeronautica. It served with the Aviazione Legionaria in the Spanish Civil War and with six foreign air forces.

Above *The Farman F221 bomber and troop transport entered service with the Armée de l'Air in 1936.*

Below *The Fiat CR32 fighter biplane saw action with the Italian Aviazione Legionaria in the Spanish Civil War.*

Fiat was not solely involved with military work in the inter-war years, its AS1 and AS2 lightplanes being built in some numbers and the G18 airliner going into service in 1937. Yet military work was its major pre-occupation. The BR20 twin-engined bomber was tested operationally in Spain and by the Japanese in China. Some 200 remained in service in June 1940 and it operated briefly against Britain later that year.

Although the G50 monoplane fighter was in service when Italy entered World War II (over 700 were built

Above Last in a long line of Fiat fighter biplanes, the CR42 saw extensive combat early in World War II.

Below The Aeritalia G222 twin-turboprop STOL transport serves with the Aeronautica Militare Italiana.

Bottom A Fiat G91 of the Italian Frecce Triolori aerobatic team.

in total), the CR42 biplane fighter was far more widely used, 1551 being built for the Regia Aeronautica between 1939 and 1943. It saw widespread service despite the fact that the biplane fighter was really an anachronism by 1940. Yet it was not until 1942 that Fiat's DB605-powered G55 Centauro monoplane fighter first flew. This promising machine did not reach front-line units until after the Armistice of 1943, when some 200 were supplied to the air arm of the Fascist RSI regime of northern Italy, which fought on alongside Germany. The most important postwar Fiat aircraft was the G91 lightweight fighter, which served with the Regia Aeronautica and West Germany's Luftwaffe in substantial numbers. The G222 STOL (short take-off and landing) transport of 1966 is also in Italian service. Fiat was absorbed by the state-owned Aeritalia concern in 1969.

FOCKE WULF

The Focke Wulf Flugzeugbau, best known for its classic Fw 190 fighter of World War II, was founded by Professor Heinrich Focke, Georg Wulf and Dr Werner Neumann in 1924. The company's early products were sports aircraft and light transports. Focke became especially interested in rotary-wing aircraft, leaving Focke Wulf in 1936 to set up the Focke Achgelis Flugzeugbau which produced the FA 61 and other early helicopters. Kurt Tank joined Focke Wulf as chief designer in 1931 and he was responsible for the company's notable warplane designs of World War II. Early Focke Wulf products for the Luftwaffe, however, were training aircraft. The Fw 44 Stieglitz two-seat biplane of 1932 served as a basic trainer throughout World War II, and the Fw 56 Stösser single-seat, high-wing monoplane of the following year was an advanced trainer. The twin-engined Fw 58 Weihe of 1935 was more versatile, being used for communications and light transport duties as well as for training.

In 1937 the Fw 187 twin-engined fighter made its maiden flight, but in spite of its promising performance under test it did not go into large-scale production. In the same year Tank's Fw 200 airliner appeared and on the eve of World War II this design was adapted to undertake the long-range maritime patrol task. Although by no means a suitable design for this role (Fw 200s suffered from structural weakness throughout their military service), the Fw 200 Condors served with distinction. Equipping Kampfgeschwader 40's I Gruppe in late 1939, the Condors moved to Bordeaux-Merignac after the fall of France. They soon became a menace to British shipping, sinking a total of 90,000 tons in August and September 1940. In the following month an Fw 200 piloted by Oberleutnant Bernhard Jope bombed and crippled the liner *Empress of Britain*, which was then finished off by a U-boat. In 1941 Condor losses on operations increased with the introduction by the British of catapult-armed merchantmen

Opposite page, top A Fiat BR20 bomber of the Japanese army air force.

Right The Focke Wulf 190A-8/U1 tandem two-seat conversion trainer was originally intended to assist Junkers Ju 87 pilots to train on the ground-attack versions of the Fw 190.

Below The Focke Wulf Fw 200 Condor maritime reconnaissance bomber entered Luftwaffe service with I/KG40 during 1940. Condors also served as VIP transports.

Bottom A Focke Wulf Fw 190A undergoes servicing at its dispersal site on a French airfield. The FW 190A first became operational with the Luftwaffe in the autumn of 1941.

(CAM-ships) and the escort carrier *Audacity*. The type served on until the end of the war, however, latterly in the transport role.

In the early summer of 1942 the Luftwaffe's battle-field reconnaissance squadrons began to replace their Henschel Hs 126s with the twin-engined Fw 189 Uhus and eventually 864 Fw 189s were built. Focke Wulf's top priority, however, was getting the Fw 190 fighter into service, and the first of these went into action against the RAF over France in the autumn of 1941. The early Fw 190As soon made their presence felt, as they outperformed the RAF's Spitfire Mk V fighters and retained this ascendancy until the Spitfire Mk IX appeared in the autumn of 1942. Numerous variants were produced, including specialized ground-attack and night-fighter versions. In the autumn of 1944 the Fw 190D-9 entered service, powered by an in-line Jumo 213 in place of the earlier Fw 190's BMW 801 radial. It proved to have an outstanding performance, but too few were available to affect the outcome of the air battles. The Ta 152H high-speed fighter development of the Fw 190D saw only limited service in 1945, but it was the first Focke Wulf fighter to use the 'Ta' prefix in acknowledgment of Tank's design work. The twin-engined Ta 154 night fighter of wooden construction was intended to emulate the Mosquito's success, but very few of them reached front-line units.

FOKKER

The name of the Dutch aircraft designer Anthony Fokker first came to prominence in the autumn of 1915, when the German army air service's Fokker Eindeckers established a hitherto unprecedented air superiority over the Western Front. The origins of the Fokker E I, the world's first successful fighter aircraft, lay in the Fokker M 5 monoplane of 1913. When this was fitted with a gun interruptor gear devised by Fokker's engineers and a Spandau machine gun in the spring of 1915 it became a formidable fighting weapon. The interruptor gear allowed the machine gun to fire through the fighter's propeller arc without hitting the revolving blades. Similar devices had been produced by Allied inventors, but it was the Germans who brought it into operational use, thereby gaining a considerable tactical advantage. With the introduction of such Allied fighters as the DH2 and Nieuport 11 on

Top *A Fokker EI fighter with wings unrigged for transport. The single, forward-firing Parabellum machine gun can be seen mounted forward of the cockpit.*

Above *Fokker Dr I Triplanes of the Imperial Army Air Service's Jasta 26 lined up for inspection in 1917. The type remained in service until the summer of 1918.*

who was killed flying a Dr I in April 1918. However, although well-liked by von Richthofen and fellow ace Werner Voss, who scored 21 victories while flying the type, it suffered from a series of structural failures and its career on the Western Front was relatively brief (November 1917 to May 1918). Greater acclaim was deserved by the Fokker D VII biplane fighter, which entered service in the spring of 1918 and was considered by many Allied and German pilots alike to be the finest fighter design of World War I. By September 1918 some 800 were in service and the type remained in production in the Netherlands after the Armistice.

The Armistice had in fact specified that all Fokker D VIIs be handed over to the Allies (the only aircraft mentioned by name in the document). In flagrant disregard of these conditions Anthony Fokker smuggled over a hundred of his aircraft from Germany to Holland. Most of these aircraft were Fokker D VIIs, but the batch also included 20 of his D VIII parasol-wing fighters. Both of these types served with the Dutch army air service in the 1920s. However, it was to be with civil transport aircraft that Fokker re-established his reputation in the 1920s. The single-engined, high-wing F II and F III transports, designed by Reinhold Platz, first appeared in 1919 and were put into production at Fokker's new works at Schiphol near Amsterdam. It is worth noting here that Anthony Fokker's chief forte was as an entrepreneur and businessman, so the famous aeroplanes that bore his name (apart from the Eindecker) were designed by his company's employees.

Fokker's new aircraft manufacturing business flourished in the 1920s. In addition to orders from the Dutch airline KLM, many foreign operators flew his transports. The F IV transport, one of the largest single-engined aircraft of its day in 1923, made the first non-stop, coast-to-coast air crossing of the United States, flown by a US Army Air Service crew. Two years later another large single-engined transport, the Fokker F VIIA, was converted into a trimotor as the F VII/3m. It was to be one of the most successful interwar civil transport aircraft, notable F VII/3ms including Kingsford-Smith's *Southern Cross* and Byrd's

the Western Front in early 1916 the Fokker Eindeckers lost their advantage, but they remained in front-line service until the end of that year on less active fronts and around 400 were built. Fokker then produced a series of biplane fighters (the D I to D VI) in 1916–17, but they were relatively undistinguished designs and saw little service.

Perhaps the most famous Fokker design of World War I was the Dr I, a triplane design inspired by the earlier Sopwith Triplane, although it was in no sense a copy. The fame of this aircraft is due to its association with the leading German ace Manfred von Richthofen,

Right *The Fokker D VII was considered by many German and Allied pilots to be the finest fighter aeroplane of World War I. It first appeared at the front in the spring of 1918 and some 50 Jastas flew the type at the time of the Armistice.*

for 32 passengers, and the scaled-down F XXII, which seated 22 passengers. However, by this time the classic Fokker construction techniques of wooden wings and metal structure, with fabric-covered fuselage, had been overtaken by American all-metal, stressed-skin airliners such as the Douglas DC-2. Consequently the F XXXVI and F XXII saw little service.

While concentrating on the production of civil airliners, Fokker had not entirely neglected military aircraft in the inter-war years. Two derivatives of the wartime Fokker D VII fighter, the D XI and D XIII, were produced for export, among the users being the German clandestine military training centre in the Soviet Union. The Fokker DC I two-seat reconnaissance aircraft appeared in 1922 and was followed by the immensely successful C V two-seater. This aeroplane not only served with the Netherlands air force and naval air service at home and in the East Indies, but it was exported to Norway, Sweden and Finland and built under licence in Italy and Switzerland. Its successor the C X first flew in 1934. Among the Fokker designs to oppose Germany's assault on the Netherlands in May 1940 were the T V bomber, the T VIII-W floatplane, the D XXI single-engined fighter and G I heavy fighter. The D XXI was in service with three fighter groups, around 30 being available to meet the German attack, and it also served with Denmark and Finland. The T VIII-W floatplane continued in production during the German occupation and was supplied to Luftwaffe maritime reconnaissance and air/sea rescue units. A Dutch-manned squadron of the RAF also flew the T VIII-W floatplane for a short period.

After the war Fokker produced the S 11 basic trainer and S 14 advanced jet trainer for the Netherlands air force. Then in 1955 the prototype of the F 27 Friendship twin-turboprop airliner took to the air and this

Top *The Fokker FVII/3m Trimotor airliner entered service with the US Army Air Corps as the C-2. The first of them to be delivered, named Bird of Paradise, made the first non-stop flight from Hawaii to California in 1927.*

Above centre *The four-engined Fokker F XXXVI airliner, with accommodation for 32 passengers and a crew of four, was outclassed by the more advanced Douglas DC-2.*

Above *The Fokker F27 Friendship twin-turboprop airliner of 1955 has enjoyed considerable success.*

Josephine Ford. The successful trimotor formula was continued with the F XII of 1931, while the F XXXII was a four-engined, high-wing transport built by Fokker's United States subsidiary. In 1934 the parent company produced the F XXXVI, with accommodation

Right *The Fokker S11 Instructor – a two-seat, piston-engined trainer – first flew in 1947 and was built for the Royal Netherlands Air Force and several foreign air arms.*

was to repeat the success of the pre-war Fokker transports. Deliveries to the airlines began in 1958, with licence production by Fairchild-Hiller in the United States. A military transport version served with the Netherlands air force and was exported in small numbers, as was a maritime reconnaissance variant. The Friendship's twin-jet successor, the F 28 Fellowship, first flew in 1967 and entered airline service two years later. Fokker currently manufactures the General Dynamics F-16 fighter under licence.

GENERAL DYNAMICS

General Dynamics, which is the successor of the Consolidated-Vultee Corporation, has produced two important warplanes for the USAF – the F-111 strike aircraft and the F-16 Fighting Falcon multi-role fighter. The F-111 was designed in response to the US Department of Defense's TFX (tactical fighter experimental) requirement, which called for a single aircraft to carry out both the USAF's interdiction bombing mission and the US Navy's fleet air defence mission. In the event it proved impossible to reconcile the two differing requirements and the US navy's F-111B fighter was cancelled. However, the USAF's F-111A went into production and entered service with the USAF in 1967. It was a radical new design in many ways, being fitted with a variable-geometry wing giving optimum flight characteristics over the entire speed range, turbofan engines with reheat to combine high performance with low fuel consumption and a terrain-following radar to enable it to operate at low level and high speed. Perhaps not surprisingly the F-111 had more than its share of development problems and the

Top *General Dynamics F-111E strike fighters serve with the USAF's 20th Tactical Fighter Wing, based at Upper Heyford in Oxfordshire.*

Above *The General Dynamics YF-16, prototype of the Fighting Falcon fighter, made its first flight on 20 January 1974.*

Below *The two-seat F-16B conversion trainer serves alongside single-seat F-16A fighters in many air forces.*

first combat detachment of six F-111s sent to Southeast Asia in 1968 lost three aircraft within the space of a few weeks. However, the F-111 weathered the storm of controversy that resulted from this inauspicious debut and when it returned to combat in 1972 it performed well. The USAF currently operates six F-111 wings, including two equipped with the FB-111 strategic bomber, and the Royal Australian Air Force also flies the type.

In 1974 General Dynamics flew the prototype of the F-16 lightweight fighter and in the following year the aircraft was selected for production in preference to the rival Northrop F-17 design. A high-performance, manoeuvrable single-seat fighter, the F-16 is intended to replace the McDonnell Douglas F-4 Phantom in USAF service, and total production may eventually exceed 2000 aircraft. In addition the F-16 has been selected to equip the air forces of Belgium, Denmark, the Netherlands and Norway, with licence production being undertaken in Europe. The fighter has also found customers outside Europe, in Israel, Egypt, Pakistan, South Korea and Venezuela. It has seen combat service with the Israeli air force against Syria and Iraq and it looks likely to emulate the success of its predecessor, the Phantom.

GLOSTER

The Gloucestershire Aircraft Co. was formed in the spring of 1917 to produce such types as the Bristol F2B Fighter and FE2b under sub-contract. After the war the firm acquired design rights for the Nighthawk

Top *Gloster Grebe fighters served with No 25 Squadron RAF from 1924 until 1929.*

Above *The Gloster SS37, which first flew in September 1934, was the prototype of the Gladiator. Production Gladiators were fitted with a more powerful Mercury engine and an enclosed cockpit.*

Below *A Gloster Meteor F Mk 8 of No 229 Operational Conversion Unit based at Chivenor in Devon.*

order, but the wooden Gambit found favour with the Japanese navy and 150 were built by Nakajima in Japan. Although overshadowed by the more famous Supermarine racing seaplanes, the Gloster III, IV, V and VI floatplanes participated in the Schneider Trophy contests between 1925 and 1929. In contrast to the Gloster VI, a sleek monoplane design, the company's next RAF fighter was the open-cockpit, biplane Gauntlet. In the spring of 1937 14 RAF squadrons flew this fighter, but they had virtually disappeared from front-line service by the outbreak of World War II, although a few saw action in the Middle East in 1940. Gauntlets also served with the air forces of Denmark and Finland. Its successor in RAF service, the Gladiator, was another biplane fighter, although it had a few concessions to modernity, such as an enclosed cockpit and four-gun armament. Gladiators began to reach the RAF fighter squadrons in 1937 and eventually 25 of them flew this aeroplane. It served during the Battle of France, in Norway, and (with one squadron only) during the Battle of Britain. The 'navalized' Sea Gladiator provided Malta's only air defence when Italy entered World War II, and Gladiators also fought in East Africa, the Western Desert and Greece. In foreign service Gladiators saw combat with the air forces of Belgium, China, Norway and Finland.

It is ironical that the company which produced the RAF's last biplane fighter also built that service's first jet fighter. In 1941 the Gloster E28/39 made its maiden flight, powered by a Whittle jet engine. This was Britain's first jet aeroplane, but it was an experimental aircraft rather than an operational fighter. The Meteor prototype of 1943 was a twin-jet aircraft armed with four 20mm cannon. Production aircraft reached No 616 Squadron in the following year and they went into action against the V1s in August 1944. Early in 1945 the squadron moved to Nijmegen in Holland, but the Meteors saw no combat with the new German jets such as the Messerschmitt Me 262. After the war the Meteor

fighter from the defunct Nieuport and General Aircraft Co. at Cricklewood and 50 of these aircraft were built for the Japanese navy as the Sparrowhawk. The Nighthawks also formed the basis for the Mars I racing aircraft and a small number of Nighthawks and the related Nightjars served with the RAF. In 1923 the Gloster Grebe fighter entered RAF service as a replacement for the Sopwith Snipe, 129 being built. Three years later it was followed by the Gamecock fighter, which eventually equipped five RAF fighter squadrons. It was also in 1926 that the Gloucestershire Aircraft Co. changed its name to the Gloster Aircraft Co.

The all-metal Goldfinch failed to receive an RAF

Below *The Grumman F2F-1 fighter biplane served with US Navy fighter squadrons from 1935 until 1940 and thereafter were used as gunnery training aircraft.*

F Mk 4 became the RAF's standard day fighter, equipping 20 squadrons. Its successor was the Meteor F Mk 8 and more than 1000 of this version were built, equipping 43 RAF squadrons. The Meteor F Mk 8s of No 77 Squadron Royal Australian Air Force saw action in the Korean War, although they were found to be no match for the MiG-15 in air-to-air combat and were relegated to ground-attack duties. Night-fighter, tactical reconnaissance and trainer versions of the Meteor also served with the RAF and all versions were exported to foreign air arms. Gloster's last design was the Javelin all-weather jet fighter, which entered service with No 46 Squadron RAF in 1956. Over 400 were built and the Javelin remained in service until 1967. By that time the Gloster Co. had been absorbed by the Hawker Siddeley group.

GRUMMAN

The Grumman company has throughout its existence been primarily concerned with building aeroplanes for the US Navy. Formed in January 1930, its first major navy contract was for the FF-1 two-seat fighter (27 produced) and the similar SF-1 Scout aircraft (33 produced). The design was also built in Canada for the RCAF, which named it the Goblin, and 40 aircraft from the Canadian production line found their way to the Republican air force in Spain. Grumman's next navy aircraft was the JF-1 Duck amphibian, which entered service in 1934 and was used throughout World War II. The F2F biplane fighter of 1933, nicknamed the 'Flying Barrel', served with US Navy fighter squadrons until 1939, while the F3F of the same year (which was also flown by the Marine Corps) proved to be the US Navy's last biplane fighter. The Grumman Goose amphibian flying boat and the larger

Widgeon were also produced at this time and they served in both civil and military versions.

In 1937 Grumman flew the prototype of a monoplane naval fighter, which was ordered into production in 1939 as the F4F-3 and later named Wildcat. The fighter was also supplied to the Fleet Air Arm, which was the first service to fly it in action. When the United States entered World War II the Wildcat was the navy's standard shipboard fighter. The F4F-4 model introduced a folding wing which eased the problem of stowage aboard carriers – especially the smaller escort carriers. Wildcats fought in the great carrier battles of Coral Sea and Midway and ashore on Guadalcanal with the US Marine Corps. Although replaced by the F6F Hellcat in 1943 aboard the larger carriers, they continued to fly from escort carriers until the end of the war. The Battle of Midway saw the combat debut of the TBF Avenger, a single-engined torpedo-bomber replacement for the Douglas Devastator. When production of this aeroplane ended no fewer than 9836 had been built and it proved to be a rugged and versatile warplane. Apart from its intended torpedo-bomber role it carried out anti-submarine patrols, day and night bombing, night-fighter direction, minelaying, and, after the war, airborne early

Left *The Grumman F4F
Wildcat fighter first reached
US Navy fighter squadrons in
late 1940. This preserved
FM-2 Wildcat, built by
General Motors, is painted in
a pre-war colour scheme.*

Below *The Grumman G-44
Widgeon amphibian first flew
in 1940 and entered service
with the US Navy as the J4F.
The example pictured was in
service in New Zealand in the
1960s.*

Bottom *Grumman F6F
Hellcat fighters (foreground)
prepare to take off from the
deck of an Essex-class carrier in
World War II. Grumman
TBF Avenger torpedo-bombers
are in the background.*

warning (AEW). Avengers were supplied to many
foreign air arms, notably the Fleet Air Arm and Royal
New Zealand Air Force, and they finally retired from
US Navy service in 1954.

The F6F Hellcat fighter began to reach the navy
fighter squadrons in early 1943 and it proved to be a
superb fighter aircraft, eventually accounting for
nearly 5000 enemy aircraft destroyed. Night-fighter
and photo reconnaissance versions were produced and
Hellcats were supplied to the Fleet Air Arm under the
Lend-Lease scheme. Production ended in 1945 after
12,272 had been built, but surprisingly it was soon
afterwards withdrawn from front-line service. Grumman's F7F Tigercat was a twin-engined fighter which
was too late for service in World War II, but it did
see action as a night fighter in Korea with the US
Marine Corps. The high-powered F8F Bearcat also
missed service in World War II and it proved to be
the last piston-engined fighter built by Grumman for
the US Navy. Although no US Navy Bearcats fought
in combat, the Armée de l'Air did use the fighter on
ground-attack sorties in Indochina.

In 1950 the Grumman Guardian entered US Navy
service in the anti-submarine role. Two versions were
built, the AF-2W 'hunter' and AF-2S 'killer', which
operated in pairs, one detecting the target and the other
attacking it. They remained in service until 1955 when
they were replaced by the S2F Tracker. The Grumman
Albatross amphibian of 1947 served with the US services as an air/sea rescue aircraft and was exported to
many nations, some of which operated it in the anti-
submarine role.

Grumman's first jet fighter was the F9F Panther,
which became operational with the US Navy in 1949.
In the following year Panthers of VF-51 and VF-52
went into action over Korea, flying from the USS *Valley Forge*, and on 9 November 1950 a Panther from
VF-111 scored the US Navy's first victory against
the MiG-15. The straight-wing F9F-5 Panther was

modified with a swept wing to produce the F9F-6 Cougar, but was too late to see combat over Korea. However, a two-seat training version was produced as the F9F-8T (redesignated TF-9J in 1962) and a small number of these operated with the US Marine Corps during the Vietnam War. In 1958 a new Grumman fighter, the F11F Tiger, entered service, but its career was brief and only some 200 were built. This disappointment was offset by the success of the S2F Tracker anti-submarine aircraft of 1954, which were assigned to specially equipped anti-submarine carriers. The basic Tracker airframe was adapted for the AEW role as the WF-1 Tracer (redesignated E-1 in 1962) and as a carrier-to-shore transport aircraft, the C-1 Trader.

The Tracker retired from front-line navy service in

1976, when replaced by the Lockheed S-3A Viking. The E-1 and C-1 were succeeded by a new Grumman design, the E-2 Hawkeye and its derivative the C-2 Greyhound. The Hawkeye has proved to be an especially effective aircraft, seeing combat in Vietnam and with the Israeli air force, and it remains in production in the 1980s. Another Vietnam War veteran is the A-6 Intruder all-weather attack aircraft, which has been modified for the tanker role as the KA-6D and for electronic warfare as the EA-6 Prowler. Grumman's OV-1 Mohawk too was used extensively in Vietnam, but with the army in the battlefield surveillance role. The latest in a long line of Grumman navy 'cats', the F-14 Tomcat variable-geometry fleet-defence fighter, forms the mainstay of the US Navy

Above *Grumman A-6E Intruder attack aircraft and an EA-6B Prowler (third from the front) are parked on the flight deck of the USS* John F. Kennedy.

Below *A Grumman F-14A Tomcat two-seat fleet air defence fighter of US Navy Fighter Squadron VF-32 pictured moments before touchdown aboard its parent carrier.*

Top right *Grumman F9F-2 aircraft of VF-112, one of the earliest Panther-equipped units to appear on the Korean battlefront in 1950.*

Right *The US Navy's standard airborne early warning aircraft of the mid-1980s is the Grumman E-2 Hawkeye. In common with many naval aircraft, the E-2's wings fold for carrier stowage.*

fighter squadrons in the 1980s and current plans call for production of some 800 of these highly sophisticated fighters. A single Tomcat can engage up to six targets at once at ranges of 200km (120 miles) thanks to its AWG-9 radar and AIM-54 Phoenix missiles. Grumman's latest venture is the conversion of the USAF's F-111A into the EF-111A electronic warfare aircraft, making use of its experience with the Prowler.

HANDLEY PAGE

The Handley Page company is chiefly remembered for the heavy bomber aircraft that it built for the Royal Air Force. Indeed its twin-engined O/100 of 1915 was the first British heavy bomber. Ordered by the Royal Naval Air Service, the prototype first flew at Hendon in Middlesex on 18 December 1915 and eventually 46 were built. The O/100 began operations with No 3 Wing RNAS, based at Luxeuil-les-Bains in France, and after that unit's disbandment in May 1917 the type operated with No 5 Wing at Dunkirk. In the autumn of 1917 O/100s of A Squadron RNAS operated alongside No 41 Wing of the Royal Flying Corps, which was flying strategic bombing missions against Germany from the Nancy region of eastern France. When this offensive was intensified, under the command of the Independent Force RAF, O/100s were joined by the more powerful O/400s in the spring of 1918. Eight

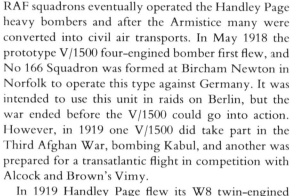

Above In 1919 the Handley Page O/400 went into service with Handley Page Transport Ltd as a civil airliner, serving such destinations as Paris, Brussels and Amsterdam.

Below The Handley Page O/400 twin-engined bomber entered service early in 1918 and by the time of the Armistice it had become the RAF's main heavy bomber.

RAF squadrons eventually operated the Handley Page heavy bombers and after the Armistice many were converted into civil air transports. In May 1918 the prototype V/1500 four-engined bomber first flew, and No 166 Squadron was formed at Bircham Newton in Norfolk to operate this type against Germany. It was intended to use this unit in raids on Berlin, but the war ended before the V/1500 could go into action. However, in 1919 one V/1500 did take part in the Third Afghan War, bombing Kabul, and another was prepared for a transatlantic flight in competition with Alcock and Brown's Vimy.

In 1919 Handley Page flew its W8 twin-engined commercial airliner and this design formed the basis for the Hyderabad bomber of 1923. Two front-line RAF units (No 99 Squadron and No 10 Squadron) flew this bomber, and it later equipped another two squadrons of the Auxiliary Air Force. The Hyderabad's successor, the Hinaidi, was of metal rather than wooden construction and served with the same units as its predecessor. A transport version, the Chitral (later renamed Clive), served with a transport flight in India, and the Hinaidi prototype took part in the Kabul airlift of 1928–9. The RAF's last biplane heavy bomber was the all-metal Heyford, which first flew in 1930 and entered service three years later. A total of 125 were built and they equipped 11 bomber squadrons, being eventually retired from front-line service in 1939.

One of the most impressive Handley Page designs of the inter-war years was not a bomber but an airliner. The four-engined HP42 first flew on 17 November 1930 and eight of them served with Imperial Airways on routes serving the European capitals, the Middle East, Africa and India. It took six and a half days to fly from London to Delhi, while from the centre of London to the centre of Paris took three and a half hours. The HP42 served with Imperial Airways until the outbreak of World War II, when they were impressed into RAF service as transport aircraft. The same duty was performed by the HP Harrow, a large, twin-engined, high-wing bomber/transport which had served in the bomber role until 1939. Harrows operated as transport aircraft throughout World War II with No 271 Squadron, taking part in the evacuation of British forces from France in 1940 and in the

Normandy, Arnhem and Rhine airborne operations of 1944.

The HP Hampden, one of Bomber Command's standard night bombers in the early years of World War II, made its first flight in June 1936. By the outbreak of war ten squadrons were equipped with the type and they took part in minelaying and night-bomber raids until they were retired from Bomber Command in September 1942. Thereafter Hampdens served as torpedo-bombers with Coastal Command and with the Royal Canadian Air Force. In all 1430 were built plus 150 examples of the unsuccessful Hereford, which was powered by two Napier Daggers in place of the Hampden's Bristol Pegasus engines. One of the four-engined heavy bombers which superseded the Hampden in Bomber Command during 1942 was the HP Halifax. The prototype first flew in September 1939, production Halifaxes entered service in November 1940 and by the spring of 1942 the type equipped 12 squadrons. Although its career was overshadowed by that of the admittedly more capable Lancaster, Halifaxes flew some 82,000 bomber sorties during World

Above *The passenger cabin of an Imperial Airways HP42 airliner was laid out like a Pullman railway carriage. The airline's motto was 'Speed without hurry'.*

Right *The Handley Page Hampden bomber first flew on 21 June 1936 and by the outbreak of World War II over 200 were in RAF service. A Hampden Mk II fitted with American Wright Cyclone engines is pictured.*

War II. The early Halifax bombers (Mks I and II) were powered by Rolls-Royce Merlins, while the later aircraft were fitted with Bristol Hercules radials. A total of 6176 Halifaxes were built, and as well as undertaking the bomber role, the type served as an anti-submarine patrol aircraft with Coastal Command, with special duties squadrons dropping supplies to Resistance forces, and as a glider tug. After the war Halifaxes served with the RAF both as transport aircraft and for meteorological reconnaissance, and a civil transport variant, the Halton, was produced.

Above *The last version of the Handley Page Halifax to go into production was a specialized glider-tug and paratroop-transport version designated Halifax A Mk IX.*

Right *The second prototype Handley Page Halifax. It first flew in August 1940 and was followed by the first production Halifax within two months.*

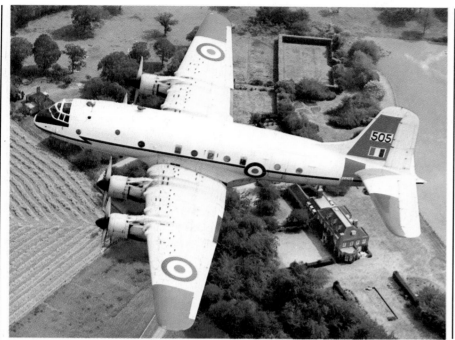

In 1946 Handley Page completed the prototype of the Hastings four-engined military transport and production versions entered service two years later, in time to participate in the Berlin airlift. Eventually 11 squadrons of RAF Transport Command flew this type and they operated all over the world until their replacement by such later types as the Blackburn Beverley, Armstrong Whitworth Argosy and Bristol Britannia between 1956 and 1968. The type served on in the bomber training role with the Bomber Command (later Strike Command) Bombing School at Lindholme in Yorkshire – otherwise known as '1066 Squadron' – until the Hastings finally retired in 1977. Its civil counterpart, the Hermes, had a much briefer career, serving with BOAC from 1950 until 1954 and thereafter with such independent operators as Silver City and Skyways until the early 1960s. The twin-engined Herald was no more successful. It first flew in August 1955 powered by four Alvis Leonides piston engines, but was then re-engined with a pair of Rolls-Royce Dart turboprops. The Dart-Herald prototype appeared in 1958, but was lost in an accident the same

Above *The HP Hastings transport entered RAF service in 1948 and served on, latterly in the bombing training role, until 1977.*

Right *The first production Herald pictured in the livery of British Air Ferries during the 1970s.*

Below *Victor SR Mk 2s of No 543 Squadron RAF operated in the strategic reconnaissance role between 1965 and 1974. The Victor remains in RAF service as an in-flight refuelling tanker aircraft.*

year. These early troubles allowed the rival Fokker F 27 to corner the market for the twin-turboprop airliner and only 48 Heralds were built, serving with British European Airways and various British independent operators. Foreign customers included Nordair of Canada, Itavia of Italy, Globe Air of Switzerland and the Royal Malaysian Air Force.

Handley Page's last aeroplane, the Victor V-bomber, entered RAF service in 1957, and the type has proved to be highly effective both in its original role as a strategic bomber and latterly as a tanker aircraft. Two bomber versions were produced, the B Mk 1 powered by four Armstrong Siddeley Sapphire turbojets and the B Mk 2 with Rolls-Royce Conway engines and a greater wingspan. The Victor was also modified to undertake strategic reconnaissance and in-flight refuelling missions and the tanker versions remain in RAF service well into the 1980s. Handley Page refused to take part in the state-sponsored mergers of the early 1960s and as a result of a lack of government contracts went bankrupt in 1969.

HAWKER

The Hawker Aircraft company, which became world-famous for its single-seat fighter aircraft, was formed as a successor to the Sopwith concern in 1920. Its early years were lean ones, with the company surviving on contracts to recondition wartime Sopwith Snipe fighters for RAF service, and in 1921 its founder, the famous test pilot Harry Hawker, was killed in an air crash. The first Hawker design, the parasol-wing Duiker reconnaissance aircraft of 1923, was a disappointment. It was followed, however, by the Woodcock night fighter, which in its Mk II version was accepted for RAF service in 1924. Two RAF units, Nos 3 and 17 Squadrons, operated Woodcocks from 1925 until 1928, and the similar Danecock was built in Denmark. The Hawker Cygnet ultra-light aircraft also belongs to this period and is noteworthy as the first example of the work of Hawker's great aircraft designer Sydney Camm.

The Hawker Heron fighter of 1925 did not go into production, but in the following year Horsley bombers for the RAF began to leave Hawker's Kingston-upon-Thames factory in Surrey. Total production of the Horsley, which served both as a day bomber and as a torpedo-bomber, was 144, and they were exported to Denmark and Greece. At the same time a small number of Tomtit trainers were built for the RAF. Following the success of the Fairey Fox, the Air Ministry issued a requirement in 1926 for a high-speed day

Top Hawker Woodcocks of No 17 Squadron RAF, based at Upavon in Wiltshire, flying in 'vic' formation in the late 1920s. The leader's aircraft is denoted by the pennant flying from its rudder.

Above The Hawker Hart day bomber first flew in 1928 and entered RAF service two years later. This example, the thirteenth production aircraft, has been preserved at the RAF Museum at Hendon.

Below Among numerous Hart Variants was the Fleet Air Arm's Osprey. This floatplane operated as a spotter aircraft in the Mediterranean.

bomber for the RAF. This resulted in the Hawker Hart of 1928, one of the classic warplanes of the inter-war years. It entered service with No 33 Squadron at Eastchurch, Hampshire, in 1930 and immediately distinguished itself on air exercises by outrunning the RAF's latest interceptor, the Bristol Bulldog. Numerous variants of the Hart were produced, including the Hart Trainer, the Demon two-seat fighter, the Osprey for Fleet Air Arm (FAA) service, the Audax and Hector for army cooperation, and the Hardy for service with the RAF in the Middle East and Africa. A developed version of the Hart bomber, the Hind, appeared in 1934, and 581 were built. The Hart and its derivatives played an important part in the RAF expansion of the late 1930s.

Despite Camm's success with the Hart, his true forte was as a fighter designer. The Hornbill of 1926 did not progress beyond prototype stage, but his Fury design of 1929 was produced in quantity for the RAF. The type entered service with No 43 Squadron in 1931 and it was joined in 1936 by the improved Fury II. A naval carrier-fighter adaptation, the Nimrod, first flew in 1931, and was produced for the FAA and Danish navy. Export sales of the Fury were made to Yugoslavia, Iran, Spain and South Africa. Further development of the Fury was directed towards producing a Fury monoplane, but this project soon evolved into an entirely new design, the eight-gun Hurricane fighter. The prototype Hurricane first flew on 6 November 1935 and was ordered in quantity by the RAF.

The Hurricane entered service with No 111 Squadron at Northolt in Middlesex at the end of 1937 and by the outbreak of war 18 squadrons were flying the type. Hurricanes saw action in France and Norway in the spring of 1940, and although outperformed by the Luftwaffe's Messerschmitt Bf 109 in many respects, they generally gave a good account of themselves. During the Battle of Britain Hurricanes outnumbered Supermarine Spitfires in Fighter Command by a proportion of about two-to-one, and Hurricanes destroyed more enemy aircraft than all other RAF fighters engaged in the battle. The Spitfire was indisputably the more advanced fighter, however, and whenever possible the RAF controllers sought to direct the Hurricane against German bombers, while leaving the

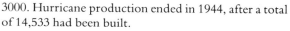

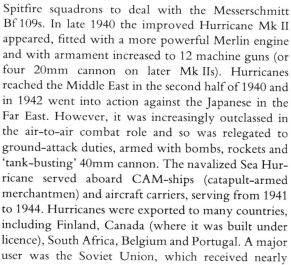

Spitfire squadrons to deal with the Messerschmitt Bf 109s. In late 1940 the improved Hurricane Mk II appeared, fitted with a more powerful Merlin engine and with armament increased to 12 machine guns (or four 20mm cannon on later Mk IIs). Hurricanes reached the Middle East in the second half of 1940 and in 1942 went into action against the Japanese in the Far East. However, it was increasingly outclassed in the air-to-air combat role and so was relegated to ground-attack duties, armed with bombs, rockets and 'tank-busting' 40mm cannon. The navalized Sea Hurricane served aboard CAM-ships (catapult-armed merchantmen) and aircraft carriers, serving from 1941 to 1944. Hurricanes were exported to many countries, including Finland, Canada (where it was built under licence), South Africa, Belgium and Portugal. A major user was the Soviet Union, which received nearly

Above left Fury II fighters of No 25 Squadron fly in echelon formation.

Top right RAF ground crew prepare a Hawker Typhoon Mk 1B of No 175 Squadron for a mission.

Above right An early production Hawker Sea Hawk F Mk 1 naval fighter approaches its parent carrier.

Below Hawker Hurricane fighters flew in every combat theatre in which the RAF was engaged in World War II. A Hurricane Mk II of No 81 Squadron is shown at Vaenga, near Murmansk, USSR.

3000. Hurricane production ended in 1944, after a total of 14,533 had been built.

In September 1941 a new Hawker fighter, the Typhoon, entered RAF service, but its early career was plagued with problems, including a series of unexplained crashes. Once its early design faults had been rectified, however, the Typhoon became a highly effective ground-attack fighter with the RAF's Second Tactical Air Force. A total of 3330 were built. Its successor, the Tempest, unlike the Typhoon, proved to be an excellent air superiority fighter. Tempest Mk V fighters first went into action against V1s in 1944, accounting for over 600 of them. They then moved to bases on the Continent and by the end of the war eight squadrons had been equipped with the type. The Tempest Mk II was too late for wartime service but served with the RAF until 1951 and was supplied to the Indian and Pakistani air forces. The FAA's piston-engined Sea Fury saw combat service during the Korean War in 1950–53.

Hawker's first jet fighter, the P1040 of 1947, did not go into RAF service, but was supplied to the FAA as the Sea Hawk. Entering service in 1953, Sea Hawks took part in the Suez operation of 1956 and were finally retired in 1960. Export versions were supplied to West Germany and the Netherlands and Sea Hawks saw action with the Indian navy against Pakistan in 1971. A swept-wing version of the P1040, designated P1052, flew in prototype form in 1948 and was followed by the entirely new P1067, which first flew in 1951. The design was ordered by the RAF as a Gloster Meteor replacement and was named the Hunter. The

One of the most radical new warplanes of the 1960s was the Harrier V/STOL fighter, the first machine of its kind to enter air force service anywhere in the world. The RAF's first front-line Harrier unit was No 1 Squadron at Wittering in Cambridgeshire and the type currently equips three RAF squadrons and an operational training unit. Harriers were supplied to the US Marine Corps as the AV-8A and also to the Spanish navy. The navalized Sea Harriers serves with the Fleet Air Arm, with which it saw action during the Falklands conflict, and will replace the Indian navy's obsolete Sea Hawks.

Two important civil designs were inherited by Hawker Siddeley from de Havilland: the Trident airliner and the HS 125 executive jet. The Trident, intended for British European Airways service, was the first three-jet airliner to fly, appearing a year before the rival Boeing 727. It began to operate scheduled services in 1964 and among its export customers was the People's Republic of China, which ordered 15. A notable achievement of the Trident was that it was the first airliner to carry out blind landings while carrying fare-paying passengers. The twin-jet HS 125 has proved to be a very popular design, with good devel-

Hunter F Mk 1 entered RAF service in 1954 with No 43 Squadron, based at Leuchars in Fifeshire. Around 1000 Hunters had been built by the time that production ended in 1960 and as well as serving with the RAF in the fighter, ground-attack, tactical reconnaissance and training roles they were exported all over the world. In 1963 the Hawker company became part of the larger Hawker Siddeley Aviation group.

HAWKER SIDDELEY

On its formation in 1963 Hawker Siddeley Aviation absorbed the Avro, de Havilland, Hawker, Armstrong Whitworth, Gloster, Folland and Blackburn companies. Among the products it took over from earlier concerns was the Sea Vixen naval all-weather fighter which had begun as a de Havilland design. The first operational Sea Vixen squadron (No 892 Squadron Fleet Air Arm) was formed in 1959, and the improved Sea Vixen F (AW) Mk 2 entered service in 1963. A total of 146 were built and the type was withdrawn from front-line service in 1972. Blackburn's Buccaneer was also manufactured by Hawker Siddeley, the S Mk 2 version appearing in 1965, and Buccaneers remain in RAF service in the mid-1980s. Another notable maritime aircraft is the Nimrod land-based ASW (anti-submarine warfare) patrol aeroplane which first flew in 1967. Based on the design of the Comet airliner, the Nimrod entered RAF service in 1969. An airborne early warning version, the AEW Mk 3, will replace the Shackletons in this role in the mid-1980s.

Top *A Hunter F(GA) Mk 9 with the chequer markings of No 43 Squadron.*

Above centre *The Hawker Hunter was exported to many*

foreign air arms, including the Sultan of Oman's air force, as shown here.

Above *A Hawker Siddeley Sea Vixen F(AW) Mk 1*

about to be catapulted from HMS Ark Royal.

Below *An RAF Hawker Siddeley Nimrod MR Mk 1 maritime patrol aircraft.*

opment potential, as both 'stretched' and re-engined versions have appeared. Intended primarily as a light transport for corporations which can afford to operate their own jets, it has also served as a military communications and training aircraft with various air forces, including the RAF. Another civil type with proven military potential is the HS 748 (originally an Avro design), which has been built as the Andover military transport for the RAF and Royal New Zealand Air Force. In 1977 Hawker Siddeley Aviation and the British Aircraft Corporation merged to form British Aerospace.

Above left The HS Harrier was the first V/STOL aircraft to enter military service. An RAF Harrier GR Mk 1 is shown firing a salvo of Matra rockets.

Above The Hawker Siddeley HS 125 executive jet first flew in 1962 and has operated with both civil and military users.

Left The Andover C Mk 1 is a military derivative of the HS 748 airliner, fitted with a rear loading ramp. It first entered service with the RAF in 1966.

Below The Trident airliner entered airline service in 1964 with British European Airways and 15 were exported to the People's Republic of China.

HEINKEL

The Ernst Heinkel Flugzeug Werke, which is primarily remembered for its He 111 bomber of World War II, was formed in 1922. Its founder had worked as an aircraft designer with the LVG and Brandenburg companies in World War I. However, until the restrictions imposed by the Treaty of Versailles were openly flouted in the mid-1930s, Heinkel and other German designers had to produce their military designs for export. Among the aeroplanes of this period were the HD 17 and HD 21 trainers, the He 1 and He 5 floatplane fighters and the He 45 reconnaissance/bomber. A number of these aircraft were clandestinely tested by the German army in the Soviet Union. One of the most important warplanes of the newly emergent Luftwaffe in 1935 was the He 51 biplane fighter, which also served as a floatplane with coastal defence flights. Heinkel He 51s equipped the Condor Legion's Jagdgruppe 88 in Spain, where the type performed indifferently and was soon replaced by the early models of the Messerschmitt Bf 109. The Heinkel He 59 floatplane had a longer career with the Luftwaffe and remained in service from the mid-1930s until 1943, latterly in the air/sea rescue role.

In December 1932 the prototype He 70 Blitz took to the air. It entered service with Lufthansa as a high-speed airliner in 1934 and also equipped a number of Luftwaffe bomber and reconnaissance units. The He 70

Top *The Heinkel He 51 fighter appeared in 1935 and became the newly formed Luftwaffe's first front-line fighter aircraft. The He 51-B illustrated served with the Condor Legion in Spain.*

Above *The high-speed Heinkel He 70 was used by Lufthansa on German internal services and operated with the Luftwaffe in the reconnaissance and bombing roles.*

Right *One of the most bizarre aircraft to see service in World War II was the Heinkel He 111Z glider tug, a five-engined aircraft incorporating two He 111H fuselages.*

served in Spain with the Condor Legion and a total of 296 of the military version were built. The He 115 of 1936 was a twin-engined floatplane which entered service with the Luftwaffe's *Küstenfliegergruppen* (coastal reconnaissance section) as a minelayer, torpedo-bomber and reconnaissance aircraft. He 115s laid magnetic mines in British coastal waters in 1939–40 and served as transports during the invasion of Norway in April 1940. One of the foreign operators of the He 115 was the Norwegian air force and these aircraft flew against German forces during the campaign. The He 115 remained in service throughout World War II and about 500 were eventually produced.

The He 111 was first flown in 1935 and the early versions were produced both as bombers and as civil transports. He 111Bs served with the Condor Legion in Spain and by the outbreak of World War II nearly 1000 had been produced. The bomber took part in the campaigns against Poland, Norway, the Low Countries and France. The early He 111 models up to the He 111J featured a glazed nose position for the observer with a stepped pilot's canopy behind it. The He 111P introduced a redesigned nose section which enclosed observer and pilot within a single transparent nose cone. By the summer of 1940, when the Battle of Britain was fought, the main production version of the Heinkel bomber was the He 111H, some 500 of which were in service. This variant was adapted as a torpedo-bomber, which saw action against the British Arctic convoys in 1942. Other versions served as paratroop transports, glider tugs and cargo transports, and in 1944 He 111Hs of III Gruppe, Kampfgeschwader 3

acted as launch aircraft for V1s directed against London. One of the He 111's last successes of the war was the attack made on Poltava on the night of 21/22 June 1944, which destroyed 43 Boeing B-17s and 15 North American P-51s of the USAAF's Eighth Air Force, which were using the Soviet airfield for 'shuttle' bombing missions. Undoubtedly the most bizarre variant of the He 111 to see operational service was the He 111Z glider-tug. This comprised two He 111 fuselages joined at the wing, by a centre section which housed a fifth engine. Crewed by seven men with the pilot in the port fuselage, the He 111Z was intended to tow the giant Me 321 cargo glider.

Unlike the Western Allies, Germany was slow to introduce a four-engined bomber design into service. The He 177 did not reach front-line units until 1942

Right *The Heinkel He 111V8 was the prototype of the P series which introduced a redesigned nose section. Some 350 He 111Ps were in Luftwaffe service at the outbreak of World War II.*

and even then its development problems had not been fully eradicated. One problem was overheating of the paired DB 605 engines. This was an unusual installation, intended to reduce drag, whereby the engines were mounted in pairs, each driving a single propeller. Thus the four-engined He 177 had the appearance of a twin-engined aircraft. This arrangement gave nothing but trouble and eventually the He 277 was produced with a conventional four-engine layout; but it was too late to see wartime service. He 177s operated as transports during the Stalingrad airlift in 1942, but it was not until the following year that the bomber version became fully operational. He 177s operated

against Britain during Operation Steinbock, the 'Little Blitz' of 1944, and flew anti-shipping missions with Kampfgeschwader 40 over the Mediterranean, while Kampfgeschwader 1 operated the bombers on the Eastern Front.

In 1942 the Heinkel He 219 twin-engined night fighter first flew and it entered operational service with I Gruppe, Nachtjagdgeschwader 1 in June 1943. Although popular with night-fighter crews because it had the necessary performance to counter the RAF's Mosquitoes, the He 219 was only built in small numbers (under 700) and so its impact on the night battles over the Reich was comparatively slight.

Right *The prototype He 177 made its first flight in November 1939. Despite its appearance, it was a four-engined bomber powered by paired Daimler Benz DB601 engines.*

Right *A Heinkel He 162 Volksjäger stands abandoned on Vienna-Schwechat airfield at the end of World War II. Despite grandiose plans for mass production, the He 162 saw no combat.*

The world's first jet aircraft, the He 178, first took to the air on 24 August 1939 under the power of an He S3 turbojet. This powerplant was produced by the German engineer von Ohain, an employee of the Heinkel company. The He 178's successful demonstration of jet-powered flight led Heinkel to develop the He 280, the first jet fighter, but this twin-jet machine did not go into production. In 1944 Heinkel successfully competed for a lightweight jet fighter requirement and this machine was put into production as the He 162. Construction of the fighter was simple, and numerous small sub-contractors were employed in its production. The prototype first flew in December 1944 and the first production aircraft appeared the following month. The *Volksjäger* (people's fighter) programme called for output to be raised to a rate of 2000 per month in May 1945. Pilots for the mass-produced fighter were to be recruited from the ranks of the Hitler Youth. By the end of the war, however, the first He 162-equipped unit (I Gruppe, Jagdgeschwader 1) was still not fully operational.

HUGHES

The first venture of the eccentric millionaire Howard Hughes into aeroplane design and construction came in 1934. Hughes assembled a small team in Los Angeles to build a racing aircraft with which he intended to establish a new world speed record for landplanes. The Hughes H-1 first flew in August 1935 and the following month it achieved an average speed of 567.13km/h (352.39mph) over a measured course with Hughes at

Above The gigantic Hughes H-4 Hercules flying boat, nicknamed the 'Spruce Goose', was intended as a long-range cargo transport. It made its first and only flight in 1946.

Below left Howard Hughes poses with his H-1 racing aeroplane, which was built in conditions of great secrecy and made its first flight in 1935.

aircraft, in which Hughes was badly injured when the prototype crashed during its first test flight in 1946. Undismayed, Hughes resumed flight testing of a second prototype in April 1947, but the XF-11 failed to attract a production order from the USAF. The last aircraft with which Hughes was personally involved was the H-4 Hercules, a giant, eight-engined wooden flying boat derisively nicknamed the 'Spruce Goose'. Intended for wartime long-range transport operations, the flying boat made its first and last flight in 1946.

Thereafter a part of Hughes's vast industrial empire remained in the aircraft manufacturing business. This was Hughes Helicopters, which in 1956 produced the Hughes 269A two-seat helicopter. The design was fur-

the controls. This was the new speed record which Hughes sought, but the H-1 finished this flight in a crash-landing, due to engine failure caused by a blocked fuel line. In the following year Hughes rebuilt the H-1 and used it to establish a new US coast-to-coast record of 7 hours 28 minutes in November 1937.

Hughes's next two aircraft were unsuccessful military designs, the D-1 and D-2 fighters. There followed the XF-11 long-range photographic reconnaissance

Above One of the most successful Hughes helicopter designs was the OH-6 Cayause (civil Model 500), which served in the scout role in Vietnam with the US Army.

ther developed into the successful Model 300 civil helicopter and the US Army's TH-55 Osage training helicopter. In 1963 there followed the army's OH-6 scout helicopter, which was used extensively in the Vietnam War. The latest Hughes helicopters are the Model 500 Defender attack helicopter, developed from the OH-6, and the very advanced AH-64 Apache all-weather attack helicopter, over 500 of which are required by the US army.

The Il-10 was a successor to the Il-2, having a more powerful engine and increased armour protection for the crew. It entered service in 1944 and remained in use until the late 1950s, over 6000 being built. In 1946 the twin-engined Il-12 transport first flew, entering service with Aeroflot in the following year. An improved version, the Il-14, appeared in 1950 and as well as operating in large numbers with Aeroflot it was widely exported. Equally successful was the Il-28 twin-engined bomber, the Soviet equivalent of the British Canberra, which first flew in 1948. Some 5000 were produced, including a torpedo-bomber version and a mailplane variant for Aeroflot. It was the Soviet air force's standard tactical bomber aircraft throughout the 1950s and 1960s.

The Il-18 four-turboprop airliner of 1957 went into service with Aeroflot in 1959. Some 900 were produced for the Soviet state airline, various foreign operators and some military users, including the Soviet air force, which flies an electronic reconnaissance version.

Above In April 1939 the Ilyushin DB-3 prototype, piloted by test pilot Vladimir Kokkinaki, attempted to fly from the Soviet Union to the United States, but it was forced to crash-land on the Canadian island of Miscou.

Left Ilyushin Il-2 ground-attack aircraft pass down a production line during World War II.

Right An Ilyushin Il-14 of the Czechoslovak state airlines.

Below An Ilyushin Il-18 four-turboprop airliner.

Bottom The twin-engined Ilyushin Il-28 was the first Soviet jet bomber and served with many foreign air arms. A Nigerian air force Il-28 is pictured.

ILYUSHIN

Sergei Ilyushin trained as an aeronautical engineer in the Soviet Zhukovskii Air Force Engineering Academy during the early 1920s. In 1933 he formed his own design team, which produced a twin-engined design that was to be developed into the DB-3 twin-engined bomber. When production of this machine ended in 1938, over 1500 had been built. The DB-3 saw service in the Russo-Finnish Winter War of 1939–40 and in the early years of the war with Germany. Its successor, which was eventually redesignated Il-4, was built in even greater numbers, production totalling over 5000. It formed the mainstay of the Soviet long-range bomber regiments in World War II and was also employed as a torpedo-bomber and minelayer. An even more widely used warplane of the World War II period was the Ilyushin Il-2 ground-attack aircraft or Shturmovik. Initially produced as a single-seater, it was later modified to accommodate a rear gunner and in this form (known as the Il-2M3) achieved considerable success. The total production figure for the Il-2 was over 36,000, reflecting not only the widespread use of this aircraft by the Soviet air force, but also the heavy combat losses suffered by the ground-attack regiments.

The airliner also formed the basis of the Il–38 maritime reconnaissance aircraft design, which is codenamed May by NATO. In 1963 the four-jet Il–62 appeared, and it was the last aircraft which Sergei Ilyushin worked on before his retirement. Two other designs have been produced by the design bureau which perpetuates Ilyushin's name. The Il–76 is a four-jet freight aircraft intended for both civil and military operation. It first flew in 1971 and military AEW (airborne early warning) and tanker versions are reported to be under development. The Il–86 of 1976 is a wide-bodied airbus with accommodation for 350 passengers.

Top The four-jet Ilyushin Il-62 airliner operates on Aeroflot's long-haul routes both within the Soviet Union and to foreign capitals.

Above The Ilyushin Il-76 freighter, which first flew in 1971, serves both with Aeroflot and with the Soviet air force's Military Transport Aviation.

Above right The IAI Arava twin-turboprop light-transport aircraft first flew in 1969.

ISRAEL AIRCRAFT INDUSTRIES

The state of Israel has made great efforts to build up an indigenous aircraft industry so that it can achieve a measure of self-sufficiency in supplying warplanes to

Below The Kfir-C2 fighter was based on the design of the Dassault Mirage III, but has numerous new features including canard foreplanes and a General Electric J79 engine.

the Israeli air force. Israel Aircraft Industries (IAI) was formed in 1976 by renaming Bedek Aviation, the earlier company having undertaken licence production and maintenance work for the Israeli air force. Its first original design, the twin-turboprop Arava light transport, appeared in 1969. It has been sold to many civil and military customers and the Israeli air force operates an electronic warfare version. Another twin-turboprop transport, the Westwind, is based on the American Rockwell Jet Commander and has been produced as an executive jet and for maritime surveillance.

The first indigenous Israeli warplane design is the IAI Kfir, a single-seat fighter based on the French Mirage III. It is powered by a General Electric J79 turbojet and much of the avionic equipment is of Israeli design and manufacture, making the Kfir more than simply an Israeli copy of the French fighter. In its Kfir-C2 version it is fitted with canard foreplanes to enhance manoeuvrability at high angles of attack. A two-seat conversion trainer version first flew in 1971 and the Kfir-C7 of 1983 has an improved navigation/attack system. Plans are well advanced for the next generation Israeli fighter, the IAI Lavi, which is expected to fly in 1985. This is intended to replace the A-4 Skyhawk and F-4 Phantom in Israeli air force service and the total requirement is for some 300 Lavi fighters.

JUNKERS

Professor Hugo Junkers was a pioneer of all-metal construction techniques for aeroplanes and the company that he founded in 1917 produced Germany's most effective bomber aircraft of World War II, the Junkers Ju 88. Junkers' J1 monoplane of 1915 was remarkably advanced, with all-metal construction and a cantilever (internally braced) wing structure. It led to a series of single- and two-seat monoplanes, which saw limited service at the end of World War I. More important was the J4 biplane, which with the military designation JI served in the low-level tactical air support role in 1918. Over 200 JIs were built and their all-metal structure and armour protection for the crews made them extremely popular.

After the Armistice Junkers concentrated on the production of all-metal civil air transport aircraft and

limited numbers of the later Ju 252, Ju 352 and Ju 90 series transports were ever used.

The Junkers Ju 86 twin-engined bomber served with Luftwaffe bomber units in the late 1930s, but only a few modified high-altitude variants saw operational service in World War II. In contrast the Ju 87 single-engined dive-bomber of 1935 played an important part in the Luftwaffe's early campaigns, acting as flying artillery in support of ground forces. In spite of the heavy losses suffered by the type in the Battle of Britain, it served on in the Mediterranean and on the Eastern Front. An anti-tank version, armed with two

his F13 design of 1919 was produced in large numbers (over 300) and served with airlines all over the world for the next 20 years. The F13 accommodated four passengers in an enclosed cabin and was flown by a crew of two. It could be fitted with wheel, float or ski undercarriages and its corrugated metal skinning was to become the hallmark of all Junkers transport aircraft of the inter-war period. These included the single-engined W33 and W34 of 1926, which were developed versions of the F13 with accommodation for up to six passengers, the G24 trimotor and the four-engined G38, with accommodation for 34 passengers. A number of military designs were built in Sweden, including the R42 bomber and the K47 two-seat fighter-bomber.

Junkers pooled its inter-war civil and military experience in 1932 to produce the Ju 52/3m, a trimotor development of the single-engined Ju 52 of 1930. In airline service the Ju 52/3m operated with Deutsche Lufthansa

and many foreign airlines. A bomber version entered service with the Luftwaffe in 1935 and served in this role during the Spanish Civil War, being eventually replaced by Do 17s and He 111s in 1937. However, it was as a military transport aircraft that the Ju 52/3m was to achieve its greatest success. Nearly 600 of these aircraft took part in the invasion of Norway in April 1940, and they went on to serve during the campaigns in the Low Countries and France, the airborne invasion of Crete and the Stalingrad airlift. Well over 4000 examples of this workhorse transport were produced and they served throughout World War II. Only

Top The Junkers J1 monoplane of 1915 was an advanced all-metal design in contrast to the wooden, fabric-covered aeroplanes of its day.

Above centre The Junkers F13 airliner of 1919 carried four passengers in an enclosed cabin, with the crew of two seated in a semi-open cockpit.

Above A Junkers Ju 52/3m trimotor at Croydon airport in 1935.

37mm cannon, was introduced in 1943 and proved to be successful against Soviet tanks until fighter opposition on the Eastern Front stiffened in 1944. More than 5700 Ju 87s were built and a measure of the aircraft's success is that the name Stuka invariably associated with it is the German term for a dive-bomber rather than the designation of the aircraft itself.

Germany's most effective and adaptable bomber aircraft of World War II was undoubtedly the twin-engined Ju 88. The prototype first flew in 1936 and deliveries to front-line units began in September 1939. By the summer of 1940 over 250 Ju 88s were in service and the Battle of Britain was the type's first real combat test. The comparatively heavy losses to RAF fighters revealed the bomber's greatest fault, its inadequate defensive armament. Nonetheless for the rest of the war Ju 88s continued to serve in the bomber role in all theatres in which the Luftwaffe was engaged, latterly reinforced by improved Ju 188s. The type proved also to be an effective anti-shipping weapon and Kampf-geschwader 30's Ju 88s enjoyed many successes against the Arctic convoys. Perhaps the strangest version of the Ju 88 was the robot aircraft carried beneath a single-engined fighter in the Mistel composite. The fighter pilot would fly the Mistel to the target area, aim and release the Ju 88 at its target and then return to base. Mistels were used operationally with limited success against warships and enemy bridges in 1944–5.

sance biplane and the Type 92 fighter of 1929 also served with the army air service, seeing action in Manchuria and China. The Ki-10 fighter of 1935 was used in combat against the Chinese and against Soviet warplanes during the Nomonhan Incident in 1938–9. A light bomber design, the Ki-32, some 850 of which were built, remained in service until the early campaigns of the Pacific War. However, the first Kawasaki design to see widespread combat service in that conflict was the Ki-48 (Allied codename Lily), a twin-engined monoplane bomber which first flew in 1939.

The twin-engined Ki-45 fighter of 1939 entered service in 1942 and was particularly active in the defence of Japan against Boeing B-29 Superfortress

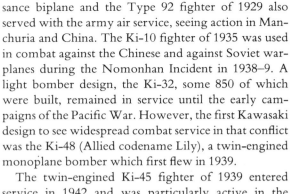

Other roles undertaken by the Ju 88 with success included reconnaissance, ground attack, day and night fighting. Camera-equipped reconnaissance versions, which were otherwise very similar to the bombers, operated from 1940 onwards, and the Ju 88 also flew weather reconnaissance sorties. Day-fighter Ju 88s proved to be a considerable danger to Allied anti-submarine aircraft over the Bay of Biscay, while the heavy-cannon-armed Ju 88P ground-attack variant operated over the Eastern Front. Towards the end of the war, night-fighter versions of the Ju 88 assumed increasing importance, and some 3900 of the total of 14,776 Ju 88s produced were earmarked for fighter or ground-attack duties.

Above In 1942 the Junkers Ju 87 dive-bomber was adapted for the anti-tank role as the Ju 87G, by fitting a pair of 37mm cannon under the wings.

Below The Junkers Ju 188, which entered Luftwaffe service in 1943, was an improved Ju 88 with a redesigned nose section, revised wing and vertical tank surfaces and more powerful engines.

raids in 1944–5. More widely used was the Ki-61 Hien (Swallow) of 1941, the first Japanese monoplane fighter to be powered by an in-line engine. Over 3000 were built and until the appearance of the Grumman F6F Hellcat and North American P-51 Mustang it could hold its own with any Allied fighter. The Ki-100 was a radial-engined development of the Hien, which saw service in the closing months of the war. The Ki-

Left The trimotor Junkers Ju 352 transport of 1943 was constructed largely of wood in order to conserve stocks of metals. Only 45 were ever built.

Above right The Kawasaki Type 88 two-seater reconnaissance bomber was the first of the company's indigenously designed aircraft to go into production.

KAWASAKI

Kawasaki is chiefly remembered as the manufacturer of some of the Japanese army air service's most successful fighter aircraft of World War II. The Kawasaki shipbuilding company first began aircraft construction in the 1920s, building a number of European designs under licence. The firm's first original design to be built in quantity was the Type 88 bomber/reconnais-

Right The Kawasaki Ki-10 fighter of 1935 was a highly manoeuvrable aeroplane which saw service with the Japanese army air force in China and against the Soviet Union in 1938-9.

102 twin-engined, high-altitude interceptor also participated in the final defence of the homeland. Since World War II Kawasaki have produced the twin-jet C-1A military transport, which first flew in 1970.

Far right *The Lavochkin La-15 jet fighter of 1948 was a contemporary of the MiG-15, but it saw only limited service with the Soviet air force.*

Below *The Kawasaki Ki-61 Hien (Swallow), codenamed Tony by the Americans, was powered by a licence-built Daimler Benz in-line engine.*

LAVOCHKIN

Semyon Lavochkin, one of the Soviet Union's most successful aircraft designers of World War II, graduated from Moscow's Technical High School as an aeronautical engineer in 1929. His first successful design, completed in partnership with Mikhail Gudkov and Vladimir Garbunov, was the I-22 single-seat, all-wooden monoplane fighter. This aircraft was ordered into production for the Soviet air force in 1939 as the LaGG-1 and it led to the improved LaGG-3. Although a robust design, the LaGG fighter was difficult to fly and proved to be unpopular with service pilots. Nevertheless, substantial numbers operated with the Soviet air force in 1941–2.

The La-5 of 1942 was a development of the LaGG-3, which was powered by a radial rather than an in-line engine, and the La-7 was a slightly modified development of the La-5. These fighters proved to be capable of taking on the Luftwaffe's Messerschmitt Bf 109 and Focke Wulf Fw 190 with some chance of success, and

Above *An LaGG-3 fighter which was captured by the Finns.*

Below *The Lavochkin La-5FN appeared in early 1943 and differed from earlier La-5s in having a cut-down rear fuselage and all-round vision cockpit canopy.*

the La-5 first went into action in late 1942 on the Stalingrad Front. Over 22,000 of the wartime Lavochkin designs were produced and they played a notable part in the Soviet air force's battles against the Luftwaffe. After the war the wooden La-7 was superseded by the metal La-9 and La-11 piston-engined fighters and the La-11 was to be the last piston-engined fighter to serve with the Soviet air force. Lavochkin designed a num-

ber of jet fighters in the postwar years, but only the La-15 (a contemporary of the MiG-15) saw service and this was only in limited numbers. Lavochkin's design bureau was closed after its leader's death in 1960.

LOCKHEED

The first Lockheed aircraft was built by the Loughead brothers in 1911, and in 1916 they formed the Loughead Aircraft Manufacturing Co., changing their name to Lockheed shortly after World War I. The company's S-1 sports biplane of 1919 was both economical and reliable but it could not compete with the flood of war-surplus aeroplanes. Consequently the company went out of business, but was reformed in 1926 to build the Vega high-wing monoplane. This high-speed airliner performed well in racing and record-breaking flights and led on to the Sirius, Altair and Orion monoplanes. In 1934 the twin-engined Model 10 Electra made its first flights, followed two years later by the smaller Model 12, both of which went into production as civil and military transports. Next came the 14-passenger Model 14, which was the fastest airliner of its day. A stretched Model 14, the Model 18 Lodestar, was built in substantial numbers (over 600) as a military transport in World War II.

In 1939 Lockheed secured an order for the Hudson maritime patrol aircraft from the British Purchasing Commission. Essentially a militarized Model 14, the Hudson served with the RAF, RAAF, RNZAF, USAAF and US Navy. Total production was 2941 and the type operated with RAF Coastal Command from 1939 to 1944, also carrying out transport duties. The military version of the Model 18, the Ventura, served briefly with the RAF in the bombing role. It was a greater success in service with the US Navy, whose PV-1 Venturas were succeeded by the improved PV-2 Harpoons. Over 1600 Venturas were built for the US Navy, plus a further 535 Harpoons.

In 1939 the prototype Lockheed Lightning fighter made its first flight. A twin-engined machine, with the tailplane carried on distinctive twin booms, the P-38 Lightning was one of the most important USAAF aeroplanes of World War II. Nearly 10,000 P-38s were built and they served in every major combat theatre in which the USAAF was engaged. Lightnings

escorted the Eighth Air Force's bombers on missions over Germany, they fought in North Africa and Italy, and in the Pacific they operated from the Aleutian Islands in the north to New Guinea in the south. The two top-scoring fighter pilots of the USAAF, Richard Bong and Thomas McGuire, flew Lightnings, and the fighter is reputed to have shot down more Japanese aircraft than any other type. Reconnaissance versions of the P-38 were built as F-4s and F-5s and some Lightnings were modified to carry a bombardier in the nose to lead formation bombing attacks. A night-fighter Lightning, fitted with a radar pod underwing and a second cockpit for its operator, saw action in the Pacific at the end of World War II.

On 9 January 1943 the four-engined Constellation airliner made its first flight and early production examples were delivered to the USAAF as C-69s. After the war it went into airline service with Trans World Airlines and the original design was stretched into the 92-seat Super Constellation, which proved to be a popular aeroplane with the airlines. Total production of the Constellation was 850, including military transport and airborne radar picket versions.

Exactly a year after the Constellation's first flight, the XP-80 Shooting Star fighter prototype first took to the air. Powered by a British Halford H1 turbojet, the P-80 was too late for combat service in World War

Top The Lockheed Altair monoplane of 1930 was one of the earliest aeroplanes to have a retractable undercarriage.

Above A Lockheed Model 14 Super Electra.

Above right The Lockheed P-38 Lightning fighter.

Below The Lockheed T-33 jet trainer was developed from the F-80 and saw widespread service.

Bottom The Lockheed Hudson served with the RAF during World War II.

II. However it did provide the USAAF, and from 1947 the newly formed USAF, with its first jet fighter, and a total of 1718 Shooting Stars were built. During the Korean War the F-80 (the P for pursuit designation gave way to F for fighter in 1948) served primarily as a ground-attack fighter, although a number of successful combats with MiG-15s were recorded. In 1948 Lockheed produced the T-33 trainer version of the F-80, which was eventually built in far greater numbers than the fighter (total production was 6377). T-33s were exported to many foreign air arms and the type remains in USAF service in the mid-1980s. Further development of the basic Shooting Star design produced the F-94 Starfire series of two-seat night fighters.

The Lockheed P2V Neptune, which for more than

20 years was to be the most important maritime patrol aircraft in NATO service, first flew on 17 May 1945. It began to equip the US Navy's patrol squadrons in 1947 and was finally replaced by the P-3 Orion in the mid-1960s. Foreign customers for the Neptune included the RAF, the Aéronavale, the Netherlands navy, the RCAF, RAAF and Japanese navy. Over 1000 Neptunes were built, including the turboprop-powered P-2J built in Japan. An even more widely used Western military aircraft is the Lockheed C-130 Hercules. The prototype first flew in August 1954 and this four-turboprop tactical transport remains in pro-

duction in the mid-1980s after some 1700 have been built. Variants of the Hercules have been produced for air refuelling, coastal surveillance, rescue, electronic warfare and weather reconnaissance. The AC-130 gunship variant, with its broadside armament of 105mm, 40mm and 20mm cannon, was built during the Vietnam War and remains in USAF service. However, it is in the transport role that the majority

Below *A Lockheed Model 749 Constellation of Trans World Airlines.*

Below right *The Lockheed U-2 strategic reconnaissance aircraft achieve notoriety in May 1960, when a CIA-operated aircraft was shot down over the Soviet Union.*

Japan, while the final version of the Starfighter, the F-104S, was produced in Italy. Two of the most publicized Lockheed aircraft of recent years have been the USAF's U-2 and SR-71 'Blackbird' strategic reconnaissance aircraft, the latter holding several world speed and altitude records. An even more exotic project is the Lockheed 'stealth' fighter, an aircraft intended to be invisible to enemy radars.

The second Lockheed aeroplane to carry the name Orion is a four-turboprop naval patrol aircraft, based on the Electra airliner of 1957. P-3 Orions entered service with the US Navy in 1962 and the type's anti-submarine warfare (ASW) equipment has since been progressively updated so that it remains a highly effective warplane more than 20 years later. Its shipboard counterpart is the S-3A Viking ASW aircraft. The mainstay of the USAF's strategic airlift force is the Lockheed C-141 Starlifter, a four-turbofan military transport, and it is supplemented by the C-5 Galaxy which can carry outsize loads. The civil L1011 Tristar wide-bodied transport has proved to be less popular than its rival DC-10, leading Lockheed into severe financial difficulties. The company has, however, overcome its problems thanks to a steady flow of military contracts.

of Hercules have served, major users including the US armed forces, Britain, Canada, Australia and New Zealand. Many other air forces have small C-130 fleets and there are a few civil operators.

The Lockheed F-104 Starfighter of 1954 had a fairly brief career in USAF service, but many were produced for the United States' NATO allies and other friendly states. A European consortium built 970 F-104Gs for the air forces of West Germany, the Netherlands, Italy, Belgium, Turkey, Greece, Denmark and Norway. Licence production also took place in Canada and

Above *The Lockheed F-104 Starfighter entered service with the USAF as an interceptor in 1958 and was later developed as a multi-role fighter for several NATO air forces. A Starfighter of the Italian air force is illustrated.*

Below *The Lockheed C-130 Hercules has remained in production since 1955 and equips many air forces.*

MACCHI

The firm of Macchi, chiefly noted for its fighter aircraft and record-breaking seaplanes, was founded in 1912 to build French Nieuport designs under licence. During World War I Macchi built the Nieuport 11 and 17 fighters for the Aeronautica Militare, as well as the Hanriot HD1. They also produced an unlicensed copy of the Austro-Hungarian Lohner flying boat, then modifying the design to produce their own L3, which was a great improvement on the Lohner. In 1916 the M5 fighter flying boat appeared and it saw considerable service in World War I. Its replacement was the M7, which served throughout the 1920s. Macchi also built larger flying boats for reconnaissance and bombing, including the M4, M8, M9 and M12.

The company's experience with flying boats and fighters made it an obvious participant in the Schneider Trophy contests and the M19 was specially designed

for the 1920 event. In 1921 a Macchi M7bis won the Schneider contest, but in the following year was beaten by the British Supermarine Sea Lion, and the M33 of 1925 was also unsuccessful. But the Macchi company's efforts were not exclusively directed towards constructing racing seaplanes, for the M18 and M24 flying boats, the M15 reconnaissance aircraft and the licence-built Nieuport NiD29 fighters were all produced at this time. In 1926 the Macchi M39, a twin-float seaplane rather than a flying boat, won the Schneider contest, but the improved M52 of 1927 lost to the Supermarine S5. Despite a brilliant performance by the M67 in 1929, Britain again won the contest, and as no other team was ready for the 1931 event, Britain won it and the Schneider Trophy outright without opposition. However, Macchi continued development of high-speed floatplanes with the M72, which set a new world speed record in 1934. The MC94 flying boat of 1936 saw limited service with the airlines, as did the MC100 of 1939.

In 1937 Macchi produced a radial-engine monoplane fighter, the MC200, which entered service with the Regia Aeronautica in 1939. Over 1000 were built and they saw service over Malta, Greece, North Africa and even on the Eastern Front. In 1941 the improved MC202 entered service. It was fitted with a German

Left The Macchi M5 flying boat fighter of World War I was the equal in performance to many land-based aeroplanes.

Below (1) The Macchi MC 205N Orione was a development of the MC 202 design, but it did not go into production.

Below (2) The Macchi MB 326 is produced in South Africa as the Impala.

Below One of two Macchi M67 floatplanes at the 1929 Schneider contest.

Bottom A Macchi MC200 Saetta in Sicily in 1940.

DB 601 in-line engine and had a more streamlined fuselage, but wings and tailplane were the same as the MC200's. The new fighter proved to be both fast and manoeuvrable and it served in Italy, North Africa and on the Eastern Front. Total production was 1105 and after the Italian Armistice of 1943 the type served with both sides, in the Co-Belligerent air force and in the Fascist Aviazione della RSI. The MC202 was certainly one of the best Italian wartime fighters, but the DB 605-powered MC205V and MC205N were even better, although only the former entered service. After

World War II Macchi built various foreign aircraft under licence, including the de Havilland Vampire, and then achieved some success with its own MB326 and MB339 trainer designs.

McDONNELL

The McDonnell company, which as the St Louis division of McDonnell Douglas is today one of the United States' foremost manufacturers of fighter aircraft, was not formed until 1939. During World War II its XP-67 escort fighter did not progress beyond the prototype stage and it was not until 1946 that a McDonnell aircraft went into production. This was the FH-1 Phantom, the US Navy's first carrier-based jet fighter. It was followed in 1949 by the improved F2H Banshee, which served with the US Navy, US Marine Corps and Royal Canadian Navy and saw combat during the Korean War. In the late 1940s McDonnell produced the F-85 Goblin fighter for the USAF. It was intended to be carried beneath a Convair B-36 bomber to provide escort for the parent craft and consequently was the smallest jet fighter ever built. The project was cancelled, however, before any F-85s entered service.

The F3H Demon fighter entered service aboard US

Navy carriers in 1957, after overcoming early development problems which had delayed its deployment for four years. It served as a missile-armed interceptor, as an attack aircraft and in the photographic reconnaissance role until its retirement in the mid-1960s. The USAF's F-101 Voodoo also entered service in 1957, serving as a tactical fighter and reconnaissance aircraft. A two-seat interceptor version was also built for service with the USAF's Aerospace Defense Command and the Canadian armed forces, these remaining in service until the early 1980s.

In 1958 the prototype of a two-seat naval interceptor first flew, entering US Navy service in 1961 as the F4H Phantom II. Redesignated F-4 in the following year, Phantoms have served aboard US Navy carriers ever since, but are due to be replaced by F-18s in the mid-1980s. The US Marine Corps has also operated the type, including the RF-4B reconnaissance version, which only that service flies. In 1961 the USAF adopted the Phantom as its standard tactical fighter and tactical reconnaissance aircraft. Phantoms of all three services were in combat over Southeast Asia and they

were flown by the major aces of both the USAF and US Navy. Phantoms have been widely exported, the most important foreign customers including the United Kingdom, West Germany, Israel and Japan.

In 1972 a new high-performance, single-seat fighter,

Top *The first variant of the McDonnell F-4E Phantom multi-role fighter to have a built-in gun armament was the USAF's F-4E, with an M61 Vulcan 20mm cannon mounted beneath the nose.*

Above centre *The two-seat McDonnell Douglas F-15B conversion trainer retained much of the combat capability of the single-seat fighter versions of the F-15 Eagle.*

Above *McDonnell F2H-2 Banshees of the US Marine Corps aboard the USS Franklin D. Roosevelt. The Banshee made its first flight in January 1947 and the type saw action in the Korean War.*

Left *The McDonnell Douglas F-18 Hornet is intended to replace Phantoms and Vought A-7s in service with the US Navy and it is also on order for the US Marine Corps.*

the F-15 Eagle, made its first flight, and deliveries of production aircraft to the USAF began two years later. Capable of flying at a speed of Mach 2·5, the Eagle is a highly manoevrable fighter primarily intended for the air superiority mission. However, the USAF will also operate it in the interceptor role and is currently evaluating the modified F-15E as a strike fighter. The service's total requirement is for over 900 Eagles, and export customers include Israel (which flew the fighter in action against Syria in 1979 and 1982), Saudi Arabia and Japan. The F-18 Hornet naval fighter entered service with the US Navy and US Marine Corps in 1982 and export versions will equip the air forces of Canada, Australia and Spain. McDonnell Douglas will also supply both the US Marine Corps and the RAF with an advanced version (designated AV-8B) of the Harrier V/STOL fighter.

MARTIN

The company founded by Glenn L. Martin in 1909 was chiefly noted for its bomber designs. However, his first contract from the US Army Air Service was for 17 Model TT trainers, which were produced in 1914–16. Then in 1918 ten twin-engined bombers, designated GMB or MB-1, were ordered. One of them completed the first flight around the borders of the United States, a distance of 15,800km (9800 miles) in 1918. Others competed in the National Air Races of 1922–4 with some success. The bomber was also ordered in small numbers by the US Navy as a torpedo-carrier. In 1920 the improved MB-2 was ordered by the USAAS, taking part in Mitchell's bombing trials against the *Ostfriesland* in the following year. A total of 130 served with the USAAS (renamed the US

Dutch operated this bomber against the Japanese in the East Indies in 1941–2. In the early 1930s Martin began building flying boats, the PM and P3M types being built for the US Navy. Then in 1935 the four-engined M-130 flying boats went into service with Pan American Airways. The M-130s operated trans-Pacific mail and passenger services until the outbreak of war with Japan.

During World War II Martin built both bombers and flying boats. Its Model 167 twin-engined bomber served with the Armée de l'Air and with the RAF as the Maryland during the early war years. The RAF also operated the twin-engined Baltimore, over 1200 of which were built. The B-26 Marauder began its operational service in 1942, flying from bases in the United Kingdom, Italy and, from mid-1944, France. Its early reputation earned it the nickname of 'Widow Maker', yet by the end of the war the Marauder was

Army Air Corps after 1926) until 1928. Martin also built various warplanes for the US Navy in the 1920s, including the MO-1 observation aircraft, the MS Scout seaplane and the SC and T3M torpedo-bombers. In the early 1930s the company produced the BM naval torpedo- and dive-bomber.

The Martin B-10 bomber of 1932 was an all-metal, twin-engined monoplane, capable of flying at a speed of more than 320km/h (200mph). The USAAC ordered 178 B-10s, which remained in service until the late 1930s, and a further 189 were built for export. The

Above *The Martin 404 twin-engined airliner appeared in 1950.*

Left *The US Army Air Corps' first all-metal monoplane bomber was the Martin B-10 of 1932.*

Below left *USAAF Martin B-26 Marauders of the 1st Tactical Air Force on a bombing mission in 1945.*

Below *The four-jet Martin P6M Seamaster flying boat.*

generally considered to be one of the best USAAF tactical bombers. The twin-engined PMB Mariner patrol flying boat also served in considerable numbers from 1941, over 1300 being built, and they remained in use in the 1950s. The huge JRM Mars of 1942 was produced in small numbers and was the US Navy's largest flying boat.

After World War II Martin produced the Mauler carrier-based attack aircraft and the Mercator patrol bomber in small numbers for the US Navy. The Model 202 twin-engined airliner appeared in 1946 and was developed into the Model 404. In 1952 the first P5M Marlin patrol flying boats were delivered and

when the last of these retired in 1966, it marked the end of the US Navy's front-line employment of flying boats. An intended successor, the four-jet P6M Seamaster, did not progress beyond prototype stage. Martin's last bomber aircraft was the USAF's B-57 variant of the British Canberra, which served from 1957 until the Air National Guard gave up its last Canberras in 1982. Today the name of Martin is primarily associated with missile and space systems.

Opposite page, top *The Martin MB-1 bomber first flew in August 1918.*

Below *The Messerschmitt Bf 109E was the Luftwaffe's standard fighter aircraft during the early campaigns of World War II, including the Battle of Britain.*

MESSERSCHMITT

The Messerschmitt company, which produced the famous Bf 109 fighter, was the largest German aircraft manufacturing business in World War II. It was formed in 1938 from the earlier Bayerische Flugzeugwerke (hence the Bf designation used for the early Messerschmitt designs). Willy Messerschmitt's early aircraft were gliders and light transports, but in 1935 he produced the Bf 109 monoplane single-engined fighter for the newly emergent Luftwaffe. The early

Above right *Underwing 30mm cannon were fitted to some Messerschmitt Bf 109G sub-variants for the bomber-destroyer role, although they seriously impaired the aircraft's manoeuvrability.*

Right *The Messerschmitt Bf 110 was intended as a Zerstörer, or heavy fighter.*

Below *This Messerschmitt Bf 109G fighter-bomber carries Jagdgeschwader 3's emblem on the engine cowling.*

Junkers Jumo-engined Bf 109B models entered service in 1937 and in the middle of that year were despatched to the Condor Legion in Spain. There they quickly regained the ascendancy lost to the Republicans' Soviet-supplied Polikarpov I-15 and I-16 fighters. By the time of the Munich Crisis in September 1938, the Luftwaffe had 171 Messerschmitt Bf 109B, C and D fighters on strength.

When Germany invaded Poland in September 1939 the early model Bf 109 fighters were giving way to the Bf 109E. Powered by a 1100hp Daimler-Benz DB 601 and armed with two wing-mounted or a single engine-mounted 20mm cannon, the Bf 109E was a formidable fighter aircraft. It easily outclassed most of the opposing fighters in the Luftwaffe's early campaigns of World War II and only when matched with the RAF's Supermarine Spitfires over Dunkirk and during the Battle of Britain was it up against an

opponent of equal calibre. During the Battle of Britain the Bf 109E's principal weakness was its short range, which limited it to flying bomber escort and fighter sweep missions only over south-east England even when operating from forward bases on the Channel coast. A fighter-bomber variant of the Bf 109E appeared during the Battle and camera-equipped tactical reconnaissance versions were also produced.

In 1941 the Luftwaffe introduced the improved Bf 109F into front-line service and during the course of the year the new fighter gradually replaced the Bf 109Es. It proved to be a match for the RAF's new Spitfire Mk V and completely outclassed the Soviet fighters encountered during the early months of the assault on the Soviet Union. Towards the end of the year Bf 109Fs reached North Africa, where Jagd-

geschwader 27 was providing fighter support for the German and Italian ground forces. The unit enjoyed considerable success against less advanced fighters such as the Curtiss Tomahawk and Hawker Hurricane, and its leading pilot, Hauptmann Hans-Joachim Marseille, became the top-scoring Luftwaffe fighter pilot in the West. The Bf 109G of 1942 was less successful, largely because it was weighed down with a heavy cannon armament and so lost the sparkling performance of the earlier fighters. Nonetheless, it was produced in greater numbers than any other model of the Bf 109 and a bewildering number of variants appeared with numerous modifications to improve performance or armament. It was in a vain attempt to rationalize this situation that the last major production model of the Bf 109, the Bf 109K, was introduced in 1944. When production of the Bf 109 ended in 1945 a total of approximately 35,000 had been built.

The Bf 110 twin-engined fighter of 1936 was intended to be a long-range escort fighter, but it did not perform well in this role. Indeed during the Battle of Britain Bf 110s themselves required a fighter escort. Despite this, a total of 6000 were produced, including fighter-bomber and reconnaissance versions, but the aircraft's most important role was to be night fighting. The Bf 110's intended successor, the Me 210, was a technical failure and so Bf 110s remained in front-line service with the *Nachtjagdgeschwaderen* until the end of World War II. The later Me 410 took over the daylight heavy fighter roles of bomber-destroyer, reconnaissance and fighter-bomber, and over 1000 were built in 1942–4.

Two of Germany's most advanced aircraft in the closing years of World War II were the Me 163 rocket fighter and the Me 262 twin-turbojet fighter. The Me 163 first went into action in the summer of 1944,

Above *The rocket-powered Messerschmitt Me 163 Komet interceptor was operated by Jagdgeschwader 400 in 1944–5.*

Opposite, top left *The Soviet MiG-15 fighter first flew in 1947. The aircraft pictured is in North Korean air force markings.*

Opposite, top right *The MiG-19 was the first supersonic fighter to serve with any air arm. A Chinese-built Shenyang F-6 is shown in service with the Pakistan air force.*

Below *The MiG-3 interceptor fighter was built in considerable numbers for the Soviet air force between 1940 and 1942.*

Bottom *This twin-jet Messerschmitt Me 262 served with Kampfgeschwader 54 in the fighter-bomber role.*

but its volatile rocket fuel made it a very dangerous aircraft to operate and only small numbers saw operational service. The Me 262 was an even more advanced design. It was powered by two Jumo 004 turbojets which gave it a top speed of 870km/h (540mph). Over 1400 were built but considerably less than half of these reached front-line units before the end of the war. Different versions of the basic interceptor were produced for the reconnaissance, fighter-bomber and night-fighter roles. However, too few were available to affect the outcome of the air battles and in any case the jet engines proved to be unreliable in service. Today the name of Messerschmitt is perpetuated by the West German Messerschmitt-Boelkow-Blohm company, specializing in helicopter construction.

MiG

The designation MiG, which has become virtually synonymous with Soviet fighter aircraft, is formed from the names of two fighter designers, Artyom Mikoyan and Mikhail Gurevich. The two men first cooperated with the design of the MiG-1 fighter of 1940. This was a fast-climbing, single-seat interceptor aircraft, but it lacked manoeuvrability and firepower. Nonetheless, over 3000 examples of the MiG-1 and the similar MiG-3 were built in 1940–42. At the time of the German invasion of the Soviet Union in June 1941 the MiG-3-equipped fighter regiments were deployed in defence of major cities. They enjoyed some success against the Luftwaffe's bombers, for example the fighter regiments defending Odessa claimed 40 Ger-

man aircraft destroyed on the first day of the campaign. However, in general the MiG fighter was outclassed by its opponents and was certainly no match for the Luftwaffe's Messerschmitt Bf 109.

In view of the design bureau's later successes, it is surprising that no other MiG fighters saw service in World War II. The next warplane to be produced for the Soviet air force was the MiG-9 of 1946. This was powered by a Soviet copy of the German BMW 003A turbojet and some 500 examples were produced. Although it was not a particularly effective design it

did provide the Soviet air force with early experience of operating turbojet fighters. The MiG-15 of 1947 was an altogether more formidable fighter. A swept-wing design, powered by the RD-45 turbojet (a Soviet copy of the Rolls-Royce Nene), MiG-15s saw considerable action in the Korean War (1950–53) against USAF North American F-86 Sabres. Although possessing a considerably better altitude performance and a heavier armament (two 23mm and one 37mm cannon on later models), the MiG-15 was consistently outfought by the pilots of the USAF. By the end of hostilities in Korea, ten MiG-15s had been lost for every F-86 Sabre destroyed by a MiG.

The MiG-17 of 1950 was an attempt to produce a supersonic development of the MiG-15. Yet although it failed in this aim, it was nevertheless an effective fighter aircraft which was produced in quantity for the Soviet air force and widely exported. All-weather fighter versions were produced, as well as the standard day fighter, and MiG-17s were built under licence in China, Poland and Czechoslovakia. In the mid-1980s it remains in service with the air force of the People's Liberation Army in China. The twin-engined MiG-19 of 1953 was the first fighter in Soviet service capable of exceeding the speed of sound in level flight. The

Above A MiG-17PF all-weather fighter of the Czech air force.

Below During its production life the MiG-21 has been progressively improved. One of the later versions is this MiG-21MF Fishbed-J.

MiG-19 had been phased out of front-line service with the Warsaw Pact by the end of the 1970s, but it remains in production in China in the mid-1980s.

The most famous of all the MiG fighters, the MiG-21, first appeared in 1956. It is of tailed-delta configuration and combines high manoeuvrability with a maximum speed of Mach 2. It has been produced in numerous versions and widely exported. The early MiG-21s were short-range interceptors suitable for use in fair weather only. Later models have an all-weather capability and undertake a secondary ground-attack mission. However, the MiG-21's lack of range is a problem which has never been satisfactorily solved. As well as the primary fighter variants, tactical reconnaissance and two-seat conversion trainers have been produced. MiG-21s have been built under licence in India, the first Soviet aircraft to be produced by a non-Communist state, and Soviet-built examples have been exported to many nations.

The MiG-23 variable-geometry-wing fighter had completely replaced the earlier MiG-21s in the Soviet air defence regiments by the early 1980s. At the same time it became the most numerous tactical fighter in the Soviet air force's Frontal Aviation command. In addition to the MiG-23 interceptor and air superiority fighter, a specialized ground-attack version, the

MiG-27, was produced. Over 2500 MiG-23s and MiG-27s were in Soviet service in the early 1980s and the type had been exported to the Soviet Union's Warsaw Pact allies and other foreign air arms.

Codenamed Foxbat by NATO, the MiG-25 high-altitude interceptor was originally produced to counter the USAF'S North American B-70 Valkyrie bomber (which in fact never entered service). The MiG-25 can reach a maximum speed of over Mach 3 and is armed with four air-to-air missiles. An improved two-seat version, able to engage low-flying targets, entered service in 1982, and the single-seat version has been modified for reconnaissance use. More than 400 Foxbats were in service with the Soviet air force in 1983, the majority of them being interceptor versions.

Although Mikoyan died in 1970 and his partner Gurevich died six years later, the MiG design bureau remains in being. Its latest fighter, the MiG-29 (NATO codename Fulcrum) was reported to be undergoing flight testing in 1983. It is a twin-engined, multi-role tactical fighter and is likely to enter service in the mid-1980s.

MIL

The Soviet helicopter designer Mikhail Mil is best remembered for his very large transport helicopters, which include the biggest machines of their kind in the world. During the mid-1930s he was involved in the design of the A-12 and A-15 autogiros and in 1947 he began the design of a three- or four-seat helicopter, which was put into production in 1949 as the Mi-1. The helicopter served both as a military liaison and observation machine and in various civil roles, including that of air ambulance, agricultural crop sprayer and traffic control. Mil's next helicopter, the Mi-4, was a

much larger rotorcraft, capable of carrying 12 passengers. Its primary role was as a military assault transport, but civil roles have included scheduled passenger services and support of construction work in undeveloped regions of the Soviet Union.

The Mi-6 heavy-lift helicopter of 1957 was the largest helicopter in the world at the time of its appearance and it was to remain the largest helicopter in operational use until 1978. Powered by twin turbines, the Mi-6 was capable of lifting an externally slung load of 9000kg (19,800lb). Its roles included civil and mili-

tary cargo transport, civil engineering support and troop transport. The Mi-10 of 1960 is a 'flying crane' development of the Mi-6, which lacks the latter design's capacious cargo cabin but can carry underslung loads of up to 8000kg (17,600lb).

In the early 1960s Mil designed turbine-powered replacements for the piston-engined Mi-1 and Mi-4. The Mi-2 light helicopter was produced in Poland, rather than in the Soviet Union. The Mi-8 cargo and personnel transport was a twin-turbine design that first flew in 1962. It could carry 32 passengers or 4000kg (8800lb) of cargo. Total production of the Mi-8 was some 1200 and the helicopter was exported to many countries for both civil and military operations. An

Above The MiG-23 Flogger-G interceptor is one of a family of Soviet fighter aircraft, which includes the Mig-27 ground-attack fighter and two-seat training aircraft.

Above The Mil Mi-4 utility and tactical troop transport helicopter with accommodation for 14 passengers first appeared in 1950. The Mi-4 pictured served with the Finnish air force.

amphibious anti-submarine helicopter version, designated Mi-14, was produced for the Soviet navy, which operates the type from shore bases.

The Mi-24 (NATO codename Hind) assault transport helicopter first appeared in 1973 and serves in considerable numbers with the Soviet air force's Frontal Aviation command in the 1980s. The Hind-A version carries a squad of troops and is heavily armed with machine guns, unguided rockets and anti-tank missiles. Specialized 'gunship' versions of the Hind are in service, armed with rapid-fire, heavy-calibre machine guns in chin turrets (mounted under the nose). In 1968

Above When the Mil Mi-6 helicopter first appeared in 1957, it was the largest machine of its kind in the world. The example illustrated is in the colours of the Soviet state airline Aeroflot.

Above right The Mitsubishi A5M Claude was the Japanese navy air force's first fighter monoplane. It saw action in China but had been largely superseded by the A6M Zero at the end of 1941.

MITSUBISHI

The Mitsubishi company's most famous aeroplane was the A6M Zero fighter of World War II, which did much to establish Japanese ascendancy in the air during the early years of the war in the Pacific. The company's first involvement with aeroplane production came in 1920 with a contract to build Nieuport trainers under licence. There followed two original designs, the 1MF1 single-seat fighter and 2MR1 reconnaissance air-

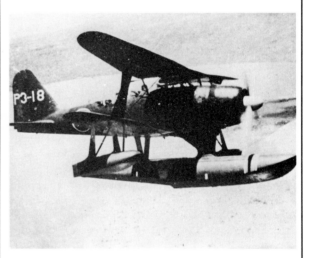

the massive Mil V-12 appeared and it remains the world's largest helicopter. It has demonstrated the ability to lift a payload of 40,205kg (88,635lb), but technical problems with the design prevented it entering service. The Mi-26 flying crane, with a payload of nearly double that of the Mi-6 and the ability to airlift 100 troops, entered service in the early 1980s. A true design pioneer, Mikhail Mil died in 1970, but the design bureau that he founded perpetuates his name.

Above The Mil Mi-8 helicopter serves with the Pakistan army as an assault transport and fulfils the same role in the Soviet air force's Frontal Aviation command.

Above right The Mitsubishi F1M floatplane, codenamed Pete by the Americans, saw considerable service in the Pacific War, operating from cruisers, seaplane tenders and coastal bases.

Left The Mil Mi-24 Hind-A assault helicopter can carry a squad of eight troops and is heavily armed with air-to-ground rockets and anti-tank missiles carried on stub wings.

craft, intended for service with the Imperial Japanese navy's first aircraft carrier, the *Hosho*. The B1M1 and B1M2 torpedo-bombers were produced in large numbers (over 400) and this type remained in service until the late 1930s. All these early naval warplanes were the work of the former Sopwith designer Herbert Smith. The company's first successful aeroplane to be produced by a Japanese designer, Joji Hattori, was the K3M crew trainer of 1930. Over 500 of these high-wing monoplanes were built and they remained in service until the end of World War II. However, foreign design influence remained strong, as was shown by the Junkers-inspired Ki-1 and Ki-2 bombers, which saw combat over China in the 1930s.

In 1934 Mitsubishi produced a long-range, land-based bomber to meet a Japanese navy requirement. This was the G3M Nell, a twin-engined aircraft, over 1000 of which were produced. The G3M's most notable achievement was the sinking of the British warships *Repulse* and *Prince of Wales* off the coast of Malaya on 10 December 1941. This attack involved a flight of 1450km (900 miles) for the bombers, which

were based near Saigon in Indochina. Similar long-distance raids had been caried out over China in the late 1930s, but the G3M's career in World War II was comparatively short as by 1943 it had been superseded by later designs. The A5M carrier-fighter's combat career was even shorter, as it only saw service briefly during the initial Japanese attack on the Philippines. Although Mitsubishi was primarily a supplier of naval aircraft, a number of types were built for the army air force. Most notable of these was the Ki-21 Sally twin-engined bomber, 2064 of which were built, and they served throughout the war. Another long-serving Mitsubishi type was the Navy's F1M Pete observation floatplane.

In 1939 the A6M Zero appeared and in the following year early production examples saw combat over China. It was the Japanese navy's standard carrier-based fighter throughout the Pacific War, taking part in all the great naval air battles, and land-based A6Ms fought over the Philippines and the East Indies. Eventually some 11,000 A6M Zeros were manufac-

tured and the type remained in production until the end of the war, although by then it was totally out-classed by such Allied fighters as the Grumman F6F Hellcat and North American P-51 Mustang. Only ten examples of the A6M's intended replacement, the A7M, were ever built. Mitsubishi's Ki-57 twin-engined transport aircraft was another type to see con-siderable wartime service and some 500 were built between 1940 and 1945. The Ki-46 Dinah reconnais-sance aircraft, also built as an interceptor, was produced in quantity (total production was 1742). It was a sleek, high-performance aeroplane with an operational range of 2475km (1540 miles).

The Mitsubishi G4M land-based bomber entered service with the Japanese navy in 1941 and remained in service until the Japanese surrender. It was the work-horse of the naval bomber squadrons and was later used as a transport and to carry the Ohka suicide aircraft. Total production was 2479, and it was two aircraft of this type that carried the Japanese delegation to the sur-render conference on the island of Ie-Shima in August 1945. Although the G4M had a maximum range of over 5950km (3700 miles), this performance was only achieved at the expense of protection for the crew and fuel tanks. Consequently losses on operations were high. In 1942 the J2M Jack, a fast-climbing interceptor, made its maiden flight. It entered service in December the following year and was primarily used to protect Japanese bases in the Pacific and for defence of the homeland. The Ki-67 Peggy bomber entered service

Above left A camouflaged Mitsubishi Ki-21 Sally moments before its destruction by a parachute-retarded fragmentation bomb. The Ki-21 was built in considerable numbers for the Japanese army air force.

Left The Mitsubishi A6M Zero fighter achieved considerable success with the Japanese navy air force in the first year of the Pacific War, operating both from aircraft carriers and shore bases.

Above The Mitsubishi J2M (American codename Jack) was a fast-climbing interceptor aircraft. It first flew in March 1942 and some 500 were built.

Left One of the fastest Japanese twin-engined aircraft of World War II was the Mitsubishi Ki-46 Dinah reconnaissance aeroplane, which first appeared in 1939.

Opposite page, bottom At the outbreak of World War II the Morane-Saulnier MS406 was the Armée de l'Air's standard fighter aircraft with over 500 of them in service.

with the army air force in 1944 and unlike most Japanese wartime aircraft it combined high performance with adequate protection for fuel tanks and crew. A total of nearly 700 had been built by the end of the war.

In the postwar years Mitsubishi has re-emerged as a major Japanese aircraft manufacturer. Apart from building American warplanes under licence, it has produced more than 500 of the indigenously designed MU-2 twin-turboprop light transport. Other original designs include the T-2 advanced jet trainer for the Air Self-Defence Force and the related F-1 close-support fighter.

MORANE-SAULNIER

The partnership between the French aviation pioneers Léon Morane and Raymond Saulnier began before World War I and during that conflict the firm became noted for such designs as the Type N monoplane fighter and the Type L parasol-wing monoplane two-seater. It was the latter type that Roland Garros flew during his early fighter combats and in which Flight Sub-Lieutenant Rex Warneford RNAS won his VC.

Above *The Morane-Saulnier Type I was a development of the Type N single-seat fighter, but only few were produced.*

Right *A Dutch-registered civil version of the Morane-Saulnier MS760 Paris, which first flew in 1954.*

Below *The Morane-Saulnier Type LA, an improved version of the Type L, first appeared in 1914.*

Another important parasol-wing monoplane, the Type AI single-seat fighter, entered French service in 1917 and more than 1200 were produced. The company continued to develop the parasol-wing formula during the inter-war years with such types as the MS225 fighter and the MS230 and MS315 trainers.

In 1935 the MS405 fighter appeared, which in its production version as the MS406 was to be the Armée de l'Air's standard single-seat fighter at the outbreak of World War II. Although eventually more than 1000 were to be built, the MS406 was completely outclassed by the German Messerschmitt Bf 109E during the Battle of France. Export customers for the MS406 included Switzerland and Finland, the Finns producing a version of the MS406 powered by captured Soviet M105P

engines in place of the standard Hispano-Suiza 12Y.

After the war Morane-Saulnier produced the MS733 Alcyon trainer for the Armée de l'Air, armed versions of which saw action in Algeria. The French armed forces and Brazil also bought the MS760 Paris twin-jet personnel transport. The company's greatest postwar success was the MS880 Rallye light aircraft for the private pilot, which first flew in 1959. Yet the popularity of this design did not prevent the disappearance of the Morane-Saulnier company in 1966.

NAKAJIMA

The Nakajima company, best known for its wartime fighters for the Japanese army air force, was founded in 1918. Most of its early business involved the licence production of such types as the Avro 504, Nieuport NiD 29 and Breguet 19 for the Japanese forces. However, the company's own Type 91 parasol-wing fighter was produced for the army in the early 1930s and eventually 450 examples were built. In the same period the

Type 94 reconnaissance biplane was built for the army and the E8N shipboard spotter aircraft for the navy. In 1937 the Ki-27 Nate fixed-undercarriage, monoplane fighter was ordered by the army. A total of more than 2000 were built and they saw action over China and over Malaya and Burma in 1941–2.

Nakajima's B5N carrier torpedo-bomber (of which 1149 were built) played a notable part in the attack on Pearl Harbor and the early Pacific War carrier battles. The Ki-49 Helen bomber was entering army service at the outbreak of war and was widely used.

Below left *The Nakajima Ki-27 Nate entered service with the Japanese army air force in 1938.*

Centre left *The Nakajima Ki-43 Oscar was produced in considerable numbers for the Japanese army air force. This ski-equipped version served in Manchuria.*

Bottom left *The most outstanding Japanese fighter of World War II in terms of performance was the army's Ki-84 Frank.*

Below *This Nieuport Nie 16 fighter of the Aviation Militaire is armed with Le Prieur incendiary rockets, which were used against enemy observation balloons.*

Bottom *The Nie 28 was used by the United States Army Air Service in France during 1918. A civil-registered example is illustrated.*

Even more significant was the Ki-43 single-seat fighter, the army's counterpart of the naval A6M Zero. This fighter achieved many successes against Allied aircraft during the early years of the Pacific War and eventually 5919 were built. The Ki-44 was primarily an interceptor fighter, which first saw action in 1942 and later played an important part in the defence of the homeland. In 1944 Nakajima produced the superb Ki-84 Frank fighter, which was the equal of any Allied fighter. When production ended at the end of the war some 3500 had been built. The company also built Japan's first jet aircraft, the Kikka, which flew in August 1945.

NIEUPORT

The name of Nieuport is invariably associated with the company's graceful single-seat fighter aircraft of World War I and the inter-war years. The Société Anonyme des Establissements Nieuport was formed in 1909 and its first designs were monoplane racers.

In 1914 the Nie 10 two-seat biplane appeared and from this design was developed the Nieuport 11 fighter of 1915, which was to succeed in mastering the German Fokker Eindecker. The type served with the French Aviation Militaire and Britain's Royal Flying Corps and Royal Naval Air Service, as did its successors the Nie 17 and Nie 24. The Nieuport 28 was less successful, but it did serve with the newly arrived US Army Air Service fighter squadron in France during 1918.

The Nieuport-Delage 29 of 1918 was too late to see wartime service, but it served with the Aviation Militaire for a decade and was exported to Belgium, Italy, Spain, Sweden and Japan. The NiD 42 and NiD 52 sesquiplane fighters (with upper wing of greater span than the lower) were built in small numbers, the latter type seeing service during the Spanish Civil War. They led to the NiD 62 series, 725 of which were built for the Armée de l'Air. This type was the standard French fighter aircraft until the late 1930s and a few remained in service at the outbreak of war in September 1939. In 1933 the company amalgamated with Loire to form Loire-Nieuport. Its last aircraft design was the LN 410 and LN 411 dive-bomber, the former being carrier-based and the latter land-based. The land-based type was in action during the Battle of France.

NORTH AMERICAN

Formed in the mid-1930s as a successor to General Aviation (formerly the American Fokker Aircraft Corporation), North American Aviation is famous for the outstanding P-51 Mustang and F-86 Sabre fighters and the AT-6 or Harvard trainer. Its first successful design was the NA-16, which was ordered for the US Army Air Corps as the BT-1 standard basic trainer. The later BC-1 introduced a retractable undercarriage and was redesigated AT-6 as an advanced trainer. It served with the USAAF and US Navy (who designated it SNJ) throughout World War II and as the RAF's Harvard it played a leading role in the Empire

Air Training Scheme. More than 16,000 were eventually built and the type remained in widespread military use until the 1960s. Less successful was the O-47 observation aircraft, which entered service in 1937 but had largely disappeared from front-line units by the time that the United States entered World War II.

In 1941 the twin-engined B-25 Mitchell medium bomber entered service with the USAAF and in the following year this type took part in the Doolittle raid on Tokyo, becoming the first American aircraft to operate against the Japanese homeland. Mitchells served with the USAAF in both the Pacific and European theatres of war and they also served with bomber units of the US Navy and US Marine Corps. Production totalled nearly 11,000 examples. In 1941 the first

Top The Nie 29 became the Aviation Militaire's standard single-seat fighter in the 1920s.

Centre The North American AT-6, known by the RAF as the Harvard, was one of the most widely used training aircraft of World War II and the immediate postwar years. This example is a civil-registered Norwegian Harvard.

Above A North American B-25D Mitchell bomber of the USAAF's 340th Bomb Group, releases its bomb load over a target in Italy.

Mustang fighters entered service with the RAF. However, it was not until the early aircraft's Allison V1710 engine had been replaced by the Rolls-Royce Merlin that the fighter realized its full potential. The Merlin-engined P-51Bs began to escort the bombers of the USAAF's Eighth Air Force from December 1943 onwards and in the following year they performed the same service for the Boeing B-29s attacking Japan. During the Korean War of 1950–53 Mustangs served as ground-attack aircraft and the F-82 Twin Mustang scored the first American aerial victory of that conflict. Over 15,500 P-51 Mustangs were built and the fighter remained in service with the USAF until 1957.

North American's B-45 Tornado was the first four-jet bomber to enter USAF service, which it did in 1948,

Above *North American P-51D Mustangs of the Italian-based 52nd Fighter Group during World War II.*

Left *The North American F-82 Twin Mustang was produced by joining two P-51Hs.*

Right *The North American OV-10 Bronco first flew in 1965.*

Above *A North American F-86F of the Japanese Air Self-Defence Force.*

Left *A North American F-100C of the USAF's Thunderbird aerobatic team.*

Below *A North American RA-5C Vigilante operating from USS America.*

and the type also served in the reconnaissance role. Another first was claimed by the FJ-1 Fury fighter, which was the first carrier fighter to serve at sea with an operational, rather than a trials, unit. However, the company's greatest success of the postwar years came with the F-86 Sabre swept-wing jet fighter, which accounted for a total of 792 MiG-15s destroyed during the Korean War for the loss of only 78 Sabres. Nearly 7000 Sabres were built by the parent company alone, with licence manufacture being undertaken in Canada, Australia, Italy and Japan. At peak strength in 1955, no fewer than 44 USAF wings operated the Sabre, which was produced in day-fighter, all-weather

fighter, tactical reconnaissance and fighter-bomber versions. A parallel design, the FJ2/FJ4 Fury carrier-fighter, was produced in quantity for the US Navy and Marine Corps. In the early 1950s both the USAF and US Navy ordered the T-28 piston-engined trainer and at the end of the decade the navy acquired the twin-jet T-2 Buckeye trainer.

The first operational fighter capable of flying at supersonic speed in level flight was the F-100 Super Sabre, which entered USAF service in 1953. Towards the end of its operational life this fighter played an important part in the war in Southeast Asia, where it was the USAF's principal close-support fighter. Another Vietnam veteran was the navy's A-5 Vigilante, originally built as a carrier-based nuclear-strike bomber, which served throughout the war as a reconnaissance aircraft. Experience in Vietnam also influenced the design of the OV-10 Bronco forward air control aircraft, which was produced for the USAF, US Navy and US Marine Corps in the late 1960s. North American's successor company, Rockwell International, is developing the new strategic bomber, the B-1B, for the USAF, and this is due to become operational in 1988.

NORTHROP

When the Northrop Aircraft Company was formed in 1929, its founder John Northrop was already an experienced designer, having worked on the Douglas World Cruiser and produced the Lockheed Vega. His first design to appear under the name of Northrop was the Alpha seven-seat airliner of 1930. This was the first

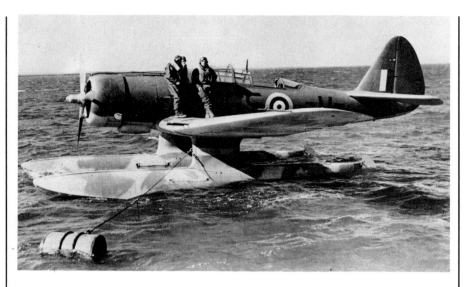

the Pacific and European theatres of war and nearly 700 were built.

In 1946 Northrop's radical new B-35 flying-wing bomber flew in prototype form. It was followed by the jet-powered YB-49 in 1947, but no production orders were received for either of these flying-wing designs. However, the USAF did order a small batch of C-125 Raider trimotor transports in 1948. In the same year the F-89 Scorpion two-seat jet night fighter first flew, and the type entered service in 1951. When Scorpion production ended in 1957 a total of 1050 had been produced. Northrop also produced the intercontinental-range Snark cruise missile for the USAF at this time.

Another substantial USAF order came in 1959, when the T-38A Talon supersonic jet trainer was put into production. A total of 1189 were built and they

metal stressed-skin aircraft to go into production, and it led to the later Beta, Delta and Gamma designs. The Northrop XBT-2 naval dive-bomber prototype was eventually developed by Douglas into the Dauntless. The same company also developed Northrop's A-17 light bomber. However, John Northrop refused to be swallowed up by the larger Douglas company and,

Above A Northrop N3PB floatplane in Iceland during World War II.

Right A Northrop F-5F of the Iranian air force. The F-5F is a two-seat trainer version of the F-5E.

serve as the standard USAF advanced jet trainer. The Talon was derived fom the N-156 private venture fighter aircraft and this machine also went into production as the F-5A Freedom Fighter. Although a few served with the USAF for combat evaluation in Vietnam, the majority of more than 1000 built were supplied to foreign air arms. Among the recipients were Canada, the Netherlands, Brazil, Greece, Jordan, Saudi Arabia and Turkey. The improved F-5E appeared in 1970 and as well as being supplied to numerous foreign air forces it was put into service with the USAF's Aggressor Squadrons to simulate Soviet fighters during air combat training. The latest member of the F-5 family, the F404-powered F-20 (formerly F-5G) Tigershark, first flew in 1982. Also under development in conditions of great secrecy is the Advanced Technology Bomber, which makes use of 'Stealth' techniques to avoid detection by enemy radars.

when his original enterprise became the Douglas El Segundo division, he broke away to form the new Northrop Aircraft Inc. in 1939. This company's first design was the N-3PB floatplane for the Norwegian government, which served with No 330 (Norwegian) Squadron of the RAF after the German invasion of Norway. More substantial orders were received for the P-61 Black Widow night fighter, which first flew in 1941. This aircraft served with the USAAF in both

Above The Northrop Alpha of 1930 was a seven-seat airliner, which went into service with Trans World Airlines.

Below The Northrop T-38A supersonic advanced trainer serves with seven USAF flying training wings. This example was supplied to the Portuguese air force.

PIPER

It has been estimated that the Piper Aircraft Corporation has been responsible for producing one out of every ten aeroplanes ever built. The foundations of this remarkable success were laid in 1930 when William Piper bought the Taylor Brothers Aircraft Corporation and began to market the high-wing Cub lightplane. This aeroplane quickly established itself as the top-selling American private aircraft, and during World War II, as the L-4 Grasshopper, it became the US Army's standard artillery-spotting and liaison light aircraft. Postwar production of the Cub continued

Left *During World War II the Piper L-4 Grasshopper, a variant of the Civil Cub, served the US Army as a liaison and artillery-spotting lightplane. This example is preserved in wartime colours.*

Below left *The Piper Tripacer of 1951 introduced a tricycle rather than a tailwheel undercarriage. As it was a relatively easy aeroplane to fly it soon achieved popularity.*

Below *The Piper Cherokee Six, a stretched version of the original PA-28, first flew in 1963. The aircraft pictured is a Canadian-registered floatplane.*

with the PA-18 and PA-21 Super Cub and by the mid-1970s over 27,000 Cubs had been manufactured. In 1952 the twin-engined PA-23 Apache appeared and its low cost won it many orders in competition with the Cessna 310 and Beech Twin Bonanza. The single-engined Tri-Pacer, fitted with a tricycle rather than a tailwheel undercarriage, was also produced in considerable numbers and it led to the Colt two-seat training aircraft of 1960.

With the Apache and Tri-Pacer both well established, Piper then produced the single-engined PA-24 Comanche. This design, with seating for four and a retractable undercarriage, filled the gap between the relatively simple Tri-Pacer and the more expensive Apache. The PA-28 Cherokee was another single-engined design, but it was simpler than the Comanche and was intended to compete with the popular Cessna 150/172 range. It quickly achieved the popularity that Piper sought, with yearly production averaging 1000. Nor was the executive market ignored, for the twin-engined Apache was refined into the Aztec for the business user. Another developing sector of general aviation was the agricultural market, and the PA-25 Pawnee of 1958 was developed for crop spraying and crop dusting. Particular attention was paid in the Pawnee's design to flight safety and this was vindicated by the type's excellent record of one fatality in 90,000 flying hours.

By the early 1960s a replacement for the Apache was needed and this emerged in 1962 as the Twin Co-

manche, based on the popular single-engined PA-24. Production of this aircraft ended in 1972 when Piper's Lock Haven plant in Pennsylvania was badly damaged by flooding. It had proved to be rather expensive for the private owner and it was replaced by the 'stretched' Cherokee Six single-engined six-seater and the twin-engined Seneca, which was also based on the Cherokee design. The six- or eight-seat PA-31 Navajo twin, in contrast, was especially aimed at the executive market and was later developed with turbo-supercharged engines and cabin pressurization for high-altitude cruising flight. Its ultimate development was the Cheyenne range of turboprop-powered executive transports. The piston-engined Navajo was developed into the Chieftain in the late 1970s, while the Cherokee was fitted with a retractable undercarriage to become the Arrow. The concept of the simple twin-engined aircraft for the private pilot has been continued with the Seminole, while an entirely new departure has pro-

Above *The twin-engined Piper Navajo, with seating for six to eight passengers.*

Below *The Piper Pawnee is designed for agricultural use.*

duced the two-seat T-tail Tomahawk, a single-engined trainer with good aerobatic capabilities. Although William Piper died in 1970, the company that he founded remains one of the world's greatest producers of light aircraft.

POLIKARPOV

The Soviet aircraft designer Nikolai Polikarpov is today best remembered for his highly manoeuvrable fighter aircraft of the inter-war years. His first fighter design, the IL-400 of 1922, proved to be a tricky aircraft to fly and only 33 of them were built. His U-2 trainer of 1926, in contrast, was a considerable success, remaining in production for a quarter of a century, during which some 40,000 were built. Later redesignated Po-2, the type saw action as a light night bomber and for agent dropping in World War II. As late as the Korean War (1950–53) it remained in service as a night nuisance raider. The R-5 reconnaissance and bomber biplane of 1930 was another successful aircraft, 6000 being built. However, fighter design was Polikarpov's primary interest. His I-3 fighter of 1928 was not as successful as the Po-2 and only about 400 were produced.

The I-5 fighter of 1930 was designed while Polikarpov and his chief assistants were in prison, this treatment presumably being intended by Stalin to stimulate their creative activity. The I-5 entered service in 1933 and over 800 were built. It was succeeded by the I-15 and I-15bis, which saw action in the Spanish Civil War and against the Japanese in China. More

Above The Polikarpov I-17 fighter of 1934 was similar to the I-16, but did not progress beyond the prototype stage.

Below The most extensively used Soviet training aircraft in World War II was the Polikarpov U-2, later redesignated Po-2.

obsolescent at the time, it was nonetheless put back into production in 1941 to meet the Soviet air force's pressing need to replace their fighter losses. No other Polikarpov design was to be produced and the design bureau was disbanded following the death of its leader in 1944.

REPUBLIC

The Republic Aviation Corportion was formed in 1939 as the successor of the Seversky Aircraft Corporation. Its most notable aircraft design was the P-47 Thunderbolt of World War II, which was built in greater numbers than any other American fighter. Alexander Seversky and his chief designer Alexander Kartveli were both Russian émigrés who had settled in the United States after the Revolution. Their SEV-3 all-metal monoplane of 1931 sold in small numbers and led to the P-35 fighter, which entered US Army Air Corps service in 1937. In spite of an export order from Sweden for the P-35, the Seversky company was forced to look for fresh financial backers. The new investors took over the firm, renamed it Republic and forced Seversky's retirement. Kartveli remained as chief designer, however, developing the P-43 Lancer fighter of 1940 for the USAAC. Although the Lancer did not see combat service with the Americans in World War II, a number supplied to the Chinese air force did operate against the Japanese.

In 1942 the first examples of Republic's massive P-47 Thunderbolt fighter entered USAAF service. The type operated with the Eighth Air Force flying bomber escort missions over Europe and in the Pacific it undertook fighter sweeps and bomber escort duties. Yet, in spite of its good performance in air-to-air combat, the Thunderbolt's chief claim to fame lay in its prowess as a fighter-bomber. When Thunderbolt production ended in December 1945, over 15,000 had been built. As well as wartime service with the USAAF, RAF, Armée de l'Air and the Soviet air force, they served on into the 1960s with many other air arms.

In 1946 the prototype of the F-84 Thunderjet first flew and this fighter saw service with the USAF in the Korean War, operating like its famous predecessor primarily in the ground-attack role. Total production was 4457 and Thunderjets were supplied to many of the United States' NATO allies and the air forces of other

than 3000 were built and a few remained in service during the early months of the war with Germany. The gull-winged I-153 of 1934 was a yet further development of the fighter biplane, which saw service in Spain and during World War II. However, it had been preceded the previous year by the I-16 fighter monoplane. Over 6500 of these were built between 1934 and 1940 and they bore the brunt of the German onslaught in June 1941. Although the type was

Above The Polikarpov I-16 was the Soviet air force's standard fighter aircraft at the time of Germany's assault on the Soviet Union in June 1941.

friendly states. The F-84F Thunderstreak was a swept-wing development of the Thunderjet, which first flew in 1951. Over 2500 were built and they too served with many of the NATO air forces. The RF-84F Thunderflash was a camera-equipped tactical reconnaissance version. Last in the line of Republic ground-attack fighters was the F-105 Thunderchief — more usually known by its nickname the Thud. This heavy-weight single-seat tactical strike fighter entered USAF service in 1958. It was primarily intended to carry out nuclear-strike missions in central Europe, flying fast and at low level. In the event, its combat service was over the jungles of Southeast Asia. F-105s bore the

Top left *The P-35 fighter was produced by the Seversky company from which Republic was formed in 1939.*

Above left *The Republic P-47 Thunderbolt first went into action with the USAAF's Eighth Air Force in 1943.*

Above right *A Republic RF-84F Thunderflash tactical reconnaissance aircraft.*

Left *A Republic F-84B Thunderjet fires a salvo of rockets at a ground target.*

Below *The Republic F-105 Thunderchief fighter bomber was primarily intended as a tactical nuclear-strike aircraft for the European theatre. An F-105D of the 36th Tactical Fighter Wing, Bitburg, in West Germany, is pictured.*

brunt of the USAF's bombing effort against North Vietnam from 1965 until they were largely replaced by McDonnell Douglas F-4 Phantoms in 1970–71. Specially equipped F-105s also undertook the Wild Weasel role — attacking North Vietnamese surface-to-air missile sites — until the final American withdrawal in 1972. By that time Republic had become a division of Fairchild Industries, but the ground-attack fighter tradition has been continued with the new company's A-10A Thunderbolt II.

ROYAL AIRCRAFT FACTORY

The Royal Aircraft Factory at Farnborough in Hampshire began its official existence in April 1912, but in fact could trace its origins to the Army Balloon Factory established in 1892. One of the factory's most famous products was the BE2 biplane of 1912, which in successively improved versions was to remain in service with the Royal Flying Corps and RAF throughout World War I, latterly as a training aircraft. Total production was over 3500, a surprisingly high figure as the BE2c was shown to be hopelessly inadequate in the observation role as early as the 'Fokker Scourge' of 1915. Its successor was the RE8 of 1916, over 4000 of which were built, and which became the workhorse reconnaissance aircraft of the RFC. Although better armed than its predecessor, it lacked the manoeuvrability necessary to evade the German fighters. During 1917-18 the RE8 was the most widely used British two-seater aircraft on the Western Front,

although very few served on with the peacetime RAF after the Armistice.

The FE2b, which began to reach RFC units in France in 1915, was intended as a fighter escort for the slower BE2s. A pusher design, its observer in the front cockpit consequently had an excellent field of fire. By mid-1917 it was outclassed in its intended role, but found a new lease of life as a night bomber. Nearly 1500 FE2s were built and the type remained in service until the end of World War I. The most successful Royal Aircraft Factory product was undoubtedly the SE5 fighter of 1916. In its improved SE5a form it served with a total of 24 RFC and RAF squadrons and over 5000 were built. The Royal Aircraft Factory became the Royal Aircraft Establishment in April 1918 and has since concentrated on research work rather than design and production.

RYAN

The Ryan Airplane Company, builders of Lindbergh's *Spirit of St Louis*, was founded by Claude Ryan in 1926 to build the M-1 three-seat high-wing monoplane. It proved to be a popular design with the companies competing for government air mail contracts and was further developed as the M-2 Bluebird. In 1927 the Ryan company accepted Charles Lindbergh's order for a transatlantic-range aeroplane based on the M-1

Above *The original BE2 two-seat observation aircraft was designed by Geoffrey de Havilland, when he worked at the Royal Aircraft Factory, Farnborough, in 1912.*

Left *The BE2 series' successor in RFC and RAF service later in World War I was the RE8, which was nicknamed 'Harry Tate' after a music hall star of the day.*

Below left *The FE2a two-seater gave the observer an excellent field of fire from the front cockpit.*

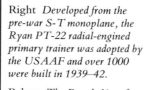

Right *Developed from the pre-war S-T monoplane, the Ryan PT-22 radial-engined primary trainer was adopted by the USAAF and over 1000 were built in 1939–42.*

Below *The Royal Aircraft Factory's SE5a was one of the finest British fighter aircraft of World War I, entering service in mid-1917 with the RFC.*

design. The Ryan NYP (New York–Paris) was built within two months and in May 1927 Lindbergh flew it from Roosevelt Field, New York, to Le Bourget, Paris, in a flight taking over 33 hours. The resultant publicity boosted Ryan's sales of the five-seat Brougham. However, the company disappeared in the Great Depression after merging with the Detroit Aircraft Corporation.

Claude Ryan continued his aviation activities by forming the Ryan Flying School at San Diego, California. In 1934 he designed and built the S-T (Sport Trainer) low-wing monoplane, which sold well to both civil and military customers. In 1939, with the approach of World War II, the US Army Air Corps ordered the Ryan trainer as the PT-16. When production ended in 1942, a total of 1179 Ryan trainers had been built in PT-16, PT-20, PT-21 and PT-22 versions. In 1944 Ryan produced the prototype of the FR-1

Fireball naval fighter, which was a composite aircraft powered by both a piston engine and a turbojet. The US Navy bought 66 Fireballs and conducted trials with them aboard various aircraft carriers in 1945–7. Unfortunately for Ryan, the faster all-jet aircraft also proved themselves, and the Fireballs were not used in service. After the war Ryan developed the Firebee drone, which was extensively used by the US forces for reconnaissance and as a target in weapons tests.

Above *The most famous Ryan aircraft was Lindbergh's NYP monoplane* Spirit of St Louis, *which was based on the company's B-1 Brougham.*

Right *The twin-engined Saab 90 Scandia airliner served with the Swedish operator ABA, but eventually all 18 built went to Brazil.*

In 1943 the Saab 21A fighter first flew, and production examples reached the Swedish air force in 1945. It was an unusual design in several ways, having its DB 605 piston engine installed as a pusher mounted between the twin tail booms, being fitted with a tricycle undercarriage and having one of the first ejector seats to be fitted to a military aircraft. After 296 Saab 21As had been produced, the design was revised to accept a de Havilland Goblin turbojet in place of the DB 605. The jet-powered version, known as the Saab 21R, first flew in 1947 and entered military service two years later. Saab's Scandia twin-engined airliner of

SAAB

The Saab company – the initials stand for Svenska Aeroplan Aktiebolaget (Swedish Aircraft Company) – was formed in April 1937. Its early products were licence-built foreign designs such as the German Junkers Ju 86 bomber and US North American NA-16 trainer. The first original Saab design was a single-engined reconnaissance bomber, the Saab 17, of 1940. The type remained in production for the Swedish air force until 1944, when 323 had been built, and was finally retired from service in 1948. Export models served with the Danish and Ethiopian air forces. In 1942 the twin-engined Saab 18 bomber made its first flight, and a total of 242 were built. They served with the Swedish air force in the bomber, reconnaissance and torpedo-bomber roles from 1944 until the early 1950s.

Above *The Saab J21 fighter of 1943 was unusual in having a tricycle undercarriage, a pusher mounted engine and one of the first ejection seats. The design was later adapted to take a DH Goblin turbojet engine.*

Above right *The Saab 91 Safir, a piston-engined training aircraft, served with the Swedish air force and several foreign air arms, including Finland's (illustrated here).*

1946 proved to be a disappointment, as only 18 were built. However, greater success was achieved with the Saab 91 Safir of 1945, which was a two- or three-seat trainer and light touring aircraft. It proved to be a popular civil and military trainer, with 320 being produced. Many served with the Swedish air force and export customers included Finland, Austria and Tunisia.

The J21R was essentially a stopgap jet fighter, and in 1968 the prototype Saab 29 appeared. This tubby swept-wing aircraft, nicknamed the Tunnan (Barrel), became operational in Sweden in 1951. A total of 665 were built, most of them serving with the Swedish air force, although 30 were exported to Austria. The Saab 29's replacement, the Saab 32 Lansen (Lance), entered service at the end of 1955. It served in the attack, all-weather fighter and reconnaissance roles until 1971 and a few of the 450 built remained in service as target tugs and electronic countermeasures trainers in the early 1980s.

In 1955 the Saab 35 Draken fighter with its distinctive 'double delta' wing platform made its maiden flight; it proved to be a highly effective fighter aircraft. In its developed Saab 35D version it was capable of a maximum speed of Mach 2, well in excess of the original Mach 1·8 speed requirement for the design. More than 600 Drakens were built for the Swedish, Finnish and Danish air forces and the type remains in front-line service in the mid-1980s. The Saab 105 jet trainer of 1963 also serves as a light attack aircraft with the Swedish air force and represents Austria's only front-line combat aircraft. The piston-engined Safari, or in its military form the Supporter, appeared in 1969 and over 150 have been built. At present Saab's most

important venture is the Viggen multi-role combat aircraft, with its distinctive canard foreplanes, which entered service with the Swedish air force in 1971. It has been specially designed for dispersed site operations from 500m (1640ft) stretches of highway, and is built in reconnaissance, attack and interceptor versions. Its intended successor, the JAS 39 Gripen, is expected to enter service in 1992.

SHORT

In 1908 the brothers Horace, Oswald and Eustace Short set up a company for the manufacture of balloons and in the following year built their first aeroplane. This machine, based on the Wright Flyer, did not fly. The brothers were more successful with six licence-built Flyers which they produced in 1910–11. They also produced a biplane of original design for J. T. C. Moore-Brabazon, which became the first all-British aeroplane to fly over a 2km (1 mile) circular course, thus winning a *Daily Mail* prize of £1000. A series of box-kite type biplanes followed, which proved to be popular machines, and they equipped the Naval Flying School at Eastchurch, Kent, in 1911. The Admiralty then ordered a number of floatplanes from Shorts and this led to substantial orders after the outbreak of World War I. The well-known Short 184 floatplane appeared in 1915 and served until the Armistice as a torpedo-bomber, reconnaissance and anti-submarine patrol aircraft. One of the type's notable exploits was the only air reconnaissance flown during the Battle of Jutland in May 1916. A landplane bomber version of the basic design served with No 3 Wing of the Royal Naval Air Service in 1916–17.

Shorts survived the postwar slump by turning their production facilities over to boatbuilding and coachwork. However, the firm's commitment to aviation remained strong and in 1920 the Silver Streak biplane appeared with an all-metal, stressed-skin fuselage. Four years later the all-metal Singapore flying boat flew for the first time, and this was used by Alan Chobham in his flight around Africa in 1927–8. The later Singapore III was built for the RAF in 1933–7 and a few remained in service as late as 1941. The Calcutta civil flying boat served with Imperial Airways between 1929 and 1936, while a military version, the Rangoon, served in small numbers with the RAF in Iraq and the United Kingdom. Unusually, the Kent flying boat built for Imperial Airways as a successor to the Calcutta formed the basis of a landplane airliner for the same operator.

In 1936 the first of the famous C-class or Empire flying boats built for Imperial Airways took to the air. Serving also with the Australian airline Qantas, their route network stretched from Southampton to Sydney, Australia. A total of 43 were built and they remained in service until as late as 1947. In 1937 the military counterpart of the Empire flying boat first

Below *The Saab 32 Lansen entered Swedish service in 1955 and served in the attack, all-weather fighter and reconnaissance roles until all had been replaced by Drakens and Viggens in 1971.*

Above *A Saab J35F Draken shows off its distinctive double-delta wing planform and armament of four Hughes AIM-4 Falcon air-to-air missiles which it carried for the interception role.*

Left *This Saab 105 served as a trainer with the Swedish air force's flight training school. Attack versions are also in Swedish and Austrian service.*

Left *The Saab 37 Viggen is a multi-role fighter, serving in the attack, interception, reconnaissance and training roles. The AJ37 pictured is an attack aircraft.*

was superseded by the more capable Avro Lancaster and Handley Page Halifax and was relegated to such duties as glider tug and parachute transport for the airborne forces.

In the postwar years Shorts built the twin-engined Sturgeon naval target tug, which was only produced in small numbers, and the even less successful Sperrin bomber and Seamew shipboard anti-submarine aircraft. In 1960 the SC1 experimental VTOL (vertical take off and landing) aircraft first got off the ground. It used a battery of four vertically mounted Rolls-Royce RB 108 turbojets for vertical lift and a fifth

flew; as the Sunderland it was to be one of the RAF's most important aircraft of World War II. Sunderlands served with RAF Coastal Command throughout the war and were credited with the destruction of 29 U-boats. Total production was 749 and the flying boat remained in RAF service until 1958. A civil version, the Sandringham, appeared after World War II and military versions were exported to Australia, Canada, New Zealand, South Africa and France. Another significant Short aeroplane of World War II was the Stirling four-engined bomber, the first of the RAF's heavy bombers to enter service. Deliveries began to RAF Bomber Command in August 1940 and total production was 2375. In the later years of the war the Stirling

Top left The Short S27 biplane, based on a Farman design, was supplied to the Admiralty in 1911.

Above left The Short 184 floatplane first flew in 1915. Total production was some 900 aeroplanes.

Above right The four-turboprop Short Belfast C Mk 1 heavy freighter served with No 53 Squadron RAF at Brize Norton, Oxfordshire, from 1966 to 1976.

RB 108 for forward flight. In 1966 the Belfast four-turboprop strategic freighter entered RAF service with No 53 Squadron, operating for a decade in the heavy-lift transport role before the fleet was sold to civil operators. The diminutive Skyvan twin-turboprop freighter enjoyed better success and is widely used by civil and military operators as a light freighter. The type has been further developed as the Sherpa commuter airliner.

Above A Short Sunderland GR Mk V flying boat lifts off from Lough Erne in Northern Ireland in 1945.

Above right The Short Skyvan twin-turboprop light cargo aircraft has served with civil and military operators in many parts of the world.

Left The Short SC1 experimental aircraft was one of the earliest jet-powered VTOL machines. It first made the transition from hovering to forward flight in April 1960.

SIKORSKY

The Russian-born aviation pioneer Igor Sikorsky built one of the first truly practical helicopters in 1939 and his company has since become one of the world's leading producers of rotorcraft. Sikorsky achieved early distinction in his native land when he designed the Bolshoi Baltiski biplane in 1913, which was the first four-engined aeroplane ever to fly. This work led to the Ilia Mourumetz four-engined bomber, more than 70 of which were built for the Imperial Russian air service in World War I. After the Revolution Sikorsky emigrated to the United States, where he founded the Sikorsky Aero Engineering Corporation in 1923. His S-29A airliner did not go into production, but the prototype was used for charter work and was eventually bought by Howard Hughes.

Left *In 1914 Sikorsky built the Ilia Mourumetz four-engined bomber, which served with the Russian Imperial Air Service during World War I.*

Below *The Sikorsky S43 flying boat amphibian first appeared in 1935 and could carry up to 19 passengers. This French-registered S43 was photographed in North Africa.*

the following year. The success of this machine resulted in an order from the USAAF for the R-4 two-seat helicopter. In 1944 an R-4 was used in Burma to rescue the crew of an aircraft crashed behind Japanese lines. R-4s also served with the US Navy and with the RAF and Fleet Air Arm in Britain. The more powerful R-6, which first flew in 1943, was also used by these services in military helicopter trials. The R-5 rescue helicopter was militarily more useful and it served with the US forces until the mid-1960s, was built in Britain as the Westland Dragonfly and, as the S-51 commercial helicopter, operated the world's first scheduled helicopter service (carrying mail) with Los Angeles Airways in 1947. Over 500 helicopters of this type were built and it saw combat in the rescue and casualty evacuation role during the Korean War.

The Sikorsky S-55, which made its first flight in 1948, was an altogether more capable helicopter than the S-51. With the military designation H-19, it went into action in Korea in 1951 with the US Army, the USAF and US Marine Corps. It could carry ten passengers plus a two-man crew, and was first used as a

The S-35 biplane of 1926 was to be used by the French air ace René Fonck for a transatlantic flight, but the aircraft crashed on take-off, and Lindbergh made his famous New York–Paris flight before a replacement could be built. Sikorsky then turned to the design of amphibian flying boats and with these he achieved considerable success. Two S-36 amphibians were built, one of which was leased by Pan American Airways, and this type was developed into the more powerful S-38 of 1928, 114 of which were built. Among the operators of the S-38 were Pan Am, Western Air Express, Curtiss Flying Service, the US Navy and US Army Air Corps. There followed small numbers of the S-39, S-40 and S-42 amphibians and then came the all-metal S-42 which pioneered Pan Am's trans-Pacific services. More than 50 of the smaller S-43s were built and the line of flying boats ended with three VS-44s, which operated a transatlantic service during World War II and one of which remained in service with Antilles Air Boats until 1971.

Sikorsky's VS-300 helicopter made its first tethered flight in September 1939 and achieved free flight in

Above *A Sikorsky S-51 operated by BEA in 1950. Designated H-5 by the USAF, the S-51 did much to pioneer helicopter operations.*

Below *The Sikorsky VS-300 was one of the first practical helicopter designs ever to fly. Its first untethered flight was made on 13 May 1940.*

troop-carrying assault transport in Korea. Total production was over 1800 and the type was built under licence in Japan, France and the United Kingdom (where it was known as the Whirlwind). The S-56 of 1953 was a heavy assault helicopter, 156 of which were built for the US Army and Marine Corps. The S-58, originally developed for anti-submarine work with the US Navy, was widely used by the American forces as the H-34 in the troop-carrying assault helicopter role. The British version, named the Wessex, served with both the RAF and Fleet Air Arm, and a French-built variant saw action in the Algerian War.

The introduction of turboshaft engines gave the helicopter sufficent reserves of power for a 'flying crane' version to be developed. The CH-54 of 1962 undertakes this role with the US Army and saw considerable service in Vietnam, where it was used to lift artillery to hilltop positions and to recover crashed aircraft. The S-62 of 1958 was a boat-hulled helicopter amphibian, which is used by the US Coast Guard (as the HH-52) and Japan as a rescue helicopter. The S-61 (US military designation H-3) Sea King of the following year is a versatile design that has been used as a shipboard anti-submarine and rescue helicopter by the US Navy and many foreign air arms. Civil versions

Left *The Sikorsky CH-54A Tarhe is a flying crane helicopter, which is operated by the US Army.*

Below *The Sikorsky S-61 of 1959 has seen extensive service. Many civil versions, including this S-61N, have been used for offshore oil rig support.*

Below centre *The Sikorsky UH-60A Black Hawk has been procured by the US Army as a successor to the Bell UH-1 helicopter.*

over 1500 H-60s in its various versions. Sikorsky have not entirely neglected the civil helicopter market, however. The S-76, which first flew in 1977, is a 12-passenger transport for commercial services or oil-rig support.

SOPWITH

The Sopwith Aviation Company, which is famous for its World War I fighter aircraft, was founded by T. O. M. Sopwith in 1912. Its first aeroplane, the single-seat Tabloid, was a highly successful racing machine and in floatplane form it won the 1913 Schneider Trophy contest for Britain. The type was also produced for the Royal Naval Air Service after the outbreak of World War I and was eventually developed into the Baby floatplane, which was widely used from ship and shore bases in 1917–18. In 1916 the RNAS adopted the oddly named 1½-Strutter, which could be flown as a single-seat bomber or as a two-seat escort fighter. The Royal Flying Corps also adopted the type and over 1000 were built for the British services. However, the French Aviation Militaire was the largest user of the 1½-Strutter, some 4200 being built in France, and some of these were supplied to the Belgian, Russian and American air arms.

The highly manoeuvrable Pup single-seat fighter first reached RNAS and RFC squadrons in France during 1916, but it was not until the following year that appreciable numbers entered service. As well as serving with fighter squadrons on the Western Front, the type was used for home defence and as a naval fighter aboard cruisers fitted with flying-off platforms above the gun turrets. Its stablemate the Triplane was flown almost exclusively by the RNAS. The first squadron became operational early in 1917 and in all six naval fighter squadrons were equipped with Triplanes. Their outstanding manoeuvrability and rate of climb inspired Fokker to produce his much better-known Dr I Triplane.

In the summer of 1917 the F1 Camel, Sopwith's best-known fighter, began to reach the British fighter squadrons in France. A difficult machine to fly, once

have played an important part in supporting offshore oil exploitation and the USAF's HH-3E Jolly Green Giant was extensively used for combat rescue in Southeast Asia. Licence production of the S-61 has been undertaken in the United Kingdom, Italy, Canada and Japan.

The much larger S-65 (US military designation H-53) serves the Marine Corps as a heavy assault transport, the navy as a minesweeping helicopter and the USAF for air rescue. The S-70 (H-60) of 1974 is another versatile helicopter, which is used by the US army as an assault transport, by the US Navy as a shipboard anti-submarine aircraft and by the USAF as a specialized rescue helicopter. The US services alone require well

operational with No 43 Squadron in September 1918. Only three operational fighter squadrons in France were fully equipped with Snipes before the Armistice. However, the aircraft was so well regarded that it was adopted as the RAF's standard fighter after the war. An armoured variant, the Salamander, was intended for the ground-attack role, but although it was ordered in quantity none served operationally. Another notable innovation that was too late to see action was the T1 Cuckoo single-seat shipboard torpedo-carrier. In 1919 Sopwith produced the Atlantic, which in May that year attempted an Atlantic crossing. It was forced to ditch in mid-ocean, however, and its crew, Harry Hawker and Lieutenant-Commander K. Mackenzie-Grieve, were fortunate to be rescued by a passing tramp steamer. The Sopwith company was forced to close in 1920, but its traditions were inherited by the Hawker company.

Above *A Sopwith Pup fighter of the RNAS fitted with a skid undercarriage for experiments in arrested landings on aircraft carriers.*

Left *The Sopwith Triplane fighter first entered service with the RNAS in November 1916. No 1 (Naval) Squadron, whose Triplanes are pictured, flew this type in France from June until December 1917.*

Opposite page, bottom *The Sopwith Tabloid served with both the Royal Flying Corps and Royal Naval Air Service in floatplane and landplane configuration early in World War I.*

Below left *A Sopwith Camel demonstrates its superb aerobatic qualities. Although a tricky aircraft for the beginner to master, the Camel proved to be a highly effective fighter.*

Below *The Spad SXIII first flew in August 1917 and swiftly became the Aviation Militaire's most important fighter aircraft. A total of 8472 were produced.*

mastered the Camel was a formidable opponent. Over 5000 Camels were built and they accounted for 1294 enemy aircraft destroyed in combat. Camels were used for ground attack, notably during the fighting to counter the German offensive of March 1918, and also as shipboard fighters and as night fighters. Among the exploits of Camel pilots was the shooting down of six enemy aircraft in one day, a feat performed by both Captain J. L. Trollope and Captain H. W. Woollett (both of No 43 Squadron) in the spring of 1918. In 1917 the 5F1 Dolphin fighter made its first flight. Over 1500 were built, but they served with only four squadrons on the Western Front from January 1918 onwards.

The last Sopwith fighter to see action over the Western Front was the 7F1 Snipe, which became

SPAD

The Spad company which produced France's finest fighter aircraft of World War I was founded in 1910 by the French pioneer Armand Deperdussin. His company, the Société pour les Appareils Deperdussin, produced monoplane racing aircraft of outstanding performance, but in 1914 it was on the verge of financial collapse. It was saved by the intervention of Louis Blériot, who renamed the concern Société pour Aviation et ses Dérivés, thus retaining the acronym Spad. The firm's chief designer was Louis Béchereau, who in 1915 produced the unusual Spad A2 two-seat fighter. In an attempt to give the gunner a clear field of fire, his cockpit was mounted ahead of the engine and propeller in this otherwise conventional tractor biplane. Although 42 Spad A2s were supplied to the Aviation Militaire and a further 57 to Russia, the type was unpopular and only a handful of the later Spad A4 were built.

The Spad SVII design of 1916 was a far more effective fighting machine. A single-seat fighter, powered initially by a 140hp Hispano-Suiza liquid-cooled engine, it was armed with a fixed forward-firing

but were exported to Warsaw Pact allies and other nations. The Indian air force operated the type against Pakistan in 1971 and Egypt also flew Su-7s in the Yom Kippur War of 1973. A developed version of the design, the Su-17, with variable-geometry outer wing panels, has a considerably improved performance and currently serves with the Warsaw Pact and other air forces. The Su-9 delta-wing interceptor was further improved to produce the Su-11, and both of these versions served with the Soviet Air Defence Forces. Their successor was the twin-engined Su-15, which first appeared in the late 1960s.

Although Sukhoi died in 1975, his bureau is still in existence and has produced the Su-24 (NATO code-name Fencer), a variable-geometry-wing strike fighter similar in concept to the USAF General Dynamics F-111. The Su-25 (NATO codename Frogfoot) was evaluated in the close-support role in Afghanistan in 1982, while the Su-27 interceptor is reported to be undergoing flight testing in the early 1980s. According to US intelligence sources this aircraft is closely comparable to the McDonnell Douglas F-15 Eagle in performance and manoeuvrability.

machine gun synchronized to fire through the propeller arc. A total of 5600 Spad SVIIs were built in France and a further 220 in Britain to equip the Royal Flying Corps fighter squadrons. The type was operated from September 1916 until mid-1917, when the improved Spad SXIII became available. The new fighter offered an increase in engine power to 220hp and an armament of two forward-firing machine guns. Total production of the Spad SXIII was 8472, and some 80 *escadrilles de chasse* flew the type. It was also exported to Belgium, Italy, Japan, Czechoslovakia and Poland and equipped squadrons of the US Army Air Service in both France and the United States. In the inter-war years the company was responsible for the Spad 61, Spad 81 and Spad 510 biplane fighters. It was nationalized in 1937.

SUKHOI

The Soviet aircraft designer Pavel Sukhoi formed his design bureau in the late 1930s, but it was not until his Su-7 appeared in the late 1950s that he enjoyed any degree of success. The two-seat Su-2 attack aircraft had been put into production in 1940, but only some 600 were built – a derisory figure by Soviet wartime production standards. There followed a series of experimental designs, none of which progressed beyond the prototype stage, and in 1949 the Sukhoi bureau was closed down.

After Stalin's death in 1953, Sukhoi was allowed to re-form his bureau and in 1956 the prototypes of the Su-7 ground-attack fighter and Su-9 interceptor appeared. Both were produced in quantity for the Soviet air force. The Su-7B and Su-7BM not only served with regiments of Frontal Aviation command,

Top left *A Spad SXIII fighter carrying the Indian's-head emblem of the US 28th Aero Squadron.*

Above centre *A two-seat Spad SXVI used by US Brigadier-General 'Billy' Mitchell.*

Above *The Sukhoi Su-15 is a standard Soviet interceptor.*

Below *The Sukhoi Su-17.*

Right The Supermarine Southampton flying boats served with five RAF squadrons between 1925 and 1937. An aircraft of No 201 Squadron, based at Calshot in Hampshire, is pictured.

SUPERMARINE

Below The RAF's Supermarine S5 racing seaplane took first and second places in the 1927 Schneider Trophy contest, which was held at Venice.

Right Supermarine Walrus spotter aircraft of the Fleet Air Arm flying in close formation.

Far right A Supermarine Spitfire Mk VB serving with No 316 (Polish) Squadron of the RAF. The Supermarine Spitfire Mk V first appeared in March 1941.

The Supermarine company is most famous as the producer of the wartime Spitfire fighter, but curiously its specialization was flying boats and floatplanes rather than high-speed landplanes. It was the successor of the World War I Pemberton-Billing company, which built the AD flying boat of 1917 to an Admiralty Air Department design. In 1922 Supermarine produced the Seagull amphibian, which served with the Fleet Air Arm (FAA) and Royal Australian Air Force. In 1925 the Southampton flying boat entered RAF service, replacing the wartime Felixstowe, and it remained in use for a decade. The Walrus of 1933 was an amphibian flying boat intended for reconnaissance duties aboard major warships. During World War II it also took on the air/sea rescue role with 11 RAF squadrons. Its successor, the Sea Otter of 1943, was the last biplane to enter RAF service. Two other biplane flying boats were built by Supermarine for the RAF: the Scapa of 1933 and the Stranraer of 1935. Stranraers remained in RAF service until 1940 and were also manufactured in Montreal by Canadian Vickers for the Royal Canadian Air Force.

The machines which gave Supermarine's designer R. J. Mitchell experience in working on high-speed aircraft were the floatplanes built to compete for the Schneider Trophy. The S4 of 1925 crashed during that contest, but the subsquent S5, S6 and S6B monoplane racers won the Trophy outright for Britain with three consecutive wins in 1927–31. The sleek lines of the racing floatplanes were preserved and immortalized in the design of the Spitfire fighter, which first flew in 1936. Unquestionably the most important fighter aircraft to serve with the RAF in World War II, the Merlin-engined Spitfire Mk I and Mk II with eight-machine-gun armament fought in the Battle of Britain in 1940. They were succeeded in the following year by the faster Mk V many of which had twin-cannon armament. Then the Spitfire Mk IX appeared in July 1942 and this proved to be the equal of the Luftwaffe's Focke Wulf Fw 190 which was a much later design than the basic Spitfire. Other versions of the Spitfire appeared for high-altitude interception and photographic reconnaissance. In 1943 the Rolls-Royce-Griffon-engined Mark XII entered service, followed by the Mk XIV with the same powerplant, and these served until the end of the war. Total production of the Spitfire was 20,334, and the type remained in front-line RAF service until 1954. A naval fighter variant, the Seafire, was developed in parallel. This type entered FAA service in 1942 and the Griffon-engined Seafire Mk 47 saw action in the Korean War.

Left *A Supermarine Scimitar F Mk 1 of HMS* Ark Royal's *No 803 Squadron.*

Below *The Supermarine Swift proved to be a failure in its intended role as fighter, but the Swift FR Mk 5 tactical reconnaissance version (pictured) served with two RAF squadrons in Germany from 1956 until 1961.*

After World War II Supermarine produced the Attacker naval jet fighter, the first of its kind in operational service with the FAA. They served from 1951 until 1957 and Attackers were exported to the Pakistan air force in 1951. The Scimitar of 1954 became the FAA's first swept-wing, single-seat fighter when it entered service in 1958. Operating in the strike fighter role, it was the first British naval aircraft to be armed with a tactical nuclear weapon. Scimitars were finally replaced by Blackburn Buccaneers in the late 1960s. The RAF's last Supermarine fighter, the Swift, did not enjoy such a long service career. The early fighters only served with one RAF unit, No 56 Squadron, and gave constant trouble leading to the cancellation of outstanding contracts in 1955. However, the fighter/reconnaissance Swift FR Mk 5 was more satisfactory and served with two RAF squadrons in 1956–61.

TUPOLEV

The Soviet aircraft designer A. N. Tupolev has given his name to some 60 Soviet aircraft, many of them bomber and transport designs. One of the earliest aircraft produced by this prolific designer was the ANT-2 of 1924, the first Soviet all-metal aircraft, which owed much to Junkers engineering techniques. The series of heavy bomber aircraft with which Tupolev was to become particularly associated began with the ANT-4 (TB-1) of 1925. Over 200 were built. There followed the scaled-up ANT-6 (TB-3), which was the largest aircraft in the world at the time of its appearance in 1930. Some 800 examples of this four-engined bomber were built and they served up to the early months of World War II in this role and thereafter as a transport aircraft. TB-3s were also used as a parachute transport during the pioneering Soviet development work on airborne forces in the 1930s, and played a notable role in Arctic exploration.

The most important Tupolev design in military service when Germany went to war with the Soviet

Below *The ANT-2, designed by Andrei Tupolev, was the first Soviet all-metal aeroplane. Its corrugated metal skinning was a construction practice borrowed from Junkers.*

1980s and the bomber is still being produced in China. The wings, tail and engines of the Tu-16 were matched to a new fuselage to produce the Tu-104 airliner of 1956. A similar conversion of the Tu-20 four-turboprop long-range bomber of 1954 produced the Tu-114 airliner. However, both these machines proved to be uneconomical to operate on commercial services. More success was achieved with the later Tu-124 and Tu-134 medium-range airliners and the long-haul Tu-154. In 1968 the Tu-144 supersonic airliner, look-

Union was the SB-2 twin-engined fast bomber. At the time of its combat debut in Spain in 1936 it could out-perform the Nationalists' Fiat CR32 and Heinkel He 51 fighters. However, by 1941 it was an obsolescent design and losses to German fighters were heavy. Its replacement was designed from a prison cell, as Tupolev and many of his design staff were arrested and

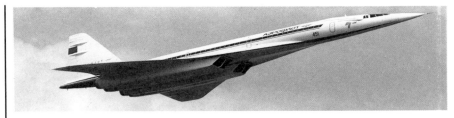

Top *The twin-engined Tupolev SB-2 bomber aircraft was built under licence by Avia in Czechoslovakia, the first Soviet-designed aeroplane to be manufactured abroad.*

Above *Looking remarkably like its Western counterpart, Concorde, the Tupolev Tu-144 proved to be a failure and was withdrawn in 1978.*

Left *A maritime reconnaissance variant of the massive Tupolev Tu-20.*

ing remarkably like the Anglo-French Concorde, made its first flight ahead of its Western rival, but its service career with Aeroflot was short.

In 1961 a new medium-range bomber appeared, the supersonic Tu-22, and it has seen limited service with the Soviet air force's Long-Range Aviation and Naval Aviation commands. At the same time the heavy-weight Tu-28P long-range fighter entered service with the Air Defence Forces. It is complemented by the Tu-124 AEW (airborne early warning) aircraft, developed from the Tu-114 airliner. The Mach 2 Tu-26 (NATO codename Backfire) entered service in 1975. This variable-geometry-wing Mach 2 bomber caused

imprisoned on orders from Stalin in 1936. The proto-type Tu-2 fast bomber flew in 1941, but production examples did not reach the Soviet air force until 1944. Its eventual success won Tupolev his freedom, and Tu-2s served on with the Soviet air force and Warsaw Pact allies into the 1950s.

In 1944 several Boeing B-29 Superfortresses force-landed in Soviet territory after raids on Japan. Tupolev was entrusted to produce a copy of the design for the Soviet air force – a more difficult task than might be imagined – and this entered service as the Tu-4 in the late 1940s. It was the first Soviet nuclear-armed stra-tegic bomber. The Tu-14 twin-jet bomber of 1947 was only a limited success and few were produced. In con-trast the Tu-16 swept-wing jet bomber, which entered service in 1955, has served in the bomber, reconnais-sance, tanker and ECM (electronic countermeasures) roles. Several hundred remain in Soviet service in the

Above left *The twin-engined Tupolev Tu-16 jet bomber first appeared in 1955 and considerable numbers remained in service with the Soviet air force during the early 1980s.*

Above *The Tupolev Tu-154 airliner, powered by three Kuznetsov turbofans, can carry 120 passengers over a maximum range of 4000km (2485 miles) and is one of the more efficient Soviet civil air transport aircraft.*

considerable concern in the West and it was feared that it even posed a threat to targets in the United States. However, its primary role is as a medium-range tactical nuclear bomber. The latest Soviet long-range bomber, codenamed Blackjack by NATO, was under-going flight testing in the early 1980s.

VICKERS

In March 1911 the Vickers engineering company formed an aviation department to manufacture the designs of the French pioneer Robert Esnault-Pelterie under licence. It was the beginning of the company that was to produce such famous bombers as the Vimy, Wellington and Valiant. One of the most significant

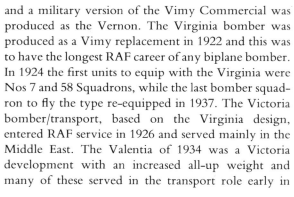

and a military version of the Vimy Commercial was produced as the Vernon. The Virginia bomber was produced as a Vimy replacement in 1922 and this was to have the longest RAF career of any biplane bomber. In 1924 the first units to equip with the Virginia were Nos 7 and 58 Squadrons, while the last bomber squadron to fly the type re-equipped in 1937. The Victoria bomber/transport, based on the Virginia design, entered RAF service in 1926 and served mainly in the Middle East. The Valentia of 1934 was a Victoria development with an increased all-up weight and many of these served in the transport role early in

early Vickers designs was the Experimental Fighter Biplane No 1 of 1913, which early in World War I was developed into the Vickers FB5 Gunbus. In mid-1915 No 11 Squadron RFC was equipped with the Gunbus and sent to France as the first unit with a primary role of air fighting, as opposed to reconnaissance of one sort or another. The type remained in front-line use until mid-1916 and was thereafter relegated to

World War II. Two very similar single-engined biplane designs, the Vildebeest torpedo-bomber and Vincent army cooperation type, entered RAF service in the early 1930s and Vildebeests of Nos 36 and 100 Squadrons saw action against the Japanese in 1941–2.

The Wellesley monoplane bomber of 1935 employed the lattice-like geodetic structure evolved by Barnes Wallis, which derived from his earlier work on airships (notably the R100). Wellesleys served briefly with RAF Bomber Command in 1937–9, but did see action in East Africa and over the eastern Mediterranean in World War II. In 1938 a flight of specially modified Wellesleys flew non-stop from Ismâ'ilîya in Egypt to Darwin, Australia, establishing a new world distance record of 11,430km (7100 miles). A more successful bomber employing Barnes Wallis's geodetic structure was the twin-engined Wellington. These entered service in 1938 and were employed on operations from 1939 until 1945. Although Bomber Command had replaced its Wellingtons with four-engined 'heavies' by 1943, they remained operational in Italy and the Far East until 1945. Wellingtons also served with Coastal Command as anti-submarine patrol aircraft, torpedo-bombers and in the DWI version as minesweepers. Total production was 11,461, and Wellingtons remained in RAF service as trainers until the early 1950s.

training duties. The FB19 fighter biplane of 1916 also served in small numbers in Macedonia, Palestine and with Home Defence squadrons. Yet undoubtedly the most successful Vickers design of the World War I period, although too late to see combat in that conflict, was the FB27 Vimy twin-engined bomber. It first flew in November 1917 and early production examples reached the Independent Force RAF in France just before the Armistice. After the war it served with six RAF bomber squadrons between 1919 and 1927, pioneered the Cairo-to-Baghdad air mail route and also served as a parachute training aircraft. However, it was the Vimy's long-range record-breaking flights that won it the greatest acclaim. The most notable were Alcock and Brown's transatlantic crossing of June 1919, the Smith brothers' England-to-Australia flight of November–December 1919, and the England-to-Cape Town flight of the following year made by Pierre van Ryneveld and Quintin Brand.

In 1919 Vickers produced an airliner version of the Vimy known as the Vimy Commercial, and this ten-passenger transport aircraft remained in service with Instone and later Imperial Airways until 1925. The same companies operated the single-engined Vulcan,

Top *The Vickers FB5, nicknamed the Gunbus, was the first effective fighter aeroplane to serve with the Royal Flying Corps. A replica, built by RAC at Weybridge, is illustrated.*

Above centre *A Vickers Wellington Mk 1C of No 311 (Czech) Squadron. The Wellington was the RAF's most effective night bomber aircraft in the early years of World War II.*

Above *The Vickers Vimy twin-engined bomber was too late to see combat in World War I, but it achieved fame with a series of record-breaking, long-distance flights in 1919–20. This is the Vimy in which Alcock and Brown made the first crossing of the Atlantic by air.*

The twin-engined Warwick, which first flew in 1939, suffered early development problems and never served in its intended bomber role. However, the Warwick GR Mk V finally reached Coastal Command air/sea rescue units towards the end of the war. The last Vickers geodetic bomber, the four-engined Windsor, was too late to see wartime service and so was not put into production. With the end of the war approaching, Vickers turned to civil aircraft and in June 1945 the prototype twin-engined Viking airliner first took to the air. A total of 163 were built and Vikings served with British European Airways, Aer

Lingus, South African Airways and various other operators including the RAF King's Flight. In 1947 the Valetta military transport appeared, based on the Viking, and 262 were produced for the RAF. It led to the Varsity trainer, which, unlike the Viking and Valetta, had a tricycle undercarriage. The 160 Varsities had a long RAF career, entering service in 1951 and not being finally retired until 1976. They provided twin-

Above Derived from the earlier Valetta transport, the RAF's Varsity was a twin-engined advanced trainer for pilots and a flying classroom for training in other aircrew specializations.

engined instruction for pilots destined to fly multi-engined aircraft and acted as flying classrooms for trainee navigators.

In 1948 Vickers produced the four-engined Viscount, the world's first turboprop-powered airliner, which had accommodation for 32 passengers. It entered service with British European Airways on a trials basis in 1950 and three years later the airline began scheduled services with the larger (47-seat) Viscount V701. Total Viscount sales were 438, to 60 different operators, including the United States airlines Capital, Northeast and Continental. The four-turboprop Vanguard of 1959 did not repeat the Viscount's considerable success, for although it was an economical

Above The Vickers Viscount four-turboprop airliner began to fly scheduled services in 1953.

Right The Voisin brothers' first successful powered flight was in this Voisin-Delagrange 1 at Bagatelle in 1907.

Below The swept-wing Valiant jet bomber was the first of the RAF's 'V-Bombers' entering service in 1955. The other components of the V-Force were the HP Victor and Avro Vulcan.

aircraft to operate, it lost out in competition with the similar Lockheed Electra. The four-engined VC10 of 1962, the last in the line of Vickers airliners, was developed under the auspices of the company's successor British Aircraft Corporation.

The Valiant bomber of 1951 was the first of the four-jet V-bombers built for the RAF. Entering service in 1955, a total of 107 were built to equip nine squadrons. Valiants operated against Egypt during the Suez Crisis of 1956 and two years later Valiant BK Mk 1s of No 214 Squadron became the RAF's first operational in-flight refuelling tanker aircraft. Valiants also took part in the British atomic weapon tests of 1956–7. In 1963 it was decided to withdraw the Valiant from service due to fatigue problems when operating the bomber at low level. It was to be the last in the line of famous Vickers bombers, for in 1963 the company was absorbed by British Aircraft Corporation as its Weybridge Division.

VOISIN

The brothers Gabriel and Charles Voisin were influential French aviation pioneers, whose company produced more than 10,000 aeroplanes between 1905 and 1918. Their first successful powered aeroplane (there had been earlier glider designs) was the Voisin Delagrange 1, a boxkite biplane of 1907. The Voisins' next machine, built to the order of Henry Farman, was the first European aeroplane to remain in the air for more than one minute. Whether this performance was due to the merits of the basic design or to Farman's modifications has long been a matter of controversy.

By the end of 1909 the Voisin company had orders for some 20 aeroplanes and they also acquired a licence to build the Wright type.

In 1912 the Aviation Militaire placed orders for 12 Voisin biplanes and with the outbreak of World War I the firm concentrated on military production. The wartime Voisins were all of basically similar configuration, with biplane wings, a central nacelle housing the crew and a pusher engine, with the cruciform tail unit carried by booms. The Type L was in service in 1914 and was used on early bomber and reconnaissance

squadrons in 1927–8. Corsairs saw action with the US Marine Corps against rebel forces in Nicaragua in 1928, and the aircraft was built by Nakajima in Japan as the Type 90 naval reconnaissance aircraft. The later O3U and SU Corsairs, were respectively shipboard and carrier-based scouting aircraft.

The SBU Scout bomber of 1935 proved to be Vought's last navy biplane design. Its successor, the SB2U Vindicator, was an all-metal monoplane scout-bomber which saw action early in the Pacific War, notably with Marine Scout Bombing Squadron VMSB-241 at Midway. Export models were supplied to the French Aéronavale and to the Fleet Air Arm as the Chesapeake. However, the Vindicator's service life was short, unlike the OS2U Kingfisher which served as an observation and scouting aircraft aboard

missions. The more powerful type 3 served with the French, Russian, Belgian, Italian and British air services and over 2000 were built. The Types 5 and 6 were essentially similar. The Voisin Type 8 and Type 10 of the late war years were used in the night-bombing role. Essentially similar to the earlier Voisins, their performance was improved by installing more powerful engines. In all, 1123 Voisin Type 8s were built and they were followed by 900 Type 10s, most of them serving with France's Aviation Militaire. Charles Voisin was killed in a car accident in 1912. His brother Gabriel abandoned aviation at the end of World War I, but lived on until 1973.

VOUGHT

The company founded by Chance Vought in 1917 specialized in the design of aeroplanes for the US Navy and was responsible for the famous F4U Corsair fighter of World War II. Its first product was the VE7 trainer, which was followed by the VE9. So efficient were these machines that some were used as operational aircraft rather than trainers. Consequently the basic design was refined to produce the UO-1 observation aircraft. These served as catapult floatplanes aboard the major American warships and a floatplane fighter version, the FU-1, served aboard the 12 US Navy battleships. The UO-1's successor was the O2U Corsair, which entered service with the battleship-based observation

Top The Voisin Type L was the chief French reconnaissance aeroplane at the outbreak of World War I. Most subsequent Voisin designs followed its general configuration.

Above left The Voisin 8 entered service with the Aviation Militaire in 1916 and served as a night bomber.

Above The Vought VE-9 training aircraft illustrated was one of 23 built for the US Army Air Service.

Below The Vought F4U Corsair fighter of World War II was characterized by its distinctive inverted gull wing, which was adopted to give adequate propeller clearance.

battleships and carriers throughout the war. The Kingfisher's main duty was spotting the fall of naval gunfire, but they also performed air/sea rescue missions.

Vought's second Corsair, the famous F4U single-seat fighter, first flew in 1940. Because of early difficulties in operating the Corsairs from aircraft carriers, they first went into service as land-based fighters with the US Marine Corps in the Solomon Islands. The Corsair was operated by the Fleet Air Arm, its first carrier operations being flown in April 1944, and the fighter was also supplied to the Royal New Zealand Air Force. Night-fighter and photographic reconnaissance versions of the Corsair were built and total production was over 12,500. Its postwar career extended into the 1960s and it saw extensive action in Korea.

Vought's first postwar naval jet, the F6U Pirate, saw only limited service, while the later F7U Cutlass equipped four US Navy fighter squadrons. The F8U Crusader first flew in 1955 and served with the US

Navy in the fighter and photographic reconnaissance roles. It operated throughout the Vietnam War and the fighter versions were credited with destroying 19 MiGs. The French navy operated Crusaders from the carriers *Clemenceau* and *Foch* and the Philippine air force operates the type as a land-based fighter. In 1965 the A-7 Corsair II (in fact it was the third Vought aircraft to be named Corsair) appeared. It was ordered by the US Navy to replace the A-4 Skyhawk and is currently that service's standard carrier-based light attack aircraft. In 1966 the USAF ordered the A-7D version of the Corsair II and these entered service in Southeast Asia in 1972. A-7s flew over 100,000 combat missions in Vietnam with the US Navy and USAF. Total production is over 1500 and A-7s have been exported to Greece and Portugal.

WESTLAND

The Westland company, which today specializes in the design and production of helicopters, was formed in World War I at Yeovil in Somerset. Its first aircraft were Short 184s, de Havilland DH4s, DH9s, and DH9As built under sub-contract. After the war small numbers of the Limousine cabin biplane were built for civil operators, as well as the Walrus fleet-spotter, based on the DH9A, for the RAF. The 1920s were lean years, with DH9A renovation for the RAF providing some bread-and-butter work for the company. Thirty of the company's own Widgeon light aircraft were also produced in the late 1920s. A turning point in Westland's fortunes was reached in 1927, when the Wapiti two-seater was ordered by the RAF as a DH9A replacement. Wapitis entered service with No 84 Squadron at Shaibah in Iraq in the following year and eventually 565 were built. They remained in use with the RAF until the late 1930s and were exported to Canada, South Africa and Australia. Follow-on orders were then received for the Wallace two-seater, 172 of which were built. In 1933 a modified Wallace and the Westland PV3 prototype torpedo-bomber became the first aeroplanes to fly over Mount Everest.

The Lysander army cooperation aircraft first flew in 1936, and this high-wing monoplane with its excellent short take-off and landing capability entered RAF service in 1938. Lysanders were heavily engaged during the Battle of France and losses were heavy (some

Top The Vought F-8 Crusader's unique variable-incidence wing is in the raised position for a catapult launch of this RF-8 photographic reconnaissance version.

Above The Vought A-7 Corsair, originally a naval aircraft, has been built as a land-based attack aircraft. This A-7H is one of 60 serving with the Greek air force.

Right The Westland Lysander army-cooperation aircraft entered RAF service in 1938.

Below An Army Air Corps Westland Scout AH Mk 1 anti-tank helicopter, armed with Nord SS-11 missiles.

80 were destroyed). Clearly the type was unsuited for its primary role, yet it continued in services as an air/sea rescue aircraft and as an agent-dropper with the Special Duties squadrons. In June 1940 the Whirlwind twin-engined, cannon-armed fighter began to equip No 263 Squadron. However, because problems with the fighter's Rolls-Royce Peregrine engines were never properly resolved, only two squadrons ever flew the Whirlwind and it went out of service in 1943. The Welkin twin-engined high-altitude fighter of 1942 was not used operationally.

Westland's last fixed-wing aircraft was the Wyvern turboprop-powered naval attack fighter, which served with the Fleet Air Arm (FAA) from 1953 until 1958 and saw action during the Suez Crisis of 1956. The company then concentrated on the production of helicopters, having acquired a licence to build the Sikorsky S-51 in 1947. Re-engined with an Alvis Leonides engine, this went into production as the Dragonfly and 139 were built. There followed the Whirlwind, based on the S-55, which was produced in piston- and turbine-engined versions. An improved Dragonfly, known as the Widgeon, sold in small numbers, and the S-58 was re-engined with turbines to produce the

Wessex for FAA and RAF service. The Scout and Wasp were basically the same design modified for army and naval use respectively. The connection with Sikorsky was maintained in 1966, when the SH-3 Sea King was put into production for the FAA and a British-developed assault helicopter version, the Commando, was also produced. Another cooperative deal resulted in the Lynx, Gazelle and Puma helicopters being built in collaboration with Aérospatiale in France. Of the three, only the Lynx was a British design but this has been developed into advanced attack helicopter and troop transport variants. A replacement for the Sea King is being designed in collaboration with Agunta of Italy.

Above left A British Army Air Corps Gazelle. The Gazelle serves with both the French and British armies.

Above This Yakovlev Yak-3 fighter fought with the Normandie-Niemen Regiment, a French volunteer unit which operated with the Soviet air force on the Eastern Front during World War II.

Below The Westland Lynx serves both with the Army Air Corps in the anti-tank role and with the Fleet Air Arm.

which in turn was modified into the Yak-9, with a lighter wing structure and greater range. This became the most widely used Soviet fighter in the later war years and a lightweight low-level fighter version was produced as the Yak-3. In the late 1940s all-metal versions of both the Yak-9 and Yak-3 served in considerable numbers with the Soviet fighter regiments. Well over 36,000 Yak fighters were built, a greater number than any other Soviet fighter design.

After the war the Yak-11 two-seat piston-engined trainer was built for the Soviet air force and its allies, 3859 being produced. The Yak-18 trainer of 1946 was also built in quantity, later versions being specialized aerobatic aircraft. The first jet-powered Yakovlev fighter, the Yak-15, also appeared in 1946 and was followed by the more powerful Yak-17 in 1947. They were essentially Yak-3 airframes adapted to take early Soviet turbojets copied from German designs. Early in the 1950s the Yakovlev design bureau produced the Yak-25 twin-engined all-weather fighter. This evolved into the Yak-28, which served in reconnaissance, strike, ECM (electronic countermeasures) and all-weather fighter roles from the early 1960s until its retirement in the early 1980s. A related design was the Yak-25RD (NATO codename Mandrake) high-

YAKOVLEV

Alexander Yakovlev is best known as the designer of a series of famous Soviet fighter aircraft in World War II. As an aeronautical engineering student in the 1920s, he designed and built several gliders and light aircraft. One of the most successful of the latter was the AIR-6, over 400 of which were built between 1933 and 1936. Even more successful was the AIR-10, which was produced as the UT-2 military trainer. Over 7000 UT-2s were built between 1937 and 1944. A single-seat aerobatic trainer version, the UT-1, was even used as a ground-attack aircraft in 1942.

With the approach of war, Yakovlev turned his attention to the design of single-seat fighter aircraft. The Yak-1 which first flew in 1940 was a low-wing monoplane powered by a Klimov M-105P in-line engine. The fighter was put into production that year and a total of 8721 were built. It led to the very similar Yak-7,

Above One of the most important training aircraft to serve with the Soviet air force in postwar years was the Yakovlev Yak-18.

Right The Yakovlev Yak-36 (codenamed Forger by NATO) is the first Soviet VTOL aircraft in operational service. It is a naval fighter-attack aircraft which flies from Kiev-class carriers.

altitude reconnaissance aircraft. The latest Yak fighter type is the VTOL (vertical take-off and landing) Yak-36 naval strike fighter which serves aboard the *Kiev* class carriers.